D1534946

Rec ͜

Axel Honneth and the Tradition of Critical Social Theory

Recognition and Power offers a critical evaluation of Axel Honneth's research program on Critical Theory, developed in his book *The Struggle for Recognition*. Editors Bert van den Brink and David Owen have brought together the leading workers in the field to review and clarify the topic of recognition, which now occupies a central place in contemporary debates in social and political theory.

Honneth's program on recognition, rooted in Hegel's work on the topic and further advanced by George Herbert Mead and Charles Taylor, offers an empirically insightful way of reflecting on emancipatory struggles for greater justice and a powerful theoretical tool for generating a conception of justice and the good that permits the normative evaluation of these struggles.

The contributors to this volume examine in particular the relationship between recognition and the other major development in critical social and political theory in recent years – the focus on power as formative of practical identities (or forms of subjectivity) proposed by Michel Foucault and further refined by theorists such as Judith Butler, James Tully, and Iris Marion Young.

Recognition and Power will be read by professionals and students in social and political philosophy and political theory.

Bert van den Brink is an associate professor of political and social philosophy at Utrecht University, The Netherlands. He is the author of *The Tragedy of Liberalism*, co-editor of *Reasons of One's Own*, and author of articles and book chapters on liberalism, democratic conflict and civility, and critical social theory.

David Owen is professor of social and political philosophy and deputy director of the Centre for Philosophy and Value at the University of Southampton. He is the author of *Maturity and Modernity; Nietzsche, Politics and Modernity*; and *Nietzsche's Genealogy of Morality*; and editor or co-editor of *Sociology after Postmodernism; Foucault contra Habermas; Max Weber's Vocation Essays*; and *Multiculturalism and Political Theory*. He has published articles and book chapters on a variety of topics in moral, social, and political philosophy.

In Memoriam
Iris Marion Young
1949–2006
Ave atque vale

Recognition and Power

*Axel Honneth and the Tradition
of Critical Social Theory*

Edited by

BERT VAN DEN BRINK
Utrecht University

DAVID OWEN
University of Southampton

CAMBRIDGE
UNIVERSITY PRESS

CAMBRIDGE UNIVERSITY PRESS

Cambridge, New York, Melbourne, Madrid, Cape Town, Singapore,
São Paulo, Delhi, Dubai, Tokyo, Mexico City

Cambridge University Press
32 Avenue of the Americas, New York, NY 10013-2473, USA

www.cambridge.org
Information on this title: www.cambridge.org/9780521184380

First published 2007
First paperback edition 2010

A catalog record for this publication is available from the British Library

Library of Congress Cataloging in Publication data

Recognition and power : Axel Honneth and the tradition of critical social theory /
edited by Bert van den Brink, David Owen.
p. cm.
Includes bibliographical references and index.
ISBN-13: 978-0-521-86445-9 (hardback)
1. Critical theory. 2. Honneth, Axel, 1949– 3. Recognition (Philosophy).
4. Power (Philosophy). I. Brink, Bert van den. II. Owen, David, 1964– III. Title.
B809.3.R42 2007
302′.1–dc22 2006022360

ISBN 978-0-521-86445-9 Hardback
ISBN 978-0-521-18438-0 Paperback

Contents

List of Figures and Tables   *page* vii

Contributors   ix

Acknowledgments   xiii

1. Introduction   1
   Bert van den Brink and David Owen

   PART I. PHILOSOPHICAL APPROACHES TO RECOGNITION

2. Analyzing Recognition: Identification, Acknowledgement,
   and Recognitive Attitudes towards Persons   33
   Heikki Ikäheimo and Arto Laitinen

3. Recognition and Reconciliation: Actualized Agency
   in Hegel's Jena *Phenomenology*   57
   Robert Pippin

4. Damaged Life: Power and Recognition
   in Adorno's Ethics   79
   Bert van den Brink

5. The Potential and the Actual: Mead, Honneth,
   and the "I"   100
   Patchen Markell

   PART II. RECOGNITION AND POWER IN SOCIAL THEORY

6. Work, Recognition, Emancipation   135
   Beate Rössler

7. "... That All Members Should be Loved
   in the Same Way ... "   164
   Lior Barshack

8. Recognition of Love's Labor: Considering Axel
   Honneth's Feminism   189
   Iris Marion Young

   PART III. RECOGNITION AND POWER IN POLITICAL THEORY

9. "To Tolerate Means to Insult": Toleration, Recognition,
   and Emancipation   215
   Rainer Forst

10. Misrecognition, Power, and Democracy   238
    Veit Bader

11. Reasonable Deliberation, Constructive Power,
    and the Struggle for Recognition   270
    Anthony Simon Laden

12. Self-Government and 'Democracy as Reflexive
    Co-operation': Reflections on Honneth's Social
    and Political Ideal   290
    David Owen

    PART IV. AXEL HONNETH ON RECOGNITION AND POWER

13. Recognition as Ideology   323
    Axel Honneth

14. Rejoinder   348
    Axel Honneth

Bibliography   371

Index   391

List of Figures and Tables

FIGURES

7.1. Corporate and Communal Bodies — *page* 178

TABLES

1.1. Honneth's Theory of Recognition — 11

10.1. Ascriptive Criteria of Allocation: Practices of Discrimination, Oppression, Exclusion: Typical Ascriptive Ideologies — 245

10.2. Basic Types of Positional Inequality and Structural Asymmetries of Power — 246

10.3. Pluralist Versus Monist Strategies — 251

Contributors

Veit Bader is a Professor of Sociology and of Social and Political Philosophy at the University of Amsterdam. His main research areas are theories of societies, social movements and collective action, and modern capitalism; ethics of migration and incorporation; and citizenship and associative democracy. Among his publications are *Racism, Ethnicity, Citizenship* (1995); *Associative Democracy: The Real Third Way* (2001) (with Paul Hirst); *Religions, Politics, and the State* [Special Volume (6/3) of *Ethical Theory and Moral Practice* (2004)]. His book *Democracy or Secularism? Associational Governance of Religious Diversity* is forthcoming. Bader has written many book chapters and articles in journals such as *Political Theory, Philosophy and Social Criticism, Citizenship Studies,* and *Ethical Theory and Moral Practice.*

Lior Barshack is an Associate Professor at the Radzyner School of Law, The Interdisciplinary Center, Herzliya, Israel. His research interests include constitutional theory, political theology, transformations in family law, and the relations between the state and the arts. Recent publications include "Constituent Power as Body: Outline of a Constitutional Theology" in 57 *University of Toronto Law Journal* (2006); "The Body Politic in Dance" in Peter Goodrich, Lior Barshack, and Anton Schutz (eds.), *Law, Text, Terror* (2006); and "The Communal Body, the Corporate Body, and the Clerical Body: An Anthropological Reading of the Gregorian Reform" in Lawrence Besserman (ed.), *Sacred and Secular in Medieval and Early Modern Cultures* (2006).

Rainer Forst is Professor of Political Theory and Philosophy at Johann Wolfgang Goethe-University in Frankfurt/Main and was the Theodor Heuss Visiting Professor of Political Science and Philosophy at the New School for Social Research (2005/06). Among his publications are *Contexts of Justice* (2002), *Toleranz im Konflikt* (2003), and *Das Recht auf Rechtfertigung* (2006).

Axel Honneth is Professor of Social Philosophy at Johann Wolfgang Goethe-University and Director of the Institute for Social Research in Frankfurt/Main. His publications include *Social Action and Human Nature* (1988) (with Hans Joas); *Critique of Power* (1990); *Struggle for Recognition* (1994); *The Fragmented World of the Social: Essays in Social and Political Philosophy* (1995); *Suffering from Indeterminacy: Spinoza Lectures* (1999); *Unsichtbarkeit. Stationen einer Theorie der Intersubjektivität* (2003); *Redistribution or Recognition? A Political-Philosophical Exchange* (2003) (with Nancy Fraser); *Verdinglichung. Eine anerkennungstheoretische Studie* (2005).

Heikki Ikäheimo is a Research Fellow of the Academy of Finland at University of Jyväskylä, Finland, and a visiting scholar at the University of Frankfurt/Main. His main fields of interest include recognition, personhood, social ontology, and Hegel's theory of subjectivity. Among his publications are *Self-Consciousness and Intersubjectivity; A Study on Hegel's Encyclopedia Philosophy of Subjective Spirit* (1830); "On the Role of Intersubjectivity in Hegel's Encyclopaedic Phenomenology and Psychology," *Bulletin of the Hegel Society of Great Britain* (2004), and "On the Genus and Species of Recognition," *Inquiry* (2002). In these publications, he has argued for an intersubjectivist reading of Hegel's encyclopedic philosophy of subjective spirit and developed a basic conceptual analysis on the phenomena of intersubjective recognition. Currently he is working on applications of the concept of recognition in theories of personhood and social ontology.

Anthony Simon Laden is an Associate Professor of Philosophy at the University of Illinois in Chicago. He is the author of *Reasonably Radical: Deliberative Liberalism and the Politics of Identity* (2001) and co-editor, with David Owen, of *Multiculturalism and Political Theory* (2006).

Arto Laitinen is a Researcher in Philosophy in the Department of Social Sciences and Philosophy at the University of Jyväskylä, Finland. He has been a visiting scholar at Oxford, Reading, Columbia, and Münster. His publications include *Strong Evaluations without Sources* (2003); a collection edited with Nicholas Smith, *Perspectives on the Philosophy of Charles Taylor* (2002); and articles entitled "Interpersonal Recognition: A Response to Value or a Precondition of Personhood?" in *Inquiry* (2002); "Interpersonal Recognition and Responsiveness to Relevant Differences" in *Critical Review of Social and Political Philosophy* (2006); with Heikki Ikäheimo and Michael Quante, "Leistungsgerechtigkeit: Ein Prinzip der Anerkennung für kulturelle Besonderheiten? in Halbig & Quante (eds.), *Axel Honneth: Sozialphilosophie zwischen Ethik und Anerkennung* (2003).

Patchen Markell is an Associate Professor of Political Science at the University of Chicago, where he teaches modern political theory. His recent publications include *Bound by Recognition* (2003) and articles in the *American Political Science Review*, *Political Theory*, and *Polity*. He is currently at work on two books: *The Architecture of the Human Condition* and *The Rule of the People: Power, Activity, and Democracy*.

David Owen is Professor of Social and Political Philosophy and Deputy Director of the Centre for Philosophy and Value at the University of Southampton. He previously taught at the Universities of Essex and Central Lancashire and was DAAD Visiting Professor in Social and Political Theory at the Johann Wolfgang Goethe-University, Frankfurt/Main in 2000. He is the author of *Maturity and Modernity* (1994); *Nietzsche, Politics, and Modernity* (1995); and *Nietzsche's Genealogy of Morality* (forthcoming). His edited or co-edited collections include *Sociology after Postmodernism* (1997), *Foucault contra Habermas* (1999), *Inhuman Futures* (2000), *Max Weber's Vocation Essays* (2004), and *Multiculturalism and Political Theory* (2006). He has published articles and book chapters on a variety of topics in moral, social, and political philosophy in such journals as *Deutsche Zeitschrift für Philosophie*, *European Journal of Philosophy*, *Nietzsche Studien*, and *Political Theory*. He is currently a member of the editorial boards of *Journal of Nietzsche Studies*, *Max Weber Studies*, and *Theory and Event*.

Robert Pippin is the Evelyn Stefanson Nef Distinguished Service Professor in the Committee on Social Thought and the Department of Philosophy, University of Chicago. His work is on the modern German philosophical tradition (Kant to the present); contemporary

Continental philosophy in general; moral theory; social and political philosophy; theories of modernity; and various topics in ancient philosophy. He also has a number of interdisciplinary interests involving philosophical issues in literature, art history, and film. His many publications include *The Persistence of Subjectivity: On the Kantian Aftermath* (2005); *Henry James and Modern Moral Life* (2000); *Idealism as Modernism: Hegelian Variations* (1997); and *Hegel's Idealism: The Satisfactions of Self-Consciousness* (1989).

Beate Rössler is an Associate Professor of Philosophy at the University of Amsterdam. She is also Socrates-Professor for the Foundations of Humanism at Leiden University. In 2003/04, she was a Fellow at the Institute of Advanced Studies (Wissenschaftskolleg) in Berlin. She has published on issues in ethics, social and political philosophy, and feminist theory. She is the editor of *Privacies: Philosophical Evaluations* (2004) and is the author of *The Value of Privacy* (2005, original German version 2001).

Bert van den Brink is an Associate Professor of Political and Social Philosophy at Utrecht University. He is the author of *The Tragedy of Liberalism* (2000), co-editor of *Reasons of One's Own* (2004), and the author of articles and book chapters on liberalism, democratic conflict and civility, and critical social theory. From 1999 to 2004 he was a Research Fellow of the Royal Netherlands Academy of Arts and Sciences. He is a member of the editorial board of *Contemporary Political Theory* and an editorial associate of *Constellations: An International Journal of Critical and Democratic Theory*.

Iris Marion Young was a Professor of Political Science at the University of Chicago. Among her books are *Inclusion and Democracy* (2000) and *On Female Body Experience* (2005). In 2006, Polity Press will issue a collection of her recent essays under the title *Global Challenges: On War, Self-Determination, and Labor Justice*.

Acknowledgments

The initial idea for this collection arose when the editors were both visitors at Goethe University, Frankfurt/Main, and participants in Axel Honneth's research colloquium in 2000. Its transition from a virtual existence to an actual existence resulted from the good will and efforts of the contributors to the volume, particularly Axel Honneth. We would like to thank them not only for their own contributions, but also for the mutual encouragement and criticism they offered each other starting from the time the contributions collected here were first presented in early drafts at the symposium *Recognition and Power* held at Utrecht University in March 2003.

That conference was made possible through the generous financial support of Utrecht University; the Department of Philosophy at Utrecht University; ZENO: The Leiden-Utrecht Research Institute for Philosophy; The Netherlands Organization for Scientific Research; The Royal Netherlands Academy of Arts and Sciences; and The Netherlands Research School in Practical Philosophy. Mathijs Peters and Mirjam Snijder assisted us in organizing the conference.

While compiling the book, we received much appreciated help in producing the bibliography from Andrew Brearley at the University of Southampton. At Utrecht University, Randy Lemaire saw to it that the pile of drafts was turned into a final manuscript. We are also indebted to Ronald Cohen for the very fine and thorough work he did in editing the manuscript.

Our editor at Cambridge University Press, Beatrice Rehl, has been a constant source of invaluable advice, patience, and care throughout the whole process, and we are grateful to her.

The death of Iris Marion Young in the summer of 2006 occurred as this volume was in the final stages of production. Iris's work combined an activist's passionate commitment to the practical redress of injustice with a philosophical acuity and capacity for conceptual innovation that not only made her one of the major voices in political theory over the last two decades but also makes reading her work such a rewarding experience. These features are readily apparent in her contribution to this volume, but so too is a further feature – namely, the spirit of generosity and care that characterized her engagement with the work of other thinkers. Her death deprives us not only of a compassionate, witty, and engaged woman, but also of a richly talented thinker whose words sparked all our imaginations.

Introduction

Bert van den Brink and David Owen

The topic of recognition now occupies a central place in contemporary debates in social and political theory. Rooted in Hegel's early Jena Writings and the famous discussion of the Master/Slave dialectic in his *Phenomenology of Spirit*, and developed in a variety of ways by George Herbert Mead, Frantz Fanon, Jean-Paul Sartre, Charles Taylor and Nancy Fraser, recognition has been given renewed expression in the ambitious third-generation program for Critical Theory developed by Axel Honneth over the past twenty years, most prominently in his classic text *The Struggle for Recognition*.[1]

Honneth's guiding thought has two aspects. First, modern ethical agency requires the formation of practical relations to self that are constituted in and through relations of recognition across three axes of self-formation: love, respect, and esteem. Second, the non-recognition or misrecognition of ethical subjects along any of these axes of self-formation is experienced as a harm or injustice that, under favourable social conditions, will motivate a struggle for recognition.

The research program that Honneth has developed is widely acknowledged as both an empirically insightful way of reflecting on emancipatory struggles for greater justice within such societies and a powerful way of generating a conception of justice and the good that permits the normative evaluation of such struggles. The aim of this volume is to offer a critical clarification and evaluation of this research

---

[1] Axel Honneth, *The Struggle for Recognition. The Moral Grammar of Social Conflicts*, transl. by Joel Anderson (Cambridge: Polity Press, 1995).

program and particularly its relationship to the other major development in critical social and political theory over recent years – the focus
on power as constitutive of practical identities (or forms of subjectivity) proposed by Michel Foucault and developed in a variety of ways
by theorists such as Judith Butler, James Tully, and Iris Marion Young.
Consider, for example, that, for Honneth, struggles for recognition are social processes in which certain groups in society contest the
predominant and, in their eyes, demeaning social standards of expectation and evaluation that ascribe to different members of society certain 'appropriate' roles, statuses, or characteristics. We can think here
both of officially sanctioned forms of unequal treatment of citizens
(apartheid, sexism) and of more informal forms of misrecognition in
everyday interaction concerning, for instance, the treatment of cultural minorities, the relation between the sexes, and so on. If we want
to understand the dynamics by which such forms of misrecognition are
kept in place, an analysis of power relations seems necessary. For both
official and more informal forms of misrecognition involve and articulate power relations that shape aspects of identity such that the identity
of those who do not have the power to co-determine the terms of their
legal and social status may come to involve an internalized sense of
their powerlessness, inferiority and 'appropriate' place in the margins
of society. Not least of the issues raised by this focus on recognition *and*
power is the problem of distinguishing between ethical and ideological – power-based – forms of recognition, a task that Honneth takes
on in his contribution to this volume.

In this Introduction, we begin with a reconstruction of the core
of Honneth's research project, before elaborating on the challenge
posed to this project by philosophical accounts of power. We end with
a brief introduction to the contributions to this volume and situate
them in relation to the problematic of recognition and power.

1. HONNETH'S THEORY OF RECOGNITION

a. The Moral Grammar of Social Conflicts

Ever since the publication of his earlier book, *The Critique of Power*,[2]
the aim of Axel Honneth's work has been to investigate the "moral

---

[2] Axel Honneth, *The Critique of Power: Reflective Stages in a Critical Social Theory*, transl. by
Kenneth Baynes (Cambridge, MA, and London: MIT Press, 1991).

grammar" of social conflicts inscribed in the institutions and social relations characteristic of modern societies. In looking for the *moral* grammar of social conflicts, Honneth rejects the notion that social conflict is to be conceived as a basic feature of the human condition that derives simply from the self-interested character of human beings. This view, which is given powerful expression by Thomas Hobbes in the early modern period,[3] radically undermined the ancient Greek-Roman idea of social and political interaction – whether in harmonious or more agonistic forms – as directed toward the common good of society's ethical life.[4] While critical of the metaphysical assumptions of Greek–Roman ethical and political thought, Honneth develops, through a reading of Hegel's early work on the concept of recognition,[5] a critique of the atomistic, instrumental-rational assumptions concerning human agency that he identifies in the tradition inaugurated by Hobbes and that he takes to inform much contemporary liberal political philosophy.[6]

At the core of Honneth's reading of Hegel is the idea that a social and political theory that works from such atomistic premises cannot account for human beings' constitutive dependency on non-instrumental social relations for the many aspects of their identities and agency that touch upon their integrity as *moral subjects and agents*. Human beings' moral subjectivity and agency stands in need of the recognitive relations of care, respect, and esteem with others in all phases and spheres of life. Such relations of recognition cannot be accounted for adequately in terms of a model of human beings as self-interested actors or, indeed, in terms of any atomistic model of

---

[3] Thomas Hobbes, *Leviathan*, ed. by Richard Tuck (Cambridge: Cambridge University Press, 1991).

[4] Honneth, *Struggle*, 7–10. Of related interest is Honneth's essay "The Limits of Liberalism: On the Political-Ethical Discussion Concerning Communitarianism," transl. by Jeremy Gaines, in Axel Honneth, *The Fragmented World of the Social: Essays in Social and Political Philosophy*, ed. by Charles W. Wright (Albany: State University of New York Press, 1995), 231–246.

[5] Honneth's reading of Hegel's early work is mainly based on *"System of Ethical Life"* (*1802/03*) and *"First Philosophy of Spirit"* (*Part III of the System of Speculative Philosophy 1803/04*), ed. and transl. by H. S. Harris and T. M. Knox (Albany, NY: State University of New York Press, 1979), and on "Jena Lectures in the Philosophy of Spirit," in *Hegel and the Human Spirit: A Translation of the Jena Lectures on the Philosophy of Spirit (1805–6) with Commentary*, ed. and transl. by Leo Rauch (Detroit: Wayne State University Press, 1983). See, for further relevant references to Hegel's early work, Honneth, *Struggle*, 183n2.

[6] Honneth, *Struggle*, 11–30 and "The Limits of Liberalism."

human agency. On the contrary, such an account requires a model of human agency as constituted in and through relations with others, where one's formation as an ethical subject and agent is dependent on the responsiveness of others with respect to *care* for one's needs and emotions, *respect* for one's moral and legal dignity, and *esteem* for one's social achievements. In the absence of such responsiveness, Honneth argues, one cannot develop the practical relations to self – self-confidence, self-respect, and self-esteem – that are crucial to one's status as a competent ethical subject and agent. As Honneth summarizes a point regarding the experience of love from Hegel's *System of Ethical Life*:

... the superiority of interpersonal relationships over instrumental acts was apparently to consist in the fact that relationships give both interlocutors the opportunity to express themselves, in encountering their partner to communication, to be the kind of person that they, from their perspective, recognize the other as being.[7]

In relations of recognition, subjects reassure others and themselves of their *similarity* with regard to their being persons who all have similar needs, capacities, and abilities, which can only be sustained and further developed through intersubjective relations. At the same time, these dependent, and in important respects, similar persons reassure themselves and others of their status as *distinct* individuals – persons whose specific needs and emotions, moral-cognitive capacities, and distinctive social traits and abilities compose their unique individualities. In sum, relations of recognition enable *alter* and *ego* to develop, through the internalization of general social standards that are responsive to individuality, both a sense of *self* and a capacity for *other-regarding*, competent moral agency. Both Hegel and Honneth defend the far-reaching claim that without such non-instrumental relations of recognition, human beings simply cannot be the beings that our best phenomenological accounts suggest they are.[8] Relations of recognition are a necessary – one is tempted

---

7 Honneth, *Struggle*, 37.
8 This is the research project presented in *Struggle*. Honneth's interpretation of Hegel along these lines is reached by means of a sociological and developmental-psychological confirmation and a systematic reconstruction and further conceptual development of Hegel's original idea.

to say a transcendental – condition of our moral subjectivity and agency.[9]

This conclusion, important as it is, does not mark the end of Hegel's and Honneth's work on recognition, but rather the establishment of their starting point. Both authors are dialectical thinkers who regard the substance of relations of recognition as historically variable and, therefore, not simply pre-given in needs and capacities that can be accounted for in terms of historically invariant anthropological categories.[10] For instance, it is quite clear that, in the course of history, understandings of what it means to receive care as an infant or a partner, to be respected as a moral subject and agent, or to be esteemed as a member of society with socially valuable traits and abilities have changed. Indeed, it seems that institutional and more informal standards of what constitutes due recognition are, and in all likelihood have always been, subject to interpretation and even contestation. To grasp the point, one need only think of, for example, the struggles by workers for fairer wages and working conditions as demanded by due recognition of the value of their work in society, or the struggles for independence by colonized people as demanded by their moral standing as human beings.[11] It is clear to see why this must be of fundamental concern to the theory of recognition. If it is true that what count as the generalized and dominant standards of recognition in a society can, from a moral point of view, be criticized as perpetuating relations of misrecognition, then it becomes necessary to understand by what social means, and in light of which criteria, misrecognized persons might claim full recognition for those needs, capacities, and abilities they feel do not receive the recognition they are due. This

---

9 Writing about a political ethic based on a theory of recognition, Honneth has recently made a claim to this effect. See Axel Honneth, "Redistribution as Recognition: A Response to Nancy Fraser," in Nancy Fraser and Axel Honneth, *Redistribution or Recognition: A Political-Philosophical Exchange*, transl. by Joel Golb, James Ingram, and Christiane Wilke (London/New York: Verso, 2003), 174.

10 Ibid., 138–150.

11 For an influential account of the social and moral logic of emancipatory struggles by the worker's movement, see, for instance, Barrington Moore, *Injustice: The Social Basis of Obedience and Revolt* (White Plains, N.Y.: M. E. Sharpe, 1978). For such struggles by colonized peoples, see, for instance, Frantz Fanon, *The Wretched of the Earth* (New York: Grove Press, 1963), and James Tully, *Strange Multiplicity: Constitutionalism in an Age of Diversity* (Cambridge/New York: Cambridge University Press, 1995).

is the point at which the idea of a *struggle* for recognition enters the scene.

We will come back later to such struggles and their historical meaning. For now, it is more important to end with a conclusion as to the *moral* grammar of social conflict. Once the notions of, first, relations of recognition as necessary conditions of moral subjectivity and agency and, second, the often-contested nature of generalized and dominant standards of recognition are accepted, it is only a small step to the insight that social conflicts that concern the adequate interpretation of such standards of recognition necessarily have a *moral* point. In conflicts over the adequate interpretation of dominant standards of recognition, members of society raise moral claims as to the adequate protection of the social conditions under which they can form, sustain, and further develop their identities as moral subjects and agents. What makes such claims moral is, first, that they concern *the social conditions of undistorted subjectivity and agency*[12] and, second, that they require of social agents *an attitude that goes beyond an immediate concern with their self-interest in being responsive to the needs of others.*[13]

b. Honneth's Project in Context

Having sketched the theoretical intuition guiding Honneth's project, it may be useful to situate Honneth's work with respect to other strands in social and political philosophy before exploring his project in more depth. This will both be helpful in bringing out the relevance of his project in contemporary debates and provide us with a bridge to the theme of recognition and power addressed in this volume. We have already noted that Honneth's work puts him in proximity with Hegel's early writings, from which the core of his theoretical project derives. More broadly, his project has an affinity with theoretical traditions that account for social conflicts in terms of struggles over the adequate interpretation of the normative standards central to a community's broad moral self-understanding or ethical life. This is a wide field, in which Kant's moral theory[14] can be placed just as easily as early

---

[12] Cf. Honneth, "Redistribution as Recognition: A Response to Nancy Fraser," 133.

[13] See Honneth's first contribution to this volume, "Recognition as Ethical Demand and Ideology."

[14] Immanuel Kant, *The Metaphysics of Morals*, transl. by Mary Gregor (Cambridge: Cambridge University Press, 1991).

Critical Theory's investigations into the paradoxes of capitalist society,[15] Michel Foucault's ethical work,[16] Jürgen Habermas's communicative ethics,[17] John Rawls' liberal theory of justice,[18] and Charles Taylor's investigations into the moral sources of modernity.[19] That this is the case is demonstrated by Honneth's engagement with these disparate theoretical stances in the articulation and development of his own project. With Kant, Habermas, and Rawls, Honneth shares a strong commitment to the notion of the autonomy of the person understood as a source of justified social claims that are brought into practices of public moral reasoning. Honneth has always stressed the importance of the public sphere as an arena in which struggles over the interpretation of standards of recognition are to be decided through public deliberation. Still, he has been remarkably consistent over the years in criticizing these authors for an understanding of autonomy that is both too narrow and too abstract (having "the character of a mere 'ought'"[20]) to inform us adequately about the way in which autonomy is thought to be embedded in the complex structures of the historically developed ethical life characteristic of modern societies. If autonomy is conceptualized in terms of following principles

---

[15] Max Horkheimer, "Traditional and Critical Theory," in Horkheimer, *Critical Theory* (New York: Herder and Herder, 1972); Max Horkheimer and Theodor W. Adorno, *Dialectic of Enlightenment*, transl. by John Cummings (New York: Continuum Publishing, 1972); Theodor W. Adorno, *Minima Moralia: Reflections from Damaged Life*, transl. by E. F. N. Jephcott (London and New York: Verso, 1974).

[16] Michel Foucault, *Ethics: Subjectivity and Truth. Essential Works of Foucault 1954–1984, volume I*, ed. by Paul Rabinow, transl. by Robert Hurley and others (New York: New Press, 1994).

[17] Jürgen Habermas, *Moral Consciousness and Communicative Action*, transl. by Christian Lenhardt and Shierry Weber Nicholson (Cambridge, UK: Polity Press, 1993); Jürgen Habermas, *Between Facts and Norms: Contributions to a Discourse Theory of Law and Democracy*, transl. by William Rehg (Cambridge: Polity Press, 1996).

[18] John Rawls, *A Theory of Justice* (Cambridge, MA: Harvard University Press, 1971); John Rawls, *Political Liberalism* (New York: Columbia University Press, 1993).

[19] Charles Taylor, *Sources of the Self: The Making of the Modern Identity* (Cambridge and New York: Cambridge University Press, 1989).

[20] Honneth, *Struggle*, 5. In his criticism of these authors, Honneth's main inspirer is, again, Hegel. The quote is taken from the first sentence of *Struggle*, which in a way says as much about Honneth's own project as Hegel's: "In his political philosophy, Hegel set out to remove the character of a mere 'ought' from the Kantian idea of individual autonomy by developing a theory that represented it as a historically effective element of social reality, and he consistently understood the solution to the problem this posed to involve the attempt to mediate between the modern doctrine of freedom and the ancient conception of politics, between morality and ethical life [*Sittlichkeit*]."

that are either derived from transcendental or formal reflections on moral-cognitive conditions of our capacity for reasonable action (Kant, Habermas), or from a thought experiment as to how we would judge questions of justice if our judgment were not tainted by knowledge about our actual position in society (Rawls), the question remains as to how such an understanding of autonomy relates to practices of self-government among distinct and fully embodied persons who strive for freedom and well-being in and through multiple social settings such as the family, civil society, the workplace, cultural life, and so on. The key point is that Honneth's focus is on the social preconditions of effective, socially embedded autonomy rather than simply on an abstract understanding of the moral-cognitive requirements of autonomy alone:

> the development and realization of individual autonomy is in a certain sense only possible when subjects have the social preconditions for realizing their life goals without unjustifiable disadvantages and with the greatest possible freedom.[21]

What relates Honneth to Horkheimer and Adorno's Critical Theory, to Foucault's studies of disciplinary and confessional practices, and to Taylor's investigations of ethical life is that their work may be said to explore these social preconditions of, and obstacles to, autonomy or self-government. Whereas Kant, Habermas, and Rawls start their theoretical projects from idealized conceptions of the autonomous and reasonable subject, and develop an ideal-conception of just and well-ordered societies from that starting point, Horkheimer and Adorno, Foucault, and Taylor start their theoretical projects from rather thick (and, for that reason, often contested) descriptions of our not so just and well-ordered societies and the many roles we play within them. They may be said to introduce individuals' striving for autonomy or self-government as an influential but hard to attain ideal in these societies. Furthermore, they do not primarily direct their reflections on the social preconditions of self-government to procedural, moral-cognitive aspects of political deliberation. Rather, they investigate – each in his own manner – the wide terrain of, for instance, intimate relations in the family, the modern understanding of sexuality, the capitalist economy, the culture industry, corrective institutions, art, and religion. They do

---

[21] Honneth, *Redistribution or Recognition*, 259.

so from perspectives that aim to unearth the socially alienating or disciplinary character of these social spheres of interaction and, in Taylor's case, their moral sources.

Through the broad scope of their investigations into the social realm, these authors develop insights into the demanding social preconditions of individual autonomy.[22] Although Honneth has criticized Horkheimer and Adorno's notion of the administered society,[23] Foucault's notion of disciplinary power,[24] and aspects of Charles Taylor's communitarian reflections on the modern identity as unnecessarily sceptical regarding either the possibility (Horkheimer, Adorno, and Foucault) or the normative weight (Taylor) of individual autonomy,[25] Honneth's approach to autonomy is perhaps closer to theirs than to the various approaches deriving from the Kantian tradition. Honneth's analytical approach to the subject is as follows. First, we ask how best to describe the multiple institutions, social practices, and mutual patterns of expectation in society that make us into the (at best partially) autonomous subjects we are. Second, we ask how an adequate account of legitimate moral expectations as to greater autonomy of subjects could be extracted from the moral grammar of the social struggles for recognition that we witness in our societies.

c. Recognition and Practical Relations-to-Self

In modern societies, Honneth distinguishes a three-fold set of socially sanctioned moral principles that circumscribe what should count as adequate recognition of members of society. He claims that these principles are not just contingent principles that express "how we do things around here." Rather, they are seen as the result of moral learning processes by which members of society, often over many generations,

---

[22] For a related insight into the required broadness of investigations into political freedom and practices of governance, see James Tully, "Political Philosophy as a Critical Activity," in: *Political Theory* 30/4 (2002), 533–555.

[23] Here, the criticism is especially directed against Horkheimer and Adorno, *Dialectic of Enlightenment*. See Axel Honneth, "From Adorno to Habermas: On the Transformation of Critical Social Theory" and "Foucault and Adorno: Two Forms of the Critique of Modernity," in: *Fragmented World*, 92–120 and 121–131. See also Honneth, *Critique of Power*, chs. 2 and 3.

[24] See Honneth, "Foucault and Adorno: Two Forms of the Critique of Modernity," in *Fragmented World*, 121–131. See also Honneth, *Critique of Power*, chs. 4–6.

[25] See Honneth, "Limits of Liberalism."

have gradually acquired knowledge of what it means to recognize each other with respect to various aspects of moral subjectivity and agency. Based on a review of historical and social theoretic research, Honneth argues that moral subjectivity and agency today require the formation of practical relations to self that are constituted in and through relations of recognition across three axes of self-formation.

The first of these axes is that of *love*, according to a principle of loving care and friendship for the concrete needs and desires of others that fosters their *self-confidence*. The second is that of *respect*, according to a principle of equal treatment with respect to every person's rights that fosters persons' *self-respect*. The third is that of *esteem*, according to a principle of achievement in the division of valuable social labour in society that fosters persons' *self-esteem*.[26] The three principles of recognition express the normative core of what in spheres of affective, moral/legal, and social relations counts as adequate recognition. And adequate recognition is understood from an ethical theory that defines the social "preconditions that must be available for individual subjects to realize their autonomy."[27] In *The Struggle for Recognition* (1995: 129), Honneth summarises his theory of the forms and aims of recognition as shown in Table 1.1. The table shows the three axes of recognition.

---

[26] Honneth's most complete systematic development of this three-fold scheme is to be found in *Struggle*, 92–139. For a recent (re)formulation, in which the historical development of the principles is discussed at length, see Honneth, "Redistribution as Recognition," 110–197.

[27] Honneth, "Redistribution as Recognition," 178. Where, in the following, Honneth's theory will be interpreted as one that reflects on conditions of autonomous agency and personhood, this is done in knowledge of a certain tension in Honneth's theory as to what is meant by such conditions. On the one hand, he speaks of the autonomy of persons as a moral-cognitive capacity that is tied to modes of recognition characteristic of modern ideals of legal equality and the forms of self-respect they allow for members of society who claim civil, political, and social rights. On the other hand, he speaks of conditions of individual or personal autonomy of persons in intimate relations and in social relations in the economic division of labour within society. In this article, the focus is on conditions of autonomy in that broader sense, where principles of equal or fair treatment of persons as self-governing subjects and agents in all spheres are at stake. See Honneth, "Redistribution as Recognition," 177–8, where Honneth uses the broad conception of conditions of autonomy, and pp. 188–9, where he uses both the broad and the narrow one. See, for another account of both the broad and the narrow sense, Honneth, "Recognition and Moral Obligation," in: *Social Research* 64/1 (1997), 16–35.

TABLE 1.1. *Honneth's Theory of Recognition*

Mode of recognition	Emotional support	Cognitive respect	Social esteem
Dimension of personality	Needs and emotions	Moral responsibility	Traits and abilities
Forms of recognition	Primary relationships (love, friendship)	Legal relations (rights)	Community of value (solidarity)
Developmental potential	–	Generalization, de-formalization	Individualization, equalization
Practical relation-to-self	Basic self-confidence	Self-respect	Self-esteem
Forms of disrespect	Abuse and rape	Denial of rights, exclusion	Denigration, insult
Threatened component of personality	Physical integrity	Social integrity	'Honour,' dignity

Basic Self-Confidence. Honneth's account of basic self-confidence is presented by reference to object-relations theory as developed by Donald Winnicott and, more recently, Jessica Benjamin. The central claim is that the relation between child and 'mother' (primary carer) can be grasped in terms of a struggle for recognition that involves the negotiation of, or continual exchange between, ego-relatedness and boundary dissolution and that

> because this relationship of recognition prepares the ground for a type of relation-to-self in which subjects acquire basic confidence in themselves, it is both conceptually and genetically prior to every other form of reciprocal recognition.[28]

The general point that Honneth draws from object-relations theory for his concern with struggles for recognition can be summarized as follows:

> Without the felt assurance that the loved one will continue to care even after he or she has become independent, it would become impossible for the loving

[28] Honneth, *Struggle*, 107.

subject to recognize that independence. Because this experience must be mutual in love relationships, recognition is here characterized by a double process, in which the other is released and, at the same time, emotionally tied to the loving subject. Thus, in speaking of recognition as a constitutive element of love, what is meant is an affirmation of independence that is guided – indeed, supported – by care.[29]

It is important to note here that while the 'mother'–child relationship is "conceptually and genetically prior to every other form of recognition" and "prepares the ground" for basic self-confidence as a practical relation-to-self, Honneth's argument is that the production and maintenance of basic self-confidence is an ongoing activity in which the loving subject's relation to parents, friends, and lovers involves a continual exchange of ego-relatedness and boundary dissolution.

Self-Respect. Honneth's argument with regard to self-respect claims that this practical relation-to-self is grounded in legal relations as a form of recognition – that is, in our reciprocal recognition of ourselves and of others as bearers of legal (and moral) rights. Central to this argument is the claim that respect as a form of recognition that is distinct from esteem emerges historically with the development of a post-conventional morality that is expressed in the idea of universal human rights. The concept of respect refers to the normative non-appraisive recognition of an individual *qua* personhood, where "personhood" refers to the idea of "moral responsibility" of the rights-bearer in reciprocal relation with other such rights-bearers. However, Honneth knows only too well that what personhood in this sense might mean in detail cannot be determined "once and for all." He stresses rather that the "... essential indeterminacy as to what constitutes the status of a responsible person leads to a structural openness on the part of modern law to a gradual increase in inclusivity and precision."[30] Given the centrality of the idea of reciprocal recognition of moral responsibility, it does not come as a surprise that Honneth claims that the exact determination of our capacities as morally responsible subjects will have to be undertaken in light of

[29] Ibid.
[30] Ibid., 110.

historically developing assumptions about what it means to participate
as a member in procedures of rational opinion- and will-formation in
society:

> The more demanding this procedure is seen to be, the more extensive the
> features will have to be that, taken together, constitute a subject's status as
> morally responsible.... The cumulative expansion of individual rights-claims,
> which is what we are dealing with in modern societies, can be understood as
> a process in which the scope of the general features of a morally responsible
> person has gradually increased, because, under the pressure for struggles for
> recognition, ever-new prerequisites for participation in rational will formation
> have to be taken into consideration.[31]

Here Honneth points to the movement from civil to political to socio-
economic rights as described by T. H. Marshall. But how are rights-
recognition and self-respect connected? The crucial argument for this
connection is the following:

> Since possessing rights means being able to raise socially accepted claims,
> they provide one with a legitimate way of making clear to oneself that one is
> respected by everyone else. What gives rights the power to enable the devel-
> opment of self-respect is the public character that rights possess in virtue of
> their empowering the bearer to engage in action that can be perceived by
> interaction partners. For, with the optional activity of taking legal recourse to
> a right, the individual now has available a symbolic means of expression whose
> social effectiveness can demonstrate to him [or her], each time anew, that he
> or she is universally recognized as a morally responsible person.[32]

Honneth concludes that legal recognition enables a person to understand herself as someone who possesses the capacities – the prerequisites of competent subjectivity and agency – that make her appear
as a full member of society who is able to participate in the processes
of will-formation by which a society gives itself the law. To the extent
that the person is now recognized as someone who can effectively
exercise her rights and thus stand up for herself in public debates in
society, legal recognition permits a form of positively relating to oneself that Honneth labels "self-respect."[33] Here, Honneth's claim is not

---

[31] Ibid., 114–15.
[32] Ibid., 120.
[33] Ibid.

that our self-respect is totally dependent on legal recognition. Rather, as Joel Anderson puts it, "only that the *fullest* form of self-respecting autonomous agency could only be realized when one is recognized as possessing the capacities of 'legal persons' – that is, of morally responsible agent."[34]

The point of this argument, then, is to suggest that we can grasp social and political conflicts over rights in terms of struggles for respect-recognition that are directed to the generalization and/or deformalization of rights.

Self-Esteem. Honneth specifies self-esteem as a practical relation-to-self in which one's distinct traits and abilities (which are not shared by all) are valued. This practical relation-to-self is formed, Honneth argues, through relations of solidarity in which individuals or groups share a common project or horizon of value. As with respect from which it is gradually disentangled, Honneth argues that social esteem is characterized by developmental potentials. He bases this claim on the historical transformation of relations of social esteem, and describes these developmental potentials in terms of processes of individualization and of equalization. Individualization refers to the process whereby social esteem becomes separated out from status-groups and is ascribed to individuals *qua* individuality – that is to say, with respect to their own unique characters or life-projects. Equalization refers to the process whereby social esteem becomes increasingly detached from forms of social hierarchy and interwoven into a pluralistic value framework. Together, Honneth argues, these processes mean that

the individual no longer has to attribute to an entire collective the respect that he or she receives for accomplishments that fit social standards but can refer them positively back to himself or herself instead. Under these altered conditions, the experience of being socially esteemed is accompanied by a felt confidence that one's achievements or abilities will be recognized as 'valuable' by other members of society. . . . To the extent to which every member of society is in a position to esteem himself or herself, one can speak of a state of societal solidarity.[35]

34 Anderson, in: Honneth, *Struggle* ("Translator's Introduction"), xv.
35 Ibid., 128–129.

He continues:

In modern societies, therefore, social relations of symmetrical esteem between individualized (and autonomous) subjects represent a pre-requisite for solidarity. In this sense, to esteem one another symmetrically means to view one another in light of values that allow the abilities and traits of the other to appear significant for shared praxis. Relationships of this sort can be said to be cases of 'solidarity,' because they inspire not just passive tolerance but felt concern for what is individual and particular about the other person.[36]

d. Moral Progress and a Conception of the Good

We have already noted that Honneth is not satisfied with accounts of recognition that are "simply derived from an anthropological theory of the person."[37] An anthropological theory cannot account for the changes with respect to standards of recognition that can be historically discerned. Indeed, Honneth stresses that

... forms of reciprocal recognition are always already institutionalized in every social reality, where internal deficits or asymmetries are indeed what can first touch off a kind of "struggle for recognition."[38]

Struggles for recognition are touched off, Honneth claims, by feelings of misrecognized persons that the institutionalized standards of recognition in society – standards that claim legal and moral legitimacy – are in fact unjust because they frustrate the formation, sustenance, and further development of valuable aspects of these persons' subjectivity and agency. The subjects' implicit or explicit knowledge of their constitutive dependency on adequate social conditions of the formation of subjectivity and agency makes such feelings possible. Shame, hurt, or indignation "are, in principle, capable of revealing to individuals the fact that certain forms of recognition are being withheld from them."[39] This may motivate them to engage in social struggles for the forms of recognition – understood as conditions of their successful autonomy – that they think are being withheld from them.

[36] Honneth, *Struggle*, 129.
[37] Honneth, "Redistribution as Recognition," 138.
[38] Ibid., 136.
[39] Honneth, *Struggle*, 136.

This moral-psychological logic behind struggles for recognition reveals that disrespected individuals can, on principle, *know* that their identity must not be thought of as something that is inalterable, or "given once and for all."[40] Furthermore, or so Honneth claims, the experience-based knowledge that persons have about their dependence on sound, autonomy-enhancing forms of recognition can spark struggles for recognition that aim at effective moral criticism of, for instance, dominant, outdated, arbitrary, or ideological forms of recognition.

In the history of modern societies, Honneth discerns a process of differentiation of the three spheres of recognition discussed in the last section. In recent years, Honneth has spelled out in more detail than before how he accounts for this process and why he understands it as representing *moral progress*. At the core of his analysis is an understanding regarding structural changes that concern the legal respect and the social esteem members of society are due. In pre-modern societies, the legal status of the individual – and thus the respect he or she was due – was rather directly tied to "the social esteem he or she enjoyed by reason of origin, age, or function."[41] With the emergence of bourgeois capitalism, this close connection loosened. Through the increasing influence of market relations and the way in which they undermined traditional social rankings,

... legal recognition split off from the hierarchical value order insofar as the individual was in principle to enjoy legal equality vis-à-vis all others.... [T]he individual could now – certainly not in actual practice, but at least according to the normative idea – know that he or she was respected as a legal person with the same rights as all other members of society, while still owing his or her social esteem to a hierarchical scale of values – which had, however, also been set on a new foundation.[42]

The legal order that developed under the pressure of struggles for recognition of value orientations associated with the bourgeois capitalist order against the feudal and absolutist socio-political order put this "hierarchical scale of values" on a new footing. Now that origin, age, or function no longer absolutely determined the legal order, a

---

40 Honneth, "Redistribution as Recognition," 138.
41 Ibid., 139.
42 Ibid., 140.

principle of "individual achievement" in the rapidly developing "industrially organized division of labor" became ever more dominant as a category according to which social status was ascribed and measured.[43] Indeed, much more than in his earlier work, Honneth sees this principle of individual achievement as the main medium through which relations of solidarity in society take shape. Relations of solidarity express the patterns of mutual esteem by which society's members recognize the validity of each other's socially valuable achievements on the capitalist market and in various social association and organizations in civil society. Taken together, the two closely intertwined developments lead Honneth to the conclusion that

One part of the honor assured by hierarchy was in a sense democratized by according all members of society equal respect for their dignity and autonomy as legal persons, while the other part was in a sense "meritocratized": each was to enjoy social esteem according to his or her achievement as a productive citizen.[44]

Finally, in his recent work, Honneth has corrected, rightly it seems, his earlier thesis from *The Struggle for Recognition* that love "does not admit of the potential for normative development."[45] He now claims that it is characteristic of modern societies that childhood is seen as an "institutionally marked off . . . phase of the life process requiring special protection."[46] For this reason, the development of a child through relations of love and care with parents or carers has been explicitly tied to special duties and social forms that enable the development of the child in the direction of specifically modern understandings of self-confidence, self-respect, and self-esteem. The structural transformations in the spheres of legal respect and social esteem made possible still another development in the sphere of love: "The relations between the sexes were gradually liberated from economic and social

---

[43] Here, following historical sociological studies that take up ideas central to Max Weber's sociology of religion, Honneth stresses the importance of the religious valorization of paid work.

[44] Ibid., 141.

[45] Honneth, *Struggle*, 176. See also "Redistribution as Recognition," 192–3, n. 35, and the scheme from *Struggle* that we have included in this Introduction in Table 1.1.

[46] Honneth, "Redistribution as Recognition," 139. Here, the main reference is to the French historian Philip Ariès, *Centuries of Childhood: A Social History of Family Life*, transl. by Robert Baldick (New York: Knopf, 1962).

pressures and thus opened up to the feeling of mutual affection."[47] This development is tied to the institution of bourgeois marriage, as based not on economic or status-related necessities or opportunities, but rather in feelings of mutual affection and love. Together, the relations between parents and children and between loving spouses gave official institutional form to persons' need of well-being for loving care by others in light of their individual need and desires.

When tied to the idea that structural transformations with regard to principles of social integration are ultimately based in struggles for recognition of identity-claims, this brief historical sketch of the development of the principles of love, equality, and achievement shows that these principles articulate the *moral point* of these identity-claims. Since the principles seem to be firmly embedded in institutional forms that foster the social conditions of agency and identity, Honneth is able to claim that

... with each newly emerging sphere of mutual recognition, another aspect of human subjectivity is revealed which individuals can now positively ascribe to themselves intersubjectively.

Honneth discerns in the moral progress that he sees in the development of modern societies *a conception of the good* to which the ideal of the *autonomy* of moral subjects and agents who are considered *equals* is central. He needs this liberal-egalitarian conception of the good in order to have a standard against which the normative evaluation of concrete claims for recognition – often phrased in terms of claims for greater justice – can be undertaken.

... we only learn which aspects of public life are important for realizing individual autonomy from a conception of personal well-being [or the good], however fragmentarily developed.[48]

This conception of well-being or the good – which is made up of Honneth's three principles of recognition – is one by which moral subjects and agents recognize in others valuable qualities such as their (capacity for) autonomy or more specific needs and abilities in the three spheres of recognition. Such valuable qualities, Honneth claims,

[47] Ibid.
[48] Honneth, "Redistribution and Recognition," 179.

neither have an ontological status that is entirely independent from the culturally specific life worlds from which we judge and act, nor are they to be understood in a strong relativistic manner – that is, as ascribed to persons from entirely contingent cultural-value schemes. Rather, he claims to have found a third way between moral realism and moral relativism by trusting on the rationality of the moral learning processes in modern life worlds through which our current conception of the ethical good – understood in terms of Honneth's three autonomy-enhancing principles of recognition – has developed.[49] He works from the heuristically necessary *assumption*[50] that moral learning processes have shown that, in all three spheres of recognition, an ethics of autonomy and equal respect can help us to recognize those valuable qualities in others by which they, as well as we, can acknowledge our own and each others' status as moral subjects and agents.

For Honneth, the conception of the good that speaks from his theory is necessarily a historically embedded one. This is to say that it has gained shape in institutions of society such as bourgeois marriage and its understandings of need and care, the liberal-democratic state and its understandings of legal rights and political participation, and capitalist markets and their understandings of the value of persons' achievements in their contribution to the market. Yet Honneth stresses that given institutional forms and patterns of expectation can hardly ever be expected to fully live up to the "surplus validity" that the principles of recognition central to his conception of the good possess. Indeed, the tension between the given, hardly ever perfect level of inclusion and individualization that given institutions grant to members of society and the moral ideal of inclusion and individualization for the sake of members' social and individual autonomy in different spheres of recognition sets

. . . a moral dialectic of the general and the particular in motion: claims are made for a particular perspective (need, life-situation, contribution) that has not yet found appropriate consideration by appeal to a general recognition principle (love, law, achievement). In order to be up to the task of critique, the theory of justice outlined here can wield the recognition principles'

---

[49] See Honneth's first contribution to this volume, "Recognition as Ethical and Ideological Demand."
[50] Honneth, "Redistribution and Recognition," 180.

surplus validity against the facticity of their social interpretation. As against the dominant interpretative praxis, it is shown that there are particular, hitherto neglected facts whose moral consideration would require an expansion of the spheres of recognition.[51]

But exactly how is this shown? And, more particularly, how are these 'facts' identified or made visible such that they 'require' an expansion of the spheres of recognition? With these questions, we are brought inevitably to consider the relation of recognition and power.

2. RECOGNITION AND POWER

Because Honneth goes much further than most authors do in ascribing moral status to actual social institutions such as the family, law, and even the capitalist economy, the question of arbitrary power relations inscribed in these institutions is never far from sight. Indeed, many of Honneth's critics make this point central to their readings of his work. He has been criticized for taking a stance that is naïve or even affirmative with regard to structural injustices as inscribed in bourgeois marriage and hidden forms of sexism, ethno-centrism, and even economic exploitation as inscribed in the institutions and social patterns of expectation and normative evaluation characteristic of Western democracies.[52] His account is perhaps peculiarly exposed to this set of concerns since – as, for example, Rainer Forst's chapter makes clear – relations of power can themselves take 'recognitive' forms that foster certain practical relations-to-self. The issue here is not merely that of forms of power that guide and circumscribe the interpretation of principles of recognition in the way that, for example, has been the case with respect to the achievement principle. In respect of this principle, Honneth acknowledges that often, "the extent to which something counts as 'achievement,' as a cooperative contribution, is defined against value standards whose normative reference point is the economic activity of the independent, middle-class, male bourgeois."[53] (And he has made similar remarks with regard to the spheres of love and law. The normative agreement over principles

---

[51] Ibid., 186.
[52] In this volume, see, for instance, the contributions of Iris Marion Young, Beate Rössler, and Veit Bader.
[53] Honneth, "Redistribution as Recognition," 141–143; "Zwischen Gerechtigkeit und affektiver Bindung. Die Familie im Brennpunkt moralischer Kontroversen," in:

of recognition is often underpinned by institutional forms that are themselves shot-through with a "thoroughly one-sided valuation" of claims to recognition.)[54] It is also an issue about the extent to which the emergence and demarcation of the principles of recognition that Honneth identifies may themselves be products of power relations.

We might consider, in this context, Michel Foucault's account of the emergence and role of the psycho-disciplines such as psychoanalysis as bound up with the establishment of a matrix of 'bio-power' that functions through the idea that there is a true self to be realized.[55] Here, a serious issue for Honneth's project is how he is to ground a way of distinguishing between ethical and ideological forms of recognition without begging the question by simply assuming that struggles for recognition represent moral learning processes. After all, if we consider the kind of struggle for recognition that Nietzsche addresses under the notion of 'the slave revolt in morals' in which the terms of moral recognition are themselves transformed, we may – if we follow Nietzsche's analysis – be somewhat sceptical of the claim that this transformation is best understood as a moral learning process that represents a form of moral progress as opposed to a process that enables a certain social group to experience a (previously lacking) feeling of power.[56] The concerns expressed by Bernard Williams in *Shame and Necessity* concerning 'progressivism' of the type that Honneth exemplifies may be seen as exhibiting a contemporary version of this Nietzschean spirit of scepticism.[57] Honneth's chapter in this volume endeavours to address such concerns.

In more formal terms, we can distinguish a number of possible critical standpoints in terms of which Honneth's project can be contested with respect to the theme of recognition and power:

1. *The critique of Honneth's appeal to, and/or use of, 'recognition' as the basic category of ethical theory.* This critique can be articulated

---

Das Andere der Gerechtigkeit. Aufsätze zur praktischen Philosophie (Frankfurt am Main: Suhrkamp, 2000, 193–215).

54 Honneth, "Redistribution as Recognition," 141.

55 Michel Foucault, *The History of Sexuality: Volume 1*, trans. R. Hurley (Harmondsworth, Penguin Books, 1979).

56 Friedrich Nietzsche, *On the Genealogy of Morality*, trans. by C. Diethe (Cambridge/New York: Cambridge University Press, 1994).

57 Bernard Williams, *Shame and Necessity* (Berkeley, University of California Press, 1993), see especially 4–12.

on the basis that the concept of recognition is not the basic category of ethical theory because it fails to capture salient features of human agency and hence renders certain forms of power invisible or because, although the concept of recognition is basic, Honneth's use of this concept misconstrues its character or because, given the relationship of our ethical concepts to current ethical experience in contemporary conditions of domination, it is 'misrecognition' that is best viewed as the basic category of ethical theory.

2. *The critique of Honneth's proposal of the theory of recognition as a monistic ethical theory.* The basic thought expressed in this criticism is that although the concept of recognition captures important features of human subjectivity and agency, it does not embrace on all the salient features. Consequently, it may leave us exposed to (or even support) certain forms of power by seeking to construe all exercises of power as being, or issuing in, forms of non-recognition or misrecognition.[58]

3. *The critique of Honneth's account of contemporary forms of recognition in terms of the three axes of love, respect, and esteem.* This criticism can take the forms of arguing *either* that there are more or less axes of recognition that Honneth identifies *or* of arguing that Honneth's specification and strict demarcation of these axes of recognition creates certain blind spots with respect to the operation of power.

4. *The critique of Honneth's account of contemporary principles of recognition as (either in part or in whole) ideological.* This criticism suggests that in some respect or other, Honneth's specification of the principle of recognition does not simply make it hard to discern certain forms of power but itself inadvertently plays the ideological role of disguising and legitimating certain operations of power.

In taking up these critical standpoints, the contributors to this volume invite Honneth to clarify, refine and defend his research programme.

---

[58] Of course, this subject relates directly to the debate between Nancy Fraser and Axel Honneth in their book *Redistribution or Recognition.* See, in that book, Nancy Fraser, "Social Justice in the Age of Identity Politics: Redistribution, Recognition, and Participation," and "Distorted Beyond all Recognition: A Rejoinder to Axel Honneth," 7–109 and 198–236, respectively.

3. THE STRUCTURE OF THE BOOK

This book has four parts. The first three address Honneth's project in terms of the philosophical foundations of his project (Part I), its implications for social theory (Part II), and its significance for political theory (Part III). In Part IV, Honneth offers both a chapter setting out his response to the challenge posed by the concept of power for his research programme and a reply to his critics.

a. Philosophical Approaches to Recognition

The four chapters in Part I address philosophical perspectives on the concept of recognition. In the opening chapter, Heikki Ikäheimo and Arto Laitinen present a conceptual analysis of Honneth's use of this concept, and in the following three chapters, Robert Pippin, Bert van den Brink, and Patchen Markell take up and challenge Honneth's conceptualization of recognition by way of analyses of philosophers who have been central to the formation of Honneth's research project: Hegel, Adorno, and Mead.

Ikäheimo and Laitinen's chapter, "Analyzing Recognition: Identification, Acknowledgment, and Recognitive Attitudes towards Persons" provides a conceptual overview and clarification of the notion of recognition with particular regard to Honneth's use of this concept. Central to their account is (1) distinguishing recognition from identification and acknowledgment, (2) arguing for Honneth's understanding of recognition in terms of an attitude towards another person that is accepted by that person, and (3) clarifying the need for a (minimally) objectivist view of misrecognition. The focus of this chapter is thus not on presenting a critical perspective on Honneth's use of the concept of recognition but on offering a lucid characterization and defence of the commitments that are at stake in this use.

By contrast, Robert Pippin in his chapter "Recognition and Reconciliation: Actualized Agency in Hegel's *Jena Phenomenology*," investigates Hegel's original arguments concerning recognition, dependence, and independence in order to determine (1) the nature of the human dependence at issue, and (2) what might serve as the successful satisfaction of this condition of dependence. Pippin's argument is that it is easier to clarify the former than the latter and, crucially, and *contra* Honneth, that such clarification leads to a rejection of the claim that Hegel's arguments concerning the nature of human dependence are based on a claim about human need that can be supported or developed through appeals to evidence in developmental or social psychology of the type that Honneth adduces in *The Struggle for Recognition*. On the contrary, Pippin argues, Hegel's theory of recognition is a distinctively philosophical response to a condition of dependence characterized by the fact that being an agent is a normative status that can be nothing other than a social status, and hence exists only if taken by other members of the society to exist. In this respect, Hegel's theory offers an account of the conditions of possibility of notions such as 'mine,' 'yours,' 'ours,' and 'theirs.' Yet, working through the implications of Hegel's expressivist understanding of agency and what it means on this account for me to understand my intentions and actions as 'mine,' Pippin goes onto argue that it is not at all clear that Hegel even offers a full account of what would count as the successful satisfaction of this condition of dependence or what the political implications of such a full account would be.

Turning to the first generation of the Frankfurt School, Bert van den Brink, in "Damaged Life," offers an analysis of the ethics of resistance to be found in Theodor W. Adorno's reflections on damaged life. Van den Brink argues that although Adorno does not (and, given his commitments to the relationship of ethical practice and ethical knowledge, cannot) develop a positive ethical theory, his reflections on false normality and its power-based pathologies, on the kinds of experience that make possible knowledge about wrong life, and on the evaluative stance from which such knowledge points in the direction of a better life, do sketch an ethos or ethics of resistance in which the concept of *mis*recognition has a significant role. However, while Adorno may be related to Honneth in terms of their scrupulous attention to experiences of misrecognition, Adorno's mistrust of what passes for contemporary ethical practices leads him, *contra* Honneth, to be wary of positing a positive theory of recognition on the basis of our current ethical concepts and categories. Thus, the key issue raised by van den Brink is that Honneth's confidence in our current forms of ethical reflection runs the risk of reification that is always present in proposing a full-blown positive theory of recognition. This raises the stakes for Honneth in that it requires that he provide grounds for this confidence that remain attentive to Adorno's concerns with regard to contemporary power relations.

We have already noted that Honneth's interpretation of Hegel differs from that offered by Pippin – as well as, we might add, Robert Brandom – in its attempt to sketch out Hegel's theory of recognition in terms of social psychology. An earlier effort at this project that has been highly influential for Honneth's own work was mounted by George Herbert Mead, and Patchen Markell, in his chapter "The Potential and the Actual: Mead, Honneth, and the 'I,'" addresses Honneth's relationship to Mead as a way of bringing into focus a problem with Honneth's understanding of recognition as responding to certain potential features of persons that are only actualized in virtue of being recognized. Markell's argument is that Honneth's use of the concepts 'potentiality' and 'actuality' is meant to resolve a problem concerning whether recognition can be at once creative and responsive and at the same time support his casting of the history of relations of recognition in teleological terms; however, by investigating how this issue is also addressed by Mead's reflections on the "I" and the "me," Markell presents a case for the claim that Honneth's use of 'potentiality' and 'actuality' both runs into a set of problems already apparent in Mead's work when Mead slips into this mode of reflection and misses another line of argument in Mead that offers a more productive route for reflecting on potentiality, actuality, and recognition. In the end, Honneth's current stance, far from resolving his dilemma, leads on Markell's account to an inability to understand certain powerful modes of response and opposition to injustice.

b. Recognition and Power in Social Theory

In Part II, the chapters focus on the viability of Honneth's theory of recognition in the terrain of social philosophy. In the opening chapter, "Work, Recognition, Emancipation," Beate Rössler takes up the cogency of Honneth's approach for dealing with issues of family work understood as housework and caring for one's own children. Rössler's concern is that by situating family work under the "achievement principle" in which esteem is related to merit, and by focusing on the concrete form of reward for achievement in terms of financial remuneration, Honneth's theory is unable to provide guidance appropriate to the specific issues raised by family work and, indeed, is ultimately unable to present a cogent case for reflecting on work in general. Beginning by presenting a *prima facie* case for a categorical distinction between family work and paid work, Rössler argues that financial remuneration is not an appropriate response to the issues of justice and the good life raised by family work, a point that she reinforces through attention to the gendered division of labour. She then demonstrates that Honneth's model conceives of family work in terms that see remuneration as the medium for conveying social recognition to family work and as such threatens both to support, rather than overcome, the gendered division of labour and to reduce the demand for recognition with respect to gainful employment (paid labour in general) to issues of remuneration. These arguments lead Rössler to suggest, following Nancy Fraser, that an adequate approach to family work – and, for that matter, paid employment – must involve an appeal to a variety of normative criteria in which recognition is only one element. The clear implication of Rössler's analysis is that Honneth's theory of recognition fails to identify forms of social power that can, consequently, be made visible only by recourse to other evaluative perspectives.

Lior Barshack in "...That All Members Should be Loved in the Same Way..." turns his attention to the relationship of love and law. Following Honneth by drawing on psychoanalytical work in the object-relations field, Barshack argues that love and law cannot be easily separated out in the way that Honneth's theory claims, and that this becomes clear once we recognize that this psychoanalytical tradition involves not only 'horizontal' relations of recognition (love, respect, esteem) but also vertical relations of recognition towards a transcendent authority (the corporate body). The point here is not only that the modern family is formed within the context of the legal arrangements of the state and is, as such, characterized by relations of both love and respect, but also that the modern state involves a corporate body characterized by both mutually dependent relations of care and respect between its members. Supporting this argument by way of recourse to, for example, liberal nationalist authors such as David Miller who stress the significance of nationality in terms of the mutual concern (and not merely respect) of citizens, Barshack argues that Honneth's strict separation of love and respect prevents his theory from being able to adequately analyse ideological movements and ground the claims of redistributive justice.

A related set of issues are raised in Iris Young's chapter, "Recognition of Love's Labor: Considering Axel Honneth's Feminism," which focuses on Honneth's conception of recognition of love and care. While giving due credit to Honneth's willingness to acknowledge the role of love and care in ethical life and his objection to the low esteem currently granted to care work within a gendered division of labour, Young notes that Honneth's explanation of the persistence of the gendered division of labour is limited to the view that certain naturalistic assumptions concerning men and women have been carried over into the modern period. This explanation, Young argues, is insufficient to account for the persistence of the gendered division of labour and, indeed, the central role it plays in reproducing a division between principles of care and of achievement that finds expression in Honneth's theory. In particular, Young argues that Honneth remains (1) subject to an ideological picture of conjugal love inherited from Rousseau and Hegel, (2) fails to appreciate the implications of the asymmetrical nature of care relationships and the difficulty of situating such relationships under the principle of esteem without separating esteem from the achievement principle to which Honneth ties it, and (3) unable to address adequately forms of power through which the gendered division of labour is reproduced.

c. Recognition and Power in Political Theory

Part III redirects attention to central topics in political philosophy: toleration, deliberation, democracy, and pluralism. In the opening chapter, "'To Tolerate Means to Insult': Toleration, Recognition, and Emancipation," Rainer Forst explores the topic of toleration with respect to the fact that toleration can be based on mutual recognition and respect but can also be a form of domination that is articulated through a form of recognition. Forst starts by sketching two accounts of toleration. On the first view – the *permission* conception of toleration – to tolerate involves extending certain legal protections to a group but making them dependent on the good will of, for example, a monarch. In this context, toleration involves a complex pattern of inclusion and exclusion in which power is articulated through different forms of recognition that grant liberties to subjects while also making them into dependent subjects. On the second view – the *respect* conception – toleration is a general rule about the way citizens respect each other as legal and political equals on the basis of an account of right and wrong that all can endorse independent of, say their religious beliefs. Forst is clear that both of these conceptions of toleration persist in contemporary democratic communities, and argues for two conclusions. First, recognition can, via the permission conception, serve as a channel for power. Second, and *contra* Honneth, recognition can, via the respect conception, serve as a vehicle of emancipation but only if it is limited to respect and not esteem for one's fellow citizens.

In "Misrecognition, Power, and Democracy," Veit Bader offers a critical assessment of Honneth's *monistic* commitment to a theory of recognition and argues for a more pluralistic approach to issues of democracy and power. Like Nancy Fraser and, in this volume, Beate Rössler, Bader takes issues of recognition and misrecognition to be significant features of contemporary politics. However, he is sceptical as to whether recognition can adequately capture all the salient forms of power that are exercised in more complex democratic societies. Moreover, like Adorno, Bader holds that a focus on misrecognition is more appropriate than the proposal of a positive theory of recognition, not least since specifications of basic forms of misrecognition may be less susceptible to reasonable disagreement than specifications of what full recognition entails. Bader moves from this initial theoretical disagreement with Honneth to an assessment of the interrelatedness of relations of misrecognition and power and experiences of social and moral incapacitation. Thereby, he becomes able to further argue for his earlier anti-monistic claims and to argue, *contra* Honneth, that an adequate treatment of the issue of social and moral incapacitation requires a pluralistic rather than a monistic approach in social theory, not least since positive theories of full recognition run the risk of treating victims of misrecognition as more incapacitated than they actually are.

Anthony Simon Laden's chapter, "Reasonable Deliberation, Constructive Power, and the Struggle for Recognition," is a demonstration of how Honneth's work on struggles for recognition may be brought into fruitful dialogue with Rawls' political liberalism. Laden constructs this dialogue by considering how political institutions might be set up so as to be responsive to struggles for recognition, and how such struggles might appeal to such responsiveness. Laden focuses on the urgent case of groups struggling for recognition who have achieved basic respect in the forms of legal status and even a degree of social esteem but lack fully equal respect in that they fail to be recognized by those who maintain power of them as fully co-equal authors of the contours of their mutual relationship. Laden's argument is that combining Honneth's work on struggles for recognition with Rawls' work on reasonable deliberation brings into relief the way in which our practical identities can be shaped by asymmetrically distributed forms of constructive social power, shows how such forms of misrecognition undermine the conditions of reasonable deliberation, and provides participants who exercise power over other's identities with motives to overcome this condition.

In the final chapter in Part III, David Owen in "Self-Government and 'Democracy as Reflexive Co-Operative'" discusses the political significance of Honneth's theory of recognition to the extent that it is inspired by an ideal of (radical) democracy as "reflexive co-operation" drawn, in large part, from the work of Dewey. Owen's critical examination demonstrates (1) how this ideal is related to the theory of recognition, and (2) how critical reflection on this theory carries some interesting, if not always fully determinate, implications for the ideal. In particular, he shows how the democratic ideal might be further developed in relation to certain problems concerning Honneth's understanding of self-confidence, self-respect, and self-esteem. In the end, he suggests that Honneth's democratic ideal can be maintained, but only if significant changes are made to the ideas of a just division of labour and Honneth's accounts of love, respect, and esteem as forms of recognition. Throughout, Owen argues that only closer attention to the unavoidable tensions between Honneth's social and political ideal on the one hand and the imperfect, non-ideal and complex societies we inhabit on the other is necessary for Honneth to make these changes.

d. Axel Honneth on Recognition and Power

In his first contribution to this volume, "Recognition as Ideology," Axel Honneth asks what may help us distinguish ethical, sound forms of recognition from ideological ones. "How is it possible," Honneth asks, "for forms wherein values are confirmed, i.e., forms of recognition, nonetheless to possess the character of being forms of domination?" Honneth starts with a useful summary of widely accepted results of the recent debate in social philosophy as to what we mean by the term 'recognition.' Here, he shows that all defensible uses of the term designate a form of interaction with which persons respond to valuable characteristics of persons or groups. After having clarified, by means of an argument from the idea that our life world is our second nature (McDowell), what he considers the best account of such responsiveness to value, Honneth argues that it is not enough to claim that 'true' forms of recognition are responsive to valuable characteristics of persons or groups. Indeed, or so Honneth claims, ideological, power-based forms of recognition too "mobilize evaluative reasons that pertain to our horizon of value." But then what is the irrationality that we associate with false ideologies of recognition? By means of a critical assessment of the recognition-order of the new capitalism and its ideals of the flexibility and entrepreneurism of the employee, Honneth argues that a criterion by which ideological forms of recognition can be identified can be found in the notion of *fulfillment in material practice* of those prospects of autonomy and well-being that the ideological vocabulary of recognition promises.

In his second contribution, "Rejoinder," Axel Honneth responds to the issues raised in the other chapters in this volume. After having accepted some of the points raised by his critics and rejected others, he concludes that although the book has not resulted in a new theory about recognition and power, progress has been made on the road towards such a theory.

PART I

PHILOSOPHICAL APPROACHES TO RECOGNITION

2

Analyzing Recognition

Identification, Acknowledgement, and Recognitive Attitudes towards Persons

Heikki Ikäheimo and Arto Laitinen

There is a wide consensus today that 'recognition' is something that we need a clear grasp of in order to understand the dynamics of political struggles and, perhaps, the constitution and dynamics of social reality more generally. Yet the discussions on recognition have so far often been conceptually rather inexplicit, in the sense that the key concepts have remained largely unexplicated or undefined. Since the English word 'recognition' is far from unambiguous, it is possible, and to our mind also actually the case, that different authors have meant different things with this word.

In what follows, we will make a number of conceptual distinctions and clarificatory proposals that are intended to bring to more sharply focus the field of phenomena that are being discussed under the catchword 'recognition.' This is meant to serve a dual purpose: to suggest a number of distinctions that are of help in formulating rival views, and to propose what strikes us as the best overall position formulated in terms of those distinctions.

We thank the editors of this volume as well as participants of the "Recognition and Power" symposium held at Utrecht University, March 13–15, 2003; participants of the workshop on recognition held at Macquarie University, November 10, 2003; participants of the Colloquium on Recognition held at the University of Jyväskylä, May 29–30, 2004; and Axel Honneth, Ariane ten Hagen, Mattias Iser, Emmanuel Renault, Hans-Christoph Schmidt am Busch, Andreas Wildt, Christopher Zurn, and other participants of Axel Honneth's research seminar in summer 2005, for helpful criticisms, comments, and questions.

Our proposals are meant to be, by and large, compatible with Axel Honneth's work on recognition, which to us is the most ambitious and differentiated account of recognition available. Where we propose something that seems to us to be in compatible with Honneth's explicit formulations, we indicate it in the footnotes. In discussing recognition, one should of course be aware of the venerable Hegelian origins of the theme, but we will pass over specific questions of Hegel interpretation in this chapter,[1] although, we will try to be faithful to Hegel's spirit in at least one sense: by endeavoring to proceed in a holistic manner, in the sense of trying to forge a conceptual overview where things hold together as systematically as possible.

1. IDENTIFICATION, ACKNOWLEDGEMENT, AND RECOGNITION

We will first distinguish between three phenomena, or constellations of phenomena, which are usually called 'recognition' and which are therefore easily run together.[2] For the sake of clarity, we will introduce a terminological distinction, and call these three different, although intricately interconnected, phenomena or constellations of phenomena, *identification, acknowledgement,* and *recognition.* Formally, identification, acknowledgement, and what we will call 'the recognitive attitude'

---

[1] On recognition in Hegel's theory of subjective spirit, see Heikki Ikäheimo, "On the Role of Intersubjectivity in Hegel's Encyclopaedic Phenomenology and Psychology," *Bulletin of the Hegel Society of Great Britain,* 49/50 (2004), 73–95. On the role of recognition in Hegel's views on agency, see Arto Laitinen "Hegel on Retrospective and Intersubjective Determination of Intention," *Bulletin of the Hegel Society of Great Britain,* 49/50 (2004), 54–72, and Robert Pippin's contribution to this volume.

[2] For predecessors or earlier versions of this distinction, see Avishai Margalit, "Recognition II: Recognizing the Brother and the Other," in *Aristotelian Society,* Supplementary Volume 75 (2001), 127–139; Heikki Ikäheimo, "On the Genus and Species of Recognition," in *Inquiry* 45 (2002), no. 4, 447–462; Heikki Ikäheimo, "Taylor on Something Called 'Recognition,'" in *Perspectives on the Philosophy of Charles Taylor,* ed. by Arto Laitinen and Nicholas H. Smith, *Acta Philosophica Fennica* 71 (Helsinki: Societas Philosophica Fennica, 2002), 99–111. For some initial steps towards distinguishing recognition (or 'acknowledgement,' as we call it here) of values and recognition of persons, see Arto Laitinen, "Interpersonal Recognition – A Response to Value or a Precondition of Personhood?" *Inquiry* 45 (2002), no. 4, 463–478, and for a more full-fledged analysis, see Arto Laitinen, "Interpersonal Recognition and Responsiveness to Relevant Differences," *Critical Review of International Social and Political Philosophy* (March 2006),Vol. 9, No. 1, 47–70.

can all be conceived as cases of some A taking B as X. In all cases, A is a person or collective of persons, but the B's and X's differ, depending on whether what is at stake is a case of identification, acknowledgement, or recognition. Also, identification, acknowledgement, and recognition are different kinds of 'takings.' Let us take a brief look at them one by one.

Identification of Anything

There is a sense of the word 'recognition' in which anything can be recognized. For this sense of 'recognition,' let us reserve the term 'identification.' Anything can be *identified* numerically, qualitatively, and generically. In other words, any B can be taken as the individual thing it is, as a thing with some particular features, and as a thing belonging to a certain genus.

The identification of persons (that is, when B is a person or a collective of persons) is a special type of identification, at least in the sense that persons have a self-identity or are self-identifying creatures. Thus, in the case of persons, we need to distinguish between *external* identifications and *self-*identifications. External identifications are made by other persons (A and B are different), self-identifications by the person herself (A and B are the same). As is well known, qualitative self-identifications are never made completely independently of qualitative identifications made by others. Our qualitative self-identities are formed in complex dialogues and struggles with the views that others have of us.

In many politically interesting cases, how something is identified is vitally important. It makes a difference, for instance, whether something is identified generically as a terrorist organization (by focusing on certain qualities or features as the defining ones) or as a resistance movement (by focusing on some other qualities or features).

Acknowledgement of 'Normative Entities'

There is, second, a sense of 'recognition' in which only something like 'normative entities' can be recognized. For this sense of 'recognition,' let us reserve the term 'acknowledgement.' We *acknowledge* norms, principles, rules, or claims as valid; reasons as good; values as genuine, and so on.[3] Formally then, in acknowledgement, the possible B's are things like norms, principles, rules, claims, reasons, values, and so on, and the possible X's are things like 'valid,' 'good,' 'genuine,' and so on.[4]

Recognition of Persons

Whereas anything can be *identified*, and whereas only normative entities can be *acknowledged*, there is a sense of the word 'recognition' in which only persons (and possibly collectivities of persons) can be *recognized*. When we see recognition as a genus consisting of the three species of love, respect, and esteem – as Axel Honneth, following Hegel, does[5] – it is obvious intuitively that recognition is not to be straightforwardly run together with identification or with acknowledgement.[6] A failure to distinguish *recognition of persons* from *identification* and from *acknowledgement* risks losing sight of their complex interconnections.[7]

---

[3] Identification is possible in relation to normative entities as well. One can identify them as what they are, or mistake them for something else: "*That* is not the categorical imperative, that is Hammurabi's law," "*That* law is 3000 years old", "that is not a moral norm, it is a legal norm." To identify a normative entity is not necessarily to acknowledge it. Acknowledging a claim includes the opinion that the claim is valid, and it includes being disposed to feel, will, and act accordingly, and being disposed to feel regret if one fails to act accordingly. As we encounter in our life-worlds a plurality of (valid) claims, often the claims one acknowledges are in conflict and the stronger ones *override* the weaker ones. That a claim is overridden does not mean that one does not acknowledge it. One can also *by mistake* act contrary to the claims one acknowledges. But if one *deliberately* violates a claim, *without any stronger reasons*, it means that one does not acknowledge the claim.

[4] How about 'acknowledging one's duties or responsibilities'? In the A-B-X-scheme, this can be understood as A's acknowledging some explicit or implicit claim concerning her duties or responsibilities as valid.

[5] See Axel Honneth, *The Struggle for Recognition: The Moral Grammar of Social Conflicts*, transl. by Joel Anderson (Cambridge, UK: Polity Press, 1995).

[6] Note for instance that whereas persons care about whether they are recognized or not, norms or values cannot care whether they are acknowledged or not. Recognition and acknowledgement have different dynamics.

[7] Distinguishing these helps in conceiving more clearly how, for instance, individual or collective identities – which are created, formed, and contested in external and internal identifications – hang together with normativity. Identities come with various kinds of normative statuses, explicit or implicit evaluations, and so on, and acknowledging these seems to be internally related to interpersonal recognition. We believe that the identification-acknowledgement-recognition-distinction will help, for example, in discerning clearly the constituents of what Louis Althusser called 'recognition' (or *reconnaissance*). See Axel Honneth's contribution to this volume.

2. INTERPERSONAL RECOGNITION: A CLOSER LOOK

In this chapter, we will focus on recognition of persons. Towards the end of the chapter, however, we will discuss one aspect of the complex interrelation between recognition of persons and acknowledgement. By 'persons' we mean only persons in flesh and blood and not juridical or institutional persons. Conceptualizing 'recognition' of institutions – states, for example – requires formulating a clear theory of institutions, but we will not discuss that field of issues here.

It may be possible to start analyzing interpersonal recognition in various ways, taking various concepts, such as statuses, actions, institutional spheres, or attitudes as the key concept. In what follows, we will analyze interpersonal recognition in terms of attitudes. We call the relevant attitudes 'recognitive attitudes' or 'attitudes of recognition,' and these are, following Honneth and Hegel, those of love, respect, and esteem. Analyzing recognition in terms of recognitive attitudes has a number of useful features.

First (2.1), it helps in distinguishing distinct attitudes of recognition from various kinds of complexes of attitudes. Second (2.2), it provides an easy way of distinguishing one-dimensional conceptions of recognition from multi-dimensional conceptions of recognition. Third (2.3), it helps in distinguishing the attitudes of recognition from the various social and institutional spheres or contexts where recognition or misrecognition takes place. Fourth (2.4), it helps in seeing how interpersonal recognition is related to action. Fifth (2.5), it helps in getting a clear view of how attitudes of recognition affect our attitudes towards ourselves. Sixth (2.6), it helps in clarifying how exactly interpersonal recognition is related to statuses in different senses of the word 'status.'

2.1. Recognitive Attitudes and Attitude-Complexes

Let us start with a question. Is a case of a person A's having a recognitive attitude towards a person B always a case of recognition? The answer depends on whether one has in mind a *monological* or a *dialogical* conception of recognition.

According to a monological conception, a mere recognitive attitude of A towards B *is* recognition irrespective of the attitudes of B towards

A or towards A's attitudes. If A, for example, respects B, this is as such a case of B's being recognized by A.

According to a dialogical conception, on the other hand, it takes the attitudes of two to constitute recognition. In other words, A's recognitive attitude of, say, respect towards B adds up to B's being recognized by A, only if B has relevant attitudes towards A or A's recognitive attitude. More specifically, according to the dialogical conception, B has to have a *recognitive* attitude towards A – she has to recognize A as a competent recognizer.[8]

Thus, according to the dialogical conception, there is no such thing as one-sided recognition. Hegel's story of the master and the slave is a case in point. In the Hegelian dialogical conception of recognition, recognition is thus what we may call a *two-way complex of recognitive attitudes*. It is worth noting that conceiving recognition along the dialogical conception as a two-way complex of recognitive attitudes is not the same as conceiving of it as a symmetrical affair. If A esteems B as an excellent doctor, it is not B's esteeming A as an excellent doctor that makes this a case of recognition according to the dialogical conception, but rather B's taking A as a competent recognizer or judge regarding the relevant matters (excellence of doctors in this case). It is only on the dialogical conception, which emphasizes the importance of the attitudes of B, that we get a clear view of the complexities of how exactly the recognitive attitudes of others may affect a persons attitudes towards herself (see 2.5).[9] Not only should we distinguish between the recognitive attitudes and the two-way complex of attitudes – which, according to the dialogical conception, recognition proper is – but we also should distinguish between the individual recognitive attitudes of a single person towards another from the (one-way) complex of attitudes that that single person has towards the other. Hence, for example, the attitude-complexes of individual family members towards each

---

[8] Elsewhere (Ikäheimo, "On the Genus and Species," 450 and note 5), we have used the terms 'recognizee-sensitive,' 'recognizee-insensitive,' and 'recognizee-centered' conception of recognition. Of these, the first is the dialogical conception and the second and third are monological conceptions. According to a 'recognizee-centered' conception of recognition, it is the viewpoint of the recognizee *alone* that counts in determining whether something is recognition or not.

[9] Compare Hegel, *Phenomenology of Spirit*, transl. by A. V. Miller (Oxford: Oxford University Press, 1977), §183 and passim.

other always contain a multitude of attitudes, and concerning of recognitive attitudes, they may contain not only love, but also respect and esteem in different degrees. It is perfectly possible, for instance, to love someone a great deal, but not to hold him in esteem much, or at all.[10] This takes us to the next distinction.

2.2. One-Dimensional versus Multi-dimensional Conceptions of Recognition

It is useful to distinguish between *one-dimensional* and *multi-dimensional* conceptions of interpersonal recognition. Following the attitude-analysis, according to a one-dimensional conception of recognition, there are not several types of recognitive attitudes, but only one type.

Thus, restricting recognition, say, to *respect* in the Kantian sense, is a one-dimensional conception of recognition. Reading the literature on 'recognition,' it is often hard to say whether an author understands recognition in a one-dimensional or a multi-dimensional way. (Add this to the fact that interpersonal recognition can easily be confused with what we renamed earlier as identification and acknowledgement.)

Axel Honneth's conception of recognition is the most explicitly multi-dimensional conception of interpersonal recognition that we are aware of, and is, in this respect, of exemplary clarity. In his view, there are three types of recognition: love, respect, and esteem. More exactly, love, respect, and esteem are types of recognitive attitudes, which, according to the dialogical conception, are potential *constituents of* different types of recognition.

Adopting a multi-dimensional conception of recognition raises the question of what it is that the various dimensions or types share. Here, views may part depending on philosophical sensibilities or background convictions. Those with a 'late-Wittgensteinian' sensibility may find this question uninteresting, thinking that whatever types of recognitive attitudes these are, they bear only a 'family resemblance' to each

---

[10] Different kinds of 'relations of recognition' can be analyzed in terms of different kinds of complexes of recognitive attitudes. What we call 'human relationships' or 'personal relationships' are essentially various kinds of relations of recognition, consisting of various kinds of complexes of recognitive attitudes. This is not to say that persons in relations of recognition have *only* recognitive attitudes towards each other, but only that the recognitive attitudes are the constitutive core of these relations.

other. Those with a more traditional sensibility, on the other hand, may not be content with such an answer, and may insist on the need for closer scrutiny. There are important philosophical questions involved in this divergence, but here we will only assume that the right way to proceed is by trial and error: by making proposals as to how the various types of recognitive attitudes might be usefully seen as *species* of a *genus*, and by finding out whether the proposals can stand critical examination.

By looking at Honneth's three types of recognitive attitude in the traditional manner, we can understand the recognitive attitude as a genus for the three species of love, respect, and esteem. What then is the definition of the genus 'recognitive attitude'? One answer, which we believe is compatible with Honneth's conception, is that the definition of the genus recognitive attitude is *taking someone as a person*. Following the A-B-X-scheme, the general term for X for all of the interpersonal recognitive attitudes is thus 'person.'[11]

Less formally, having a recognitive attitude towards someone is relating to her as to a person, or having a 'personalizing attitude' towards her. This way of looking at recognition has interesting implications. As is widely agreed by philosophers following Wittgenstein's reflections on "an attitude towards a soul" in *Philosophical Investigations* and elsewhere, the traditional formulation of the problem of other minds, other 'souls,' or persons centrally as a problem of knowledge or justified belief does not grasp the most fundamental ways of relating to others as to persons. For instance, Stanley Cavell talks of *acknowledging* persons or personhood.[12] In our terms, this view can be formulated as

---

[11] Laitinen ("Social Equality, Recognition and Preconditions of Good Life," unpublished ms.) has put forward the suggestion that in mutual recognition, the participants take each others to be recognizers of some kind (persons, groups, states, and so on), and thus the genus is something more general than 'taking as a person' – namely, 'taking as a recognizer.' Seen this way, 'taking as a person' and 'taking as a legitimate state' are two cases of this general attitude.

[12] See Stanley Cavell, "Knowing and Acknowledging," in *Must We Mean What We Say: A Book of Essays* (Cambridge: Cambridge University Press, 1976), 238–266. Cavell does not distinguish terminologically between 'acknowledgement' and 'recognition' in the way we do. See also Brandom's usage of "acknowledgement" and "recognition" in Robert Brandom, *Making it Explicit* (Cambridge, MA: Harvard University Press, 1994). On Wittgenstein on attitudes towards a soul, see, for example, Simo Säätelä, "Human Beings and Automatons," in *Persons – An Interdisciplinary Dialogue*, Papers

saying that the most fundamental way of taking someone as a person is not (or at least not only) *identifying generically* someone as a person, but rather *recognizing* someone as a person, or having a recognitive attitude/attitudes towards her.[13]

Hegel shows no particular interest in the traditional formulation of the problem of other minds, and there is reason to believe that his theory of recognition, among other things, involves more or less the same kind of shift in the discussion as the one made by Wittgenstein and his followers. Following Honneth's three-dimensional reconstruction of Hegel's concept of recognition and our attitude-analysis, the three recognitive attitudes can be seen as three different ways or modes of 'taking' someone as a person in three respective dimensions of personhood.[14]

This way of thinking specifies the relevant concepts of love, respect, and esteem. *Respect* in the relevant sense is hence a way of taking someone as a person. By contrast, speaking about, say, 'having respect towards the forces of nature,' either involves some other concept of respect or then reveals a personalizing attitude towards nature. Also, we may value anything, but in the relevant sense, we only hold in *esteem* what we take to be a person. Finally, since *loving* in the relevant sense is also a species of taking someone as a person, it differs from 'loving' in a non-personalizing sense in which people may declare that they 'love,' say, summer nights or Italian food.

If love, respect, and esteem, on the relevant conceptions, turn out to be the *only* species of recognitive attitude, then taking someone as a person, or relating towards someone as to a person (or, having a

---

of the 25th International Wittgenstein Symposium, ed. by Christian Kanzian, Josef Quitterer, and Edmund Runggaldier (The Austrian Ludwig Wittgenstein Society, 2002).

[13] One way to read this would be that personhood is nothing more than the status of being an object of personifying (that is, recognitive) attitudes and treatment. This is not our line of thought, as will hopefully become clear in Section 3. We leave open here the question of whether taking someone as a person involves also identification, and if so, what exact role identification, has in the general phenomenon. It may well be that the answer will be different in the cases of love, respect, and esteem.

[14] See Ikäheimo, "On the Genus and Species," for an attempt at a more detailed analysis, where X is divided into C and D, where C is a placeholder for the different 'attributes' attributed to B in A's recognitive attitudes, and where D is a placeholder for the respective dimensions of B's personhood.

'personalizing attitude' toward someone) is always a case of loving, respecting, or holding in esteem, or a mixture of these. If this is so, then love, respect, and esteem are arguably what Wittgenstein was after in his reflections on the "attitude towards a soul." But if we adopt the dialogical conception of recognition, then the definition of the genus recognitive attitude – taking someone as a person – is not exactly the definition of the genus recognition. What then is the definition of recognition as such? We propose that it is something along the lines of *taking someone as a person, the content of which is understood and which is accepted by the other person*. We will return to this shortly (in 2.4).

2.3. Recognitive Attitudes versus Social and Institutional Spheres

Another useful feature of the attitude-analysis of recognition is that it enables one to make a clear distinction between recognition in its various types or species, on the one hand, and the various social and institutional *spheres* or *contexts*, where recognition may take place, on the other.

It also enables one to think more precisely how these spheres themselves may be constituted by attitudes of recognition. Hence, for example, although attitudes of love between individuals are certainly of central importance in *families*, and can be even taken to be constitutive of a family *as a family*, attitudes of respect and esteem between family members are still far from unimportant for everything that takes place in a family. Indeed, from a rights point of view, one can even argue that a family ceases to exist as a family, if the family members do not respect each other as having certain relevant rights and responsibilities. And, legally speaking, the family is a juridical institution, whose existence depends on the recognitive attitudes of the society, or members of the society, institutionalized in laws and decrees.[15] The relation between distinct attitudes of recognition, on the one hand, and social

---

[15] Think of the juridical status of same sex relationships. Without the institutionalization of relevant rights and responsibilities, a same sex relationship will not count as a family juridically, however close to ideal it may be 'ethically' – for example, by involving deep mutual love, respect, and esteem.

or institutional spheres, on the other, is extremely complicated, and it takes careful case studies to see exactly how attitudes of recognition and different social and institutional spheres are related.[16]

2.4. Recognitive Attitudes, Action, and Understanding

Conceptualizing recognition in terms of attitudes may sound to some as an overly 'theoretical' approach. Isn't recognition something more active or dynamic or practical than just attitudes? Isn't it a matter of actions or acts of recognition?

First, 'attitudes' should not be understood in any implausibly 'representationalist' or 'mentalist' or 'atomistic' manner. The relations-to-world of a person – from pre-linguistic coping and vague background understandings to clear and distinct beliefs – are that person's 'takes,' 'views,' 'understandings,' 'stances,' 'intentions,' or 'attitudes' towards the world. The points from hermeneutical phenomenology – that the views implicit in know-how or emotion-laden understandings are often hard to articulate or identify – are well taken. We do not restrict the term 'attitude' to the already linguistically articulated and clearly individuated opinions only, but intend it to cover implicit understandings and presuppositions as well. In the world, we encounter other persons, and we have and form various kinds of 'attitudes' towards other persons: not only explicit ones, but also implicit 'background' attitudes.

Let us analyze next how the recognitive attitudes relate to actions, expressions and understanding. It is a given in the philosophy of action

---

[16] At least on a superficial reading, Honneth's way of connecting each of the three types of recognition to one respective institutional sphere of recognition in Axel Honneth, *The Struggle for Recognition: The Moral Grammar of Social Conflicts*, transl. by Joel Anderson (Cambridge, UK: Polity Press, 1995), chapter 5, had a tendency to cover up this distinction, but the defect is easily corrected. Perhaps one could say that a different recognitive attitude is *dominant* in the constitution of these different spheres. In any case, as Honneth has subsequently pointed out, institutional complexes or spheres rarely instantiate only one 'recognition principle' (Nancy Fraser and Axel Honneth, *Redistribution or Recognition? A Political-Philosophical Exchange* (London: Verso Books, 2003), 146. On the dynamics and frictions of love and respect in the family, see Honneth's "Zwischen Gerechtigkeit und affektiver Bindung. Die Familie im Brennpunkt moralischer Kontroversen" and "Liebe und Moral. Zum moralischen Gehalt affektiver Bindungen," in Honneth, *Das Andere der Gerechtigkeit* (Frankfurt am Main: Suhrkamp, 2000), 193–215 and 216–236.

that actions differ from natural events in that actions are something that we understand as effects, externalizations, or embodiments of intentions or attitudes of persons. A special case of action is action that is performed *in order to express* one's intentions or attitudes to other persons. Concentrating on the recognitive attitudes, we may mean by an 'act of recognition' in a broad sense any act or action that in one way or another is motivated by them. But in a more limited sense, only those actions of A that she performs *in order to express* her love, respect, or esteem towards B, are 'acts of recognition.' We believe that it is important not to identify the immense variety of social actions or practices, in which attitudes of recognition have some motivating role, with 'acts of recognition' in this limited sense.[17]

Coming back to the definition of recognition that we proposed earlier ("taking someone as a person, the content of which is understood and which is accepted by the other person"), what does it take for B to *understand* A's attitudes of recognition towards her? Obviously A does not necessarily have to *say* to B that she, for example, holds B in esteem for something in order for B to be able to understand A's attitude-complex towards her as including the attitude of esteem. More generally, it is not necessary that A in any way deliberately act with the intention of expressing, or in order to express, her attitudes to B.

Fully understanding any action of a person involves understanding the motives or motivating reasons for the action. The motives or reasons that motivate the actions of persons can tell us of their attitudes towards, in principle, anything that is relevant for the action.

---

[17] Some of Honneth's formulations are to our mind somewhat misleading in this respect – for instance, when he writes, "whether we are talking of gestures, speech acts, or institutional measures, these expressions and procedures are cases of 'recognition' only if their primary purpose is directed in some positive manner towards the existence of another person or group" (Honneth, "Grounding Recognition," 506). As we see it, this formulation is inaccurate, first, in that it limits 'acts of recognition' to an unnecessarily limited subgroup of actions: we take it that recognitive attitudes may importantly determine or modify an action, (1) even if anything like affirming the existence of others is not the *primary* purpose of the action, and (2) even if *expressing* recognitive attitudes is not among the purposes of the action at all. Second, the formulation is in our view inaccurate more generally in making actions of whatever kind a necessary constituent of recognition: we argue that actions – also according to the dialogical conception – are not a necessary constituent of recognition at all. Rather, the recognitive attitudes that *are* a necessary constituent of recognition are motivators of actions. And of course actions are an important – but clearly not the only – index through which we try to read each others' attitudes.

Why does A help B, when B has hard times in her life? There are of course many possible explanations, but one candidate is that A loves B. A does not need to say this to B for B to be able in principle to tell. Or what does it tell B of A's attitudes towards her that A always asks for B's help when there is some especially difficult work to be done at the office? Well, possibly that A holds B in esteem for her abilities and achievements in similar tasks. A does not have to give B a medal or a gold watch 'in recognition of' B's contributions for B to be able in principle to understand A's attitude-complex towards her as including the recognitive attitude of esteem. Similarly with respect.

Sometimes, of course, it may make a big difference whether A deliberately expresses or communicates her attitudes to B or not. Let us assume that A and B are colleagues and A does not hold B in *esteem* for her abilities and achievements, since from A's point of view, what B does is mostly useless or even harmful. If A says this to B, the reason may be that she, however, *respects* B as someone who ought to be criticized and who may be able to learn from criticism. Also, it may be that A's communicating the criticism to B explicitly is motivated by the fact that A sincerely *cares about* B and hence about how she manages in her life and work.[18] If A does not bother to communicate her lack of esteem for B to B, but B understands it from her behavior, B may wonder whether A even respects B, or whether A cares at all about B. And so on. The point is that our omissions, too, may 'communicate' our attitudes, and the choice between expressive action and omission may sometimes make a difference.

Needless to say, we are not always sincere in expressing or communicating our attitudes. What may seem to be an 'act of recognition' in the limited sense is not a genuine act of recognition (at least in the limited sense) if it is not a sincere attempt to communicate one's true attitudes: a 'respectful' bow can be insincere and so can, say, the giving of a gold watch to a retiring worker 'in recognition of' her indispensable contributions. Even in these cases, B may still be able to read from A's other actions whether, and to what extent, A *really* loves, respects or esteems her.[19]

---

[18] Following Aristotle's core meaning of *philia*, caring about someone *for her own sake* is loving her. See Ikäheimo, "On the Genus and Species."

[19] A fake act of recognition in the narrow sense can be a genuine act of recognition in the broader sense: A may hide some of her real attitudes towards B behind polite words because she does not want to hurt B's feelings or pride unnecessarily.

Further, it is possible that A has recognitive attitudes towards B, but these do not lead A into any kind of action in which these attitudes are detectable by B. There are at least two types of cases like this. In the first type, A's recognitive attitude towards B has the kind of role in A's motivational set that would lead A into a particular action, if only A were not for some reason incapable of so acting. A might be, for instance, completely paralyzed physically. In the second type, A does have recognitive attitudes towards B, but these attitudes do not have the kind of role in A's motivational set that will lead A into acting 'out of recognition' towards B even if she is physically capable of doing so. A may have stronger motivation to act otherwise. Take the extreme case in which A has to choose between saving B, whom she deeply loves, and saving the world, and A chooses the latter option. If, by some terrible twist of fate, saving the world demands of A that she does not even express her attitude of love towards B (for instance, by saying or otherwise showing that she is deeply sorry), A's love towards B does not necessarily show in any way at all in A's actions.

In both types of cases, it *may* still be that B is able to understand or detect A's recognitive attitudes towards her in A's *feelings or emotions*, say, of grief or anxiety – to the extent that these show in some other way than in A's actions. It is often vitally important to know that someone loves, respects, or esteems me, even if she has absolutely no way of acting out of these attitudes towards me.[20]

Understanding the attitudes of others is always fallible, and we can easily be seriously mistaken about the recognitive attitudes of others towards ourselves – say, by interpreting sincere praise as sarcasm or sarcasm as praise. Generally speaking, for genuine recognition to take place, B cannot be seriously mistaken about A's real attitudes towards her. If B just imagines that A has recognitive attitudes towards B, no genuine understanding takes place and we do not have a case of recognition but, at most, imagined recognition. This may be the case, even

---

[20] The phrase acting (or doing) something 'out of recognition' towards someone can perhaps be understood in a strict sense in which a recognitive attitude is a primary motive for a token of action, and in a looser sense in which a recognitive attitude motivationally or in some other way modifies an action (for example, its manner). In a very general sense, there are arguably no actions of persons that would not fit the bill in some respect, since arguably any actions of persons are somehow modified by some attitudes of recognition towards some other persons. See also note 17.

if A does in fact have recognitive attitudes towards B. Understanding someone's attitudes is not just imagining nor just successfully guessing them.[21]

2.5. Acceptance, Internalization, and Autonomy

Attitudes have propositional or judgmental content. Thus, B's understanding A's attitude towards B involves B's understanding the judgmental content of the attitude. But what is it to 'accept' the recognitive attitude in a relevant sense? Remember that according to the Hegelian dialogical conception of recognition, B has to have a *recognitive* attitude towards A in order for B to be recognized by A. It seems not to be enough that B accepts *the content* of A's attitude in the sense of *just agreeing with* it. B may well agree with the judgements of persons whom she does not respect at all as competent judges in the matters in hand: they just happen to be right this time, but whatever they said wouldn't change B's view. Accepting the attitude should then be seen as something more demanding than just agreeing with the content. On the other hand, it is not necessary that B fully agree with every detail of A's view. What matters is rather that B accepts the fact that the view has a point or is a reasonable one, or is a view to be taken seriously, or is one from which one could learn something. Let us hence redefine the acceptance-clause so that in the relevant sense, B only accepts the attitudes of A to the extent that she *respects* A as a *competent judge* in the matter in hand.[22]

---

[21] This is not to say, for instance, that 'imagined recognition' is totally inconsequential for the self-conception of a person. For example, Axel Honneth speaks of the importance of recognition from *imagined others* for the capability to transcend the prevailing status quo of recognitive relations. (see Honneth, *Struggle*, 85). It may be important for an individual (or a group of individuals), who in given circumstances fare badly in terms of recognition, to be able to imagine another situation, where she (or they) would receive more, or more adequate, recognition. If one wants to understand recognition as genuinely dialogical, as we do, it should be emphasized, however, that recognition from imagined others (as well as felt 'recognition' based on imagined attitudes of real others) is just what it is, *imagined recognition*, not recognition proper.

[22] Ikäheimo has earlier tried two other formulations for the definition of recognition according to the dialogical conception: "taking another person as a person that is understood as such taking and accepted by the other person" (Ikäheimo, "On the Genus and Species") and "taking another person as a person that is understood as such taking and the content of which is accepted by the other person" (Heikki Ikäheimo, "Taylor"). Both of these seem to get things slightly wrong. First, it is better

The extent to which we generally respect others as competent judges in the relevant matters affects the extent to which we accept their recognitive attitudes towards us, and hence the extent to which these may affect our attitudes towards ourselves.[23] If someone does not accept anyone's views towards herself, then she does not receive recognition from anyone. Usually we are *more or less* open to the attitudes of particular others, or respect particular others as *more or less* capable of making judgements about us in this or that matter. An extreme case of lack of respect for others in the sense of not accepting anyone's views on oneself is a serious pathology, and anyone knows, or at least can imagine, different variations of cases like this.

On the other hand, it is possible that a person 'accepts' the attitudes of others towards oneself in the sense of just more or less uncritically 'internalizing' them as her self-attitudes. It seems counterintuitive that this would be a genuine case of recognition.[24] Let us therefore refine the acceptance-clause further in such a way that at least extreme cases of uncritical *internalization* of the attitudes of recognition towards

---

to say "the *content* of which is understood . . ." since this emphasizes the possibility of intricate misunderstandings of what exactly others think of us. Second, it is better not to say "and the *content* of which is accepted by the other person" but rather "and *which* is accepted by the other person," to emphasize that accepting in the relevant sense is not just agreeing with the content, but involves respect towards A, whose attitude has the content in question. Hence, the proposal "taking someone as a person, the content of which is understood and which is accepted by the other person."

[23] Note that your judgments about the competence of some particular other in judging you may change when you find that her judgment on a particular issue concerning you was more (or less) perspicacious than what you would have expected from her, or what you first thought. This implies that 'agreeing with' the content of the other's judgment does not necessarily mean agreeing from the start, but often also coming to agree with. One way in which the views of others about ourselves affect us is by changing our own views about ourselves (another is strengthening views that we already held). The changes are sometimes instantaneous, sometimes very slow: think of meditating on something that your grandmother said about you years ago and only now seeing the wisdom of it. Note also that agreeing on the relevant kinds of judgments is hardly ever a matter of all or nothing. Agreement allows for degrees, and the degree may change: you might, for instance, have first thought that there just might be a grain of truth in someone's judgment about you, and later come to think that there is actually much more truth in it than just a grain.

[24] This was a problem in Honneth's earlier reliance on G. H. Mead's to some extent mechanistic, 'internalization' model (in Honneth, *Struggle*). Subsequently, Honneth has explicitly backed away from Mead's social psychology. See "Grounding Recognition: A Rejoinder to Critical Questions," in *Inquiry* 45 (2002), no. 4, 499–520, especially 502–3.

oneself do not involve *acceptance* in the required sense, and that these cases are hence not genuine cases of recognition. This way of thinking implies that the degree of B's cognitive autonomy affects the degree to which B can be genuinely recognized by A. Whereas we can internalize views even under hypnosis or other kinds of psychic manipulation, accepting views in the relevant sense implies the capacity to reflect on their validity. The acceptance-clause thus rules out at least extreme cases of indoctrination, but it naturally does not imply B's infallibility. It is indeed a very important form of finite autonomy to be capable of evaluating the validity of the attitudes of others towards oneself. Some degree of this capability clearly seems to be a necessary condition for recognition in the dialogical sense to take place.

Another way of stating the same point is that we are able to respect others as competent judges only to the extent that we are ourselves competent judges of their competence. Unequal competences or unequal levels of cognitive autonomy bring their own complexity to relations of recognition, but a general truth seems to be that for B's recognition by A to take place, at least B has to be cognitively autonomous enough, B has to respect A as cognitively autonomous enough, and B has to take herself as *fallible* enough to let the attitudes of A towards B count. Recognition according to the dialogical conception takes place among rational but fallible persons in the space of reasons.

2.6. Statuses and Attitudes

Sometimes recognition is analyzed in terms of statuses, or 'granting statuses.' We see no reason to think that this idiom would in principle be incompatible with analyzing recognition in terms of recognitive attitudes. How one should see the relationship of statuses and recognitive attitudes, however, depends on what exactly one means by 'status.'

What kind of a thing is a status? There seem to be at least three different approaches to this question. In one meaning or usage of the word 'status,' statuses are 'official' statuses that are granted by appropriate authorities in performatives, in accordance with appropriate rules or norms. One gets the status of 'citizen' or 'legally wedded husband' only in specific institutionalized procedures. Such official statuses, once granted, have normative implications for the rights, responsibilities, and normative powers of the status-holding individuals, and appropriate recognition of these individuals must take them somehow into account. The normative powers of the appropriate authorities doing the 'grantings' or performatives depend in complex ways on recognition (as well as on the acknowledgement of norms constituting the respective institutions).

Second, in another meaning or usage of the word 'status,' the state of 'being recognized' (*Anerkanntsein*) is a status. If recognition is analyzed in terms of recognitive attitudes, then in this idiom, being loved, being respected, and being esteemed are, as such, statuses. Since recognitive attitudes are not as easily detectable as are official grantings or performatives, it may be a matter of hermeneutical interpretation as to which statuses a given person has in this sense. Jill may, for instance, have the status of being deeply loved by Jack, as well as the statuses of being greatly esteemed by Bill and seriously disrespected by her colleagues.

Third, in yet another meaning or usage of the term 'status,' statuses are independent both of official grantings and of attitudes of recognition. One can, for instance, have a normative theory of personhood, according to which personhood as such includes normative statuses, which are not dependent on official grantings or on recognitive attitudes, but which ought to be taken somehow into account 'officially' as well as in the recognitive attitudes towards persons. In this idiom, one might say, for instance, that states that do not respect all of its citizens equally ought to do so, because of the 'moral status' of persons.

In all of these senses of the word 'status,' statuses are somehow related to recognitive attitudes, but how exactly depends on what sense of the word 'status' one has in mind.[25] What holds for the attitude-analysis of recognition, holds also for possible status-analyses of recognition. Neither will be capable of grasping social reality in its full complexity if the central concepts are not being defined clearly enough.

If we read her right, Nancy Fraser in her 'status-model' of recognition sees recognition primarily in terms of 'cultural' status – namely, the status that members of some groups have according to established

---

[25] For instance, whereas attitudes in the first two senses are constitutive of statuses, in the third sense attitudes are only responsive to statuses.

and often stereotypical cultural patterns of value.[26] In the three senses of 'status' that we have distinguished, Fraser seems to be speaking of status mostly in the second sense: the state of being recognized (or misrecognized) by some recognizers, who rely on the established cultural patterns of value.

Making the point either in terms of statuses or in terms of attitudes comes down to the same thing: *status* in this sense is the state of being seen in certain lights and treated accordingly – that is, the state of being an object of certain kinds of *attitudes*.[27] In a Honnethian or any multidimensional view, there are as many types of statuses of *Anerkanntsein* as there are types of recognitive attitudes: for Honneth, love, respect, and esteem (with all their possible variations).

3. ANALYZING MISRECOGNITION

Just as it is sometimes quite hard to tell what exactly a theorist means by the term 'recognition,' it is often equally hard, or even harder, to tell what exactly a theorist means by the term 'misrecognition.' As people may mean by the word 'recognition' either what we renamed in the beginning as *identification, acknowledgement,* or *recognition* (or any combination of these), they may also mean by 'misrecognition' either something like *misidentification, 'misacknowledgement,'* or *misrecognition* (or any combination of these). Since all of these cover an enormous

---

[26] See Fraser's contributions to Fraser and Honneth, *Redistribution or Recognition?*

[27] It is also possible to make 'detached' judgments that *according to a specific cultural pattern of value,* the person X is of lesser worth than Y, even when one does not share that view oneself. Indeed, criticism of established cultural patterns is possible only because critics (say, feminists) too can see what things look like according to a specific cultural pattern (say, a male chauvinist one). Because of this, we can distinguish between a genuine status of being recognized (or misrecognized) by real persons from the 'detached' judgement concerning a status that one could have 'according to some cultural pattern of value.' The detached judgements can be correct even if no one really acknowledges the views of that cultural pattern; people may be aware of well-known stereotypes that 'float around' even if no one seems to know whether anyone sincerely accepts them (say, that blondes in general are less bright). What matters in social criticism is those cultural patterns that shape the attitudes and action of real flesh and blood persons, and thus what matters is the genuine 'status' of being recognized (or misrecognized) that one has because of the attitudes of others.

range of phenomena, the interrelations of which are, to say the least, very complex, the possibilities of misunderstandings and unfruitful confusions are numerous.

In what follows, we will outline one possible way of thinking about misrecognition as distinguished from misacknowledgement and misidentification. It will, however, turn out that misrecognition of persons is intimately connected with misacknowledgement of claims.

A recognitive attitude in the sense of taking something as a person is, as we said, not (or at least not only) a matter of believing that it is a person – that is, of identifying it generically as a person. As we see them, love, respect, and esteem as the species of the recognitive attitude of taking someone as a person can be characterized as ways of *responding to* the personhood of someone in corresponding dimensions of her personhood, not only cognitively but also conatively and emotionally. In recognizing someone as a person, we adopt a basic way of being towards that person, which shapes all our specific responses. We experience those responses as subject to claims that the other's personhood presents us with. Let us think of recognitive attitudes as responding to someone's personhood in terms of *acknowledging claims*. Thought of in this way, we really recognize someone as a person only if we acknowledge claims of her personhood, or, to put it slightly differently, if we acknowledge claims that her personhood presents us with. From this point of view, a case of misrecognition can be seen as a case where claims of B's personhood are not appropriately or adequately acknowledged by A.[28]

Let us consider that the 'claims' of B's personhood are real features of the lifeworld, which are in principle independent of whether anyone 'makes' or expresses these claims, as well as independent of what A or B think that the claims of B's personhood are. Because of this, it is possible for both A and B to be mistaken about what the claims of B's personhood to be acknowledged (or the 'true' claims) really are.

---

[28] Note that here we are analyzing misrecognition only in terms of the attitudes of A. In thus abstracting from the attitudes of B in the characterization of misrecognition, we are in fact presenting a *monological* conception of misrecognition and hence only part of the story. A full catalogue of different types of misrecognition on the *dialogical* conception, including all the ways in which also the attitudes of B can add up to something going wrong in terms of recognition between A and B is beyond the scope of this chapter.

This way of thinking about misrecognition is neutral as regards the question of *what* exactly the true claims of this or that person, group of persons, or of persons in general are, and also about *how* exactly it is that we can know what they are in each case. If successful, it is also neutral as regards questions of how exactly things such as values, evaluative properties, reasons, norms, and so on are related to claims of personhood in particular cases, or in general.[29]

Thus, this way of thinking is meant to be largely neutral as regards different positions in ethical and political theory. It recognizes, for instance, that the true claims originate from prior collective development.[30] It is not *wholly* neutral, however, since it assumes that there is

---

[29] For some suggestions on how such claims are related to values or evaluative features that persons instantiate, see Arto Laitinen, "Interpersonal Recognition" and Laitinen, *Strong Evaluation Without Sources. On Charles Taylor's Philosophical Anthropology and Cultural Moral Realism.* (Jyväskylä: *Jyväskylä Studies in Education, Psychology and Social Research* 224, 2003). There seems to be an important connection between something being good or valuable and its providing reasons for action (for engaging with it, protecting it, and so on) and thus presenting demands or claims for agents. Some theorists (for example, Scanlon) see reasons as primary and say that something is valuable because it provides reasons for action, others (for example, Raz) see evaluative features as primary and say that something provides reasons for action because it is valuable. Whatever the precise relation between reasons and values, features of other persons are something that demand or invite certain kinds of responses, and thus generate claims on us.

[30] The Hegelian view of the centrality of historical development is in different forms stressed – for instance, in Honneth's "moderate value realism" (see Honneth, "Grounding Recognition," and Honneth, "Between Hermeneutics and Hegelianism: J. McDowell and the Challenge of Moral Realism," in *Reading McDowell. On Mind and World*, ed. by Nicholas H. Smith, (London/New York: Routledge, 2002)); in Joseph Raz's (see *The Practice of Value* [Oxford: Oxford University Press, 2003]) thesis of the social dependence of many values; and in Robert Pippin's take on the relevance of Hegel (see, for example, his contribution to this volume). Laitinen (in "Interpersonal Recognition" and in *Strong Evaluation*) defends a historically sensitive or 'culturalist' variant of realism, and emphasizes that not all norms and values guiding recognition can be generated by previous acts of recognition or acknowledgement. In this text, we try to steer a middle ground between a projectivist version of what Honneth calls the "attribution model" and a Platonist version of what he calls the "perception model" of recognition, the first of which he attributes to Ikäheimo and the second to Laitinen (see Axel Honneth, "Grounding Recognition"; Ikäheimo, "On the Genus and Species"; and Laitinen, "Interpersonal Recognition"). Ikäheimo did not mean his analysis of recognition to have the projectivist implications or connotations that Honneth reads into it, and therefore wants here to put more emphasis on an objectivist way of looking at recognition and misrecognition – something that his analysis did not rule out, but that admittedly was not discussed explicitly enough in it. Laitinen did indeed defend a non-projectivist model, and in that sense a "perception-model"

in principle an objective truth about whether something is a case of appropriate recognition or misrecognition – however complex the issue may be or however difficult it often may be to judge. This way of thinking of recognition and misrecognition is hence *objectivist* in the minimal sense, which is necessary for making the distinction between cases of appropriate recognition and cases of misrecognition. This means that it is incompatible with possible views, according to which A's acknowledging a particular claim of B's personhood in one way or another produces the acknowledged claim, or is sufficient for its validity. It is also incompatible with the banality of saying that whatever B takes as recognition is recognition and whatever B takes as misrecognition is misrecognition.

The objectivist way of looking at recognition and misrecognition maintains the important intuition that what B takes as appropriate or adequate recognition of herself by A may in fact, from an 'objective point of view,' be misrecognition. Similarly, it maintains the intuition that what B takes as misrecognition of herself by A is, from an 'objective point of view,' not necessarily misrecognition.

It may be, for instance, that B takes herself as a relatively insignificant contributor to the good of A and thus thinks that her actions do not present A with claims that A ought to acknowledge by holding B in esteem, at least to any great extent. Or B may think that she is mostly incapable of taking part in communal decision making with A and that her inferior degree of rationality hence does not present A with a claim that A ought to acknowledge by respecting B as a full partner in decision making.

But if, in fact, B's contributions to the good of A are more important than B thinks, or if, in fact, B is more capable of taking part in communal decision making than B thinks, then something that B takes as adequate or appropriate recognition on the part of A may, from an objective point of view, be misrecognition. In other words, something that B thought of as appropriate or adequate acknowledgement of the claims of her personhood perhaps was not appropriate or adequate,

---

of adequate recognition. Honneth is further right in his critical note that in Laitinen, "Interpersonal Recognition," there is not much in terms of explaining how such a perception-model can avoid the excesses of Platonism. Such an analysis is attempted in chapters 6–13 of Laitinen, *Strong Evaluation*.

since B was wrong or misled about what the true claims of her personhood are.

On the other hand, it may be that B takes herself as an indispensably important contributor to the good of A and thus thinks that her indispensability presents A with the claim that A ought to acknowledge by holding B greatly in esteem, and by somehow acting accordingly (for instance, by expressing gratitude). Or B may think that she is perfectly capable of taking part in communal decision making and that her rationality presents A with a claim that A ought to acknowledge by respecting B as a full partner in decision making.

But if, in fact, B's contributions to the good of A are less important than B thinks, or if, in fact, B is less capable of taking part in communal decision making than B thinks, then what B takes as misrecognition on the part of A is, from an objective point of view, not necessarily misrecognition.[31] In other words, what B thought of as inappropriate or inadequate acknowledgement of the claims of her personhood on the part of A perhaps was not inappropriate or inadequate, since B was wrong or misled about what the true claims of her personhood are.

As we see it, talking about an 'objective point of view' does not as such imply anything else than the minimal sense of objectivism, which we usually take for granted in our moral and political life. We are constantly engaged in struggles for recognition, as well as in disputes over recognition and misrecognition, in which we presuppose *de facto* that there is some (however contested and difficult to find out) fact of the matter as to whether something really is a case of adequate or appropriate recognition or rather one of misrecognition.[32] If, or when, we do not make this presumption, we are in danger of collapsing the

---

[31] Note that according to the dialogical conception of recognition, as we formulated it, it does not seem to be recognition either, since the acceptance-condition is not fulfilled.

[32] In addition to the perspectives of A and B, and the 'objective point of view,' the prevailing rules and norms in a society provide one further perspective from which the adequacy of recognition can be assessed. The prevailing norms need not be norms that the persons A and B wholeheartedly acknowledge, and they need not be the most adequate norms available. Yet, A may behave towards B in accordance with the prevailing norms of that society (say, because A falsely assumes that B wants to be treated that way, or because it is easier or less risky). Such cases are not cases of misrecognition according to the society, but they may be misrecognition according to both A and B, and they may be 'really' cases of misrecognition in the objective sense.

distinction between struggles for recognition and strategic struggles. Here we simply assume that this is an undesired consequence for theorists who are discussing struggles and demands for 'recognition' in ethical, political, and social theory.

Let us make one more point about the critical potential of conceptualizing interpersonal recognition in terms of acknowledging claims of personhood in the 'objectivist' mode. As has often been emphasized (by both Axel Honneth and Nancy Fraser, for instance, in different ways[33]), critical theory cannot contend with simply taking for granted the normative validity of the various demands for recognition voiced in the political arena or social life more generally. Feelings or experiences of misrecognition – whether explicitly articulated as demands for recognition or just prevailing as more or less vague feelings of discontent – are a crucially important index for identifying possible cases of misrecognition, but feelings or experiences are not, simply as such, authoritative. It is important for critical theory to be able to articulate the exact content of feelings and experiences of misrecognition and of demands for recognition so that their possible normative weight can be discussed and decided upon in collective discourses. This certainly requires that the *subjects* of these feelings, experiences, and demands are seriously respected as communication partners, but it does not mean that their viewpoint alone decides the truth of the matter in each case.

In fact, there seems to be no reason to think that desires, demands or expectations for recognition are in principle any less vulnerable to ideological distortion, manipulation, or indoctrination than other parts of our self-relations, world-relations, or interpersonal relations. It is because of the central role of recognition and recognitive expectations in structuring social life and social reality as a whole that critical theorists need well worked out and thoroughly scrutinized conceptual tools for understanding recognition in all its complexity. In this respect, Axel Honneth's work on recognition provides critical theory with an enormously fruitful starting point and deserves serious theoretical scrutiny, constructive criticism, and further elaboration.

[33] See their contributions to Fraser and Honneth, *Redistribution or Recognition?*

3

Recognition and Reconciliation

Actualized Agency in Hegel's Jena *Phenomenology*

Robert Pippin

I. LIBERAL POLITICS AND THE POLITICS OF RECOGNITION

Most modern liberal versions of the state depend on a philosophically ambitious theory about the nature of human individuality and its
normatively relevant implications. It is often assumed that contrasting
theories about the ultimacy of inter-subjective relations and the deriva-
tive or secondary status of individuality are potentially if not actually
illiberal, and Hegel's putative "organic" theory of the state is often
cited as an example. A major arena for such disputes has been the
claim by such neo-Hegelians as Charles Taylor and Axel Honneth that
the key liberal notion of the "free and rational individual" depends
for its possibility on a social condition of great political relevance:
"mutual recognition." In the following, I return to the sources of this
dispute (a dispute sometimes called postmodern "identity" politics) in
Hegel's original arguments about "dependence" and "independence,"
and investigate what according to Hegel is the exact nature of the
human dependence at issue and what might count as the successful
satisfaction of this condition of dependence. It is, I argue, much easier to see what Hegel's answer is to the former question than to the
latter.

We need first a general, admittedly high-altitude survey of the landscape occupied by "liberal versions of the state." This is not easy to
do; versions of liberal political theory have become ever more various. There are autonomy liberals, value-neutral liberals, skeptical

liberals, relativist liberals, libertarian liberals, welfarist liberals, and more recently liberal or value pluralists. But it remains the case that a set of recognizable, underlying commitments characterizes the Western liberal democratic tradition, and that there are two main sorts of theoretical justifications for these commitments and their practical extensions. The common orientation has to do with the pre-eminence and in some sense the theoretical "ultimacy" of the human individual mentioned earlier, and so with the equality of worth of each, qua individual. This commitment is understood to require a limited and accountable state (accountable to the "consent of the governed"), equality before the law, and in most versions, significant and extensive property rights. The theoretical considerations advanced to support such a conception of political life amount to two different ways to claim that such arrangements are *rational*.

One set of such arguments relies on a pragmatic or a broadly consequentialist form of reasoning and is oriented from what are taken to be empirical facts and the empirical consequences of certain arrangements of power. One argues that under a liberal political arrangement, we will all simply be better off – that is, more prosperous, more secure, better able to achieve whatever ends we set for ourselves, and perhaps also more likely to advance culturally. (J. S. Mill is the champion of this group.) Or one argues, somewhat less ambitiously, that in order to retain and develop what we have already achieved in any pre-civil situation, it is pragmatically reasonable to designate an umpire or sovereign, in a fiduciary relation with his subjects, with sufficient power to resolve disputes (Locke), but answerable to his clients if he fails to perform these functions. Or one argues, with something like an absolute minimum of assumptions, that we know at least that we will all be drastically worse off without an all-powerful "monster" or leviathan sovereign to enforce order (Hobbes). The idea is that no one could be presumed to want or will anything without wanting or willing what is practically necessary for the achievement of any end, and that this general interest in the success of what we attempt can be shown to yield tacit or active consent to such an arrangement, to the state or civil order. On this interest-based conception of political life, the problem of politics is a rational cooperation problem, and it has thus been given new life recently with the growing sophistication and popularity of rational choice models of reasoning. Perhaps the most influential contemporary proponent of this brand of liberalism is David Gauthier.

On the other hand, a robust theory of original *moral* entitlements – rights – is invoked to justify the moral unacceptability of a state of nature, or, said the other way around, to justify the claim that we have a duty to leave the state of nature and to establish a civil order. The state's monopoly on coercive force is justified because these claims of moral entitlement – rights claims – are justified. In this case, the basic argument is that no one could be presumed to want or will anything without implicitly claiming to be entitled to such a pursuit (that is, each has a presumptive right to non-interference), and that such an entitlement claim is not one that could be consistently denied to all others. And, the argument continues, the only possible realization of a situation wherein such equal rights claims could be secured is one where we give up the right to decide in our own case and submit to the rule of law. Such appeals to a "rational will" as the source of the state's coercive authority (by virtue of its protection of basic entitlements) are (1) often ascribed to Rousseau and to Kant's position in his "Doctrine of Right," (2) is quite prominent in the rhetoric of the French Revolution and its declaration of the rights of man, and (3) is a major component, in quite different ways, in the contemporary theories of John Rawls, Ronald Dworkin, Otfried Höffe, and Jürgen Habermas.

These categories are of course idealizations. In some positions, there is considerable overlap and intermingling of such strategic and normative reasoning. (The cases of Locke and Rawls are the most obvious.) But the distinctions are stable enough for us to be able to identify an *alternative* modern tradition, which, by being alternative, is often just thereby (and too hastily) considered non- or anti-liberal (or anti-individualist). The problems raised by this alternative tradition involve a critique of the putative "*ultimacy*" or *original* status of the individual and the implications that follow for politics if that ultimacy is denied in favor of some more complicated view of the "logic," let us say, of original relations of dependence and independence among persons. Obviously one such implication might be that the legitimacy of the state's coercive power could not be wholly defended by appeal to what an adult person would will, either in a strategic sense or, more broadly, by appeal to what such a person could be argued to be rationally committed to. The claim is that such a picture of the rational individual is a "cropped" picture, that we have arbitrarily excluded from the frame original and prior inter-subjective relations, which, because these are necessary for the possible existence and exercise of any individual will, cannot be a standard subject of rational negotiation *for* individuals but which cannot be justifiably ignored. Under the influence of this distorted or cropped picture, we would falsely conclude that all relations to others are results of volition or consensus, either ex ante or post facto as a matter of reflective endorsement, and thereby we would in our theory of political life and its authority fail to acknowledge properly such pre-volitional, unavoidable, necessary ties to others (not ones we could adopt or reject as a matter of choice).

As Axel Honneth has pointed out, such a fantastic, atomistic ideal of a boot-strapping, wholly self-defining and self-determining subject is bound to produce various social pathologies of a distinctly Hegelian or dialectical sort.[1] By this I mean that we will have adopted as an ideal (not just in our political lives but comprehensively) a norm of self-determination and self-authorship that cannot possibly be fulfilled and cannot even be action-guiding. It will remain formal, abstract, and empty, and in trying unsuccessfully to fulfill it we will successively undermine its authority. We will, in Honneth's fine phrase, "*suffer* from indeterminacy." (Hegel documents a number of these pathologies in his *Phenomenology*: the "frenzy of self-conceit," the "beautiful soul," and an unavoidable hypocrisy.)

By contrast, a new and different sort of claim for ultimacy in *inter-subjective relations* would form the basis of such an alternative political reflection, and the most important aspect of this relation is often a form of original, unavoidable *social dependence*. It is, so goes the claim, by ignoring or denying such original relations in a fantasy of self-reliance that we end up in those distorted or even pathological relations to others, even to ourselves.[2] As we shall see, at its most ambitiously dialectical

---

[1] I mean especially Axel Honneth, *The Struggle for Recognition: The Moral Grammar of Social Conflicts*, trans. Joel Anderson (Cambridge, MA: MIT Press, 1996), and *Suffering from Indeterminacy: An Attempt at a Reactivation of Hegel's Philosophy of Right*. Introduction by Beate Rössler; trans. Jack Ben-Levi (Assen: Van Gorcum, 2000). (SI hereafter.)

[2] The implication that follows from putting together these two claims about "suffering from indeterminacy" and the priority of original inter-subjective relations of dependence is that such relations provide the determinate content for modern ideals of equality, individual dignity, mutual respect, and the like. (It must always be in terms of such dependence that we understand what it is to respect each other, acknowledge

the full claim is that acknowledging, acting in the light of, such relations of dependence is a necessary condition for the achievement of true independence, or true "self-realization," or "actualized," "concrete" freedom. And, to anticipate again, this idea amounts to what is at once one of the most noble and most abused notions of nineteenth-century European thought. The claim of such original dependence leads to a charge much more radical than one of unfairness or injustice if there is freedom for some and unfreedom for many others. The idea is that I cannot be properly said *to be free* unless others are free, that my freedom depends on theirs, reciprocally.[3] (In the version of the claim that I am interested in, being a free agent – an actual or successful agent – is said to depend on being recognized as one by others whose free bestowal of this recognition depends in turn on their being recognized as such free bestowers.)[4] This is why it is argued that an understanding of the nature of *this* sort of dependence – unavoidable dependence on recognition by others – ought to guide all reflection on both the powers and limits of sovereign authority.

This tradition is again associated with the Rousseau of *The Social Contract*. (Rousseau seems to have managed to express and defend almost all the alternatives in modern social and political theory.) This is the Rousseau who argued passionately against the enslaving effects of modern social dependence but for the creation of a new form of artificial dependence that would count as the creation of a collective independence, *the citizen*, or the famous exchange of natural freedom for civil freedom. But it is most apparent in Fichte's 1796 *Grundlage* and of course in Hegel's Jena writings and his Jena *Phenomenology*, and in the left-Hegelian tradition inspired by Hegel's gripping account of "the struggle to the death for recognition" and the internal paradoxes of the Master-Slave dialectic. This tradition too has its contemporary resonances. The most well-known appearance of this sort of claim

dignity, and so forth.) This is a consequence that Honneth accepts in SI, but it opens the door to the question about how we evaluate such social communities once we have eliminated all reliance on methodological individualism, on "what rational individuals would will." I discuss this issue further below.

3 Honneth, SI, 21.

4 I defend this at greater length in "What is the Question for Which Hegel's 'Theory of Recognition' is the Answer?" in: *The European Journal of Philosophy* 8/2 (August 2000), and in a different way in *Henry James and Modern Moral Life* (Cambridge: Cambridge University Press, 2000).

is in the various "communitarian" reactions to Rawls' work, and in
some neo-Aristotelean work (MacIntyre), but the most worked out
and thoughtful reflections on the theme can be found in the recent
work of Charles Taylor and Axel Honneth.

II. THE LIBERAL REJOINDER AND THE CORE ISSUE

This – these strands of liberal thought and this counter-strand that concedes the existence of rights-bearing independent, self-determining
individuals but denies their theoretical ultimacy – forms the context
for the issue in Hegel I want eventually to raise. Of course, the thematic itself is a sprawling and barely manageable one, since it quickly
spills over into claims about social psychology, developmental psychology, theories of modernity, and philosophical anthropology. But the
heart of the matter clearly concerns how we are to understand two
issues: the basic claim about an "original" relation of dependence on
others (what *sort* of dependence we are talking about, how it is to be
related to claims for independence), and secondly, in what sense we
are to draw political implications from such an understanding (and
I mean especially implications about the coercive use of the state's
monopoly on violence). What I want to claim is that Hegel's argument
for a particular sort of original dependence necessary for the possibility of individuality – recognitional dependence – is not based on a
claim about human need, or derived from evidence in developmental
or social psychology. It involves a distinctly philosophical claim, a shift
in our understanding of individuality, from viewing it as a kind of ultimate given to regarding it as a kind of achievement, and to regarding
it as a normative status, not a fact of the matter, whether empirical
or metaphysical. Understanding how Hegel wants to free us from one
picture and suggest another way of looking at the issue will make the
relevance of this recognitional dependence much easier to see. With
respect to the question of what Hegel's position is on the second issue –
what political implications follow from this transformation – the issue
is murkier, even somewhat mysterious, and I want only to make a few
closing suggestions about what we seem left with.

In general, this – the status of the claim for some inter-subjective
ultimacy – is the core issue because it is obviously open to a defender of
some version of classical liberal theory to claim that any such putative

dependence or inter-subjective bond, even if it is true that it is original and unavoidable, is irrelevant to mature political reflection. *However* "I" got to be the concrete "me" that I am, however dependent in such a process and even in the present on others in a variety of contexts, that "I" is now, qua adult agent, quite capable of a complete reflective detachment from any such commitments and attachments and dependencies that may have arisen. No such attachment or dependence can be counted as of value to me unless it can pass what has been called a "reflective endorsement" test *by me*,[5] unless I can "stand back" from such involvements and decide whether I ought to be so attached. And underlying such a claim is a view of the possible worth or value of my achievements to me. To be so valuable – so goes this style of thought – they must be due *to* me, must be experienced as the result of *my* will and initiative and talent. And so my claims on you and yours on me as civil beings should then be limited to what can be shown to be necessary for each of us to have a sphere of activity wherein such will might be exercised. To be a liberal in this sense is to forego "your" approval or recognition or in some large measure even your assistance. Giving up at some point in one's life such dependencies, *being able to act without requiring the recognition, approval or in some sense the assistance of others, is to assume the role of an adult responsible individual* – to grow up, one can imagine a Thatcherite liberal insisting impatiently. For those on this side of the issue, anything less than such a commitment, especially any claim that my status or worth depends on its effective acknowledgement by others (not just on their non-interference), would be a recipe for "group think," social conformism, and ultimately quite illegitimate restrictions on individual liberty in the name of what is supposed to be such originally necessary dependence.

It may be that one manifestation of such non-interference might be a callous indifference, resulting in the humiliating invisibility suffered by, say, Ralph Ellison's *Invisible Man*. But even if that is considered a wrong, our Thatcherite might concede only that it is a moral wrong, a failure of charity and not a politically correctable wrong, as if some "right" to visibility that had been violated. And it is not enough

---

[5] Cf. the use of this phrase in work by Christine Korsgaard, especially *The Sources of Normativity* (Cambridge: Cambridge University Press, 1996).

just to show that without reliance on, or trust in, the already ongoing social practices, institutions, and norms into which one has been socialized, there could be no determinative content to ideals such as self-determination or self-realization, or ideals at all for that matter. Establishing that might just mean that we are *worse* off philosophically, "stuck" with a contingent social content that we experience as unavoidable but reflectively unredeemable, the Heideggerean cage of *das Man* rather than the Hegelian liberation of *Sittlichkeit*. If the indeterminacy criticism holds, we will also clearly need an account of the rationality of specific, modern institutions, and some way to do justice to the subjective element in our acceptance and embodiment of these norms, some explanation of how *we have made them ours* that does not revert again to the individualist reflective endorsement model and does not settle for a matter of fact habituation.

The rejoinder to all this by any proponent of "recognitional" politics clearly will turn on the argument for something like the *ultimacy* of such dependence (or a claim in social ontology) and so the *necessity* of acknowledging its indispensability in our political theory. (That is, the normative necessity of so doing, a requirement that will constitute a claim for the rationality of such acknowledgment.) It will thus rest on the claim that the sort of detachment and endorsement spoken of earlier is not only impossible, but is a dangerous fantasy, leading to the pathological indeterminacy already noted. However, even if this can be established, the *political* implications of such an unavoidable dependence will have to be drawn carefully. After all, the language of "social harm" arising from mis-recognition suggests a consequentialist form of reasoning, an argument about the weight of various social goods with, apparently, an additional claim that esteem and self-worth (and the social acknowledgement they depend on) have *more weight* than has hitherto been conceded. (Since we are talking ultimately about the use of the state's coercive force to prohibit such a harm, we will need a very *strong* argument to show that such injuries are not just unfortunate, subject to moral disapproval, but must be subject to legislative remedy, are in some way components of the common good.) That would suggest one form of an extension of the "original dependence" claim that would be consistent with, a kind of addendum to, the empirical form of liberal reasoning noted earlier. But the language of ultimacy and undeniability also suggests a case based on some entitlement claim, as if the wrong in question were a moral injury, of the general sort Kant argued against by denying we should ever use another merely as a means, should ever withhold respect for another's "incomparable" worth. This sort of claim for a kind of *"right to be recognized"* implies another direction altogether, one consistent with, a kind of addendum to, the rights-based liberalism noted above. And again we would face the problem of showing some claim on others to be an entitlement requiring coercive enforcement and not just a claim that we ought, in some general moral sense, to respect.

III. THE HEGELIAN POSITION

As already noted, these sorts of doubts about the ultimacy of liberal individualism have a complex historical origin. What I want to do now is concentrate on one aspect of this pedigree – Hegel's, in his Jena *Phenomenology* – not only because his account there of something like the unfolding drama of the struggle for recognition has been so independently influential, but because his account, by virtue of what Hegel says and what he doesn't say, raises in an interesting way both the sorts of questions just noted – what *sort* of claim on others is the claim for recognition, and what, if any, are its *political* dimensions.

To understand Hegel's position, we need to begin again with the fundamental issue in the difference between liberal and "recognitional" politics. (For the moment, we can just let this latter stand for a conception of politics that does not tie any claim to legitimacy and justice to the interests or rights claims of sovereign rational individuals and what they have or would or must rationally will, and all this because of some claim of prior or pre-volitional dependence that requires political acknowledgement, the non-acknowledgement of which counts as a wrong.) We could put the basic problem of the independence/dependence relation in a way familiar from Kant's *Rechtslehre*: that it concerns what I can justifiably claim as mine, not yours, and the conditions under which such a distinction is possible. At this quite primary level, we should begin by noting that the basic starting points of modern political reflection – mine, yours, and ours – do not refer to empirical facts that can be read directly off the social world. They involve the establishment of normative statuses; what we mean by "mine" invokes a norm – it appeals to what is rightfully mine;

we are not pointing to any empirical fact. (As Kant noted in the *Recht-slehre*, intelligible beings, beings responsive to reasons, are not limited in possession to what they can physically hold. They can establish rational relations with others and therewith intelligible or "noumenal" possession.) And if our original dispute is about the "ultimacy of individuality," then that will have to be a dispute about the bases of such a *normative claim of content*. So, the question of my distinctness as a human individual is not the sort that can be settled by a DNA test, but concerns the extent of my (putatively) rightful exclusion of your and any else's interference. This seems primarily a worry about property, but, given the kind of worries about the psychology of dependence first voiced in Rousseau's *Second Discourse*, the issue is much broader. Given how materially dependent we have become (thanks to the division of labor and the growing distance between civilized life and any possible self-sufficiency), especially how dependent in the long process of human maturation, *whatever* we value in the ends we set and the views we espouse, *whatever* we "guard" as rightfully "ours," are, we come more and more to suspect, likely to be an inevitable reflection of such dependence and the conformity it enforces, however much it might feel like our own intimate self. Rousseau goes so far as to claim the following.

The Savage lives in himself; sociable man, always outside himself, is capable of living only in the opinion of others; and so to speak, derives the sentiment of his own existence solely from their judgment.[6]

We can thus now see that the underlying problem pointed to – the normative status of "mine" in all its senses – appears as the problem of freedom, understood broadly as the ability to see myself in my own deeds, to experience such deeds as the products of my will, not the forces of social necessity; in a word *as mine*. Secondly, this notion of non-alienated freedom would also involve understanding the deeds as reflections of what *I* most value, as genuine expressions of my view of the good, or whatever; as manifestations of what is rightfully and originally mine. (If I *can* experience the deeds as products of my will, but also regard them as violations of my own views of what ought to be done or never ought to be done, then I am alienated from my own

---

[6] Jean-Jacques Rousseau, *The First and Second Discourses*, edited and translated by Victor Gourevitch (New York: Harper and Row, 1986), 199.

deeds in another way.) Fulfilling such conditions is what amounts to practical success as a determinate agent, a free being. (All this, while conceding that there is clearly a possible difference between what I consciously take myself to value, and what in fact counts as "rightfully and originally" my commitments. In this admittedly paradoxical sense, I can be "alienated" from what I truly value, while regarding myself as free in this "expressive" sense.)

And this provides the opportunity for a full if very provisional summation of what I take to be Hegel's whole claim about this matter. For it is this "success" as an agent that, according to Hegel's position in the Jena *Phenomenology*, requires as its conditions, that others (1) recognize me as having the social status and identity I attribute to myself; (2) recognize the deed as falling under the act-description that I invoke; and (3) recognize me as acting on the intention I attribute to myself. In general, this success requires that I am taken by others to have the intentions and commitments that I take myself to have, and so *to be doing* what I take myself to be doing.[7] (By contrast, I can claim to be a knight and to be engaging in acts of chivalry, but if the social world in which I live cannot recognize such a status or such deeds, then I am a comic imitation of a knight, a Don Quixote.) To say everything at once: Hegel's eventual claim will be that these three conditions of successful agency (or, as he often says, "actual," *wirklich* agency) cannot be satisfied unless individuals are understood as participants in an ethical form of life, *Sittlichkeit*, and finally in a certain historical form of ethical life, in such relations of recognition can be genuinely mutual, where that means that the bestowers of recognition are themselves actually free, where the inter-subjective recognitional (sometimes called "communicative") relation is sustained in a reciprocal way.

But clearly this is to say so much at once as to strain the patience of any audience. But underlying the manifold of issues just presented one can still detect, I hope, what I have been calling the core, or basic, issue. For Hegel is clearly treating the basic notion of individuality as an *achievement*, a result of a complex inter-subjective dynamic, and not

---

[7] Such a subject "perceives itself just as it is experienced by others, and the perceiving is just existence which has become a self." *Phänomenologie des Geistes* in *Hauptwerke in sechs Bänden*, Bd. 2 (Hamburg: Felix Meiner, 1999), 351; *Phenomenology of Spirit*, transl. by A. V. Miller (Oxford: The Clarendon Press, 1977), 395.

a matter of mere biological uniqueness (which he calls "particularity").
True individuals are *agents* in Hegel's account, in non-alienated relations with their deeds and commitments. (Said more precisely, they
are "actual" agents, and Hegel seems to conceive of such a state as having gradations, levels.) And clearly what is driving his argument about
social dependence is the claim that this status as an agent is, can be
nothing other than, a social status, and a social status exists by being
taken to exist by members of some community. A priest, a knight, a
statesman, a citizen are not, that is, natural kinds. One exists as such
a kind by being treated as one, according to the rules of that community. And the radicality of Hegel's suggestion is that we treat being a
concrete subject of a life, a free being, the same way. It is in this sense
that being an individual already presupposes a complex recognitional
status.

IV. HEGEL'S NARRATIVE

Why should we believe that we are dependent in just this way, that
individuality, or being an individual subject, should be understood
this way (as a "normative status" dependent on social recognition),
and that there are both social and political conditions without which
we could not become the individual subjects of our own lives?

Hegel has, when all is said and done, two main kinds of answers to
this question. One is systematic and is to be found in his *Encyclopedia*.
That answer is extremely comprehensive and ranges from his treatment of relata and their relations, the logic of same and other, the
category of actuality, and especially the transition in the third part, on
"Geist," from a doctrine of "subjective" spirit to a doctrine of "objective" spirit. Once that is understood, the status of the claims in Objective Spirit (otherwise known as his *Philosophy of Right*) can be properly
assessed, especially the key claim for our purposes: "The sphere of
right and that of morality cannot exist independently [*kann nicht für
sich existieren*]; they must have the ethical [*das Sittliche*] as their support and foundation [*zum Träger und zur Grundlage*]."[8] This is, in the

---

[8] *Grundlinien der Philosophie des Rechts*, in G. W. F. Hegel, *Jubiläumsausgabe in zwanzig
    Bände*, Bd. VII , ed. H. Glockner (Stuttgart: Frommans Verlag, 1952) (Werke, here-
    after), p. 225 (§141Z); *Elements of the Philosophy of Right*, ed. Allen Wood, trans. H. B.
    Nisbet (Cambridge: Cambridge University Press, 1991), 186.

language of *The Philosophy of Right*, the claim for the priority of inter-subjective relations over liberal notions of individual entitlement and responsibility.

But there is also a better known phenomenological case as well as systematic case for these claims, and that involves an unusual narrative developmental logic that is difficult to summarize economically. This narrative – surely one of the most original and exciting "accounts" ever presented in philosophy – can for our purposes be isolated as beginning with the introduction of a social conception of self-consciousness in Chapter Four of the *Phenomenology* (PhG hereafter), especially with the introduction of the theme in the first section there, "Independence and Dependence of Self-consciousness," and the famous struggle and Master-Slave sections. It then extends throughout the chapter on "Reason," a good deal of which describes what are in effect attempts to avoid the messiness of such social struggle by appeal to an accessible abstract, formal status, The View From Nowhere, the rational point of view. The story here is a story of various *failures* in inhabiting such a status. And Hegel then describes something like the return (in his narrative) of a beautiful version of such a social reality in the first section of the chapter about spirit (on Greek ethical life), but then that chapter too continues the *via negativa*, an account of Western cultural and political history as a history of failed sociality, mis-recognition, naïve assumptions of self-sufficiency, and so forth. ("Self-Alienated Spirit," "the Terror," "dissemblance," "hypocrisy," "the beautiful soul.") (Hegel thus treats the two dominant forms of the modern Western fantasy of individual self-sufficiency: the Enlightenment and romantic notions of individual authenticity.) The Spirit narrative clearly is meant to suggest an experiential path from the one-sidedness of the ancient Greek form of a recognitive community, with a level of social integration that could not properly account for claims of individual conscience, to a modern, conversely one-sided moralism, reliant too much on the private voice of conscience, unwilling to act in a way that would subject its deed to the judgment of others, or stuck in a fierce judgmental hard-heartedness about the necessary wickedness of all actual deeds. These last are all treated as prototypical modern fantasies of normative or rational self-sufficiency. And they clearly raise the question of what would break the hold of such fantasies on the modern imagination. Quite surprisingly, though, we do not find in the Jena PhG the account that played a major role in Hegel's Jena lectures on spirit – the return of a modern, successful picture of sociality, the family, labor, the modern state – successful, mutual recognition, and so the achievement of a reflective, socially mediated form of subjectivity. There is no such discussion of ethical life (*Sittlichkeit*); only a fairly abstract treatment of the social and mostly philosophical dimensions of religion.

I won't try for a comprehensive view of this narrative, but I will try first to isolate what seems to me one critical element in the answer to the question just posed (why believe any of these claims about the necessity of recognition?), and then to conclude with some remarks about the relevance of the discussion of "forgiveness" to the account of spirit and ultimately to its political dimension.

To understand the fulcrum on which this account pivots – the account of practical reason in Chapter Five, we need to reiterate that the topic of the PhG concerns the "conditions for the possibility of normativity" in human experience. I mean that Hegel has tried to show that the essential dimension of all human mindedness – consciousness – is such a normative dimension. We are being educated to see that thinking, reasoning, believing, deciding, resolving, and so on should not be understood as primarily or essentially mere mental events occurring at a time. They are that, but that is the wrong category with which to understand them *as practices*. As practices, activities aimed at getting something right, at finding the right course of action, their intelligibility requires attention to the rules and purpose of this practice, and the subjects of these activities should be understood as purposive rule-followers. In the Hegelian story of our mental life, what is "happening" is happening because of a subject determining that it shall; a subject taking a stand in a way, for which one is answerable. It is not simply to come to be in a state. This is what is eventually called the inherently self-conscious dimension of human mindedness. In consciousness of an object, one is not just differentially responsive to the external world; one is holding oneself to a normative claim about some object or state. (This is the clear descendent of that Kantian claim that all cognitive awareness is a judging, indeed an apperceptive judging.)[9] One is subject to any such claim *only by holding oneself to it*, and what we will see is that also necessarily involved in "really" so being bound

---

[9] This is admittedly a controversial reading. For a defense of it, see my *Hegel's Idealism: The Satisfactions of Self-Consciousness* (Cambridge: Cambridge University Press, 1989).

to such a claim – for any successful committing – is being held to it by others. This will eventually mean that it is only within some form of social relation that the inescapable phenomenological features of self-consciousness (especially the claim to normative legitimacy) can be accounted for.

This means that, in Hegel's language, in any such commitment to a claim or course of action, there is a possible gap between my own self-certainty, my subjective take on what is happening and what is called for, and the "truth," often manifest when it is apparent that others attribute to me commitments and implications of commitments other than those I attribute to myself. The experience of such a gap, itself a kind of social pathology, is what Hegel appeals to as the engine for conceptual and social change, a struggle or striving for reconciliation and mutuality in such a context.[10]

This is the kind of problem that is at issue in the second half of Chapter Five, when Hegel pursues what I have been calling his critique of the ultimacy of individuality into an area where the privileged and prior status of the individual or first-person point of view seems intuitively strongest: the dependence of outer manifestations of the subject's will on the inner intentions of that subject. These passages represent the most radical of the implications that follow from what is in effect Hegel's attempt to alter that relation of priority and to argue for the reciprocal dependence of the "inner" on the "outer."

What Hegel attempts to show in a variety of contexts, against a variety of inner-oriented positions is that we cannot determine what actually *was* a subject's intention or motivating reason by relying on some sort of introspection, by somehow looking more deeply *into* the agent's soul, or by some sincerity test. "By their fruits shall ye know them,"[11] Hegel quotes, and Hegel would add "*only* by their fruits or deeds."

---

[10] Indeed this gap helps one understand what would otherwise be somewhat paradoxical in the whole account given thus far of the priority of recognitional dependence in the possibility of true individuality. The question would be: must I not *already be* a free, self-determining being to be properly responsive to any such inter-subjective exchange with another, and to be capable of bestowing the kind of recognition that would count for another as constitutive of his or her individuality? And the answer would be that such a self-ascription must always be *provisional*, mere self-certainty, something challengeable and correctable "socially." I develop this claim more fully in a forthcoming book, *Hegel's Practical Philosophy: Rational Agency as Ethical Life.*

[11] *Enzyklopädie der philosophischen Wissenschaften*, I, in Werke, Bd. 8 §140, (EL) 277; *Hegel's Logic*, transl. William Wallace (Oxford: The Clarendon Press, 1975), 199.

Only as manifested or expressed in a social space shared by others, subject to their "takes" on what happened, can one (*even* the subject himself) retrospectively determine what must have been intended. And of course it seems a bit paradoxical to claim that we can only know what we intended to do after we have actually acted and in a way dependent on the reactions of others, but there is little doubt that Hegel holds something like such a position. (Consider: "Ethical Self-consciousness now learns *from its deed* the developed nature of what it actually did . . .")[12]

Hegel is clearly anticipating here the account of "action as expression," familiar after Wittgenstein II, von Wright's *Explanation and Understanding,* Anscombe's *Intention,* and Charles Taylor's work. But the way Hegel formulates his own position, with its claim about retrospective determination and narrative logic, is quite distinctive. Formulations of that account show up frequently in a wide variety of Hegelian texts. "An individual cannot know who he is before he has made himself into actuality through action."[13] And that "A human being – as he is externally, i.e. in his actions, so is he inwardly; and when he is virtuous, moral, etc. only inwardly, i.e. only in intentions, dispositions and when his externalities are not identical with this, then the one is as hollow and empty as the other."[14]

However, the most concentrated and richest discussion occurs in the *Phenomenology,* in the sections whose titles are already both a concise summation of Hegel's view of the nature of agency and a direct reference to our theme. After Hegel had in "Observing Reason" demonstrated (to his satisfaction) the self-contradiction involved in the reduction of mindedness to a thing or property of things (its reduction to mere "externality"), he turns to the equally one-sided attempt to give some sort of causal and conceptual priority to "the internal" in sections called "The Actualization [*Verwirklichung*] of Rational Self-Consciousness through Itself" and "Individuality, which is itself in and for itself real."[15]

---

[12] PhG, 255; 283.

[13] PhG, 218; 240.

[14] EL, 274; 197.

[15] Miller's translation rightly captures Hegel's suspicion about such a possible position, "Individuality which takes itself to be real in and for itself," but there is no "takes itself" in the German.

What Hegel tries to show in these passages is that the actual deed negates and transcends that aspect of the intention understood as separable as cause, understood as the mere occurrence of a somatic desire or passion, as well as the idea that one's real intention can only be partly expressed in a deed, and so remains in itself inexpressible, "*unaussprechlich.*" Contrary to both views: "the individual human being *is what the deed is.*" All, such that if a person's deed, also called his "Werk," is contrasted with the "inner possibility" then it is the work or deed that "must be regarded as his true actuality, even if he deceives himself on this point, and turning away from his action into himself, fancies that in this inner sense he is something else than what he is in the deed (*That*)."[16]

Finally, there is an implication about this position that Hegel eagerly accepts, most prominently in the "die Sache selbst" section. For if there is *no* way to determine what an agent intended prior to and separate from the deed, if it's only and wholly "in the deed" that we can make such a determination, then not only are we faced with an unusual retrospective determination of intention, even for the agent, it also follows that we cannot specify *the action* by reference to such a separate intention. What *I* take the act to be, its point, purpose, and implication, now has none of the privileged authority we intuitively attribute to the agent. In such an account, I don't exercise any kind of proprietary ownership of the deed, cannot unilaterally determine "what was done." This is, as it were, up for negotiation within some concrete social community, the participants of which must determine what sort of deed "*that*" would be in our practices, how our rules apply. *My intention is thus doubly "real": it is out there "in" the deed, and the deed is essentially out there "for others."* In describing agents who pride themselves on "not caring what people think," and for "having integrity" and for "believing in themselves no matter what the critics say" and so forth, who believe that there is a *Sache selbst*, determined by my intention, Hegel notes that

... in doing something, and thus bringing themselves out into the light of day, they directly contradict by their deed their pretence of wanting to exclude the glare of publicity and participation by all and sundry. Actualization is,

---

[16] PhG, 178–9; 195.

on the contrary, a display [*Ausstellung*] of what is one's own in the element of universality whereby it becomes and should become the affair [*Sache*] of everyone.[17]

From the viewpoint of such a Mr. Integrity, Hegel reports, this would look like "flies" hurrying along to "freshly poured milk," busying themselves with another's business, but Hegel rejects this attitude and insists that with all action "something has been opened up that is for others as well, or is a subject-matter on its own account."[18]

If this is so, then Hegel is claiming there to be a far deeper level of human dependence than would be claimed by mutual commitment to an ideal communicative exchange, or mutual obligation to a moral law. The content of one's status as individual, and not just the linguistic form of its expression, also is taken to reflect such recognitional dependence. This has nothing to do with some sort of complete absorption of individuality into inter-subjective determinations, and Hegel's politics retains a liberal basis in determinate individuals. He may have re-interpreted *what it is* to be an individual, treating it now as the achievement of a kind of capacity, a capacity especially to negotiate successfully various boundary problems in the play of an acknowledgement of social dependence and the inevitability of individual self-assertion. But he celebrates constantly the Christian principle of subjectivity as the heart and soul of modernity's achievement and attacks only what he regards as naïve and dangerous exaggerations of subjective self-sufficiency, even as he also locates the achievement of such individuality within an inter-subjective struggle. All of which just adds to the stakes involved in asking what acting in the light of such dependence would be like.

V. FORGIVENESS?

So, where *is* all this emphasis on so many modes of social dependence leading? What would be the *right* account of something like the appropriate dependence on such social recognition in the determination of what is mine, even in this deeply "inward" sense of "my own intention"?

---

[17] PhG, 227; 251.
[18] Ibid.

What is the political relevance of this altered sense of "mine," "yours," and "ours"?

So far, we just seem to have learned these two things: A self-image never realized in social space, never expressed in public action, a conception of individuality as socially independent and original, has to count more as a fantasy than self-knowledge, or at least as merely provisional, even though when expressed in action, the public deed cannot be said to be exclusively owned by the subject, to have the meaning that the subject insists on. It is "up for grabs" in a certain sense. One's individuality becomes a social fact through action, and its meaning can then no longer be tied to the privately formulated intention or will of the agent alone.

And yet, on the other hand, there are clearly people whose self-image, whose practical identity, has been formed so extensively by the expectations and demands and reactions of others that, while their own self-image does circulate successfully in society, their view of themselves is indeed very well mirrored in how they are regarded and treated, it has to be said that one has only become the person "they" want one to be, that one does not have one's own identity, has not become who one is. As noted earlier, this type of slavish conformism has to count as just as much a failure to become an individual as the fantasy-indulging narcissist we just discussed. Hence the suggestion that individuality amounts to the capacity to set and maintain a boundary that is of the sort consistent with all others doing likewise and so sustainable in mutual recognition.[19]

In what amounts to the closing section of the narrative account of sociality in the *Phenomenology*, Hegel's remarks are quite elliptical and do not help the reader much draw these two insights together.[20] One could argue that the incomplete and somewhat chaotic state of the PhG indicates that Hegel simply postponed until later his official discussion of "objective spirit" and that, if interested in Hegelian-rational institutions as answers to such questions, we should consult those later

---

[19] Why there has to be *that* sort of constraint is clearly an independent and arguable issue.

[20] The succeeding account of religion treats it much more as philosophically "representative" than as the social phenomenon that interested the young Hegel.

texts, the 1817 and then later versions of the *Encyclopedia* and the 1820 *Philosophy of Right*.

That may be, but the way that Hegel, in effect, leaves his narrative "hanging" at the end of the chapter on *Geist* does not suggest any possible institutional resolution, and it is hard to imagine one with the resources he gives us. Instead of such an institutional direction, he concludes with an enigmatic discussion of something like a spiritual possibility, a quasi-religious "conversion experience," in a community: "forgiveness." Left at *that*, such a culmination might well return us again to the liberal rejoinder mentioned some time ago – we may have demonstrated the centrality, essentiality even, of forms of mutual recognition for a satisfying human life, but these are largely ethical matters that are not proper subjects for political remedy, that they lead us closer to moral and religious practices than to any program for social reform, perhaps lead us to consider transformations in a form of life that are entirely independent of, prior to, any exercise of human will.

The last sections of the spirit chapter present what is in effect Hegel's last treatment of what I've been calling various modern fantasies of self-sufficiency: a fanatically self-righteous conscience, a "beautiful soul" unwilling ever to act and so to sully its pure standards, and the dissembler, who tries to reconcile its particularity with what could be shared by all by endless sophistical qualifications and reformulations of his maxim for action. Hegel describes this as a situation of inevitable guilt and the drama that he narrates leaves us only with the option of "confessing" such guilt to others whom we hope will reciprocate in a gesture that will undermine any such pretended independence and will re-affirm in mutual forgiveness our inevitable dependence.

This moment of confession and, after an initial moment of hard-hearted resistance, forgiveness, do sound very much like some moment of "release" from the grip of the ideal of self-sufficiency and fantastic independence, but there is no institutional manifestation in this account of a possible (and, it sounds like, very idealized) moral community. Moreover, there is very little in the account of modern institutions in Objective Spirit that seems in any way connected with a "hard-heart" breaking, and mutual forgiveness occurring, even in the famous supercession of morality by *Sittlichkeit*.

Let me conclude with a literary analogy in order to make this point. The situation we are left with sounds very much like the final act of

King Lear and, frustratingly, so does the "resolution." The Hegelian elements are all in place. Lear plays the part of an "acting conscious-ness" with dirty hands. He is dying without a male heir and must do what he can to leave the kingdom divided in ways that will not invite invasion by Burgundy, France, and others. He enacts in the division of his kingdom the dependence of his personal and familial life on a shared political world. Cordelia is the initially hard-hearted moralist or even beautiful soul, who finds her father's intermingling of these acts of private love with the public demands of this recognitive community unforgivable. (Lear seems to think of speech as inherently duplicitous, the price we pay for our dependence and vulnerability. Cordelia, rashly, thinks speech, the public enactments of dependence, is dispensable; that *silent* love is love enough.) We all know the catastrophe that ensues from these two fixed positions. In finally losing his status as king, in learning that his social status is not absolute, that it cannot obliterate the bonds of private love, Lear becomes a father again, the true nature of our manifold dependences revealed to him; and with the "breaking of Cordelia's hard heart," she becomes again his loving daughter and they can both express mutual forgiveness in lines as heart-breaking as any in literature. *But there is nowhere for any of this to go.* Lear's famous words evoke the exclusively personal moments of con-version and redemption possible within the cage of social necessity.

> No, no. Come, let's away to prison.
> We two alone will sing like birds i' th' cage.
> When thou dost ask me blessing, I'll kneel down
> And ask of thee forgiveness; so we'll live,
> And pray, and sing, and tell old tales, and laugh
> At gilded butterflies . . . [21]

And when Kent begins the political restoration at the end of the play, we are left with the same feeling of unsatisfactory tidying up that, I would suggest, we experience when we turn from the *Phenomenology* to

---

[21] . . . and hear poor rogues
Talk of court news, and we'll talk with them too –
Who loses and who wins, who's in, who's out,
And take upon's the mystery of things
As if we were God's spies; and we'll wear out
In a walled prison packs and sects of great ones
That ebb and flow by th' moon.

the account of modern institutions in the account of *Objective Spirit*. The conversion and transformation that occur, as figures in general for collapse of the aspiration to self-sufficient individuality, seem to present something profoundly transforming and pre-institutional. But what?

Some see all this as evidence of the "tragic nature of all social action" for Hegel, comprising both a universal dimension and an inevitable transgression of such a law. But that is Hegel read through Adorno, in my view.[22] The aspiration for a culminating reconciliation is everywhere in Hegel, but everywhere elusive. The solution to the problem he presents us with is not to abandon that hope, but to try to understand what he meant, and especially to try to find the links between that aspiration and his theory of the state, both because the relation seems mysterious and because what Hegel has written about it has inspired some of the most intense criticism of his position. Here is a frequent image that testifies to the depth of the problem as Hegel saw it and that he invoked throughout his career, early and late. In his *Lectures on Aesthetics*, Hegel claims that Spirit, human being itself, *is* a "wound" that spirit inflicts on itself, but which it can heal itself,[23] and in doing so reiterates what he had claimed at the end of this chapter of the PhG, many years before, when he had promised us even more: "The wounds of spirit heal, and leave no scars behind."[24]

---

[22] I am here disagreeing with Jay Bernstein, "Confession and Forgiveness: Hegel's Poetics of Action," in *Beyond Representation: Philosophy and Poetic Imagination*, ed. Richard Eldridge (Cambridge: Cambridge University Press, 1996), 34–65.

[23] G. W. F. Hegel, *Aesthetics: Lectures on Fine Arts*, 2 volumes, transl. T. M. Knox (Oxford: The Clarendon Press, 1975). 98.

[24] PhG, 360; 407.

4

Damaged Life

Power and Recognition in Adorno's Ethics

Bert van den Brink

Theodor W. Adorno's most well-known statement about ethics probably is "Es gibt kein richtiges Leben im falschen"; "There is no way of living a false life correctly."[1] This is Adorno's answer to the old question in ethics and social philosophy as to whether good, just, well-ordered lives can be led in societies that are neither good nor just nor well-ordered. Adorno has important things to say about the fatal dynamics between the *false* – damaged, distorted – social and cultural conditions modern individuals live under, on the one hand, and these individuals' (in)ability to recognize themselves and others as moral

---

[1] Theodor W. Adorno, *Minima Moralia: Reflections from Damaged Life*, transl. by E. F. N. Jephcott (New York: Verso, 1978), A (aphorism) 18. This work will be referred to as 'MM' throughout this chapter. Jephcott translates Adorno's words as "A wrong life cannot be lived rightly." I follow James Gordon Finlayson's translation in his "Adorno and the Ethical and the Ineffable," *European Journal of Philosophy* 10:1 (2002): 1–25. Finlayson's translation of the German 'richtig' as 'correct' rather than 'right' and 'falsch' as 'false' rather than 'wrong' has the advantage of not suggesting that Adorno is primarily interested in justice and not so much in the good, in virtue, and in human flourishing. In fact, as we will see, he is interested in all of this, and more. I thank Finlayson for pointing this out to me.

I thank David Owen, Gordon Finlayson, Mathijs Peters, the participants in the conference on "Recognition and Power" (Utrecht University, 2003), and two anonymous reviewers for Cambridge University Press for their invaluable remarks on an earlier draft of this chapter. Of course, I am entirely responsible for not having been able to put to rest all their questions and worries.

and ethical agents, on the other.[2] Since Adorno accounts for false life in terms of a theory of rationality according to which the control of inner nature, social relationships, and of the external physical world determines humans' chances at survival, there is not much room in Adorno's modern world for forms of recognition of self and others as beings with a non-instrumental, moral status. Here we find a link between Adorno's account of power understood as rational control (*Herrschaft*) and his account of recognition. We will see that insofar as Adorno has an account of recognition at all, it is an account of moments of intersubjective responsiveness towards genuine needs of self and other that escape false rationality. But recognition is always momentary, an escape from reification that cannot be stabilized and institutionalized, cannot be turned into a trustworthy disposition for action that would escape the way false life shapes us.

We may conjecture that Adorno would have been highly skeptical of Axel Honneth's claim that a formal yet comprehensive conception of ethical life that encompasses "the qualitative conditions for self-realization"[3] can somehow be "abstracted from the plurality of all particular forms of life" in our societies[4] and be made socially effective by means of justly ordered institutions.[5] Indeed, I will argue that, as seen from Adorno's perspective, Honneth's attempt at abstracting three core principles of recognition from his analysis of ethical life – institutionally anchored principles of love, respect, and achievement[6] – is in danger of theoretically capturing valuable forms of recognition the wrong way. According to Adorno, recognition and the kind of social reconciliation it promises is not to be thought of as an institutionally stabilized – and in that way controllable – state that warrants social justice, but as a *moment of responsiveness to otherness* that escapes

---

[2] I include both sides of the well-known distinction between 'moral' and 'ethical' agency here – agency directed towards justice and agency directed towards the good life, respectively – not because Adorno uses the distinction in that way (he does not), but because it is important to stress that according to Adorno, correct living ('richtiges Leben') always encompasses both dimensions.

[3] Axel Honneth, *The Struggle for Recognition: The Moral Grammar of Social Conflicts*, transl. by Joel Anderson (Cambridge: Polity, 1996), 175.

[4] Ibid.

[5] See, especially, Axel Honneth, *Redistribution as Recognition, A Response to Nancy Fraser*, in Nancy Fraser and Axel Honneth, *Redistribution or Recognition: A Political-Philosophical Exchange*, transl. by Joel Golb, James Ingram, and Christiane Wilke, London/New York: Verso, 2003, pp. 110–197.

[6] Ibid., 137–44.

wrong life and the (false) forms of justice and freedom it claims to protect. Because the stress on responsiveness to value and otherness is not at all at odds with Honneth's theory of recognition, but his theory is affirmative of the ethical life of modern society, it seems worthwhile to reconstruct Adorno's worries about a full-blown theory of recognition such as Honneth's, and offer what we find as a message in a bottle on the shore of contemporary critical social theory.

In his social theory, Adorno has been said to sketch a physiognomy of capitalist and totalitarian forms of life (rather than a convincing social theoretical explanation of how these life forms came about). These forms of life are characterized by reification of individuals' relations to themselves, to others, and to the external world.[7] Despite the devastating portrayal of forms of life and their incapacitating consequences for human agency, Adorno never stops pointing to the possibility of a state of freedom, of human flourishing, that has overcome reification – a state of redemption or reconciliation that, throughout his career, he has tried to unearth from the ruins of failed Enlightenment. However, this 'pointing to' remains notoriously vague. We know that the positive notion of freedom would involve realizing our capacity for reason by overcoming instrumental rationality and its identity thinking – that turns all true ends into means for controlling the world. This instrumental rationality keeps our relations to ourselves, to others, and to the non-human world reified. But Adorno does not spell out a positive notion of freedom. Lacking any firm knowledge about what it would mean to reason in such a way in practice, this very spelling out would involve a use of concepts that cannot escape the pitfalls of identity thinking. Rather, insofar as Adorno suggests that correct living is possible for human beings at all, he does so by focusing on the role that ineffable insights – insights by which we are shown something "that one cannot put into words," that "cannot be thought,"[8] as in aesthetic experiences or in experiences of love[9] – play in generating at least the hope that non-reified uses of reason are a possibility.[10]

---

[7] See Axel Honneth's "A Physiognomy of the Capitalist Form of Life: A Sketch of Adorno's Social Theory," *Constellations* 12 (2005): 50–64.

[8] Finlayson, "Adorno and the Ethical and the Ineffable": 14.

[9] For love see Honneth, "Physiognomy of Capitalism": 62f.

[10] For an excellent account of the role of the ineffable in Adorno's ethical thought, see Finlayson, "Adorno on the Ethical and the Ineffable."

Despite what we might call the utter helplessness of Adorno's utopian thought – how could we have insights about things that cannot be thought? – his physiognomy of false life and false rationality never resulted in a systematic plea for resignation on the individual level. Perhaps the recent interest in Adorno's ethical writings can be explained by the fact that in this work, more than in his other work, he not only presents a devastating physiognomy of modern life forms, but also presents a normative ethics: an *ethics of resistance* against the life forms in which our reification is embedded. What is so interesting about this ethics is that it tries to tell us something about what it would mean to develop a halfway respectable ethical attitude *vis-à-vis* modern society even in the knowledge that it is a false society. It is his focus on the space between that of failure and resignation, on the one hand, and that of the full enjoyment of justice and human flourishing, on the other hand, that is so fascinating about Adorno's ethics.

Of course, Adorno lived and worked in another era than ours. We feel shame, horror, and moral confusion when we read his reflections on the darkest sides of that era, especially the Holocaust. Still, most of us do not subscribe to his totalizing claims about the capitalist economy, mass culture, and political totalitarianism. And this for good reasons: as I have argued elsewhere, Adorno's most famous philosophical work must be considered sociologically naïve, and is perhaps better understood as an almost artistic expression of deep worries about Western culture than as an academic work.[11] For that reason, it would not make much sense to strictly 'compare' Adorno's ethical work with that of Honneth, which neither is sociologically naïve nor can be understood as an artistic approach to ethical questions. I will rather reconstruct what I think Adorno has to say about the connection between false social relations and recognition, and let it stand opposed to Honneth's view.

I will start with some reflections on that peculiar statement, "There is no way of living a false life correctly." I will then go on to argue that Adorno sketches the contours of an *ethics of resistance* against power relations that stands in the way of sound ethical relations. Finally, I will reconstruct Adorno's ideas about power relations, the ethical

---

[11] Bert van den Brink, "Gesellschaftstheorie und Übertreibungskunst: Für eine alternative Lesart der 'Dialektik der Aufklärung,'" *Neue Rundschau* 108/1 (1997): 37–59.

experiences that open up knowledge about false life and its power relations, and the notions of redemption and recognition that inspire such knowledge. We will find some interesting similarities with some aspects of Honneth's theory – especially the moral-psychological ones – and many differences with respect to the question as to whether a comprehensive ethical theory of recognition can be developed at all.

FALSE LIFE

It is important to stress from the outset that Adorno's observation that there is no way in which a false life can be lived correctly is not meant to say that, in false life, individuals should give up on the aspiration to lead good and just lives. The observation is a descriptive, phenomenological one, not a call for resignation. Objectively, the conditions for leading a good or right life are no longer given – if they ever where. The dominant economic and bureaucratic institutions of society have maneuvered ethical life into a *private* existence, isolated from the main economic-bureaucratic scene of society. Still, as seen from our best accounts of what makes life worthwhile, ethical life – *Sittlichkeit* – is the true locus of human life, of humanity. It is the setting in which values and practices such as love, family, friendship, art, justice, politics, reconciliation, work, trade, and commerce have their proper place and are given their social meaning. Where ethical life is seen as having its proper place in private life alone, it can no longer fulfill its integrative and meaning-giving role for the whole of society. That is the message that the subtitle of *Minima Moralia: Reflections from Damaged Life* is meant to convey. Where ethical life is understood as part of private life only, it is *damaged*.

Damaged ethical life is not an intact miniature version of what it would be if its integrity were not damaged. It is faced with structural distortions. It is now best conceptualized as a *refuge* for those who feel "homeless" in society (MM, A18). Time and again we see Adorno stressing that institutions such as work, trade, commerce, politics, private possessions, and even the family are no longer primarily means to the end of leading a good life. The instrumentalist and strategic logic of economic gain and the exercise of bureaucratic power reign supreme in the main institutions of society. This logic invades 'private' ethical existence. As Adorno describes it, individual members of society are mainly there to serve the instrumental and strategic requirements of these institutions. As a consequence, they start mimicking economic and bureaucratic forms of rationality in the spheres of love, friendship, leisure, art, intellectual life, and so on. By this logic of estrangement, individuals' undisturbed experience of the independent ethical goods these practices harbor has come under threat. The larger suggestion in the background is that there is an inversion of means and ends at work in the history of the human species. Private ethical existence has largely become a *means* that helps perpetuate the *ends* of repressive capitalist consumer society, fascist political ideologies, and their disenchanted, non-ethical forms of rationality.

In the very aphorism about false life, Adorno states that

The best mode of conduct, in face of all this, still seems an uncommitted, suspended one: to lead a private life, as far as the social order and one's own needs will tolerate nothing else, but not to attach weight to it as to something still socially substantial and individually appropriate. (MM, A18)

Private existence is the last refuge of ethical life. We can try to live a pleasant, a fulfilling life there. But,

[P]rivate existence, in striving to resemble one worthy of man, betrays the latter, since any resemblance is withdrawn from general realization, which yet more than ever before has need of independent thought. (MM, A6)

Despite his compassion for the individual who endures her estranged state without great expectations, Adorno is looking for a way in which individuals may learn to reflect on, resist, and – as a utopian hope at least – even change the objective powers they live under and are formed by – in search of a life "worthy of man."[12]

J. M. Bernstein has recently pointed out that in the background of Adorno's analysis, a "meta-ethical" position is at work that resembles a position of moral realism we know from the broad Aristotelian tradition. "Adorno presupposes," he writes,

---

[12] Theodor W. Adorno, *Probleme der Moralphilosophie*, in *Nachgelassene Schriften*, Vol. 10 (Frankfurt am Main: Suhrkamp, 1996), Lectures 1, 2, 16, 17. Cf. Stefan Müller-Doohm, *Die Soziologie Theodor W. Adornos* (Frankfurt am Main: Campus, 2000,) 188–198.

that ethical thought is a reflective articulation of ethical experience, which itself is structured through ethical practices.... [T]he provenance of the meaning and force of moral terms are the practices of the community deploying them, and [...] outside these practices, and the history they sediment and report, such terms lose their force.[13]

This helps explain why Adorno holds that ethical life is in such a desperate state. Not only is it a damaged, partly disenchanted, privatized, and powerless residue of what it is supposed to be. But what is more, for those who are aware of this in their ethical *thought*, there are no clear and meaningful guidelines for a better life to be taken from it.[14] If the material basis of ethical *experience* in authoritative practices and traditions is damaged, ethical subjects and ethical theorists must remain without firm orientation in their ethical *reflection*.[15] One does not get the impression that Adorno longs for safe, unquestioned horizons of ethical thought. Not melancholy for a traditional idea of community, but for adequate conditions for the practice-based grammar of ethical experience and reflection that breathe through his sentences. The ethical subject is in a crisis that is akin to the one sketched by Nietzsche and Weber. As Nietzsche puts it in his God is dead passage: "How could we drink up the sea? Who gave us the sponge to wipe away the whole horizon?"[16]

Now, as with Nietzsche, Adorno's way to proceed is to put the damaged subject at centre stage of his reflections. Only the damaged subject can *experience* and – albeit imperfectly – *reflect* upon the damages that are done to its life. Access to the object of her reflection is gained through damaged experience. The subject is caught in contradictions of ethical life. She is told by society to lead a good life, but may sense that ethical life in this society cannot be good. She is told about the value of moral autonomy, but may sense that she is not able to endorse herself the laws she lives under. She is told that love and family

[13] J. M. Bernstein, *Adorno: Ethics and Disenchantment* (New York/Cambridge: Cambridge University Press, 2001), 41.
[14] See Adorno, *Probleme der Moralphilosophie*, lecture 1, for a very clear statement to this effect.
[15] Bernstein, *Adorno*, p. 41.
[16] Friedrich Nietzsche, *The Gay Science*, transl. by W. Kaufmann (New York: Random House, 1974), para. 125.

are great values, but may sense that the conditions for experiencing the independent values of love and family life are under threat. Adorno continuously stresses that the knowledge we can still gain about the ruins of ethical life is best gained through the experience of the damaged subject, whose experience, we might say, is constituted by these ruins of ethical life.

In a passage in which he argues against Hegel, Adorno comments on this strategy. Since Hegel's days, he observes,

> ... the individual has gained as much in richness, differentiation and vigour as, on the other hand, the socialization of society has enfeebled and undermined him. In the period of his decay, the individual's experience of himself and what he encounters contributes once more to knowledge, which he had merely obscured as long as he continued unshaken to construe himself positively as the dominant category. (MM, dedication)

Since Hegel, the individual has been rebelling, protesting against its estranged predicament ever stronger. This is where Adorno puts his understanding not of Hegel's *dialectical method* but rather of what he sees as his *political thought* upside down. Rather than seeing the individual as someone who is formed and tutored by the ethical life of larger society, he presents the rebelling, protesting individual *as a last ethical hope* against larger society, which can no longer be understood in terms of an ethical life at all. Adorno quotes Hegel *against himself* exactly in order to stress the importance of negativity for the dialectical method. The quote is from *The Phenomenology of Mind.* "The life of the mind," Hegel writes,

> only attains its truth when discovering itself in absolute desolation. The mind is not this power as a positive which turns away from the negative, as when we say of something that it is null, or false, so much for that and now for something else; it is this power only when looking the negative in the face, dwelling upon it.[17]

The damaged life of the individual is presented as the last refuge not just of homeless members of society but also as the source of, the epistemological entrance to, ethical reflection and social criticism. We must now ask what form that reflection and critique takes.

---

[17] G. W. F. Hegel, *The Phenomenology of Mind*, transl. by J. B. Baillie (London: Allen & Unwin, 1966), 112, quoted from MM, dedication.

DOES ADORNO HAVE AN ETHICS AT ALL?

The first question that has to be addressed is whether it is at all appropriate to talk about Adorno's ethics. For Adorno, an ethics, in the sense of a positive ethical doctrine about right living, would presuppose a form of moral experience that connects theoretical and doctrinal generalizations about morality with a great sensitivity to particulars: to concrete "others" of generalizing moral thought such as objects, suffering individuals and animals, languages and vocabularies, social practices and traditions, that are crushed or ignored by the evaluative and normative concepts of the general theory or doctrine.[18] For Adorno, such particulars have a certain holiness or inviolability that has to be treated with respect. A dialectical doctrine that wants to pay such respect to particulars would never take a definite form, for it would have to be continuously aware of the harm to particulars that generalizations do; it would have to correct itself indefinitely. Openness to particulars, to negativity, presupposes a non-identitarian way of thinking – a mode of thought that does not assume that a concept fully captures and thereby determines its object. In *Minima Moralia*, Adorno has interesting things to say about the generalizing conceptual categorization of women, blacks, and Jews in society, and how it systematically silences, marginalizes, or deforms their individual and collective voices, their self-ascriptions, their repressed longings, needs, and identities. Here, he does not just caution against straightforward discrimination. He also notes that seemingly humane liberal theories of equality distort reality; make social injustices invisible by talking about the victims of such injustices *as if they were* equals – which, in fact, they are not. Such theories, Adorno holds, easily turn into ideology because their soothing insights do not reflect sufficiently on the structural wrongs in wider society that frustrate our understanding of equality, difference, and justice in the first place.

For Adorno to straightforwardly develop a positive ethical theory would be to make a mockery of his own insights. His sociological analysis of society forbids him to take that route. Bernstein reminds us that according to Adorno, sensitivity to particulars has "migrated into the marginalized domain of art," and is hardly an aspect of ethical

---

[18] Cf. Bernstein, *Adorno*, p. 33.

practice.[19] Given the state of the ethical practices Adorno analyses, he chooses to focus on the task of cautioning against identitarian modes of thought and the many forms they take. His aim is not to develop a positive ethical theory, but to free our moral sensitivities – to the extent possible – from a predicament of reification that is *caused* by socio-economic and power-political structures, but which at the experiential and epistemological levels *results* in the reification of our capacity to reflect adequately on our situation.[20]

There is a second reason why it is problematic to speak of Adorno's ethics. It has to do with vocabulary. In his 1963 lectures on *Probleme der Moralphilosophie*, Adorno sees himself confronted by the dilemma of calling his subject matter either *Moral* – morality – or *Ethik* – ethics. According to Adorno, the term 'morality' stands for a generalizing, universalistic doctrine of ethical rules and prescripts, whereas the term 'ethics' stands for a private morality of the good life. So to call the subject matter of his reflections *ethics* might be misconstrued as an affirmation of the privatization of ethical life. Although Adorno stresses that calling it morality has problems of its own, especially problems concerning the dangers of identitarian thinking, he still prefers to speak of morality rather than ethics. That, he says, reminds us of the importance of relating particular ethical experience and thought to universals as well as to questions that concern all of society. In the background here is Adorno's deep dislike of the existentialist understanding of ethics as an 'authentic' *ethics of self-realization* that, as he sees it, creates itself from nowhere and posits itself in non-dialectical opposition to larger society. Existentialism, understood in this way, comes down to robbing ethical life of its potential for resistance.[21]

So let it be granted that Adorno has no ethics in the sense of a full-blown ethical doctrine or a private ethics of the good life. Still, I will argue that he does sketch the contours of what we can term an ethical-political *attitude*. Such an ethical-political attitude does not so much provide direct guidelines for action, but rather for a mode of ethical and philosophical perception, contemplation, and insecure attempts

---

[19] See ibid., pp. 34–35, n62.
[20] Cf. Gillian Rose, *The Melancholy Science: An Introduction to the Thought of Theodor W. Adorno* (New York: Columbia University Press, 1997), Chs. 2 & 3.
[21] Adorno, *Probleme der Moralphilosophie*, 21–23, 26, 261–262.

at action. It is a *critical attitude*, and can be safeguarded against false understandings of the term "ethics." For instance, we may think of the way in which Michel Foucault has reflected on an ethical attitude in his later work. This use has been further developed, for instance, in James Tully's and David Owen's recent work in political philosophy.[22] Foucault's rudimentary description of the starting point of this critical attitude expresses quite clearly, albeit rudimentarily, the inevitable ethical-political aspect of the attitude meant here. He describes that starting point, famously, as *the will "Not to be governed like that, by that, in name of those principles."*[23] In light of these similarities, and given the Kantian, Rawlsian, and Habermasian overtones in *our* use of the term 'morality' in political ethics, it seems justified to speak of Adorno's ethics of resistance.

ADORNO'S ETHICS OF RESISTANCE

In reading *Minima Moralia* and *Probleme der Moralphilosophie* with an eye to such a critical attitude, I was struck by a threefold set of observations scattered through Adorno's ethical writings that I think can help us understand his thought. These observations show interesting parallels with the moral psychology underlying Axel Honneth's theory of recognition.[24] First, there are observations about *false normality* and its power-based pathologies. In Honneth's theory, this would be the level of the phenomenological descriptions of misrecognition.[25] Second, there are observations about *the kinds of experiences* that open individuals unto *cognitions* about false life and its pathologies. In Honneth's work, too, we see great sensitivity to the way in which the damaged subject, exactly in virtue of its learning that it *is* damaged, can gain new knowledge about itself and its relation to the social world.[26] Third, there are observations about the evaluative stance from which our

[22] James Tully, "The Agonic Freedom of Citizens," *Economy and Society* 28/2 (1999): 161–182; David Owen, *Nietzsche, Politics, and Modernity* (London, Thousand Oaks: Sage, 1995), 132–169.
[23] Michel Foucault, "What is Critique?" transl. by Kevin Paul Geiman, in *What is Enlightenment: Eighteenth-Century Answers and Twentieth-Century Questions* (Berkeley: University of California Press, 1996), 384.
[24] See Honneth, *Struggle*, 131–140, 160–171.
[25] Honneth, "Redistribution as Recognition," pp. 114ff.
[26] See, for instance, Honneth, *Struggle*, 135–139.

cognitions about social pathologies begin to point in the direction of a better life. This evaluative stance, I will argue, holds a place for an ideal of *recognition*. Again we see affinities between Adorno and Honneth, this time because Honneth has tied the evaluative stance from which he analyses the social world to a formal conception of the good life that is conceptualized in terms of ideals of recognition.

Normality. Looking at the false normality in society, Adorno sees oppression. Oppression may be overt, as in the observations of the situation of women, blacks, and Jews who rebel against their identifiable oppressors. It may also be hidden, as in the many aphorisms about seemingly happy people in trains, in their homes, in cinemas, in adolescent culture, in the laboratories of academia, and who, with smiles on their faces, are leading damaged existences. Let me call the first group the *unhappily oppressed*, the second the *happily oppressed*. In this second group, the exercise of power has reached its peak:

A breed of men has secretly grown up that hungers for the compulsion and restriction imposed by the absurd persistence of domination. (MM, A80)

Both the happily and the unhappily oppressed are victims of power-relations that are based in the socio-economic basis of society, on the one hand, and the identitarian mode of thinking that is its result, on the other. Either latently or manifestly, people suffer from the distorted images of human worth they have internalized with the help of consumer society, the culture industry, false gurus, charismatic politicians, and psychotherapists. The happily oppressed are in Adorno's observations almost always those who gain fruits from consumer society or from political totalitarianism. They are bourgeois and working-class people with jobs, homes, cars, and all the other stabilizing sedatives consumer society has to offer. In overtly totalitarian societies, they may be "backwoodsmen" turned into "blond beasts" (MM, A66). Because they think that commonsense and morality are on their side, they may see it as their duty to lend a hand in the correction of those – the unhappily oppressed – who claim to *know* about their desperate state. If at all, only members of this latter group will come to rebel against their predicament. Sometimes, Adorno describes them as doing this for the straightforward reason that they are less well-placed in consumer society or in totalitarian society than others (cf. 'workers movement,' MM, A57; 'savages,' MM, A32). Sometimes, however, people rebel because they truly sense the estranged state they are in. Only in them does rebellion against oppression lead to a glimpse of freedom, of resistance, of human agency. Their resistance may focus on the oppressed individual's own predicament, the predicament of a group she genuinely identifies with, or the situation of society at large. Only a form of protest that focuses on all these aspects does not affirm false life.

By way of internalization of false images, oppressed individuals are fatally led away from the individuals they *could become* if their larger home, ethical life were not damaged (on the importance of 'becoming' for dialectical thought, see MM, A47). One passage in which we can get a good impression of what this means is aphorism 59 of *Minima Moralia*, which addresses the position of women in society. Its title is *Seit ich ihn Gesehen*. "*Since I set eyes on him*" (the line stems from the romantic poet Adelbert von Chamisso). In the poem, the words "Since I set eyes on him" are followed by "I seem to have gone blind." This all too common experience of everyone who has ever been in love is used to sketch the logic of power through *mis*recognition in the relation between the sexes. Let me quote from the aphorism at some length:

The feminine character, and the ideal of femininity on which it is modeled, are products of masculine society. The image of undistorted nature arises only in distortion, as its opposite. Where it claims to be humane, masculine society imperiously breeds in woman its own corrective, and shows itself through this limitation implacably the master. The feminine character is a negative imprint of domination. But therefore equally bad. Whatever is in the context of bourgeois delusion called nature, is merely the scar of social mutilation. If the psychoanalytical theory is correct that women experience their physical constitution as a consequence of castration, their neurosis gives them an inkling of the truth. The woman who feels herself a wound when she bleeds knows more about herself that the one who imagines herself a flower because that suits her husband.

Let us suspend for a while our initial reaction that, in this reflection, Adorno may well victimize, incapacitate the women he reflects on much more than is sociologically or psychologically warranted. My aim is not to investigate Adorno's possibly failed conception of the types of women he sketches. It is rather to bring out his ideas as to what it means to *mis*recognize a person and the evaluative qualities that characterize her.

Adorno suggests that the woman "who feels herself a wound when she bleeds" latently knows about her situation. She has been disciplined into a functional role that perpetuates masculine domination. In order to hide this from her sight, society *has led her to believe* that she is an innocent flower, unspoiled by larger civilization. To put it in recognition-theoretical terms: the dominant patterns of social evaluation in society recognize a woman either as a natural flower, or condemn her for being a failed attempt at femininity. Both are forms of *mis*recognition, of course, but one of the things we can learn from Adorno is that it is very hard to see this, as long as we trust on dominant patterns of social evaluation.

Note the terms used here. Whereas the woman who experiences a wound is said to *feel* her predicament, the flower woman is said to *imagine* her own state. The *feeling* is a *bodily experience* through which, in the metaphor used, female experience cries over its social castration. The flower woman, on the other hand, is able to happily *imagine* her own state, because she simply feels no pain. She is provided by consumer society, by the culture industry, by women's magazines with more than enough *images* of unspoiled nature to fantasize about her happiness. But her internalization of male standards – that is, standards of manipulative, strategic rationality – comes to the fore in her relation to men. With barely concealed self-hatred – a self-hatred that perhaps illustrates his own difficult relation to various archetypes of femininity – Adorno observes:

> The femininity which appeals to instinct, is always exactly what every woman has to force herself by violence – masculine violence – to be: a she-man. One need only have experienced, as jealous male, how such feminine women have their femininity at their finger-tips – deploying it just where needed, flashing their eyes, using their impulsiveness – to know how things stand with the sheltered unconscious, unmarred by intellect. Just this unscathed purity is the product of the ego, of censorship, of intellect, which is why it submits so unrestingly to the reality principle of the rational order. (ibid)

The message may be clear: the unspoiled flower has internalized all tricks, tact, and instrumentality she needs in order to play and thereby affirm the social game. False normality is a set of relations of power through *mis*recognition between society's institutions and the happily oppressed (the flower woman and dominant men), on the one hand, and the unhappily oppressed who latently *know* about their predicament, but do not find social recognition, on the other.

Experience and Cognition. The unhappily oppressed experience *pain*, either bodily, or in their self-understandings, or both. Because of this, they are caught in contradictions that open them up to their false predicament. Through the complexities of love, marriage, divorce, gender, home-ownership, unemployment, and enforced group membership they are caught in the midst of the remaining havens of halfway valuable private existence, on the one hand, and the social pathologies that undermine them, on the other. The value of objective goods of love, friendship, bodily experience, having a place of one's own, a fulfilling working environment, and a sense of social belonging become visible only to those who are robbed even of the securities of a stable private ethical existence. At least three aspects play a role in the experience at stake, and the tragic epistemology of extremes – *only those who suffer will know about their predicament* – that Adorno seems to associate it with. It concerns, first, false images of oneself that one has internalized through false social relations – for instance, the image of the natural flower. Second, it concerns remainders of true ethical experience in the margins of such relations, such as a sense of femininity or love that escapes false images and touches on the uniqueness of the person one is, or could become. Third, it concerns the experience of loss of access to the institutions in which such experiences can be tied to non-pathological social forms (forms that would make the longing for becoming who one is possible), such as the family or relationships of love and friendship. A reflection on these three material aspects of a negative ethical experience may give rise to questions about, first, the value of dominant images, such as that of the natural flower. Second, experience raises questions as to the objective factors that threaten the remainders of ethical good in private existence – for instance, institutions such as the economy, law, and politics. Third, the experience raises questions as to the nature of the good and the institutional forms that would be needed in order to reinstate social forms in which the ethical good could be experienced in undamaged ways.

Now, for these questions to make sense, it is imperative that the bodily and mental substratum of the 'normalized' subject not be totally identified *with* the normalized subject.[27] Indeed, the bodily and mental substratum of the normalized subject must harbor a source of vitality and reflexive resistance to the dominant images the normalized subject has internalized. The tension involved here Adorno describes as one between death and vitality (MM, A36). His rhetorical strategy of inversion of familiar terms[28] reaches its peak here. *What from the perspective of wrong life looks vital is ethically dead; what looks ethically deformed wins the vital possibility of being opened unto knowledge of the "mimicry with the inorganic" of wrong life* (ibid.):

> The very people who burst with proofs of exuberant vitality could easily be taken for prepared corpses, from whom the news of their not-quite-successful decease has been withheld for reasons of population policy.

In the background here is a psychoanalytical understanding of neurosis. A neurosis is caused by a tension, a conflict in which instinctual drives are being repressed. But in *unreflected* damaged life – the life of the happily oppressed – even resistance against the repression of drives, through which a neurosis becomes visible and can be treated, has disappeared. By internalizing a conception of rationality that ignores the emotions, the subject has internalized an attitude of non-resistance. Drives and longings are being deformed and satisfied through consumption of goods and images offered by the culture industry and totalitarian political structures. The vital drives and emotions that co-constitute real conflicts become so repressed that their resistance-enabling force is "castrated" (ibid.). This results in a conclusion also known from the study on *The Authoritarian Personality*: "The absence of conflicts reflects a predetermined outcome, the *a priori* triumph of collective authority, not a cure effected by knowledge" (ibid.). The unhappily oppressed, the outcasts and refugees who have no access to the unquestioned satisfactions of false life, are the ones who get in touch with their neurosis and who therefore get a chance to at least become aware of their own pathologies and those of larger society.

---

[27] For a complete argument to this effect, regarding the work of Foucault, see Judith Butler, "Subjection, Resistance, Resignification," in *The Psychic Life of Power* (Stanford: Stanford University Press, 1997, 83–105).

[28] See Rose, *Melancholy Science*, Ch. 2.

Cognition and Recognition. But from which evaluative stance might negative experiences turn into positive cognitions that can point to the contours of a better life? I noted earlier that there are experiences of genuine ethical value even in false life. In love, we find the experience that the object of our love has a value of its own, which is not reducible to anything we might want to project onto it or manipulate. Through marriage and the family, an institution that is stabilized by the partners' fidelity and loyalty to each other, members of a family find a social environment that has a value of its own, which again is not reducible to its value as a production site of laborers, employees, consumers, and political subjects.[29] In intellectual life, private existence offers a place for the objectively valuable attitude of contemplation that respects it objects. The damaged private life of the refugee is the place from which Adorno himself develops his ethical thought. He reflects on his own situation and that of others who are in the midst of the ruins of ethical life. Fragmentary but positive understandings of human worth can be taken from these ruins.

Adorno's observations sail between the Scylla of true openness to, and respect for, the object of an individual's feelings, wants, and contemplations, and the Charybdis of their socially imposed occupation by false images and expectations. But again, Adorno does not claim that these impositions necessarily make unspoiled experience of the good of the object, of the genuine value of the other impossible. The evaluative stance from which he judges false life is inspired by his openness to the independent good of objects, persons and relationships understood as 'others' of his reflections.[30]

In the final aphorism of *Minima Moralia* (MM, A153), Adorno states that

The only philosophy that can be responsibly practiced in face of despair is the attempt to contemplate all things as they would present themselves from the standpoint of redemption.

So despite all his stress on the importance of negativity, Adorno needs a positive notion of redemption. This cannot be a formal but comprehensive conception of ethical life, such as Axel Honneth's in the final

---

[29] Compare Bernstein, *Adorno*, 45ff. and Müller-Doohm, *Soziologie*, 196ff.
[30] Cf. Bernstein, *ibid.*

chapter of *The Struggle for Recognition*. Honneth takes his conception of ethical life from "the plurality of all forms of life" . . . "at the highest level of development of each."[31] Honneth has enough trust in the soundness of *institutionalized ethical relations* in family, law, and relations of solidarity to attempt the formulation of a positive notion of ethical life. As we have seen, Adorno does not. He has some trust in undistorted experiences of love, fidelity, friendship, and contemplation in private life. But for him, law, and social solidarity in wider society are too much tainted by false totality to inform us about their hidden value (see MM, A100). Again, Adorno has recourse not so much to *social forms* but rather to moments in *individual experience*.

Scattered through his ethical work, we find indications of how a conception of redemptive recognition can be taken from non-identitarian ways of perception and thinking. Sometimes, it is packed in descriptions of misrecognition – for instance, in aphorism 68, "People are looking at you":

The possibility of pogroms is decided in the moment when the gaze of a fatally-wounded animal falls on a human being. The defiance with which he repels this gaze – 'after all, it is only an animal' – reappears irresistibly in cruelties done to human beings, the perpetrators having again and again to reassure themselves that it is 'only an animal,' because they could never fully believe this even of animals.

And a few sentences after this he observes that

. . . those in power perceive as human only their own reflected image, instead of reflecting back the human as precisely what is different.

Patient perception, non-identitarian openness to the independence, the otherness, the suffering of what it fragile and vulnerable is the cornerstone of Adorno's notion of redemption and of his notion of recognition. Recognition *is* the reflecting-back of difference, the respectful affirmation of what is of independent, ungraspable value, and goodness in the fragile other. The object, the dying animal, the human being who is not marginalized or made identical to dominant conceptions will "disclose" itself as what it is or could become, "in the long contemplative look" in which "the urge towards the object is always

---

[31] Honneth, *Struggle*, 175.

deflected, reflected" (MM, A54). From the reflecting-back of otherness of the external and the internal world, Adorno expects redemption both from social and conceptual reification. And although he does not often extend this notion of redemptive recognition to an ideal of society as a whole, there is a passage where he does:

> An emancipated society ... would not be a unitary state, but the realization of universality in the reconciliation of differences. Politics that are still seriously concerned with such a society ought not, therefore, propound the abstract equality of men even as an idea. Instead, they should point to the bad equality today, the identity of those with interests in films and in weapons, and conceive the better state as one in which people could be different without fear. (MM, A66)

So an ideal of a society *without fear*, in which institutions and individuals would recognize the *difference* rather than the proclaimed identity of their others is central to Adorno's evaluative stance. Being without fear is being free to unfold oneself without being afraid that what unfolds will be denounced when it does not itself denounce otherness. Adorno's hope is that this rudimentary type of recognition breaks with identitarian power-relations that make individuals internalize false images of themselves. If images develop in an open dialectical dynamic between subject and object, there will be room for less-unitary patterns of social evaluation in society. Adorno does not tell us how we might reach such a society open to otherness. But his ethics of resistance to false life is clearly inspired by it.

The final question we have to answer is whether this resistance is merely contemplative or whether it also takes a political form. It is predominantly contemplative, and harbors hardly any calls for social or political action. But note that this is not to say that contemplations on damaged life can afford to look away from social and political power relations. The contemplative nature of Adorno's ethics is founded in the lack of any clear calls for action, not in any restrictions of its subject matter. Still, in his 1963 lectures on moral philosophy, Adorno tells his students that "today, right living would consist in resistance against those social forms of wrong life that developed consciousness critically dissolves."[32] And at the end of the final lecture, he even states that

---

[32] Adorno, *Probleme der Moralphilosophie*, p. 249 (my translation).

questions of right or good living must be understood as political questions, which concern the way in which we shape our common world. Although it would be tempting to develop from those few passages a positive, action-guiding, ethical-political perspective, which extends to legal relations and relations of solidarity, it would not be true to Adorno.

LESSONS FOR AXEL HONNETH'S THEORY OF RECOGNITION

We have seen that there are parallels between Adorno's and Honneth's thought on ethical experience and cognitive access to instances of *mis*recognition. But Adorno's analysis of ethical life and his theory of society do not leave room for developing a positive, comprehensive theory of recognition that spells out a positive notion of ethical life. Good and bad forms of recognition are so much entangled in social practices that it is not clear how one could abstract the good from these practices without including some of the bad. For Adorno, recognition and reconciliation are not institutionally stabilized *states* but *moments of responsiveness to otherness* that escape, at least in our experience, the entanglement of good and bad in ethical life. Even if we do not agree with Adorno's deeply pessimistic outlook, we should see his ethical writings as a reminder of the dangers of reification that are always involved in theorizing from a fully fleshed-out theory and its normative categories.

In this point, we find the most important lesson for Axel Honneth's theory of recognition. Honneth has embraced the normative core of ideals of romantic love, individual rights, and the principle of achievement in economy and society to such an extent that the only kinds of criticism of modern societies that remain open to him are internal criticisms of already established evaluative standards. He conceptualizes members of society as fellow citizens, participating in a never-ending game of collective self-interpretation. At stake is the question of to what extent we live up to shared ideals of mutual recognition. There is not much theoretical room for the possibility that some members of society – let alone non-members who are still subject to the institutions of social, economic, and political power of society – may have good reasons to doubt in any far-reaching sense whether the 'shared' ideals of recognition in modern societies are sound. This aspect of trust in the ethical integrity of received standards of recognition in Honneth's theory would greatly worry Adorno. He would not trust in the moral progress in our lifeworlds that Honneth assumes is implicit in struggles for recognition in liberal-democratic societies.[33] "Resistance against those social forms of wrong life that developed consciousness critically dissolves" is an ideal that Honneth shares with Adorno, of course. The main difference with Adorno is that Honneth claims that one needs a positive formulation of the structural elements of ethical life before one can develop reasonable critiques of society at all. In the quest for an intelligible starting point for social criticism, it remains unclear why that affirmative approach should be less in danger of lending us shaky and controversial foundations for critique than would trusting in the unruly, inconsistent, but creative action of those who, like Adorno, have a never-ending urge to simply fight the machine.

[33] See Honneth's contribution to the present volume, "Recognition as Idedology," (Chapter 13) and the Introduction to the volume.

5

The Potential and the Actual

Mead, Honneth, and the "I"

Patchen Markell

There is no such thing as the "eye"; there is only the seeing.

John Dewey

1

Among the most compelling features of Axel Honneth's work is his commitment to the integration of ethical and political philosophy with the study of actually existing forms of experience, motivation, and social struggle. The idea of recognition serves as his bridge between these levels of analysis: for Honneth, recognition is what we owe to each other, yet it is also that toward which our social interactions are already oriented, however imperfectly.[1] One aim of this chapter is to identify a serious difficulty in this effort to anchor normative analysis

yep

[1] See, for example, Honneth's "Author's Introduction," in *The Fragmented World of the Social: Essays in Social and Political Philosophy*, ed. Charles W. Wright (Albany: SUNY Press, 1995), xv.

For helpful conversations and comments on earlier versions of this chapter, I thank Bert van den Brink, Carolyn Eastman, Leonard Feldman, Michaele Ferguson, Andrea Frank, Jason Frank, Jill Frank, Rachel Havrelock, Jeff Lomonaco, Eric MacGilvray, Kevin Murphy, David Owen, Alexander Wendt, Elizabeth Wingrove, and Deva Woodly, as well as audiences at the 2004 Western Political Science Association meeting, the 2004 American Political Science Association meeting, the Stockholm University Political Science Department, and the Chicago Center for Contemporary Theory.

in social reality.[2] To bring this problem into view, I consider an elegant answer that Honneth and Arto Laitinen have recently proposed to a puzzling question about the nature of recognition: is recognition a response to something that already exists, or does it bring something new into being? Their answer, which turns on a distinction between "potentiality" and "actuality," does not escape the problem it is meant to solve; instead, I shall suggest, this particular use of the concepts of potentiality and actuality drives a wedge between the levels of analysis Honneth aims to hold together, securing recognition's grounding as a <u>normative concept only</u> by making it unnecessarily difficult to grasp certain powerful modes of response and opposition to injustice.

This chapter also has a second, interpretive purpose. The foregoing difficulty did not make its appearance suddenly in Honneth's recent work, nor is it unique to him; thus, in spelling out this problem, I also trace it back to Honneth's appropriation of the social psychology of the American pragmatist George Herbert Mead. In his effort to account for the ongoing emergence of struggles for recognition, Honneth draws extensively upon Mead's famous (and famously slippery) distinction between two aspects of the self – the "I" and the "me" – reading Mead's terms as instantiations of a broader conceptual distinction between potentiality and actuality. I do not argue that Honneth has gotten Mead wrong, but I do suggest that the slipperiness of Mead's concepts is meaningful in ways that many of his readers, Honneth included, have not noticed. Setting Mead's social psychology against the background of the work of William James and John Dewey, I argue that the understanding of the "I" and the "me" that Honneth takes from Mead actually represents Mead's own partial slide away from a different, more promising way of using those terms; that this slide is evidence of a tension in Mead's work that anticipates the difficulty I identify within Honneth's project; and that a recovery of Mead's alternative sense of the terms "I" and "me" can productively recast our thinking about potentiality, actuality, and recognition.

---

[2] This way of framing the argument is indebted to Nikolas Kompridis, "From Reason to Self-Realization? Axel Honneth and the 'Ethical Turn' in Critical Theory," *Critical Horizons* 5/1 (Summer 2004), 323–60.

2

In his contribution to a 2002 symposium on Axel Honneth's work, Arto Laitinen poses a fundamental question about the nature of an act of recognition: "Is recognition a matter of responding to something pre-existing or does recognition bring about its objects (for example by granting a status)?"[3] Neither view, he suggests, seems satisfactory on its own. If recognition were "nothing but a response to pre-existing features," then recognition would have "no role to play" in the constitution of, for instance, the personhood of human organisms: persons would be persons quite apart from their being recognized as such. Yet if recognition were "pure creation," then "even stones would be persons if recognized as persons" and, presumably, human beings simply would not in any sense be persons, would have no claim to personhood, unless they were so recognized.[4] How can recognition matter – how can it, literally, make a difference – while also being subject to some criterion that would make it possible to distinguish recognition from misrecognition?

To cut through this conceptual knot, Laitinen introduces a distinction between the "potential" and the "actual," and uses this distinction to establish a division of labor within the work performed by the concept of recognition. In the case of personhood, he suggests, the pre-existing features that recognition recognizes – and which serve as the criterion of the adequacy of an act of recognition – are certain capacities that mark out some, but not all, entities as "potential persons." At the same time, this potential personhood becomes actual only when it is recognized by others. In this way, Laitinen concludes, "there is no paradox in recognition being both a response to evaluative features and a precondition of personhood."[5] Given Honneth's own intellectual genealogy – he places his project in a line of descent that reaches back through Hegel to Aristotle's understanding

---

[3] Arto Laitinen, "Interpersonal Recognition: A Response to Value or a Precondition of Personhood," in *Inquiry* 45 (2002): 463. For a different treatment of the same question, see Patchen Markell, *Bound by Recognition* (Princeton: Princeton University Press, 2003), especially chap. 2; "The Recognition of Politics: A Comment on Emcke and Tully," *Constellations* 7/4 (December 2000), 496–506.

[4] Laitinen, "Interpersonal Recognition," 473.

[5] Ibid., 474.

of social development as an unfolding or actualization[6] – it is not surprising that in his response to Laitinen, Honneth endorses this general approach to the problem. Because the "evaluative qualities that, by the standards of our lifeworld, human subjects already possess" are nevertheless "actually available to them only once they can identify with them," recognition transforms potentiality into actuality by facilitating the wholehearted identification of subjects with their own capabilities.[7]

Honneth's phrase "by the standards of our lifeworld" is worth lingering over, for it signals an important difference between Laitinen's and Honneth's use of the concepts of potentiality and actuality; and it also marks the first stirrings of a tension within Honneth's project. Honneth's reference to "our lifeworld" indicates that, for him, the "evaluative qualities" to which an act of recognition responds exist within a "historically alterable" social milieu, not in some otherworldly space of "immutable and objective" values.[8] This view reflects Honneth's broader commitment to a practice of critical theory that takes its cue from existing social relations; and, like other aspects of his work – such as his interest in the emergence of social movements out of everyday experiences of disrespect – it seems to suggest that potentiality must be located in some sense *within* the actual. Yet Laitinen's and Honneth's aim in invoking the concepts of potentiality and actuality – to sort out how "recognition" can both respond to an existing feature and bring something new into being – seems to demand a sharper separation between these terms; and this need to preserve the conceptual

---

[6] On the transformations this theme undergoes from Aristotle to Hegel, see Axel Honneth, *The Struggle for Recognition: The Moral Grammar of Social Conflicts*, trans. Joel Anderson (Cambridge, MA: MIT Press, 1996), 15–30; on the differences between Hegel's approach and Honneth's, see ibid., 59–70; *Suffering from Indeterminacy: An Attempt at a Reactualization of Hegel's Philosophy of Right*, trans. Jack Ben-Levi (Assen, Netherlands: Van Gorcum, 2000); and "Redistribution as Recognition: A Response to Nancy Fraser," in Nancy Fraser and Axel Honneth, *Redistribution or Recognition? A Political-Philosophical Exchange* (New York: Verso, 2003), 143–47.

[7] Honneth, "Grounding Recognition: A Rejoinder to Critical Questions," in: *Inquiry* 45 (2002), 510; this essay has now been incorporated into the new German edition of *The Struggle for Recognition*. See *Kampf um Anerkennung. Zur moralischen Grammatik sozialer Konflikte. Mit einem neuen Nachwort* (Frankfurt am Main: Suhrkamp Verlag, 2004).

[8] Ibid., 508. Honneth emphasizes the same point in "Recognition as Ideology" (in this volume).

division of labor between "potentiality" and "actuality" pulls Honneth in a dramatically different direction.[9]

Recall the stakes of the problem. If potentiality is to serve as the criterion of proper recognition, it cannot be mixed up with the actuality it is supposed to govern without risking a dangerous form of relativism. Honneth sees this threat lurking in his own invocation of a historically alterable lifeworld; to fend it off, he falls back on the thought that relations of recognition are not only historical but *progressive* – that is, that they can be judged in a transhistorically valid way according to whether they constitute an advance along a "developmental path."[10] Yet this move reintroduces a stark distinction between the potential and the actual, for this progressive trajectory must be anchored somewhere; and Honneth anchors it in the idea of a general human "capacity for autonomy," which stands behind the permutations of history, providing the standard by which they may be evaluated.[11] By the same token, if recognition is to retain its importance, it must be able to bring something into being that is somehow beyond potentiality – indeed, it must be able to serve as the otherwise missing link between these terms, lending the merely potential an actuality it cannot achieve on its own. Honneth's turn to the notion of historical progress helps keep potentiality and actuality separate in this sense, too. For Honneth, progress takes place when recognition is extended either to formerly obscure human powers, or to previously unrecognized persons or groups;[12] and although the general norms of recognition that are employed in these cases are in a sense actualized – they belong to an existing lifeworld[13] – this is true only with respect to already-recognized powers and persons. The principle that workers ought to be recognized for their contributions to society, for example, is first actualized with respect to predominantly male wage laborers; and this makes the principle available to be extended to predominantly female unpaid careworkers.[14]

---

9 Thanks to Bert van den Brink for encouraging me to clarify this point.

10 Honneth, "Grounding Recognition," 509; see also "Recognition as Ideology" (in this volume).

11 Honneth, "Grounding Recognition," 511.

12 Honneth, "Redistribution as Recognition," 186.

13 Although, again, this for Honneth is ultimately insufficient to render them valid: such norms are still grounded in a potentiality that lies behind the shifting configurations of the lifeworld.

14 Ibid., 154–55.

For those who stand (at best) on the cusp of recognition, potentiality remains divorced from actuality: that is precisely why recognition matters, and why it can serve as the vehicle of historical development.

But does it make sense to think of potentiality and actuality as divorced in these ways? Potentiality, for instance, is supposed to serve as the criterion of proper recognition – yet it is not clear how we are supposed to know or assess potentiality (either the general potentiality of human beings for autonomy, or the specific, as-yet unrecognized potentiality of another person or group) apart from its actualization; that is, apart from the activities in which it is expressed.[15] Conversely, recognition is also supposed to function as the actualization of potentiality – but here, too, the strict separation between the merely potential and the actual becomes self-defeating. In suggesting that potentialities need to be supplemented by something further before they can be realized – that our powers are only "available" to us when they are recognized by others – this approach converts pure or mere potentiality into its opposite: incapacity. In Honneth's terms, "the evaluative qualities that subjects already have to 'possess,' according to this model, would then be conceived of as potentialities that recognitional responses transform into actual capacities."[16] But this means that, prior to their recognition, our potentialities are not actual – that is, that we do not possess but lack the power to do certain things. Indeed, if the absence of recognition by definition leaves its victims stunted and undeveloped – potential persons *only* – then it would seem, ironically,

---

[15] As Jill Frank has argued, Aristotle himself represents potentiality and actuality as mutually constitutive, not wholly different: many capabilities are acquired and maintained precisely through activity, and all potentialities must also be in some sense actual even when they are not being put to work. For Frank, this circularity, and the consequent impossibility of having access to potentiality as such, helps explain why Aristotle's only reliable criterion for recognizing "natural" slaves turns out to have everything to do with actuality or activity – with whether people consistently act in slavish ways without being compelled to do so by force or accident. And this, in turn, suggests that Aristotle is concerned not with shoring up an existing practice of enslavement by grounding it in some transhistorical account of the unalterably distinct capabilities of different groups of people, but rather with reminding his audience of Athenian citizens of the vulnerability of their own natures to the slow but real transformations effected by the activities they undertake. Jill Frank, "Citizens, Slaves, and Foreigners: Aristotle on Human Nature," *American Political Science Review* 98/1 (February 2004), 91–104; see also her *A Democracy of Distinction: Aristotle and the Work of Politics* (Chicago: University of Chicago Press, 2005).
[16] Honneth, "Grounding Recognition," 510.

that to have a justifiable claim to recognition is also to be unable to demonstrate it, at least without the assistance of those who have already actualized their powers, and so can testify to your equal personhood with unequalled confidence and maturity.

This conceptual point has important political implications. While a strict division of labor between the potential and the actual may ultimately be impossible to sustain, the pretense of such a distinction has long served to justify a further division of labor, and hierarchy, between rulers and ruled. One familiar defense of dominion over others rests on the claim that, if people undertake activities for which they are not suited, monstrous disorder may result: a central task of rulership, on this view, is to preempt such disorderly activity by acting as a sort of gatekeeper between the potential and the actual, making authoritative assessments of the underlying potentialities of the various members of a society, and using these to determine the distribution of rights, resources, and responsibilities.[17] And while this is by no means Honneth's or Laitinen's intention, their turn to a strict distinction between the potential and the actual risks importing this fundamental inequality into the logic of recognition. As long as acts of recognition are conceived as the transfer points at which potentiality – initially unavailable to those who bear it – is assessed and recognized by others, and thereby (and only then) made actual, even the most expansive, egalitarian grant of recognition will remain just that: a *grant*, performed by already-privileged agents whose authority is not in question, its egalitarianism framed and partially betrayed by a certain structure of condescension.[18]

An alternative configuration of the concepts of potentiality and actuality might attenuate rather than reinforce the strict division of labor between these ideas, treating actuality or activity not only as the realization of a potential already present in advance, but also as the

---

[17] See, for example, Dante Alighieri's characterization of the monarch as the one who is best able to "dispose" others to virtue – which also means to bring them from potentiality to actuality (*Dante's Monarchia*, trans. Richard Kay [Toronto: Pontifical Institute of Mediaeval Studies, 1998], 1.13); or John Stuart Mill's defense of imperial rule as a way of tailoring forms of government to the capacities of peoples (Considerations on Representative Government, in *On Liberty and Other Essays*, ed. John Gray [New York: Oxford University Press, 1998], e.g. chap. 2).

[18] On condescension and (anti-)democratic politics, see Don Herzog, *Poisoning the Minds of the Lower Orders* (Princeton: Princeton University Press, 1998), 206ff.

open-ended medium through which potentiality itself is reproduced (and transformed in unforeseen ways) and known (though never more than tentatively). On this view, of course, potentiality could not serve as an independent criterion by which to assess the propriety of any given act of recognition; nor could it serve to anchor transhistorical claims about the progressive trajectory of the development of relations of recognition. Moreover, on such a view, being unable to identify fully with one's own capabilities would not represent a lack of actuality: rather, it would have to be seen as an ordinary and unavoidable condition of human agency.[19] Yet precisely because it does not treat non- or misrecognition as tantamount to impotence, such an approach might make it easier to fulfill another of Honneth's own aims: to grasp the emergence and significance of opposition to unjust relations of recognition undertaken by those who suffer such injustice. To flesh out this alternative to the idea of recognition as the actualization of an as-yet unrealized potential, to understand how it becomes obscured, and to defend this view of what is at stake in the choice between the two approaches, I turn now, via Honneth, to the work of George Herbert Mead.

3

In a 1925 letter to his daughter-in-law Irene, Mead wrote that his social psychology could be understood as "an attempt to do from my own standpoint what Hegel undertook in his *Phenomenology*."[20] The affinity between Mead and Hegel is one of the anchors of Axel Honneth's *The Struggle for Recognition*, which, along with the work of Hans Joas, Jürgen Habermas, and others, has helped to re-establish connections between Mead's work and European philosophy and social theory.[21]

---

[19] In *Bound by Recognition*, I characterize this ordinary condition of activity as the "impropriety" of action, which is closely related to what Hannah Arendt call action's "nonsovereign" character (pp. 63–64).

[20] "I hope," he added, "it won't be as inscrutable." George Herbert Mead to Irene Tufts Mead, September 10, 1925, The George Herbert Mead Papers, University of Chicago, Regenstein Library, Special Collections, Box 1a, Folder 13 (italicized *"Phenomenology"* and apostrophe in "won't" added).

[21] For Habermas's central engagements with Mead, see *The Theory of Communicative Action*, vol. 2, "Lifeworld and System: A Critique of Functionalist Reason," trans. Thomas McCarthy (Boston: Beacon Press, 1989), 1–111; and "Individuation through

Honneth draws on Mead to help reconstruct a Hegelian account of recognition that is less bound to the horizons of idealist philosophy, and more amenable to verification through empirical research, than Hegel's own.[22] But Mead does more for Honneth than translate Hegel into a postmetaphysical vocabulary. His social psychology also helps Honneth negotiate two further problems that he encounters in the course of this reconstruction – problems that, it should be noticed, are parallel in structure to the tension between recognition understood as a response to something pre-existing, and recognition understood as a creative act.

The first problem concerns the meaning of individual autonomy and its relationship to collective life in the wake of what Honneth calls the "crisis in the classical concept of the human subject."[23] The aim of Honneth's account of recognition, like Hegel's, is not to subordinate individual freedom to larger social purposes, but rather to spell out the social conditions under which individual freedom can be secured: on this account, individuality and social integration can be understood as mutually sustaining, not irreconcilably conflicting, values.[24]

Socialization: On George Herbert Mead's Theory of Subjectivity," in *Postmetaphysical Thinking: Philosophical Essays*, trans. William Mark Hohengarten (Cambridge, MA: MIT Press, 1992); for Joas's, see *G. H. Mead*; and *Pragmatism and Social Theory*. See also Ernst Tugendhat, *Self-Consciousness and Self-Determination*, trans. Paul Stern (Cambridge, MA: MIT Press, 1986); Mitchell Aboulafia, *The Mediating Self: Mead, Sartre, and Self-Determination* (New Haven: Yale University Press, 1986); and *The Cosmopolitan Self: George Herbert Mead and Continental Philosophy* (Urbana: University of Illinois Press, 2001).

[22] Honneth, *Struggle for Recognition*, 71–72. For Honneth's use of Mead, see in general *Struggle for Recognition*, chap. 4; "Decentered Autonomy: The Subject After the Fall," in *Fragmented World of the Social*; and Axel Honneth and Hans Joas, *Social Action and Human Nature*, trans. Raymond Meyer (Cambridge: Cambridge University Press, 1988). Although Honneth has recently turned partly away from Mead, Mead's work remains a useful heuristic through which to approach Honneth's view of recognition, for as Honneth concedes, that view still depends on finding a functional equivalent to Mead's concept of the "I." ("Grounding Recognition," 502–503). This has led Honneth both to Castoriadis's notion of the "monadic core of the psyche" and to ideas of the "id" as a residuum left over after the intersubjective structuring of the psyche, which provides subjects with a submerged connection to an early (if not original) experience of omnipotent symbiosis ("Grounding Recognition," 502–504; "Postmodern Identity and Object-Relations Theory: On the Seeming Obsolescence of Psychoanalysis," *Philosophical Explorations* 3 [September 1999], 225–42). See also n. 38.

[23] Honneth, "Decentered Autonomy," 261.

[24] See, for example, Honneth, *Struggle for Recognition*, 5; for Honneth's reading of the *Philosophy of Right* in these terms, see *Suffering from Indeterminacy*.

The question, however, is *where* this individual autonomy – understood both as a source of value and as a locus of power – is to be located; and this question becomes especially acute once we have taken account of the "century-long critique of the classical notion of autonomy," which has shown that "the human subject is no longer to be grasped as one completely transparent to herself or as a being in command of herself."[25] Why wouldn't a Hegelian account of intersubjective recognition as the crucible of subject-formation – itself an important part of this "decentering" of the subject – reduce individuals to functions of the social matrix in which they are situated, undermining the possibility of accounting for and valuing individual autonomy?[26]

The second problem arises out of Honneth's appropriation of the teleological tradition of Aristotle and Hegel. On the one hand, the concepts of potentiality and actuality would seem to point toward the thought of finality. That at which actualization aims is a state of full development: for individual agents and groups, the very assertion of a claim for recognition involves the projection of a possible future community in which a certain potential, currently obstructed, could be realized; likewise, to understand the larger history of relations of recognition as a progressive unfolding, one must at least be able to imagine a "hypothetical" and "approximate end-state" to this developmental process.[27] On the other hand, Honneth is also sensitive to the open-ended character of individual and collective self-actualization: he insists that struggles for recognition must be regarded as "permanent" features of social life, not temporary phenomena that are to be passed through on the way to a future free of conflict once and for all.[28] But how can struggles for recognition be extended into an infinite future without conceiving of their aims as subject to the play of intersubjective interaction, thereby losing the compass of historical progress?

To deal with these problems, Honneth draws on Mead's distinction between two aspects or "phases" of the self, the "me" and the "I." On Honneth's reading of Mead, the "me" is the "representative of the

---

[25] Honneth, "Decentered Autonomy," 262.
[26] For a critical discussion of Mead and Honneth focused around the perils of "strong intersubjectivism," see Whitebook, "Mutual Recognition and the Work of the Negative."
[27] Honneth, *Struggle for Recognition*, 83; 168–69.
[28] Honneth, "Grounding Recognition," 502; cf. "Redistribution as Recognition," 187.

community" within the self: it is the product of the act of looking at oneself through the eyes of others, internalizing the evaluations that characterize an existing regime of recognition.[29] Indeed, for Mead, subjects can only acquire self-consciousness by taking up the points of view of the others with whom they interact; and it is this thesis that, for Honneth, aligns Mead with the intersubjectivism of Hegel.[30] Yet Mead does not reduce the self to the "me"; instead, he also ascribes to the self the power of reacting against and resisting the social judgments and conventions that the "me" embodies. This "creative potential" is represented by the "I," which, in Honneth's words, names "a reservoir of psychical energies that supply every subject with a plurality of untapped possibilities for identity-formation."[31] Struggles for recognition can therefore be understood as conflicts that arise out of the ongoing "friction" between the "me" and this "I."[32] As Honneth puts it:

Mead thus introduces into the practical relation-to-self a tension between the internalized collective will and the claims of individuation, a tension that has to lead to a moral conflict between the subject and the subject's social environment. For in order to be able to put into action the demands surging within, one needs, in principle, the approval of all other members of society, since their collective will controls one's own action as an internalized norm. The existence of the 'me' forces one to fight, in the interests of one's 'I', for new forms of social recognition.[33]

For Honneth, this way of reading Mead's distinction suggests answers to both of the foregoing problems. First, this distinction promises to salvage the notion of individuality without lapsing back into the classical idea of the autonomous subject, for the "I," on Honneth's reading of Mead, does not represent anything like the self's immediate awareness of itself: instead, Honneth suggests, it is "hardly different from the 'unconscious' in psychoanalysis."[34] The reason subjects cannot be thoroughly reduced to effects of the relations of intersubjective recognition in which they are situated, for Honneth, is not

[29] Honneth, *Struggle for Recognition*, 82.
[30] Ibid., 75–80.
[31] Ibid., 80, 82.
[32] Ibid., 82.
[33] Ibid., 83.
[34] Honneth, "Decentered Autonomy," 267; see also *Struggle for Recognition*, 81.

that there is some sovereign core to the self, but rather that subjects are "decentered" in two different ways. We are always situated within intersubjective systems of meaning that are not wholly at our disposal: this decentering is the one captured in the idea of the "me," which expresses our fundamental self-exteriority in language and society. Yet we are also always bearers of inner psychic impulses that exceed our awareness and control: this "decentering" is the one captured in the notion of the "I" as an unconscious seat of creative responses.[35] It is because these are fundamentally *separate* decenterings – because the "I" and the "me" are independent, though they interact – that the "I" can serve as the locus of an individuality irreducible to the "collective will" embodied in the "me."[36]

Second, the distinction between the "me" and the "I" also helps Honneth negotiate the problem of teleology, and in a parallel way. The separateness of these two aspects of the self, one might say, is a version of what I earlier called the division of labor between the concepts of actuality and potentiality: on the one hand, the "me" represents actuality, in the sense that the self needs its "approval" – needs the support of really existing relations of recognition – in order to be able to put its impulses into action; on the other hand, the "I" represents potentiality, the domain of not-yet-realized possibilities. It is because this "I" is independent of the "me," capable of reacting back against it and making demands upon it, that we can speak of progress in the development of relations of recognition: different formations of the "me" can be more or less accommodating of the new possibilities that arise through this "I." At the same time, because the "I" is by definition a wellspring of *surplus* potentiality, which manifests itself in "impulsiveness and creativity," the process of actualizing this "creative potential" must always be incomplete, vulnerable to the "continual rebellion" of

---

[35] Honneth, "Decentered Autonomy," 266–67.

[36] As Honneth puts it, the philosophy of language and psychoanalysis have attacked the classical notion of subjectivity "from two sides" ("Decentered Autonomy," 262). It is worth noting an important exception to this scheme: Lacanian psychoanalysis, which proceeds in part by reading the unconscious as a dimension of the subject's decentering in language. See, for example, "The Instance of the Letter in the Unconscious," in *Écrits: A Selection*, trans. Bruce Fink (New York: Norton, 2004). For a suggestive discussion of Lacan and Mead in the context of a critique of Habermas, see Peter Dews, "Communicative Paradigms and Subjectivity: Habermas, Mead, and Lacan," in *Habermas: A Critical Reader*, ed. Peter Dews (Oxford: Blackwell, 1999).

the inexhaustible "I" against "established forms of recognition."[37] The "I" can thus serve both as the independent criterion by which existing relations of recognition – actuality – can be judged, and the source of infinite challenges to existing relations of recognition.[38]

But is this the right way to understand what Mead means by the "I"? To be sure, this reading is quite widely accepted. For Honneth, the "I" is a site of inexhaustible inner potentiality, and the recognition granted by the social "me" is the means through which this potential is (or is not) actualized. Likewise, Habermas characterizes the "I" as "the pressure of presocial, natural drives" as well as "creative fantasy," the site of "unconscious powers of spontaneous deviation" that work to resist and transform the socially conservative force of the "me," which represents "what already exists."[39] And, similarly, Hans Joas describes the "I" as "the endowment of the human being with impulses," which serve as the source of spontaneity and creativity.[40] In these cases and others, the "I" is understood as something like a *source* or *seat* within

---

[37] Honneth, *Struggle for Recognition*, 82, 80; "Grounding Recognition," 502.

[38] In a recent exchange with Joel Whitebook, Honneth seems to back away from this claim about the separateness of the "I" (or more accurately, given his shift away from Mead, of one of its successor concepts). Pressed by Whitebook to concede that this individuating force (whatever it is called) must mark the limit of intersubjectivism, Honneth instead argues that this "antisocial" tendency to rebel against given relations of recognition is not "asocial" but intersubjective all the way down: although its bearer may experience it as an urge to recover an original condition of omnipotent symbiosis, an observer can see that even that original condition arose out of the interaction of two subjects – paradigmatically, the mother and the infant. (Axel Honneth, "Facetten des vorsozialen Selbst: Eine Erwiderung auf Joel Whitebook," *Psyche* 55 [August 2001], 798–800; replying to Whitebook, "Mutual Recognition and the Work of the Negative.") But as Honneth himself acknowledges, "it is entirely unclear how these antisocial impulses are to be connected to the moral experiences we have in mind" with the idea of recognition ("Grounding Recognition," 504). I have argued elsewhere that it is precisely such efforts to "recover" a supposed original condition of omnipotence that are often at the root of injustice in relations of identity and difference: they constitute misrecognitions in the sense of failures to acknowledge the fundamentally non-sovereign character of human agency (Markell, *Bound by Recognition*); and the gap Honneth identifies between the observer's knowledge that "symbiosis" is intersubjective all the way down and the subject's imagination of it as a sort of omnipotence is the symptom of this misrecognition. As long as our understanding of what would count as morally successful recognition requires thinking of the "I" or of potentiality as in some sense independent of any intersubjective relations, we will be unable to diagnose this sort of misrecognition, because we will be performing it ourselves.

[39] Habermas, "Individuation through Socialization," 180.

[40] Joas, *G. H. Mead*, 118.

the individual of creativity, novelty, spontaneity, or resistance to social norms.[41] Yet many of Mead's characterizations of the "I" are subtly but importantly different. For instance, Mead repeatedly characterizes the "I" as an agent's "action" or "actual response" to a situation presented by the "me"; he calls the "I" the "act itself"; and he claims that "the possibilities of the 'I' belong to that which is actually going on, taking place."[42] On these characterizations, it would seem highly problematic to describe the "I" as a source of infinite potentiality that needs to be actualized through recognition: to the contrary, Mead here seems to be characterizing the "I" precisely as activity or actuality, *energeia*.[43]

My point in invoking these passages is not to suggest that Honneth has simply misunderstood Mead, for as we shall see, his interpretation of the distinction between the "I" and the "me" also has a sound basis in Mead's writings. Indeed, as Honneth and others have noted, Mead's use of the language of the "I" and the "me" is quite slippery.[44] But while many readers treat this as an invitation to refine Mead's concepts for him – as if the problem were merely one of imprecision – I shall suggest that this ambiguity is not accidental: it is the symptom

---

[41] Thus Joel Whitebook also calls the "I" a "source of individuation," though his own view seems to be that Mead has no well-fleshed-out account of exactly what this "source" consists in ("Mutual Recognition and the Work of the Negative," 274, 276–78); and Mitchell Aboulafia, who does not use psychoanalytic language to describe the "I," and who is sharply critical of Habermas's reading of the "I," nevertheless still refers to it as the "home of the individual's novel responses" and "the source of one's awareness of the social me" (*The Cosmopolitan Self, 14*).

[42] George Herbert Mead, *Mind, Self, and Society from the Standpoint of a Social Behaviorist*, ed. Charles W. Morris (Chicago: University of Chicago Press, 1934), 175, 277, 279. For a similar observation, focused on Mead's characterization "I" as the "response," see J. David Lewis, "A Social Behaviorist Interpretation of the Medean 'I'," in: *Philosophy, Social Theory, and the Thought of George Herbert Mead*, ed. Mitchell Aboulafia (Albany: SUNY Press, 1991), 114.

[43] This alternative mapping receives further support from Mead's courses at the University of Chicago on Aristotle's *Metaphysics*; student notes survive from two such courses, one in Winter 1925, another in Spring 1928. Rightly or wrongly, Mead seems to have thought that for Aristotle, "potentiality" is something fixed that exists in advance of its actualization; that for Aristotle, "only the actualization of [what is potentially there] is in any sense a process"; that, for this reason, "the novel has no importance for Aristotle"; and that this was precisely what differentiated Aristotle's thought from his own and Dewey's. (The George Herbert Mead Papers, University of Chicago, Regenstein Library, Special Collections, box 6, folder 7, 240; see also box 6, folder 2, 131.)

[44] Honneth, *Struggle for Recognition*, 81; see also Lewis, "A Social Behaviorist Interpretation of the Medean 'I'," 114; Aboulafia, *The Mediating Self*, 25–26.

of an unresolved tension between two elements within Mead's work, which Honneth, in skillfully extracting a relatively consistent view of the "I" and the "me" out of Mead's texts, inadvertently inherits. Like Honneth, Mead is deeply concerned with the problem of the relationship between the individual and the community; and his writings do often seem to address this problem by embracing a neo-Hegelian view of social and political development as the progressive realization of social harmony. At the same time, drawing in part on the work of William James and John Dewey – and in particular on work of Dewey's undertaken at a moment at which he was questioning aspects of his own Hegelianism – Mead develops an understanding of activity, and of the roots of the phenomenon of novelty, that is in fact deeply at odds with that neo-Hegelian progressivism, and which stands in productive counterpoint to the view of recognition as the actualization of an unrealized potential. To draw this perspective out, however, and to see how it comes to be displaced within Mead's writings, we need to consider some of the immediate intellectual background to Mead's social psychology.

4

The distinction between the "I" and the "me" was not George Herbert Mead's invention. It was an adaptation of terminology introduced by William James in *The Principles of Psychology*.[45] James begins chapter 10 of that work, on "The Consciousness of Self," with an account of what he calls "the empirical self or me." Among the constituents of this empirical self, one in particular – which James calls the "social self" – anticipates the idea of the "me" as a kind of internalized "representative of the community" within the individual that Honneth will later draw from Mead. Indeed, James even describes "a man's social self" as "the recognition he gets from his mates."[46] Yet James's distinction between the "I" and the "me" does not exactly correspond to the difference between the point of view of the individual and that of society, for

45 William James, *The Principles of Psychology*, vol. 1 (New York: Henry Holt, 1890), chap. 10; on Mead's adaptation of the terms, see Joas, *G. H. Mead*, chap. 4; Gary A. Cook, *George Herbert Mead: The Making of a Social Pragmatist* (Urbana: University of Illinois Press, 1993), 54–55.
46 James, *Psychology*, vol. 1, 293.

James's "me" includes much more than just this "social self." It also refers to the "material self" – which, for James, means one's body, clothes, property, and even family – as well as the "spiritual self," or "a man's inner or subjective being, his psychic faculties or dispositions, taken concretely."[47] Even when we forego actual social recognition for the sake of a "potential" social self, James explains, this potential self, too, belongs to the "empirical self" or "me."[48] What makes all of these things constituents of the "me" is simply that they are all objects, whether inner or outer, present or aspirational. One might say that on James's account, the "me" is nothing but a certain declension of the self – the "objective person."[49]

Early in the same chapter (10), James also entertains the possibility that there might be a further constituent of the "me," which he calls "the pure Ego." This refers not to psychic life in its concreteness, but rather to the "bare principle of personal Unity," the "self of all the other selves" in virtue of which the rest of the "me" hangs together.[50] As James proceeds, however, this idea of the "pure Ego" proves troublesome, because it does not seem to be an object like the other parts of the "me."[51] To be sure, he concedes, we have a feeling of this unity of the self, and we are inclined us to say that behind that feeling rests some object, some "Arch-Ego," that accounts for it: "the 'Soul' of Metaphysics and the 'Transcendental Ego' of Kantian Philosophy," he concludes, are "but attempts to satisfy this urgent demand of common-sense."[52] For James, however, this feeling of unity need not be ascribed to an underlying thing: it can simply be understood as the feeling of the *activity* of thinking, of a continuous "stream of thought" through which the self *qua* subject apprehends, organizes, and cares for itself *qua* object.[53] This is a difficult thought to hang onto, because – as he had

---

[47] Ibid., 292–3.

[48] For instance, James observes that at the extreme we may be driven by the desire to realize a potential self "*worthy* of approving recognition by the highest *possible* judging companion [i.e., God], if such companion there be. This self is the true, the intimate, the ultimate, the permanent Me which I seek" (ibid., 315–16).

[49] Ibid., 371; cf. 319.

[50] Ibid., 297.

[51] See, for example, James's argument that the pure Ego can never be the object of "self-love" (ibid., 317–25).

[52] Ibid., 338–39.

[53] See James's summary of the chapter at ibid., 400–401.

explained in the immediately preceding chapter of the *Psychology* – something in us resists seeing thought as a continuous flow: we feel instead that it must be punctual, chain-like, "chopped up in bits."[54] Indeed, our very language grants a kind of privilege to the "substantive" parts of the stream of thought – its "perchings" or "resting-places" – over against its "transitive" parts, or "places of flight,"[55] which are peculiarly elusive:

> Let anyone try to cut a thought across in the middle and get a look at its section, and he will see how difficult the introspective observation of the transitive tracts is. The rush of the thought is so headlong that it almost always brings us up at the conclusion before we can arrest it. Or if our purpose is nimble enough and we do arrest it, it ceases forthwith to be itself. As a snowflake crystal caught in the warm hand is no longer a crystal but a drop, so, instead of catching the feeling of relation moving to its term, we find we have caught some substantive thing, usually the last word we were pronouncing, statically taken, and with its function, tendency, and particular meaning in the sentence quite evaporated. The attempt at introspective analysis in these cases is in fact like seizing a spinning top to catch its motion, or trying to turn up the gas quickly enough to see how the darkness looks.[56]

Analogously, James implies, the tradition of philosophical speculation about the "pure Ego" tries to grasp the activity of thought, but in doing so it freezes this activity into a thing of one sort or another – it makes it into a component of the objective "me." In response to this problem, James introduces the term "I" to name this "passing subjective Thought," and to mark the irreducible difference between the active, thinking subject and the self understood as an "objective person" or "me."[57] "Personality," he concludes, "implies the incessant presence" of both.[58]

James's concern to avoid reducing the continuous activity of thought to a chain or series of separate mental states, and his related view of the "I" and the "me" as aspects of a single self rather than discrete entities, influenced Mead both directly and through the work

---

[54] Ibid., 239.
[55] Ibid., 243.
[56] Ibid., 244.
[57] Ibid., 371; see also 400–401.
[58] Ibid., 371.

of his colleague John Dewey. One obvious point of connection is Dewey's influential 1896 article, "The Reflex Arc Concept in Psychology," which criticized the commonplace view of human behavior as a matter of motor responses to sensory stimuli.[59] Just as for James we misunderstand consciousness when we treat it as a chain of punctual states, for Dewey we misunderstand behavior by treating stimulus and response as "separate and complete entities in themselves," rather than as functional phases of an ongoing, purposive activity.[60] On Dewey's account, by contrast, a stimulus is just that phase of activity which "sets the problem" for an agent, through which an agent establishes the situation or conditions to which he must respond; a response is simply how, given the situation, the agent continues or completes the activity. In principle, any slice of activity could be treated under either aspect,[61] although strictly speaking it is only in a situation of practical breakdown that we really ought to speak of "stimulus" and "response" at all, because it is only then that the distinction makes any difference – yet it is also precisely in such contexts that we are most likely to misunderstand the conscious distinction between "stimulus" and "response," to treat it as an ontological disjunction rather than as the symptom of a conflict within a course of action.[62]

Dewey's "Reflex Arc" essay reflects the powerful influence that James's *Psychology* had begun to exert upon Dewey in the 1890s. But part of the importance of James's work for Dewey in this period – not fully reflected in the "Reflex Arc" essay on its own – lay in the critical distance it began to give him from certain aspects of the neo-Hegelianism of Thomas Hill Green and others with which he had aligned himself in the 1880s. This effect can be seen more clearly in the 1893 essay "Self-Realization as the Moral Ideal," which not only spells out a critique

---

[59] On the influence of James's *Principles* on Dewey's turn away from idealist psychology, see Andrew J. Reck, "The Influence of William James on John Dewey in Psychology," in *Transactions of the Charles S. Peirce Society* 20/2 (Spring 1984): 95–98, 105–107. On this period in Dewey's intellectual development, see Alan Ryan, *John Dewey and the High Tide of American Liberalism* (New York: Norton, 1995), esp. 85–99.

[60] John Dewey, "The Reflex Arc Concept in Psychology," in *The Early Works, 1882–1898*, vol. 5 (Carbondale: Southern Illinois University Press, 1972), 97, 104.

[61] Ibid., 107–108.

[62] Ibid., 106–109.

of Green, but does so precisely by way of the categories of actuality and potentiality.[63] In his *Prolegomena to Ethics*, Green had argued that moral progress in human affairs consisted in the gradual realization of certain "definite capabilities" that we possess in virtue of a "divine principle" that actualizes itself through us.[64] Although Dewey had once embraced a similar view, he now takes a different position. Conceding that talk of capacities and their realization makes practical sense, he nevertheless insists that such capacities must not be misunderstood as properties that exist anywhere outside of or apart from actuality or activity. For instance, if a parent or educator speaks of a child's unrealized artistic capacity, "it is not a case of contrast between an actuality which is definite, and a presupposed but unknown capacity, but between *a smaller and a larger view* of the actuality."[65] The adult notices something in the child that the child has not yet seen, but this something is not "the artistic capacity of the child, *in general*"; instead, it is some feature of what the child is already doing, such as "the fact that even *now* he has a certain quickness, vividness, and plasticity of vision."[66] Dewey thus concludes that talk of "capacity" is simply a kind of abstraction (sometimes useful, but potentially misleading) from the field of activity:

In the act of vision, for example, the thing that seems nearest us, that which claims continuously our attention, is the eye itself. We thus come to abstract the eye from all special acts of seeing; we make the eye the *essential* thing in sight, and conceive of the *circumstances* of vision as indeed circumstances; as more or less accidental concomitants of the permanent eye. Of course, there is no such thing as the eye in general; in reality, the actual fact is always an act of seeing, and the "circumstances" are just as "necessary" and "essential" parts

---

[63] John Dewey, "Self-Realization as the Moral Ideal," in *The Early Works, 1882–1898*, vol. 4 (Carbondale: Southern Illinois University Press, 1971). On the continuity of James's work with Dewey's "Reflex Arc" paper, and on the intersection between Dewey's reading of James and his critique of Hegelianism (including a discussion of "Self-Realization"), see Reck, "The Influence of William James." For a broader discussion of Dewey's trajectory that emphasizes the relative continuity of some elements of Hegelianism in his thought, see Eric A. MacGilvray, *Reconstructing Public Reason* (Cambridge, MA: Harvard University Press, 2004), chap. 5.

[64] Thomas Hill Green, *Prolegomena to Ethics*, ed. A. C. Bradley, 3rd ed. (Oxford: Clarendon Press, 1890), 189–90. This work was first published posthumously in 1883.

[65] Dewey, "Self-Realization," 45 (emphasis in original).

[66] Ibid., 46 (emphasis in original).

of the activity as is the eye itself. Or more truly, there is no such thing as the "eye"; there is only the seeing.[67]

The accent in this last sentence should be placed on the word "thing," not "eye": Dewey's point is not to deny the utility of the idea of potentiality *tout court*, but rather to insist that potentiality is immanent *to* actuality, thereby detaching the ideal of "self-realization" from its fixed moorings in some notion of a pure potentiality, or of a self "in itself" that needed to be unfolded in action into a more explicit and fully articulated form, and reconceiving it as a matter of "finding the self in the activity called for by the situation."[68]

Still, however much this move might have cut against aspects of Dewey's youthful version of Hegelianism, that strain of thought did not disappear from his work. As Eric MacGilvray has pointed out, for example, Dewey's political theory continued to be organized around the ideal of the democratic public, in which individuals would recognize the ultimate harmony of their own aims and interests with those of the larger community: this ideal, he wrote, was simply the "tendency and movement" of community life "carried to its final limit, viewed as completed, perfected."[69] A similar tension between the impulse to locate potentiality within actuality or activity and the urge to find a more secure guarantee of the prospect of social reconciliation also causes trouble for Mead's version – or versions – of the distinction between the "I" and the "me."

5

Mead first distinguishes between the "I" and the "me" in a long 1903 article called "The Definition of the Psychical," in which he draws on both James and Dewey to propose a new way of thinking about the domain of psychology; that is, about the nature of "subjectivity."[70] The

---

[67] Ibid., 47 (emphasis in original).

[68] Ibid., 50–51.

[69] John Dewey, *The Public and its Problems*, in: *The Later Works, 1925–1953*, vol. 2 (Carbondale: Southern Illinois University Press, 1981), 328; MacGilvray, *Reconstructing Public Reason*, chap. 5.

[70] George Herbert Mead, "The Definition of the Psychical," in University of Chicago, *The Decennial Publications*, 1st ser., vol. 3 (Chicago: University of Chicago Press, 1903). On the importance of this text in Mead's development see Joas, *G. H. Mead*, chap. 4;

idea of objectivity, he begins, can easily be expressed in terms of its relation to human conduct: "We know what we mean when we assert that we have an object before us," he says, because "we can act with reference to it." By contrast, subjectivity is typically "identified with the consciousness of the individual *qua* individual"; and this, unfortunately, leads us to think of psychology as concerned with something altogether separate from action, for action "takes place in a common world into which inference and interpretation have transmuted all that belonged solely to the individual subjectively considered."[71] Mead's challenge in "The Definition of the Psychical" is thus to account for subjectivity in terms of its role in conduct, and thereby to do away with the false appearance of a radical gulf between the world of observable behavior and the mysterious inner world of the psychical. Psychology ought to be able to study "states which do not have to be caught from behind, as they whisk around the corner, and studied in the faint aromas which they leave behind them."[72]

To accomplish this, Mead draws upon Dewey's claim that "stimulus" and "response" first appear as such in situations of practical conflict. Dewey had described such cases as instances of "disintegration": when action breaks down, so does the field of objects that make up the actor's situation, for these were only integrated in virtue of their functional relationship to conduct.[73] Such cases demand the "reconstitution" or "reconstruction" of the suddenly problematic objects – that is, the recovery of some sort of connection between these objects and a course of action.[74] The "psychical," Mead suggests, is our name for where we find ourselves in such cases of disintegration, when we are (in Hans Joas's phrase) "thrown back upon" our

---

Cook, *George Herbert Mead*, 49–54. Three years earlier Mead had also discussed Dewey's article, but without connecting it to James's distinction between the "I" and the "me," in "Suggestions toward a Theory of the Philosophical Disciplines," *Selected Writings*, ed. Andrew J. Reck (Chicago: University of Chicago Press, 1984).

[71] Mead, "Definition of the Psychical," 77.

[72] Ibid., 100–101.

[73] Dewey, "Reflex Arc," 109. See also 106: "But now take a child who, upon reaching for bright light . . . has sometimes had a delightful exercise, sometimes found something good to eat and sometimes burned himself. *Now the response is not only uncertain, but the stimulus is equally uncertain; one is uncertain only in so far as the other is*" (emphasis added).

[74] Dewey uses "reconstitution" at "Reflex Arc," 109; Mead uses both "reconstitution" and "reconstruction" in glossing Dewey at "Definition of the Psychical," 101.

subjectivity.[75] It is the phase of our activity that has the function of letting us go on in the face of a conflict or an interruption, in the same way that the "response," for Dewey, is the phase of our activity that has the function of solving the problem set by the stimulus. Mead then immediately connects this functional approach to the psychical to James's account of the stream of thought: although under ordinary circumstances we may misunderstand the stream of thought by reducing it to its substantive parts, in situations of practical breakdown – where the substantive parts of thought have come uncoupled from the world of objects – the stream, with its otherwise easy-to-miss transitive parts, its "swirl and eddy of current," is "unmistakably present" to us as we grope toward a reconstruction.[76] Finally, this reference to the "stream of thought" carries Mead on to the distinction between the "I" and the "me." The individual understood as a "me," Mead observes, cannot provide the "positive touch of reconstruction" needed in a situation of breakdown, for the "me" is the "empirical self," and thus part of the very world of objects that calls for reconstitution.[77] Beyond the "me," then, the self must also be the point of emergence of novelty; it must be "the act that makes use of all the data that reflection can present, but uses them merely as the conditions of a new world that cannot possibly be foretold from them." This "reconstructive activity," Mead concludes, "is identified with the subject 'I' as distinct from the object 'me.'"[78]

In the years after the publication of "The Definition of the Psychical," however, Mead's uses of the terms "I" and the "me" underwent two crucial transformations, evident both in his published articles and in the late lectures that were posthumously published, on the basis of student notes, under the title *Mind, Self, and Society*. The first major change centered on the question of whether the activity of the "I" could be experienced directly. The root of the problem had already been visible in James's *Psychology*: even as he suggested that trying to capture the activity of thinking in introspection was "like seizing a spinning top to catch its motion," James still seemed to hold that the right

---

[75] Mead, "Definition of the Psychical," 101; Joas, *G. H. Mead*, 81.
[76] Mead, "Definition of the Psychical," 101–102.
[77] Ibid., 108.
[78] Ibid., 109.

kind of introspective attention could produce a direct experience of the stream.[79] Likewise, in "The Definition of the Psychical," Mead had suggested that the activity of the "I" belonged to "a field of immediate experience within reflection that is open to direct observation."[80] By the time he published "The Mechanism of Social Consciousness" and "The Social Self" in 1912 and 1913, by contrast, Mead had concluded that the self could only ever appear in consciousness as an object, and therefore as a "me"; the "I," precisely because it was not an object, necessarily remained "beyond the range of immediate experience."[81] Mead makes the same point at length in *Mind, Self, and Society*, still echoing James: the elusiveness of the "I," he suggests at one point, consists in the fact that "I cannot turn around quick enough to catch myself."[82]

Importantly, both in the published articles and in *Mind, Self, and Society*, Mead often represents this elusiveness as a function of the temporality of activity. The reason the "I" cannot be experienced directly, Mead says, is simply that "we cannot present the response while we are responding," and although we can observe what we have done in memory, even that does not exactly give us the "I," but instead converts the "I" into an object, a "me."[83] This association of the "I" with a present, ongoing, and as yet incomplete activity is also what makes the "I" a site of uncertainty and novelty. At the moment of an actor's response to a situation, "what that response will be he does not know and nobody else knows."[84] This is not just a matter of the limits to our calculative powers: the claim, as in "The Definition of the Psychical," is that the activity of the "I" is the point of emergence of the new. Moreover, by "novelty"

---

79 "Within each personal consciousness," he wrote, "thought *feels* continuous." James, *Psychology*, vol. 1, 237 (emphasis added).

80 Mead, "Definition of the Psychical," 109.

81 George Herbert Mead, "The Mechanism of Social Consciousness," in *Selected Writings*, ed. Andrew J. Reck (Chicago: University of Chicago Press, 1964), 140; cf. "The Social Self," in *Selected Writings*, 142–43. Joas dates this shift more precisely, finding the earliest evidence of it in a review essays of 1905: see *G. H. Mead*, 91–93; and cf. Cook, *George Herbert Mead*, 63–64.

82 Mead, *Mind, Self, and Society*, 174.

83 Mead, "The Mechanism of Social Consciousness," 140; *Mind, Self, and Society*, 174. Cf. *Mind, Self, and Society*, 196: "It is only after we have acted that we know what we have done; it is only after we have spoken that we know what we have said."

84 Mead, *Mind, Self, and Society*, 175.

Mead does not refer to some exceptional subset of human conduct that breaks radically with expectations: at least at certain points, he seems to suggest that novelty is a feature of the "I," and of activity, as such. Even in the case of a person who is "simply carrying out the process of walking," he suggests, "the very taking of his expected steps" nevertheless puts him in a situation that is "in a certain sense novel." The "I" is, one might say, a name for this irreducibility of the response to the antecedent situation.[85]

The second major transformation in Mead's approach concerned the social or intersubjective nature of selfhood. In James's *Psychology*, as we have seen, the "social self" – the self as seen and regarded by others – was merely one of several dimensions of the "empirical self" or "me." Likewise, in "The Definition of the Psychical," Mead mentioned social interaction only to illustrate his broader claims about reconstructive activity, not to account for the emergence of selfhood as such.[86] Soon, however, he began to turn in the direction of a more thoroughly social psychology, declaring in a 1908 article, for example, that "there must be other selves if one's own is to exist."[87] Here and over the next several years, Mead worked out the basic components of the theory of symbolic interaction for which he remains most famous, in which he argues that the reflexivity involved in

---

[85] Ibid., 177. On the similarities between Mead's view of novelty and Arendt's account of "natality," see Mitchell Aboulafia, *The Cosmopolitan Self*, 51; although I would emphasize more strongly than Aboulafia that novelty is not only a matter of unexpectedness, or of the qualitative difference between one moment and the next, for both Arendt and Mead seem to be concerned with locating novelty precisely in events that are wholly expected, and so in resisting the equivalence of "the new" with some specific subset of happenings that express discontinuity. That equivalence seems to me to fall into what Hans Joas has called the "fallacy of misplaced concreteness" – that is, the effort to "grasp the creativity of action by attributing creative features to a certain concrete type of action" (*The Creativity of Action*, trans. Jeremy Gaines and Paul Keast [Chicago: University of Chicago Press, 1996], 116). See also Hannah Arendt, "Understanding and Politics," in *Essays in Understanding, 1930–1954*, ed. Jerome Kohn (New York: Harcourt, Brace and Co., 1994), 320; and my "Arendt on Democratic Rule" (unpublished MS).

[86] Mead, "Definition of the Psychical," 106; Joas characterizes the 1903 essay as "essentially monologic" (*G. H. Mead*, 87).

[87] George Herbert Mead, "Social Psychology as a Counterpart to Physiological Psychology," in: *Selected Writings*, 103; for a fuller account of this transition in Mead's writings, see Joas, *G. H. Mead*, chap. 5.

selfhood consists in taking the perspectives of others upon one's own conduct:

> The individual experiences himself as such, not directly, but only indirectly, from the particular standpoints of other individual members of the same social group, or from the generalized standpoint of the group as a whole to which he belongs. For he enters his own experience as a self or individual, not directly or immediately, not by becoming a subject to himself, but only in so far as he first becomes an object to himself just as other individuals are objects to him or in his experience; and he becomes an object to himself only by taking the attitudes of other individuals toward himself within a social environment or context of experience and behavior in which both he and they are involved.[88]

As social interaction becomes fundamental to Mead's account of self-hood in this way, it also becomes fundamental to what Mead means by the term "me." Now, the social self is not just one constituent of the "me," but its very basis. The "me" is the self of which one becomes aware by assuming the "organized set of attitudes" of others; it is the object-self constituted by being recognized and responded to in certain ways.[89]

It would be easy to understand these two transformations as wholly complementary: the rigorous denial of the possibility of directly experiencing oneself as an "I" seems to underline the necessity of seeing oneself as a "me" through the eyes of others, and vice versa.[90] Yet the intersection of these two developments was not so harmonious: to the contrary, it lay the groundwork for the central ambiguity that afflicts Mead's use of the terms "I" and "me" in *Mind, Self, and Society*. The problem is that by equating the "me" with the "social self," Mead effectively collapses two quite distinct issues. On the one hand, there is the issue of the relationship between subjectivity and objectivity, which James, Dewey, and Mead had approached by conceiving of subjectivity as an activity, as a kind of *doing* that cannot be captured in an objective representation. On the other hand, there is the issue of the relationship of the individual to the larger society or community; and for Mead, who like Dewey was an active reformer – he was involved in

---

[88] Mead, *Mind, Self, and Society*, 138.
[89] Ibid., 175; see also similar formulations at 176, 196.
[90] See, for example, the presentations of these developments in Cook, *George Herbert Mead*, 62–66; Joas, *G. H. Mead*, 109–111.

the settlement house movement, in educational reform, and in mediating industrial conflict – this was not only a theoretical matter but also the practical problem of the day.[91] As I have suggested, on this issue, Dewey had continued to rely on the very notion of the actualization of a prior potentiality against which he had seemed to be struggling in his work of the 1890s; and Mead did the same, passionately describing the "ultimate goal of human progress" in terms of the elimination of barriers to mutual perspective-taking, such that persons could understand themselves and each other at once as distinct individuals and as members of a complex, functionally integrated whole.[92] In *Mind, Self, and Society*, these two issues blur, and the second threatens to displace the first.

The clearest symptom of this blurring can be found in Mead's shifting use of the term "me." As I have noted, in *Mind, Self, and Society*, Mead sometimes uses this term in a way that is continuous with his and James's earlier distinction between the subject "I" and the object "me." The "me," on this use, refers to the self as seen or regarded by others. Strictly speaking, it is a representation, not an agent, although this representation can be prescriptive in character, and thereby make reference to action: in looking at myself through the eyes of my teammates, for instance, I may see myself as the one who is supposed to throw the ball a certain way.[93] Mead follows this use most rigorously in the earliest extended discussion of the "I" and the "me" in these lectures; as he proceeds, however, he begins to describe the "me" as a kind of agency – both the agency of society speaking in and through the individual, and the agency of the individual insofar as he acts in accordance with conventional social norms. At first, the slide is barely perceptible: Mead shifts from suggesting that the "me" is the object-self of which one becomes aware in taking the attitudes of others, to saying that these attitudes *themselves*, which "stand for others in the community," are the "me."[94] But as Mead proceeds, the transformation

[91] On Mead's (and Dewey's) involvement in social reform see Andrew Feffer, *The Chicago Pragmatists and American Progressivism* (Ithaca: Cornell University Press, 1993).

[92] Mead, *Mind, Self, and Society*, 310.

[93] Ibid., 175. Cook emphasizes this aspect of Mead's use of the "me," but passes over Mead's own departures from this use, speaking instead of "Mead's view" as though it were "easily misunderstood" but nevertheless consistent: *George Herbert Mead*, 64–65.

[94] Mead, *Mind, Self, and Society*, 194; cf. 176; 186.

accelerates: he tells us that the "me" is a conventional, habitual individual," which has "those habits, those responses which everybody has" or "whose ideas are exactly the same as those of his neighbors"; he says that, "if we use a Freudian expression, the 'me' is in a certain sense a censor," which "determines the sort of expression that can take place, sets the stage, and gives the cue"; he tells us that "social control is the expression of the 'me' over against the 'I'"; and he suggests that the "values" of the "me" are "the values that belong to society" as opposed to those that belong to the individual.[95]

This same realignment also affects Mead's understanding of the "I." Often, as I have indicated, Mead characterizes the "I" as an "action," an "actual response," or an "act itself."[96] Yet just as the "me" sometimes seems to take on agency in addition to objecthood, the "I" sometimes seems to take on objecthood in addition to agency. It becomes not simply the response but "that which is responsible for the response," as J. David Lewis puts it;[97] or, even more strongly, it becomes the "definite personality" that the individual asserts over against the power of society embodied in the "me," and which the individual seeks to protect by demanding transformations in existing social norms or laws.[98] It is at this point, however, that Mead's blurring begins to cause serious trouble, for while this emerging use of the "I" might seem to suggest a self-possessed individual, confidently defending his own distinctiveness against the incursions of conventionalism, this would contradict Mead's earlier suggestion that the "I" is a site of the emergence of the new, unknown to the individual who is its bearer as much as to the others who encounter him. The very move by which Mead gets theoretical leverage on the problem of the relation of individuality to social integration, in other words, seems as though it might drive him back toward thinking of the "I" as a kind of self-present, classically autonomous individual. The only way to avoid this consequence is to reassert the elusiveness of the "I" – but now that elusiveness will have to be conceived in a new way, one that is compatible with conceiving

---

95 Ibid., 197, 199, 210, 214.
96 Ibid., 175, 277, 279.
97 Lewis, "A Social Behaviorist Interpretation of the Meadian 'I'," 114.
98 Mead, *Mind, Self, and Society*, 199–200. For James, and for Mead at other moments, this "definite personality," as a self-image put into competition with the image others have of you, would have been considered an alternative "me," not an "I."

the "I" and the "me" as the individual's assertion of his distinctiveness and the force of communal expectations, respectively.

Ultimately, I think, it is this imperative that underwrites the version of the "I" and the "me" that has – for better or for worse – been taken up by Mead's most influential contemporary readers: the version in which the "I" represents an unconscious seat or source of new possibilities within the individual, a site of unactualized potentiality that can resist the power of the community that speaks through the "me." If the distinction between the "I" and the "me" no longer refers to the difference between activity and objecthood, but rather to two full-blown agencies-*cum*-objects within the self, each of which makes demands upon the other and competes with the other to define the terms of the individual's being and his place within society, then the elusiveness of the "I" will have to be understood as a matter of the particular kind of *thing* the "I" is, rather than as a function of the temporal character of the "I" as activity. Although the individual, as the bearer of an "I," asserts his own distinctive aims over against the conventions of the community, those aims are never wholly transparent even to him; and this must be because they belong to, or arise out of, a constitutively opaque domain or ground within the person. At times, Mead does indeed seem understand the elusiveness of the "I" as a matter of the welling-up of a mysterious source of novelty within the individual – the individual *as opposed to* society, and, perhaps some individuals more than others: the artist whose self-expression shatters conventions; the impulsive rebel against the "forms of polite society"; the inventor.[99] In an oft-quoted passage, he writes that "the possibilities of the self that lie beyond our own immediate presentation" are "in a certain sense the most fascinating contents that we can contemplate, so far as we can get hold of them";[100] here, Mead seems to be grasping for a substantive, forgetting his own (and James's and Dewey's) lessons. Still, Mead remains more equivocal on this point than his readers acknowledge. In the same paragraph, he also insists that "the possibilities of the 'I' belong to that which is actually going on, taking place"; and this phrase recalls Dewey's effort to make potentiality immanent to activity more than it anticipates Honneth's suggestion that the

---

[99] Ibid., 209, 210, 214.
[100] Ibid., 204; Honneth quotes this passage at *Struggle for Recognition*, 82.

"inner demands surging within" the individual cannot be "put into action" – that they remain merely potential – until they are recognized by others.[101]

6

What are the consequences of this transformation of the meaning of the terms "I" and "me?" Although Mead's slide was motivated in part by the desire to use these concepts to understand the relationship between individuality and community, he might have gotten more traction on this question by holding onto the original sense of the distinction between the "I" and the "me," whose theoretical productivity lies precisely in the fact that it cuts across this other conceptual axis. The "I" and the "me," Mead suggests, are phases in an ongoing process, in a "conversation of gestures [that] has been internalized within an organic form."[102] The participants in this conversation are the individual and the community (or, more broadly, that group of others with which the individual interacts), although in the internalized form of this conversation, both roles are played by the same actor, thanks to the capacity of the individual organism to take the attitudes of others.[103] But the phases of this process are not the same as its participants. Just as, for Dewey, "stimulus" and "response" refer to functional categories rather than distinct things, such that one moment's "response" may be the next moment's "stimulus,"[104] so too each moment in the self's ongoing internal conversation can be grasped equally as "I" and as "me." Mead captures half of this point when he says that the "I," the constitutively open and uncertain activity of response to a situation, is forever being converted into a "me," objectified in retrospect and through the reactions of others.[105] By the same token, though, the very act of taking the attitudes of others, which Mead says "gives [the individual] his 'me,'" is itself a present activity undertaken by the "I," a response to the previous moment's stimulus, subject to the same constitutive uncertainty and openness – as indeed are the actual responses

---

[101] Mead, *Mind, Self, and Society*, 204; Honneth, *Struggle for Recognition*, 82.
[102] Mead, *Mind, Self, and Society*, 178.
[103] See, for example, ibid., 186.
[104] Dewey, "Reflex Arc," 106–107.
[105] *Mead, Mind, Self, and Society*, 174.

to our conduct performed by those others with whom we interact: we see ourselves, in an important sense, through the "I's" of others.[106]

Ironically, then, to map the distinction between the "I" and the "me" directly onto the distinction between the individual and the community is to reinscribe a fundamental separation between these latter two terms. It is to locate the unpredictable power of novelty exclusively in some region of the individual supposedly insulated from, and therefore capable of resisting, the force of social expectations; and it is, likewise, to treat society or community as nothing more (or less) than a predictably monolithic enforcer of conformity. But it was just this sort of view – which perpetuates a gap in the name of bridging it – that Mead had meant his account of the "social self" to overcome. Even the most isolated artist and the most anti-orthodox actor are still the bearers of social selves –"individual reflections" of the ongoing social process in which they are situated[107] – and their creative powers, while in one sense localized *in them*, are in another sense functions of their participation in an open-ended intersubjective activity, located less in them than in the world they share, in one mode or another, with others.

This suggests a second consequence of this transformation in the meaning of the terms "I" and "me." Just as this shift installs a fundamental separation between the individual and society, it also helps to underwrite a fundamental division between the potential and the actual, treating the "I" as a kind of mysterious inner potentiality that only becomes actual once it is recognized in and through the intersubjective "me." But is it right to think that our potentialities are only

---

[106] At times, Mead – already sliding toward the equation of the "me" with the "community" – seems to deny this, suggesting that we are, somehow, *certain* about how others will respond to our acts (*Mind, Self, and Society*, 176, 187); at other times, however, Mead acknowledges that the uncertainty involved in the "response" extends to others as well –" what he is going to do he does not know, nor does anybody else" (p. 177). The implications of this come out most clearly in Mead's discussion of "meaning" early in *Mind, Self, and Society*, where he suggests that the meaning of each organism's act depends on a subsequent and unpredictable response of another, potentially *ad infinitum*: "the act or adjustive response of the second organism gives to the gesture of the first organism the meaning that it has"; it is an "interpretation" of that gesture. On this view, the act of taking the attitude of the other cannot simply be a matter of *predicting* accurately how the other will respond: it is itself a move in the ongoing play of mutual interpretation, through which a "meaning" emerges that exists only in the intersubjective "field of experience" (p. 78).

[107] Mead, *Mind, Self, and Society*, 201.

available to us once we can identify with them wholeheartedly, thanks to their actualization in a regime of intersubjective recognition? Surely recognition can often make a crucial difference to how well or poorly our action goes. One lesson of Mead's claim that "the possibilities of the 'I' belong to that which is actually going on," however, is that potentiality is never cut off from actuality in this way. The initiation of a new possibility does not require an impossibly long leap from mere potentiality – from a potentiality that is not yet really available to us – into actuality; nor does it require that this gulf be spanned by a gate-keeper between the potential and the actual, who makes assessments of capability and parcels out recognition accordingly. That should be a reassuring conclusion for those who, like Honneth, wish to give theoretical accounts of the possibility of resistance to injustice, for it means that the victims of injustice cannot be quite as thoroughly deprived of agency – of power *already actual* – as those who dominate them might wish.

A brief example will illustrate the sort of response to injustice that risks being obscured by a rigid division of labor between the potential and the actual. Much of the public work of the abolitionist orator and author Frederick Douglass, born a slave in Maryland, aimed, as he once put it, to "wring from a reluctant public the all-important confession, that we are men."[108] But how was this to be accomplished? In his famous 1852 speech "The Meaning of July Fourth for the Negro," Douglass explicitly refused to "argue" or "prove" that "the slave is a man."[109] He did so on the grounds that "the point is conceded already" in slaveholders' own practice of subjecting slaves to government and punishment by laws: "when you can point to any such laws in reference

---

[108] Frederick Douglass, "What Are the Colored People Doing for Themselves," *The North Star* (July 14, 1848), in *The Life and Writings of Frederick Douglass*, vol. 1, *Early Years, 1817–1949*, ed. Philip S. Foner (New York: International Publishers," 1950), 320; I owe this passage to Robert Fanuzzi, *Abolition's Public Sphere* (Minneapolis: University of Minnesota Press, 2003), 96. On the gendering of Douglass's language of "manhood," see Jenny Franchot, "The Punishment of Esther: Frederick Douglass and the Construction of the Feminine"; and Richard Yarborough, "Race, Violence, and Manhood: The Masculine Ideal in Frederick Douglass's 'The Heroic Slave'," both in Eric J. Sundquist, ed., *Frederick Douglass: New Literary and Historical Essays* (Cambridge: Cambridge University Press, 1990).

[109] Frederick Douglass, "The Meaning of July Fourth for the Negro," in *The Life and Writings of Frederick Douglass*, vol. 2, *Pre-Civil War Decade, 1850–1860*, ed. Philip S. Foner (New York: International Publishers, 1950), 190.

to the beasts of the field," he said bitingly, "then I may consent to argue the manhood of the slave."[110] The most Douglass was willing to offer in the way of evidence – beyond the example of his own eloquence[111] – was a rich recitation (still bookended by indignation) of the activities *already* being undertaken by the "negro race":

> Is it not astonishing that, while we are ploughing, planting, and reaping, using all kinds of mechanical tools, erecting houses, constructing bridges, building ships, working in metals of brass, iron, copper, silver, and gold; that, while we are reading, writing and cyphering, acting as clerks, merchants and secretaries, having among us lawyers, doctors, ministers, poets, authors, editors, orators, and teachers; that, while we are engaged in all manner of enterprises common to other men, digging gold in California, capturing the whale in the Pacific, feeding sheep and cattle on the hill-side, living, moving, acting, thinking, planning, living in families as husbands, wives, and children, and, above all, confessing and worshipping the Christian's God, and looking hopefully for life and immortality beyond the grave, we are called upon to prove that we are men![112]

Douglass's refusal to "prove" the manhood of the slave was more than just a *praeteritio*. It was a refusal to conduct the argument over slavery in the infantilizing terms of potentiality alone. The misrecognition involved in enslavement, Douglass suggested, was not merely a pervasive false belief in the nonhumanity of the enslaved: instead, it was a contradiction within the actual, a disavowal on the part of slaveholders of part of the meaning of their own practices, which called for "scorching irony, not convincing argument."[113] Douglass thus offers more than an example of partial independence of agency from recognition: he also offers a different way of parsing injustice itself, which does not depend upon the appeal to potentiality *per se*, prior to its actualization, as a criterion with which to distinguish between just and unjust forms of recognition, much less upon the thought that the history of relations of recognition represent a kind of progressive unfolding of a general

---

[110] Ibid., 191.
[111] For an account of Douglass's exemplarity, which focuses on the rhetorical power of his bodily presence, see Fanuzzi, *Abolition's Public Sphere*, chap. 3.
[112] Douglass, "Meaning of July Fourth," 191.
[113] Ibid., 192. Douglass's refusal here seems to me echoed in Stanley Cavell, *The Claim of Reason: Wittgenstein, Skepticism, Morality, and Tragedy* (Oxford: Oxford University Press, 1982), 376.

human potentiality. From this perspective, injustice is a matter of what I have elsewhere called "a failure of acknowledgment" – a failure to see and respond to the conditions of one's own action – rather than a failure to recognize the qualities of others'; and the question that seemed to require Honneth's invocation of the distinction between the potential and the actual, about whether recognition responds to those qualities or creates them, is, fortunately, beside the point.[114]

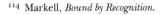

[114] Markell, *Bound by Recognition.*

PART II

RECOGNITION AND POWER IN SOCIAL THEORY

6

Work, Recognition, Emancipation

Beate Rössler

The recognition paradigm plays an important role in current philosophical social criticism. It has dominated the sociocritical landscape ever since the communication theory paradigm of the conflicts between system and life world vanished without much ado – for reasons awaiting closer interpretation – from the scene of theoretical discourse. For the paradigm of recognition, social criticism rests on a normative conception of the intersubjective formation of successful individual identities in concrete social contexts. From the outset, the concept of recognition, as a moral concept, aims to forge a link between the perspectives of social theory and a theoretical understanding of successful identity development. Social conflicts and struggles must be interpreted as conflicts in the struggle for recognition; social pathologies have to be understood as arising from the lack or denial of social recognition. The most articulate representative of this theory of recognition is certainly Axel Honneth.

I owe many thanks to a number of people: to David Owen and Bert van den Brink for inviting me to the conference on *Recognition and Power*; to Lutz Wingert and Martina Herrmann for inviting me to give a paper at Dortmund University and for critical remarks on an earlier version of this chapter; to Zhiyuan Cui, Peter Hall, Susan James, Heike Paul, and Dominique Pestre – all of them members of a discussion group at the Institute for Advanced Study (Wissenschaftskolleg) Berlin in 2004 – for a very helpful (and rather critical) discussion of an earlier version of this chapter; and finally to the Wissenschaftskolleg in Berlin, which provided perfect conditions for thinking and writing – and for conversations (not only) on work and justice.

In this chapter, I want to analyze the theory of recognition from a very specific perspective: the perspective of labour. Thus, I will ask what the sociocritical paradigm of recognition contributes to the empirical and normative problems connected with the transformation of the "labour society." What interests me in particular is the way in which the theory of recognition stakes a position on the traditional issue of the lack of social recognition afforded to domestic family work, and how it criticizes the de facto power relations expressed in the gender-specific division of labour.

My purpose here is not to rehabilitate the concept of labour for and in social criticism: I do not intend to argue that the category of labour should advance again to the forefront of sociocritical categories.[1] Rather, I am interested in finding out what categories, concepts, and normative principles are needed for social criticism to be able to describe, analyze, and criticize work relations, the division of labour, the remuneration of labour, and structures of work in general. This seems important since "labour," gainful employment, and "family work," still hold a central social function, for the reproduction of societies as well as for each individual (good) life.

I will defend the following thesis: Although social recognition of family work has to be a central aim of any social criticism, the arguments that are put forward within the paradigm of recognition – by, for instance, Axel Honneth or Friedrich Kambartel[2] – for the social-as-*financial* recognition of family work fail, on normative as well as on empirical grounds. Family work demands, I want to show, a different form of social recognition than paid work; they should not be seen simply as equivalent forms of socially necessary achievements.

I will discuss these questions in the following order: first, I will briefly say something about the terminology I use when I speak of

---

[1] In the sense of liberation from or of work; cf., for instance, T. W. Adorno, *Minima Moralia. Reflections from Damaged Life* (London: Verso, 1984), para. 72.

[2] Cf. Axel Honneth & Nancy Fraser, *Redistribution or Recognition? A Political-Philosophical Exchange* (London: Verso, 2003); F. Kambartel, *Philosophie und politische Oekonomie* (Goettingen: Wallstein: 1998); A. Krebs, *Arbeit und Liebe. Die philosophischen Grundlagen sozialer Gerechtigkeit* (Frankfurt/M.: Suhrkamp, 2002); of these, only Honneth defends a substantial and general theory of recognition in the sense sketched in my introductory paragraph. Still, these theories are all theories of *recognition of family work*. I shall focus on Honneth's theory in the discussion of problems of the recognition of work, or achievement, in general.

labour, gainful employment, and family work. This first step thus sets the scene for the discussion of the normative problems involved in the recognition of gainful employment and of family work (1). In the steps that follow, I will look more closely at the arguments put forward by the recognition theory in favour of social recognition of family work in the form of financial recognition (steps 2–4). Finally, I will sketch a societal model that makes a categorial difference between gainful employment and family work, for reasons of justice as well as for reasons of a good, rewarding life and that allows for different forms of recognition of family work and gainful employment.

1. WORK, GAINFUL EMPLOYMENT, AND FAMILY WORK

The history of the concept of labour shows that definitions of labour and the functions assigned to it have varied historically as much as the resulting evaluations.[3] Labour or work are thoroughly historical categories with changing meanings. However, from the eighteenth century on, there is a relatively stable permanent core to these changing meanings that Kocka has summarized in the following way: "Labour has a purpose (goal, end) beyond itself: the purpose of creating, achieving, performing; labour is always connected with obligation or necessity; labour is always toilsome, involves overcoming resistance, requires effort and a minimum of persistance beyond the point where it ceases being merely pleasant."[4]

In contrast to this very general idea of the meaning of labour, our present usage of gainful employment has its roots, as is well known, only

---

3 For the following, cf. esp. J. Kocka, "Erwerbsarbeit ist nur ein historisches Konstrukt," *Frankfurter Rundschau* (9.5.2000); J. Kocka, "Arbeit frueher, heute, morgen: Zur Neuartigkeit der Gegenwart," in J. Kocka & C. Offe (eds.), *Geschichte und Zukunft der Arbeit* (Frankfurt/New York: Campus, 1998); W. Conze, "Arbeit," in O. von Brunner & W. Conze & R. Koselleck (eds.) *Geschichtliche Grundbegriffe* (Stuttgart: Klei Cotta Verlag, 1997 [1979ff]); R. Castel, *Les Metamorphoses de la Question Sociale* (Paris: Gallimard, 1999); C. Offe, "Anmerkungen zur Gegenwart der Arbeit," in J. Kocka & C. Offe (eds.), *Geschichte und Zukunft der Arbeit* (Frankfurt/New York: Campus, 1998); cf. also Ulrich Beck (ed.), *Die Zukunft von Arbeit und Demokratie* (Frankfurt/M.: Suhrkamp, 2000).

4 Kocka, "Erwerbsarbeit ist nur ein historisches Konstrukt"; Kocka championed the theory that the labour society, as we know it, is relatively young. The normal labour model of the so-called *male breadwinner*, so familiar to us, has existed only since 1950, and then only until around 1975, when it again fell into decline as a result of the flexibilities and structural unemployment arising with the end of the industrial society.

in the nineteenth century, when the meaning of gainful employment was categorially transformed by the "social revolutionary invention" of the work contract.[5] Gainful employment can now be understood in abstract and formal terms as the achievement or the exercise of activities for remuneration on the basis of a contract between the offerer and buyer of these activities or achievements. Gainful employment as such assumes extremely diverse forms, but shares several features. It is typically market-contingent (male) professional work organized in companies, which means that it is (mostly) based on a separation between private domestic work and public paid work. It is also (mostly) understood as work performed for others, as (generally understood) achievement for and in society.[6]

This rather general and vague idea of what counts as work or gainful employment in contemporary market societies is, I think, all we need when we want to talk about the normative issues involved in the questions of whether or not family work should be paid for; or how to justly distribute the existing work there is in a given society. I do not think that these normative issues can be solved in a plausible or interesting way by defining more precisely what exactly work or labour is (as opposed to, for instance, interaction; or to practice).[7] What tends to happen in cases where more specific definitions are sought after is that we are not confronted with mere definitions but with stipulations that are normatively heavily loaded and tend to prejudge – by stipulation – a lot of the normative issues that should be solved by arguing instead.

---

[5] Offe, "Anmerkungen zur Gegenwart der Arbeit," 496.

[6] Ibid., 495. The question of whether the work is (still) "male" is contested; cf. for some statistics *The Economist* July 23, 2005 p. 54f; *NRC Handelsblad* 21.01.2006 7; for the European countries, also U. Gerhard et al. (eds.), *Erwerbstaetige Muetter. Ein europaeischer Vergleich* (Muenchen: Beck, 2003), 214.

[7] Cf. Muirhead's convincing strategy of not precisely defining gainful employment but describing it with the aid of Wittgensteinian family similarities (R. Muirhead, *Just Work* [Cambridge, Harvard University Press, 2004]); cf. also S. Schlothfeld, "Braucht der Mensch Arbeit? Zur normativen Relevanz von Beduerfnissen," *Deutsche Zeitschrift fuer Philosophie* 49/5 (2001). But cf., in contrast, the plea for definition in Krebs, *Arbeit und Liebe*, 24ff. Dahrendorf's lapidary dictum that work should be "objectively meaningful and subjectively satisfactory" seems to me still unsurpassed (cf. R. Dahrendorf, "Wenn der Arbeitsgesellschaft die Arbeit ausgeht," in J. Matthes (ed.), *Krise der Arbeitsgesellschaft? Verhandlungen des 21. Deutschen Soziologentages in Bamberg 1982*, [Frankfurt/M.: Campus, 1983]).

Still, the idea of contractual work carries with it, in fact, some normative weight, discernible in everyday discourse as well as in the sociophilosophical literature, roughly from the nineteenth century onwards. We can reconstruct the following three normative elements in the concept of gainful employment. First, the idea of self-preservation through acquisition of property, or the economic aspect: work should be paid (adequately) and should offer the possibility of satisfying one's own needs. Second, the idea of self-realization in the purposeful pursuit of external goals and their realization: work is good for self-realization and should therefore be self-determined. And finally, the idea of inclusion in a context of social cooperation and the securing of social recognition by means of inclusion into a system of social needs in which one is contributing toward the satisfaction of these needs: work ensures recognition by carrying out a socially relevant achievement. Note that I do not think that these normative elements are part of the definition of what counts as paid work in our societies. I only want to point out, that these are ideas that seem to be – trivially as well as fundamentally – connected to paid work in Western societies.

One can discern here three historical traditions – however modified: the Lockean tradition of determining labour as a means to secure and maintain property;[8] the Hegelian tradition of social recognition in bourgeois society;[9] and the (early) Marxian tradition of the idea of self-realization in and through work.[10] In Section 5 of this chapter, I will come back to these normative elements in conceptions of gainful employment and the historical traditions that accompany them. But

---

[8] Cf. Locke's *Second Treatise*, para. 27; for more on Locke, cf. also Hannah Arendt, *The Human Condition* (Chicago: Chicago UP, 1998).

[9] Cf. Hegel's *Philosophy of Right*, para. 191ff; for more on Hegel, cf. Axel Honneth, *Kampf um Anerkennung. Zur moralischen Grammatik sozialer Konflikte*, (Frankfurt/M.: Suhrkamp, 1991); for the different approaches, cf. also S. Guertler, "Drei philosophische Argumente fuer ein Recht auf Arbeit," in *Deutsche Zeitschrift fuer Philosophie* 48/6 (2000).

[10] Cf. Marx, Parisian Manuscripts; cf. also Axel Honneth, "Arbeit und instrumentelles Handeln," in Axel Honneth & U. Jaeggi (eds.), *Arbeit, Handlung, Normativitaet* (Frankfurt/M.: Suhrkamp, 1980); G. A. Cohen, *History, Labour and Freedom. Themes from Marx* (Oxford: Clarendon Press, 1988); T. Jefferson & J. E. King, "'Never Intended To Be A Theory Of Everything': Domestic Labour in Neoclassical and Marxian Economics," in *Feminist Economics* 7/3 (2001); E. M. Lange, "Glueck, Sinn und Arbeit," in *Rechtsphilosophische Hefte*, Band 5 (1996).

first let me return to the issue between contractual work – gainful employment on the one hand – and family work – care-work – on the other.

What is at issue when we talk about, for instance, the question of whether or not family work should be paid for is not whether or not family work is work or labour. It obviously is, in a general sense. The question is, rather, whether it should be counted as a service for society for which the society should pay. Given the financial plight many women with children find themselves in, the question becomes even more pressing. One solution to these problems of injustice and the lack of societal recognition would be to pay for the family work.

And this is precisely why the theory of recognition (especially influential in Germany) argues that family labour should be understood as socially relevant and of equal value as gainful employment, and therefore deserving of remuneration; but also the other way around: family work must be remunerated in order to receive social recognition. It is this position that I would like to discuss within the framework of a general discussion of the theory of recognition.

What counts as "family work"? I understand "family work" as the housekeeping and caretaking activities that people who live with children perform, with their own children (however broadly defined) and in their own household. Families are understood here as long-term domestic relations in which children grow up and are brought up.[11] I use this concept of family work to differentiate it from plain housework, which also piles up in childless households but does not really differ from normal work for oneself, on the one hand. On the other hand, it has to be separated from care-work in general, which, for example, involves the care of needy (elderly or sick) persons living in the household. I consider the general issue of *care* to be different – phenomenologically (in terms of, for instance, the sort of activities involved, and also in terms of the psychological involvement and motivation of the caring subjects) and normatively (in terms of the duties involved, but

---

[11] See Iris Marion Young, *Intersecting Voices. Dilemmas of Gender, Political Philosophy, and Policy* (New Jersey: Princeton University Press, 1997), 196; for other definitions, cf. Krebs, *Arbeit und Liebe*; F. Kambartel, *Philosophie und politische Oekonomie* (Goettingen: Wallstein 1998); A. Gorz, *Reclaiming Work. Beyond the Wage-Based Society* (Cambridge, UK. Polity Press, 1999); D. E. Bubeck, *Care, Gender, and Justice* (Oxford: Clarendon Press, 1995), 128ff.

also in terms of the possible contribution to the caring subject's good life) – from the care and the upbringing of children.[12] Family work in the sense described is obviously not only a private pleasure but also comprises services necessary for society, for its biological and symbolic reproduction. The question then is: should it be remunerated?

2. THE DIFFERENT RATIONALITIES OF FAMILY WORK AND PAID WORK

I would like to explain, in a first step, why family work, although socially necessary, resists being economized according to the gainful employment model. What I point out in this section, in a (modest) quasi-phenomenological way, is that family work, in contrast to paid work, follows a fundamentally different logic, a fundamentally different rationality.[13] And with this we see a first argument against the "recognition theory" model of family work.

Family work allows no eight-hour day; it offers no free weekends, no five-day week, no fixed holidays a year, no paid sick leave. What can be called a different rationality owes at least prima facie to the fact that family work is not really operationalizable, cannot be stipulated in a contract, for those who work in their own families. Living with one's own child can at times be extremely anarchic and can easily take up twenty-four hours in a day. In other words, no beginning or end can be structured into the working day. An infant, for instance, needs and expects care all day long. It is hard to imagine a contract stipulating working hours here – at least not for the caretaking parents, and we are only concerned here with them.

---

[12] The care of, for instance, elderly parents cannot be compared to the care of children – not least because of the possibly different motives involved. The moral problem appears to be a different one (hence also the question of whether care and custody services should be remunerated). Therefore, I feel justified in dealing here only with family work as defined earlier. And I consider it begging the question to lump together all "care work."

[13] For the following, cf. D. Perrons, "Care, Paid Work, and Leisure: Rounding the Triangle," in *Feminist Economics* 6/1) (2000); J. A. Nelson, "Of Markets and Martyrs: Is it O.K. to Pay Well for Care?" in *Feminist Economics* 5/3 (1999); I. Ostner & B. Pieper (eds.), *Arbeitsbereich Familie. Umrisse einer Theorie der Privatheit* (Frankfurt/M.: Campus, 1980); K. Hausen, "Arbeit und Geschlecht," in J. Kocka & C. Offe (eds.), *Geschichte und Zukunft der Arbeit* (Frankfurt/New York: Campus, 1998).

The objection that this is also true of many paid jobs is inadequate for two reasons. The nature of academic work, for instance, is admittedly such that on occasion it can occupy whole days and nights. But this work is not needed to satisfy any direct needs. And of course there are sensitive jobs (in the laboratory or with machines) that must be performed twenty-four hours a day. But these can easily be divided into shifts and performed by different people without any, so to speak, emotional residual claims – I will speak more about this affective or emotional aspect later.

The salary model for domestic childcare work, however, has to turn family work into an eight-hour day. That this is hopelessly inadequate becomes clear when Leipert and Opielka's proposal (adopted by Krebs) for calculating a childcare salary assumes that "the average amount of time spent by parents in caring for a child between the ages of 0 and 3" is around "eight hours a day."[14] *The average amount of time spent by parents*: one naturally wonders where the infant should go for the remaining sixteen hours of the day. Even if we consider a contract model to be possible, it is entirely unclear how this model would define and "recognize" the remaining hours of childcare.

Nor, on the other hand, can an eight-hour day represent very well life with an older child: in this case, the distinction between family work and leisure time is not always clear. As the sociologist Diane Perrons points out in her analysis of childcare work – and again we are only interested here in childcare work involving one's own children – reading a children's book aloud all afternoon long cannot necessarily be defined as work, nor reading the newspaper at the playground while keeping half an eye on the sandbox.[15]

These are all objections or reasons that we can call reasons of operationalizability or objectivizability. Let me now name two more powerful, categorial objections. The position of monetary recognition ignores one phenomenon in its analysis of the situation of women or parents with children: namely, that children are also an infinite source of pleasure and narcissistic satisfaction. This aspect, which appears to go unnoticed in the talk about family *labour*, the *labour* of pregnancy, birth *labour*, involves a very specific mixture of love and difficult

---

[14] Krebs, *Arbeit und Liebe*, 82
[15] Cf. Perrons, "Care, Paid Work, and Leisure"; but cf. differently Bubeck, *Care, Gender, and Justice* and her concept of exploitation, cf. 18off.

times – labour and personal interaction that characterizes family work. True, this interaction is labour, but labour that is also a satisfying and loving interaction.[16] To maintain that such labour is not performed *merely* out of love (but, for instance, out of an accepted sense of duty or for narcissist motives) does not mean that the subjects involved would find it appropriate to be paid for the labour. The motivational involvement as well as the activity itself obviously begs for a more differentiated definition.[17]

Of course, one could object that these complex motives, like the mixture of labour and interaction, also characterize various forms of paid work, such as many jobs in the field of education for instance.[18] This is certainly correct, but the analogy still has its limits: namely, when it involves the question of full responsibility, the question of motivation (as a rule, we do not love the children we professionally look after as we love our own), and the question of describing one's (social) role (described by oneself as well as by the society), which differs categorially depending on whether a woman sees herself (and is seen by the society) as, for example, mother or teacher.

But even though love and affection play crucial roles in family work, it remains entirely obvious that family work is (very often) hard work and that many women have to do this work in a financially very difficult and/or financially dependent situation. Still one might ask whether *financial* recognition of family work would be the right way out.

And here we reach the second categorial reason against the model of financial recognition: housework and childcare work or family work arise also, and especially, when the professional workday is *over*. If the financial recognition model of family work assumes that – in general – women are paid for eight hours at home while – in general – men are engaged in a "normal," out-of-house, eight-hour paid-work day, then what actually happens with the children during the remaining sixteen hours of the day? Who takes care of the remaining emotional (and other) tasks that cannot be handed over to other people in the next shift? This again appears to be a private matter, a hobby, leisure time,

---

[16] Habermas' opposition of labour versus interaction therefore does not prove to be very helpful; cf. Jürgen Habermas, *Technik und Wissenschaft als Ideologie* (Frankfurt/M.: Suhrkamp, 1968).

[17] Cf. also B. Stiegler, "Mutter, Kind und Vater Staat," in *Digitale Bibliothek der Friedrich-Ebert-Stiftung*, http://library.fes.de (2002).

[18] Cf. Nelson, "Of Markets and Martyrs."

not necessary to society and therefore not interesting. The question of who is responsible for the children during *these* hours does not appear to be relevant in the model of financial recognition.

But let me point out one last problem: when one reads biographical accounts (often in a slightly defamiliarized fictional form[19]) written by so-called housewives who are "only" responsible for children and the household; when one reads these accounts that describe the isolation, the meaninglessness, the torture of constant repetition in housekeeping and family work; when one imagines *this* aspect of family work, which is nothing but work and is often perceived as meaningless work, then these accounts do not exactly give the impression that women are demanding social recognition in the form of financial recognition for their work at home. Social recognition of family work only appears to be part of the problem here. A more appropriate interpretation of such experiences would be that these women expect something *more* from their lives than family work, something that might also provide more social recognition, but in particular, something that a person can describe as rewarding. I find the attempt to reconstruct only the desire for monetary recognition of family work from such personal accounts extremely problematic.

All this serves not only to clearly indicate the different interests and needs underlying family work, on the one hand, and paid work, on the other, but also points out that people performing family childcare work are involved in their work in a significantly different way than they are with the activities of paid work. These specific differences pertaining to involvement, motivation, task definition from the subjective first-person perspective can be read as an indication that both forms of work or activities – paid work and family work – demand different forms of recognition and can be valued and regarded as different elements of a good and rewarding life. I shall come back to this.

3. THE ARGUMENT FROM OVERCOMING THE GENDER-SPECIFIC DIVISION OF LABOUR

But let us assume for the moment – and for the sake of the argument – that the argument of the categorial difference between the activities

---

[19] Cf. the classic Betty Friedan, *The Feminine Mystique* (New York: W. W. Norton & Co., 1983); cf. critically Bubeck, *Care, Gender, and Justice*, 45; cf. Muirhead, *Just Work*.

is not convincing, and let us look again more closely at the argument for the financial recognition of family work, focusing here on the problem of the gendered division of labour.

On the one hand, payment for domestic family work should secure the economic independence of caretaking women. On the other hand, in the latest discussions, the central arguments for the claim that family work must be financed by society and the state are arguments from justice theory arguing that it is a socially (necessary) achievement.[20] Only in this way, so the argument goes, can we create more justice in the distribution of labour and recognition. Only when family work receives social (financial) recognition as work will men also participate in housekeeping and family work. In other words, only when this work gains economic recognition will it be possible to overcome the gender-specific division of labour.

Now I consider both social recognition of family work and breaking down the gender-specific division of labour to be major goals in creating a just society. But that the *monetary* recognition model of family work can contribute to achieving these goals appears to me highly unlikely. In my view, the foremost point of criticism is as follows: housekeeping and family work do not receive the same social recognition, not because these activities are unpaid but because it is work performed by women. The decisive argument, therefore, is that the lack of recognition afforded to family work has nothing to do with the fact that it is *unpaid* work, but with the fact that *women* perform the work. Nothing will change in terms of the social recognition accorded this work until men also participate in it.

We must follow the idea in reverse logic: family work is largely denied social recognition *because* bringing up children and doing the wash are typical female activities and *because* a separation between (female) private and (male) public activities has existed since about the nineteenth century.[21] Payment will do nothing, or at least not much, to change

---

[20] For the following, cf. Kambartel, *Philosophie und politische Oekonomie*, 74ff; Krebs, *Arbeit und Liebe*, 71ff et passim; Honneth & Fraser, *Redistribution or Recognition?* 141, 153ff., 263f; in *Kampf um Anerkennung*, Honneth does not deal with family or reproductive *work*; cf. S. Schlothfeld, "Braucht der Mensch Arbeit? Zur normativen Relevanz von Beduerfnissen," *Deutsche Zeitschrift fuer Philosophie* 49/5 (2001), critical of the concept of recognition and very illuminating on the concept of need.

[21] I have explored this sex-specific coding of private female and public male activities in more depth in my book, Beate Rössler, *The Value of Privacy* (Cambridge: Polity Press, 2005).

this – even if, and this is naturally an important point that must be taken seriously, it could contribute at least to a certain economic independence for women engaged in child care. To give weight to the argument of reverse logic, it suffices to look at the relevant empirical studies that show that the entry of women into an occupational group is directly connected with the loss of status of this occupational group – and vice versa.[22] For instance, the movement away from the male secretary to today's (female) secretary shows the decline in this occupation's status as more and more women entered the profession. Numerous historical and sociological studies have explored this process.[23]

In my view, these empirical references significantly weaken the argument that paying women for family work will promote its social recognition. Such an argument underestimates the power structures and the historically developed role assignments within a society. It also underestimates the power of the *naturalized ideology* that desires to maintain the hierarchy in the relationship between the sexes, and to continue reproducing it.[24] The relationship between the sexes must also be seen as a power relationship. Certainly, it is a power relationship that must be defined as a general ideology, as a very efficient, culturally determined value-system and disciplining role assignment to whose proliferation both men and women contribute. Precisely for this reason, gender relations cannot be simply rewritten as social recognition relations without analyzing them as nearly naturalized structures.[25] It has long been the case that the gender-specific distribution of private and public work is enmeshed in a social value system in which, as a rule, despite the major changes we have witnessed in the relationships between the sexes since the 1960s, so-called private housekeeping and childcare activities still qualify as female, and are negatively evaluated in terms of social relevance by comparison with remunerative occupations.

---

[22] Honneth also points this out; it is interesting that he does not see this as an argument against the (possibility of financial) recognition of the achievement of family work; cf. A. Wetterer (ed.), *Die soziale Konstruktion von Geschlecht in Professionalisierungsprozessen* (Frankfurt/M.: Campus, 1995).

[23] In general, cf. J. Laufer e.a. (ed.), *Le Travail du Genre. Les Sciences Sociales du Travail a l'épreuve des Différences de Sexe* (Paris: La Découverte, 2003).

[24] I borrow this concept from Scott although he advocates a far more optimistic version of such an ideology than I do; cf. J. Scott, *Domination and the Arts of Resistance. Hidden Transcripts* (New Haven: Yale University Press, 1990).

[25] Cf. for a more detailed analysis again, Rössler, *Privacy*.

For every subversion of these role assignments and evaluations, there still exists, implicitly or explicitly, a societal demand to legitimize it: thus, for instance, the problem of the "compatibility" of children and career is understood as a problem exclusive to women. This value system is so deeply rooted in the culture that any attempt to "restructure" relations without analyzing and critically examining this system is naive.

Axel Honneth, of course, knows all this and, in his exchange with Nancy Fraser, writes very articulately on the repressive character of this value system; the problem is, however, that the "struggle for recognition" of family work is, in his theory of recognition, conceptualized (and conceptualizable) only as a struggle for recognition of a socially relevant achievement – and as an achievement that should be financially recognized. Therefore, this struggle for recognition seems from the start to be a struggle aiming at the wrong goal. The "achievement" of family work should not only be seen as an achievement in need of financial recognition, but of rather different forms of recognition. Furthermore, and importantly, recognition might not even solve all the problems here: the question of the subject's being involved in very different activities and practices might be a question of the critique and development of (elements of) the good life, not necessarily representable in terms of recognition. I shall come back to this problem later.

Let me, however, elaborate a little further on the problematic of the value-system. Empirically, one would probably have to say that paying domestic family work would be more likely to *reinforce* the gender-specific division of labour. Any reluctant male partner will be able to continue avoiding childcare and housekeeping responsibilities, now subjectively armed with better reasons than ever by being able to point out that, after all, his wife is being paid for that work. Women will still be left to do the second shift alone, as Arlene Hochschild so depressingly and accurately described it.[26] And finally, returning to a career, even if special financial resources are provided for it, will meet with ever-greater difficulties in our increasingly complex knowledge society.

But we should particularly view with scepticism the emancipatory impulse that will supposedly arise from the financial recognition of

[26] A. Hochschild, *The Second Shift* (London: Piatkus, 1990).

family work. Arguments for paying family work frequently draw from –
and in the framework of the aforementioned value-system – precisely
those cultural interpretive patterns and symbolic resources that will
not help overcome the gender-specific division of labour. Interestingly,
the rhetoric of compensating women who stay at home to tend to children emphasises and supports the myth of the sacrificing mother that
is still dominant (not only) in (German) cultural discourse: she does
the work, while the egoistic dinks ("double income no kids") are the
real free riders in society because they intend to let other people's children pay for their pensions. Mothers should at least be paid for this
sacrifice. If one perceives family- or childcare work (only or foremost)
as a service to society, this reconstruction of women's role appears to
be logical and inevitable: her identity must then be constructed as one
who tends children and thereby performs a service for society, and
if this work is not appropriately compensated, she becomes a victim
exploited by society.[27] In this interpretive regime, women's experiences can only be reconstructed as the experiences of victims. The
cultural interpretation drawn on here is the traditional image of the
suffering, exploited woman. The argument of paying women for their
work does not circumvent this image: on the contrary, it serves to confirm it, since paying female family work cannot be justified in any other
image or tradition.[28]

---

[27] At this point, liberal feminist theories of financial recognition and Marxist theories
of exploitation happily meet. Cf. Krebs, *Arbeit und Liebe*, and Bubeck, *Care, Gender,
and Justice*.

[28] The German discussion of the "childcare salary" is quite unusual within the international discussion (cf. B. Stiegler, "Mutter, Kind und Vater Staat," in *Digitale Bibliothek
der Friedrich-Ebert-Stiftung*, http://library.fes.de [2002]; U. Gerhard et al. [eds.], *Erwerbstaetige Muetter. Ein europaeischer Vergleich* [Muenchen: Beck, 2003]; cf. E. Trzcinski,
"Family Policy in Germany: A Feminist Dilemma?" in *Feminist Economics* 6/1 [2000];
cf. also B. Vinken, *Die deutsche Mutter. Der lange Schatten eines Mythos* [Muenchen: Piper,
2001]). In comparison with European and other countries, Germany is an exception in providing comparatively magnanimous financial security for pregnant women
and women with small children. Historically, this can be elucidated by the development of different welfare state models: F.-X. Kaufmann, *Varianten des Wohlfahrtstaats.
Der deutsche Sozialstaat im internationalen Vergleich* (Frankfurt/M.: Suhrkamp, 2003);
G. Esping-Andersen, *The Three Worlds of Welfare Capitalism* (Cambridge: Polity Press,
1990); A. V. Doorne-Huyskes, "The Unpaid Work of Mothers and Housewives in the
Different Types of Welfare States," in L. Koslowski & A. Foellesdal (eds.) *Restructuring
the Welfare State* (Berlin: Springer, 1997). Aside from this, however, one must realize
that these specific regulations are steeped in a tradition and ideology that takes for

Thus, it seems right to criticise a society for its lack of recognition of family work, and it seems equally right to describe the women's movements' fight against the gender-specific division of labour as a struggle. But it seems to be short-sighted to conceive of all socially necessary achievements in the same way, and to overlook the categorial difference that different sorts of achievements might – (partly) independently of questions of recognition – contribute to the self-understanding, the identify, the good life of a person.

4. THE ARGUMENT FROM RECOGNITION

So far, we have looked at the demand for financial recognition of family work from the perspective of a – modest – phenomenology and from the perspective of the gender-specific division of labour. Let us now look more closely at the concept of recognition itself. In particular, we should look at how the theory of recognition understands its demand for the remuneration of family work.[29] I would like to briefly retrace steps in the argument.

In the first step, family work and paid work are each defined so that they both represent the same form of work: for Kambartel and Krebs, for instance, "work" means participation in a social exchange of services; and this in turn is defined to encompass those activities whose cessation would produce a social need for a substitute.[30] Honneth, on the other hand, has no precise definition of the concept of labour, but it is clear that labour is theoretically replaced with the concept of achievement (*Leistung*): recognition of achievement, then, is the

---

granted, more than is the case in other European countries, that the place of the woman is at home.

[29] Cf. Kambartel, *Philosophie und politische Oekonomie*, 74ff and critical I. Kurz-Scherf, "Kritik an Kambartels Arbeit und Praxis," in *Deutsche Zeitschrift fuer Philosophie* 41/2 (1993); Krebs, *Arbeit und Liebe*, 71ff et passim; cf. Honneth in *Redistribution or Recognition?* 141, 263, which differs from "Arbeit und instrumentelles Handeln," where Honneth, unlike Habermas, still demands that the concept of labor be given a central value in any theory of society; but work is now conceptualized as an achievement that deserves social recognition.

[30] This is obviously a very questionable definition: for one, because not every domestic work producing a social need for a substitute has formerly been care-work in the relevant sense; for example, to name but one example, the appearance of ironing services, even though ironing was classic spouse work and has nothing to do with caretaking.

demand that social conditions must satisfy. Where achievement (work) as such is not recognized, or only inadequately and inappropriately, identities, individual personalities, are impeded in their healthy development and social conflicts arise.[31]

The second step maintains that participation in socially relevant work (as defined here) is a major source of social recognition in the labour society. And the third step argues that remuneration is the medium for conveying social recognition to work; therefore, work must be remunerated so that family work, which is socially necessary work, earns appropriate recognition, and for approximately eight hours a day in accordance with an average paid work day.

We have already seen, however, that the objectification of family work into a verifiable eight-hour day is not so simple. Two more considerations speak against this monetary recognition model: the first (a) is based on a version of the commodification objection; the second (b) on a criticism of certain understandings of the recognition of alienated labour.

(a) "No other nexus between people . . . than callous 'cash payment'" is how the Communist Manifesto describes the ultimate commodification of personal relations in bourgeois capitalist society. In Marx and Engels's most popular work, written and repeatedly revised in the late nineteenth century, the authors denounce conditions in bourgeois capitalist society that lead to, and have already led to, a complete alienation of social relations. Prominent here is the condition of the bourgeois family. In fact, this quotation from the manifesto refers to the family, for Marx and Engels saw in their lifetime the complete commodification of family relations. They describe how capitalism has dissolved the family[32] because the proletarian cannot afford a family, being forced to sell his own labour on the labour market as the only commodity he can dispose of, and the bourgeois seek

---

[31] Cf. Honneth, *Redistribution or Recognition?* esp. 153ff., where struggles for redistribution are interpreted as struggles for adequate recognition of (labour) achievement. Cf. critical H. C. Schmidt am Busch, "Marktwirtschaft und Anerkennung. Zu Axel Honneths Theorie sozialer Wertschaetzung," in C. Halbig & M. Quante (eds.), *Axel Honneth: Sozialphilosophie zwischen Kritik und Anerkennung* (Muenster: LIT, 2004).

[32] Karl Marx & Friedrich Engels, *Manifest der Kommunistischen Partei* (Stuttgart, Reclam, 1969), 42; cf. I. Fetscher, "Nachwort," in the same volume.

their pleasure with prostitutes or by seducing the women of other men.[33] Capitalist society, so reads the diagnosis, leads to the general commodification of human relations, making it impossible to have non-alienated relationships.

For a long time it was – and some argue that it still is – very contentious as to whether or not the Marxist paradigm could be used to analyse domestic labour and the situation of the family in capitalism,[34] but the discussion mostly centred around the question whether or not domestic labour could count as "labour" and whether or not, therefore, women were, as domestic workers and as carers, exploited. The issue of alienation and commodification, in contrast, did not play a central role in these discussions.[35]

Even if one is rather sceptical of the Marxian paradigm of the labour theory of value in general, one can still agree with his insistence on (family) relationships as categorially evading monetarization; and one can then try to reconstruct the distinction between family work and paid work within a *different* paradigm – for instance, the paradigm of the differentiation between system and life world. The Habermasian reconstruction of categorially differing action orientations, integration mechanisms, and forms of interaction appears to provide exactly this possibility: to describe efforts to monetarize family care-work as the colonialization of the life world, as an infringement of the regulating medium money on the communicative-oriented relationships within the family, on life world rationalities. In any case, this reconstruction stands up better than the Marxian one. But it is still inadequate for comprehending and reconstructing the complex relationship between family work and paid work. For one, it is inadequate because if the life world is understood purely as a sphere oriented toward communicative acts, then phenomena such as the gender-specific division of labour cannot be analysed as a historically developed unjust labour division and role assignment, and neither

---

[33] Cf. Fetscher "Nachwort," 86.
[34] Cf. Bubeck, *Care, Gender, and Justice*, ch 1–3; N. Folbre, *Who Pays for the Kids? Gender and the Structure of Constraint* (London: Routledge, 1994); Jefferson & King "'Never Intended To Be A Theory Of Everything.'"
[35] For the commodification objection, cf. also E. Anderson, *Value in Ethics and Economics* (Cambridge: Harvard University Press, 1993), 150ff, although she is not talking here about the commodification of child care.

can the *work aspect* of family work be seen as a justice-relevant societal achievement.

Second, it is inadequate because obviously not every monetarization of relationships in the life world represents a commodification or colonialization of life world rationalities. This can be seen by looking at outsourced childcare, whether in nurseries, daycare centres, or in schools. Even the care of very young children in private or state-organized institutions can not be seen as a pathology of actions or relationships, as recent studies again very clearly demonstrate.[36] If someone cares for other people's children and receives financial recompensation for a service performed, on no account should it be implied that this relationship is reified.[37] We saw earlier, by briefly citing the example of educational occupations, that we need to differentiate categorially with regard to the responsibilities, role definitions, motivations, and life-forms between professional care-work on the one hand and care for and work with one's own children on the other.

Therefore, not every monetarization, juridification, or "formal organization" of life world relationships represents a disruption of the life world or its pathologization.[38] We ought to be able to theoretically and categorially differentiate between those life-world relationships or activities and ways of acting that can be regulated by the medium of money without deformation and those for which monetarization would inappropriately shape these relationships and activities.[39]

Honneth, of course, would be the first to acknowledge this.[40] He has written extensively on the different forms of recognition of love, right,

---

[36] If one reads the studies, especially those conducted in the United States, that compare small children (three months to four years old) cared for by outsiders with those cared for by their mother or parents, one's common sense is confirmed. See M. Dornes, "Frisst die Emanzipation ihre Kinder?" in A. Honneth (ed.) *Befreiung aus der Muendigkeit. Paradoxien des gegenwaertigen Kapitalismus* (Frankfurt/M.: Campus, 2002), who discusses the most recent studies of this topic.

[37] Cf. Nelson, "Of Markets and Martyrs."

[38] According to Habermas himself in Jürgen Habermas, *Between Facts and Norms: Contributions to a Discourse Theory of Law and Democracy* (Cambridge: MIT Press, 1998).

[39] Cf. Jürgen Habermas, *Theorie des kommunikativen Handelns* (Frankfurt/M: Suhrkamp, 1981). Interestingly enough, the theorem of the colonialization of the life world seems closer to Marx than to the recognition theory. This is ironic if one recalls Honneth's critique in "Arbeit und instrumentelles Handeln" of Habermas.

[40] By contrast, cf. Krebs, *Arbeit und Liebe*, 255ff. 280ff.

and solidarity. He has also written on the danger of encroachments of the idea of rights upon the sphere of the family.[41] But he does not seem to be aware of the danger of the principle of achievement encroaching upon the family, or personal relations. Nonetheless, it should now be apparent that the proposal for the *monetary recognition* of family work represents a step backwards in the history of theory. It seems difficult to describe the categorial distinction between family work and gainful employment adequately and comprehensively within the paradigm of recognition if work is achievement, family care-work is understood as such an achievement, and the social recognition of achievement is its remuneration.

If we return to the description of the different logics or rationalities of paid work and family work as I illustrated them at the beginning of the chapter, then it becomes clear that it is the *difference* between that peculiar mixture of toil and pleasure, work and play, love and narcissism, the special form of interaction in the relationship to one's own children on the one hand and paid work on the other, that precisely cannot be reconstructed if both forms of labour are forced into the same mode of (financial) recognition. Rather, one has to say that they at least deserve and expect *different* forms of recognition and that they cannot, as the theory of recognition tends to do, be tied up together by remuneration.[42] This becomes even more obvious if we remind ourselves of the underlying aim of recognition – namely, healthy identity development, the successful development of personalities – because then one can see that the forms of recognition involved in family work and gainful employment respectively have to be different for the simple reason that these aspects of a subjects' identity differ fundamentally (from a descriptive as well as from a normative

---

[41] Cf. Honneth, *Kampf um Anerkennung*, and Axel Honneth, "Antworten auf die Beitraege der Kolloquiumsteilnehmer," in C. Halbig & M. Quante (eds.), *Axel Honneth: Sozialphilosophie zwischen Kritik und Anerkennung* (Muenster: LIT, 2004).

[42] Honneth himself pointed out the difference between legal relationships and the affective relationships of love. If the three dimensions of recognition – which he has developed systematically in his *Struggle For Recognition* – are seen as constitutive for the respective relational structures, then Honneth should distance intra-family relationships of love not only from the law but also from the social recognition of achievement, instead of lumping them together with love. Cf. Honneth, "Antworten."

perspective); the identities seem to be involved in very different ways.[43]

(b) Let us now take another look at the recognition theory argument, this time solely with respect to its understanding of gainful employment. The recognition paradigm, it seems, cannot adequately do justice to a reconstruction of *gainful employment* and its role and function either, since the demand for recognition (of work, of achievement) cannot only be understood as a matter of monetary remuneration. The critique of forms of employment and their concrete circumstances, of undignified work, of alienated labour,. the normative differentiation between meaningful and meaningless work, between "clean" and "dirty" or "hard" work (Walzer), can only be carried out within the paradigm of recognition if it goes beyond formal monetary recognition. Otherwise, "dirty," "undignified" work would only have to be paid well enough in order to lie beyond the criticism of recognition theory.[44] At first this seems pragmatically convincing, but in terms of social criticism this is unsatisfactory. If social recognition and its denial involves the dignity and autonomy of the subjects, then it seems implausible to assume that the dignity of work could be based on monetary compensation only.

Of course this does not mean that paid work in, say, a German garbage collection company must necessarily be regarded as totally heteronomous or undignified.[45] It only means that the appropriateness, the self-determination, the "dignity" of work relations cannot be reduced to financial recognition. Rather, one should (also) assume the opposite perspective: even well-paid achievements can at times be performed under "undignified" conditions. From the perspective of dignity or the self-determination of employees, working conditions and relations can be perceived, described, and criticized

43 Cf. Honneth, *Redistribution or Recognition?* 177, where he explains the "for the sake of" social justice as the healthy development of individual personalities and individual identities.

44 Cf. Krebs, *Arbeit und Liebe*, 201, advocating this solution, following Michael Walzer, *Spheres of Justice. A Defense of Pluralism and Equality* (New York: Basic Books, 1983), Ch. 6.

45 In particular, garbage collection in Germany enjoys comparatively good working conditions; cf. Muirhead's description of work in a grape-processing plant in Muirhead, *Just Work*, 196, and his sensitive analysis of undignified work; cf. A. Schwartz, "Meaningful Work," in *Ethics* 92/4 (1982).

in ways that remain invisible in a framework of merely financial "recognition."

The theory of recognition could counter this argument by pointing out, firstly, that next to the social recognition of achievement subjects can also insist on their equal (social) rights, which are obviously also valid in the sphere of recognition of achievement and must not be violated here, either. This is surely right with regard to securing (basic) economic justice. But one might want to insist that not every form of alienation necessarily has to be seen as a matter of a violation of rights; alienation, by contrast, should also be traceable on a different level than on the level of rights.

The theory of recognition could claim, secondly, that it only refers to the recognition of those achievements, relationships, or activities that promote the attainment of autonomy – or a healthy identity – or at least do not hinder it. However, such a position seems to require a different course of argument: in this case, the attainment of autonomy itself and only indirectly the conveying of recognition will determine what undignified work conditions are or how family work contributes to the good life, and so on. It will then be clear that of course social recognition is a necessary condition for attaining autonomy, but not a condition to which all other conditions of succeeding autonomy can be reduced. And then the normative content of social criticism would no longer be sought in the concept of recognition (alone), but (also) in the concept of the successful attainment of autonomy and the good life and the many varied and diverse conditions in the social world – with its many different practices – in which it must be situated.

At this point, a more general problem in the theory of recognition emerges: Honneth writes in his critique of the "Habermasian communicative grounding of historical materialism" that it admittedly "(has) the merit of directing attention to the no longer class specifically attributable structures of an evolutionary determined process of communicative liberation. But its categorial weakness [in Honneth's view] is that it structures its basic concepts from the outset in such a way that the process of liberation from the alienated work relations which Marx had in mind seems now to have become historically superfluous."[46] It seems as though this argument could be turned against Honneth

---

[46] Honneth, "Arbeit und instrumentelles Handeln," 225.

himself: any critique of alienated work as such seems very difficult in the theory of recognition precisely because it "has structured its concepts from the outset in such a way" that such a critique does not find a place there. The basic concepts of recognition, achievement, solidarity no longer draw attention to alienation as a feature of work. But, normatively and empirically, self-determination as an element of the working condition can be decoupled from (monetary) recognition. There seems, contra the theory of recognition, no possibility, and no need, to reduce one of these aspects to the other. I shall come back to this problem in the final section.

5. LABOUR, JUSTICE, EMANCIPATION

Paid work and family work must apparently be reconstructed and defined differently than seems possible within the paradigm of recognition. Let me briefly summarize the arguments from the perspective of family work (a), and then from the perspective of gainful employment (b).

(a) The adequate form of recognition, and therefore justice, in family work, cannot be achieved by applying economic rationality to family interactions, but only by overcoming the gender-specific division of labour and by enabling women to get gainful employment. This argument is clearly a moral-rights based argument: The gender-specific division of labour in liberal societies is unjust because work in the family is not *recognized* as socially relevant work and because it assigns women (and men) to specific areas of work and thus prevents them from enjoying the same freedom to live their lives. Equal rights and equal liberties for men and women to live their own lives is, after all, the constitutive idea of liberal democracies.

The *normative societal model* to which social criticism should orient itself here is therefore not one in which family work, even if remunerated, is performed only or mostly by women, and paid work, in contrast, only or mostly by men.[47] It is also not a model that would give women and men equal opportunities for participating in gainful employment

---

[47] Fraser differentiates between three such models. Cf. Nancy Fraser, "After The Family Wage: A Post-Industrial Thought Experiment," in Nancy Fraser, *Justice Interruptus* (New York: Routledge, 1997). Cf. also Bubeck, *Care, Gender, and Justice*, 259f.

by fully socializing family work.[48] Adjusting the female biography to conform to the (normative) male biography is not exactly what one would imagine as a rich life capable of satisfying very different human needs and interests. The elimination of one kind of work – in this case family work – does appear in this respect "to be more just" than the strict gender-specific separation of the first model, but it does not necessarily bring one closer to the diversified, successful life.

Only a *third model* offers a just distribution of gainful employment together with the idea of a just distribution of family work, and therefore also an opportunity to overcome the gender-specific division of labour. This model – first developed by Nancy Fraser – envisages a radical reduction of time spent in gainful employment, along with sufficient provision of good *social, state-financed child care* for the period of parental employment *and* the equal distribution of family work among both sexes. Only with such a model does it become clear that we cannot talk about justice in gainful employment and its distribution without taking family work into account: equal participation in public gainful employment is only possible when private family work is also carried out in an equal manner.

For this model, too, social recognition of family work is important. But the form this recognition would take is different: it would be manifest, for instance, in the availability of very good crèches and pre-school arrangements, as well as equally good after-school facilities for older children. It would be manifest in the high salary of caretakers at the crèche and of teachers; it would be manifest in the self-evident equal distribution of care and family work between men and women; it would be manifest generally in the role that children play in the society and in the male (as well as female) responsibility for general care-work.

But this model does not provide payment for family work and does not see family work as work that should be financially rewarded. Nonetheless, financial security, economic justice, and the economic independence of women with children are central concerns here too. But financial security would be guaranteed by gainful employment,

---

[48] Cf. for a discussion of the Swedish model A. Nyberg, "From Foster Mothers to Child Care Centers: A History of Working Mothers and Child Care in Sweden," in *Feminist Economics* 6/1 (2000); also H. Haeussermann & W. Siebel (eds.), *Dienstleistungsgesellschaften* (Frankfurt/M.: Suhrkamp, 1995).

and not by paid family work. Also, parents would be given, for instance, tax relief – but, again, according to the idea of *compensation* (no one should be financially punished for having children) and not according to the logic of *reward*. For it is only this model that normatively assumes that family work satisfies different interests and needs than gainful employment does, but that both – and much more – can constitute a rich and rewarding (good) life. [49] Both questions – the question of justice in the distribution of work and the question of the greatest possible varied, rewarding (good) life – can only be answered, and the according demands can only be realized, in tandem.

(b) But let us return to *gainful employment*. At the beginning of this chapter, I described not only how three normative aspects of gainful employment can be reconstructed in sociophilosophical terms, but also the way in which they are relevant in pre-scientific, everyday discourse. These three normative ideas, still extant in late-modern, market-shaped conditions of gainful employment, I describe as social recognition (aa); as self-determination or self-realization through work (bb); and as the possibility of acquiring property – that is, economic security (cc).

(aa) The social critical paradigm of recognition thus takes care of *one* element in the normative concept of labour: the social recognition of achievement.[50] Here I would like to briefly address the concept of achievement ("Leistung") itself. In Honneth's theory, it is supposed to carry the entire weight of social criticism in the area of economic and working life.[51] Yet it seems not exactly clear how: for under (capitalist) market relations, it is the market that determines which achievements are paid and how. Honneth, however, claims, "that the normative idea of "merit/desert" or "performance" restricts, delimits ("einhegt") the market development from the outside (...)."[52] Of course, there is a notorious ambiguity in the concept of achievement ("Leistung"): what defines achievement – that which it achieves, or the individual effort?

[49] Cf. Fraser, "After The Family Wage." Cf. also M. Seel, *Versuch ueber die Form des Gluecks. Studien zur Ethik* (Frankfurt/M.: Suhrkamp, 1995).

[50] Cf. also Schmidt am Busch, "Marktwirtschaft und Anerkennung."

[51] Cf. especially Honneth, *Redistribution or Recognition?* 140ff. 150ff et passim; and Honneth, "Antworten," 118 in his response to Schmidt am Busch, "Marktwirtschaft und Anerkennung."

[52] Honneth, "Antworten," 118.

But achievement, no matter how defined, seems dependent on the respective market and power relations in which it is carried out. It is not clear how the concept of achievement can be used normatively as a principle to criticize market relations on the one hand, and bring about social recognition – determined and defined precisely through market relations – on the other.

It is important to note, though, that Honneth insists on the idea of (social) rights to constrain the possible excesses of an unmediated application of the principle of achievement. Struggles for recognition of hitherto unrecognized achievements can in fact take two forms: a struggle for social rights and a struggle for economic re-distributions.[53] However, if the achievement-principle is constrained on the one hand by (social) rights (but where exactly does the right take over from achievement?) and if it is not valid regarding family work – as a principle of achievement seeking financial recognition – on the other hand, then it begins to look a bit murky as to where precisely the (normative) force of the concept of achievement still exists.

Furthermore, and this is another problematic point, the concept and idea of social recognition by and in gainful employment can be understood in very different ways. Let me very briefly draw a distinction between four possible interpretations: at a general level, the social recognition that subjects initially seek in and through gainful employment is certainly inclusion in the social world of employment. At first glance, this form of recognition does not necessarily appear to be connected to the size of wages or salaries. Of importance here is simply being paid as a gainfully employed member of society.[54] A second form of desired social recognition can be perceived by looking more closely at the work situation itself, for gainful employment is also quite obviously about recognition in direct social contacts at the level of the specific job – that is, in contacts with colleagues.[55] A third form can be described by actually looking at the size of wages or salaries, since one form of social recognition appears to be directly linked to

---

[53] Cf. Honneth, *Redistribution or Recognition?* 154.

[54] For studies on unemployment, ostracization from society, etc., cf. S. Schlothfeld, "Braucht der Mensch Arbeit? Zur normativen Relevanz von Beduerfnissen," in *Deutsche Zeitschrift fuer Philosophie* 49/5 (2001); Pierre Bourdieu et al., *La Misère du Monde* (Paris: Seuil, 1998).

[55] Cf. e.g. Perrons, "Care, Paid Work, and Leisure," 110.

the (market-dependent, contingent) amount of the payment received for achievement. Finally, the fourth form one should differentiate is the social prestige – to a certain degree independent of salary size – attached to some professions: in Germany, for example (still) attached to the profession of clergymen.[56] Social recognition of gainful employment can therefore be interpreted in very different ways. Thus, when persons seek social recognition, it is not readily apparent how these four forms should be weighted and described within the paradigm of recognition. What is clear, however, is that a subject's identity is not only constituted, or formed, by the financial recognition that is manifest in the size of a salary. For this reason, a potential *critique* of existing recognition relations and conditions must treat these four aspects differently, since each might develop an entirely different critical potential. All of these forms of recognition might be relevant for a healthy identity as a member of the society, but they certainly play very different roles. And none of these forms of social recognition touches on the problem of whether or not the achievement itself is satisfying: this question is certainly not completely independent of the perspective of social recognition but it obviously still has its own and independent weight.

(bb) Let me therefore come to the second normative moment in the concept of labour: the perspective of self-realization through self-determined work – or work at least not only and entirely determined by others.[57] With this seemingly old-fashioned concept, I would like to capture and describe the dimension of employment that is a source of self-respect for subjects precisely because work affords them the opportunity to do something that they can do (well) and in which they have (at least minimal or basic) interest in its achievement, and under conditions that they normatively – at least partly or to a certain extent – want and are able to influence. In my view, Muirhead very convincingly describes this aspect of work as "fit": the activity must be such that it accommodates, or "fits," the subject in a relevant way.[58] Naturally, this normative aspect of gainful employment overlaps with the two

---

[56] Cf. Honneth, *Redistribution or Recognition?* 147ff, for the historical emergence of the modern concept of achievement (the *Leistungsprinzip*).

[57] For more on this topic and on the role of work in the good life, cf. Seel, *Versuch ueber die Form des Gluecks.*

[58] Muirhead, *Just Work.*

other normative moments, because the conditions of self-determined work are directly connected with social recognition and the economic justice of work. This focus on self-determination enables us to better understand those aspects of work conditions described as undignified, "dirty," and alienated.[59] These experiences can often be described without regard to payment of "achievement" or its social recognition, since they contain a *potential critique* of existing work relations and working conditions that cannot be captured by the dimensions of receiving recognition from others for an achievement.

(cc) Let me explain lastly – and briefly – the third normative element in the concept of work, the idea of acquiring property. I want to go beyond the Lockean idea here and argue tentativeley that (*pace* Locke) this normative element implies an idea of economic justice. We have seen already that in the theory of recognition rights constrain the market and the principle of achievement – although it is not totally clear precisely how we have to conceive of the relation between those two forms of recognition. But even if subjects do have social rights as a basic social and economic protection we still are, in capitalist societies, confronted with immense economic injustices and inequalities of income, inequalities that might not be criticisable in terms of the recognition of achievement. For Honneth, social justice starts from an "egalitarian idea of autonomy" and seeks to guarantee an "egalitarian *Sittlichkeit*." Social justice, he argues, contains the three elements of love, equality, and merit/achievement: these principles are meant to secure the idea that in the different spheres, the subjects, in different ways, can pursue their autonomy.[60]

But even if one – as I do – agrees with Honneth's aims here, it seems rather questionable whether the principle of achievement, or a principle of merit, can be of value in securing a plausible standard of economic justice. A more substantial idea of economic justice, however, seems not to be expressible by means of the principle of recognition of achievement. This might be taken as an indication that economic

---

[59] It is this perspective that Muirhead emphasizes with the idea that the appropriate "fit" must exist between person and work, Muirhead, *Just Work*; my remarks on the problem are obviously very sketchy; cf. also Schwartz, "Meaningful Work"; cf. also R. Sennett, *The Corrosion of Character: The Personal Consequences of Work in the New Capitalism* (New York: W. W. Norton, 1998).

[60] Honneth, *Redistribution or Recognition?* 177ff.

justice needs something more and something different than the idea of recognition of achievement.[61] If this is right, however, then the theory of recognition needs more than the tools it has at its disposal in order to achieve its own goals.

Let me conclude: The concept of recognition should not be the sole nor the primary concept that social criticism uses in order to comprehend and criticize work structures and the function of labour in society. It seems more plausible that social criticism should draw on concepts of successful autonomy, of the good and rewarding life, of the equal value of freedom – on a broader and maybe more differentiated normative vocabulary. Labour (or achievement) cuts across the different spheres separated by the theory of recognition, and carries with it normative demands not representable in recognition theory. But even if this only begins to indicate the direction in which the criticism of "labour" – family work and gainful employment – should develop, I have nonetheless attempted to describe two arguments against the recognition theory version of the concept of labour. The first showed that the theory of recognition cannot fully criticize unjust social conditions – regarding the gender-specific division of labour as well as economic injustices. The second showed that the recognition paradigm can only inadequately comprehend how (unalienated) gainful employment and family work can contribute to the good life, each in a categorially different way.

But only with and in these two perspectives could the critique of work relations regain an emancipatory potential. Thus, the discussion and analysis of the concept of labour affords us the opportunity to address central social problems: emancipation does not only mean greater freedom in the sense of equal opportunities to live one's life, to be able to take advantage of the options available in society, and thus overcome the structural obstacles to this "equal value of freedom."

---

[61] A richer idea of an equal value of freedom, for instance, would be a candidate; Honneth refers approvingly to Rawls and his list of basic goods but without mentioning the difference-principle in Honneth, *Redistribution or Recognition?* 178. I do not think, by the way, that Fraser's idea of participatory equality is of much help here; I also think that her earlier idea of individual freedom and the good life, which she discusses in Fraser, "After The Family Wage," is much richer and more encompassing and therefore more plausible than the later idea; but I do not discuss Fraser's theory here; cf. especially Honneth, *Redistribution or Recognition?* 279ff.

Emancipation also means overcoming the structural distortions or repressive structures that prevent us from enjoying the good life and from satisfying the different needs that enable us to live a good, a rewarding life. In *this* double sense, labour still harbours an emancipatory potential.[62]

---

[62] Cf., in contrast, Jürgen Habermas, "Die Krise des Wohlfartsstaates und die Erschoepfung utopischer Energien," in Jürgen Habermas, *Die neue Unuebersichtlichkeit* (Frankfurt/M.: Suhrkamp, 1985).

7

"... That All Members Should be Loved
in the Same Way..."

Lior Barshack

In *The Struggle for Recognition*, Axel Honneth offered an account of the birth, development, and possible demise of the self in the different circles of social interaction. The book's contribution to social theory consists both in advancing concrete views on issues such as the nature of esteem, rights, and respect, and in resetting general agendas and reorienting modes of approach. Thus, Honneth's model brought psychoanalysis back to the center of critical theory after a period of divorce between the two. His account of political conflict as a struggle for recognition calls for novel readings of left- and right-wing ideologies and notions of justice. In this chapter, I will follow these and other directions indicated by Honneth, while departing from assumptions concerning the nature of recognition that differ from Honneth's own assumptions.

According to Honneth, different forms of mutual recognition such as love and legal respect correspond to different spheres of interaction (family, civil society, state) and are constitutive of different aspects of personhood. Honneth's scheme of overlapping tripartite distinctions derives from Hegel's theory of recognition, but Honneth's appropriation of psychoanalytic theory calls these distinctions into question.

The title of this chapter is from Sigmund Freud, "Group Psychology and the Analysis of the Ego," in section IX of *The Standard Edition of the Complete Psychological Works of Sigmund Freud* (hereafter: *SE*), Vol. 18 (London: Hogarth, 1955), 65–143, at 121. I am grateful to the editors for helpful comments on an early draft of this chapter.

From the perspective of fairly standard psychoanalytic theory, love and legal respect appear as general features, rather than distinct types, of mutual recognition. While each is more easily discernible in one sphere – love in the private sphere and law in the public sphere – they can be regarded as complementary aspects of a single process, which precedes the division of recognition into specialized forms in different spheres.

In the long tradition of theological reflection on law and love, both human interaction and the relation between man and God were at stake. Law and love competed over the regulation of horizontal, social relations and of the vertical man-God relation. In this chapter, I will outline a view of recognition according to which (1) horizontal relations among individuals in any social sphere assume vertical relations of recognition with a superimposed authority, and (2) love coincides with legal respect along both horizontal and vertical axes of recognition. Mutual recognition combines love and legal respect among individuals, and between these individuals and an authority they commonly accept. As a third party to relations of recognition, authority functions as a shared object of love and legal respect through which recognition is transmitted from one individual to another. Such a view of authority has been explicitly expounded by Freud in his group psychology.

My argument for the coincidence of law and love and the triangular structure of relations of recognition will not proceed in a particularly philosophical manner. It will draw eclectically on different perspectives in legal and social thought, starting with a rough construal of the psychoanalytic – in particular, Kleinian – view of the coincidence of law and love and of the role of law-giving authority as a third party in relations of recognition. In the psychoanalytic reflection on law, the triangular structure of legal relations and law's structuring role in love relations were often taken for granted. Honneth's own notion of love is consistent with views of the love relation as legally mediated. His account revolves around the idea of love as "refracted" symbiosis – a metaphor I shall borrow and employ in the chapter. The refraction of symbiosis in love was generally considered in psychoanalytic theory as the work of law, the latter being viewed as the anchor of individual autonomy. To the extent that respect for autonomy is an ingredient of love, so is legal mediation.

I. LAW AND SEPARATION

Psychoanalytic thought offers only some among many conceptualizations of the contribution of law to the attainment and protection of autonomy. Modern legal and social theory inherited from Rousseau and Hegel a view of the rule of law as the condition and consummation of individual autonomy. In a Hegelian vein, Honneth's theory of recognition affirms the contribution of the law to the enhancement of autonomy in the sphere of civil society. It can hardly be contested that as a system of individual rights and duties the law entrenches individual autonomy vis-à-vis communal pressures by setting high standards of individual responsibility and delineating realms of individual sovereignty and negative liberty. However, the struggle between the law and destructive aspirations for communal oneness is waged also in smaller circles of interaction, such as intimate relations. Already the earliest processes of individuation may involve the parallel inner and outer institution of the law.

Within the psychoanalytic tradition, Freud himself did not accord the law a crucial role in early processes of separation. In Freud's model, law and interdiction make their appearance following the wake of the Oedipus complex, as the keys to its resolution. They play no prominent role in pre-oedipal processes of individuation. Later psychoanalytic thinkers conceived of law and its internal institution – the superego – as conditions for individuation. They repeatedly distinguished between primary relations of violent fusion, on the one hand, and law-bound love relations among autonomous individuals, on the other hand, as two fundamental patterns of human interaction.[1] Love and separation were seen as dependent upon the inner institution of the superego, and on its social institution in the form of political and religious authority. According to this line of thought, the recognition of boundaries and renunciation of primary omnipotence in the process of individuation present themselves as superimposed norms that must be obeyed

---

[1] According to Fromm, for example, in "contrast to [sado-masochistic] symbiotic union, mature love is union under the condition of preserving one's integrity, one's individuality." Erich Fromm, *The Art of Loving* (New York: Harper, 1962), 20. For Fromm's accounts of totalitarianism as a social condition of sado-masochistic fusion, see, for example, Erich Fromm, *Escape from Freedom* (New York: Farrar and Rinehart, 1941), 141; *Man for Himself* (New York: Holt, Rinehart and Winston, 1947), 151.

by mother and child, and in a social context by all group members. Separation has to be prescribed by an omnipotent authority that is external and superior to the horizontal bond. Primary omnipotence can be given up by being relegated to a superior authority, which is powerful enough to command renunciation and offer protection to the individual in return. As in Hobbes's version of the passage from the state of nature to political society, primary/natural omnipotence is renounced by being condensed and stored in the figure of the sovereign.

For the authority of law to be constructed through the imaginary projection of 'natural' omnipotence, the latter – the state of absolute, lawless union – need not exist in time, in the same way that for Hobbes the passage from the state of nature to the commonwealth is notional rather than historical.[2] The temporal authority of law derives from the image of an atemporal lawless omnipotence that never fully corresponds to reality. The consolidation of law and separation takes place in time, but it does not depart from an actual state of absolute oneness. Nor is it a unidirectional process of development, but a phase in a repetitive cycle of entrenchment and relaxation of separation.

Law's externality to the mother-child dyad, and to the community, allows it to empower its individual subjects and anchor their finitude without engulfing them in a total union with Power. Furthermore, law's externality establishes a form of equality that is essential to the attainment of separation. The law is not imposed by the mother on the child – or by some members of society on others – but superimposed upon both, forming a tripolar relation. Despite their manifest inequality, mother and child are equal before the law. The law postulates the equal moral worth of the mother's and child's autonomy. Equality before the law conditions the passage from violent fusion to separation, because it tames the extreme experiences that, according to authors such as Fromm and Klein, repeatedly launch and threaten to perpetuate relations of violent fusion: experiences of boundless omnipotence, on the one hand, and of helplessness, dependence and inferiority, on the other. As Freud pointed out in his discussion of large

---

[2] Freud's concept of primary unity of self and world has been repeatedly challenged, but the process of development from an early stage of bare individuation to fuller separation is recognized by different schools, which describe it in different theoretical terms. Honneth, for example, adopts the terminology proposed by Winnicott of a passage from absolute to relative dependence.

groups in *Group Psychology*, the equality before the law that conditions interpersonal separation comprises the fiction of being equally loved by that third party.

Before moving on to Freud's views on love, a few words on his and Klein's understanding of the superego, familiar as it may be to many readers. The idea that individuation proceeds through the transformation of imaginary merger and omnipotence into the life-asserting violence of the law forms part of Klein's theory of the superego, which develops the views on the origin of the superego presented by Freud in "The Ego and the Id." According to Freud, the superego originates in the renunciation of a sexual relation to an external object and the subsequent internalization of that object. While for Freud the institution of the law follows, rather than conditions, individuation, the law was still considered in Freudian theory as enhancing individual autonomy: the superego constitutes a critical agency that reduces dependence on external authority, consolidates ego boundaries, and curbs aspirations for merger. Furthermore, according to Freud, the superego consolidates autonomy by subordinating to its own ends symbiotic and destructive forces, which need to be redirected once the external object has been renounced. Aggression is appropriated by the law, and released through the moral sadism that the superego exhibits towards the ego. An analogous economy of violence is often observed in the social sphere, where the legal system is thought to give destructive social forces a potentially constructive outlet. Freud's account of the formation of the superego as a response to the Oedipus complex seems applicable to pre-oedipal processes. Individuation, according to such a view, is accomplished through the transformation of primary boundlessness into the figure of a law-giving authority. Melanie Klein's theory can be construed as affirming such a view of individuation.

According to Klein, separation proceeds through the internalization and consolidation of loving and nourishing objects. The incorporation of predominantly benevolent objects, which depends on the availability of parental love, allows the self to establish and consolidate boundaries. By virtue of these internalized fortifications the self can give up recourse to merger with protective, life-giving external objects. It can also, according to Klein, shield itself against the imaginary invasion of dangerous objects from the outer world, and gradually come to recognize itself and the other as separate, demarcated wholes. Following the installation of an inner protective authority, the self can make the renunciations necessary for individuation. The incorporated, empowering objects that sustain interpersonal separation form the core of the *superego*, issuing commands to live and care for the livelihood and welfare of others. Following Freud, Klein held that the superego integrates and tames destructive aspirations by releasing them through the life-affirming violence of law and morality.

The continuity of the inner, political, and religious instances of the law reflects the law's essential thirdness. In order to anchor the respective autonomy of mother and child and the equal worth of their autonomy, the commands of the superego have to be perceived by both parties as originating outside of their relationship, and as equally binding upon both. Without equality before the law, domination and infringement of boundaries will be perpetuated.[3] The fiction of the externality of the law did not receive due emphasis within the Kleinian tradition. While Klein recognized the role of the father as symbol of the authority vested in the superego, it was Freud who fully perceived the continuity of the superego with totemic political and religious authority – that is, the axiom of the external and superior origin of the superego's commands.

Klein showed that the self can recognize its own separateness and integrity only if it recognizes the other's. Without such recognition, the other will continue to be experienced as an extension of the self, haunted by the alternating fantasies of all-embracing omnipotence and helpless penetrability. Furthermore, from a Kleinian perspective, autonomy depends not only on recognizing the other's autonomy, but also on the other's recognition of one's own. To attain separation – between mother and child or members of a larger group – participants in any sphere have to refrain from using each other as mere extensions

---

[3] Axel Honneth (*The Struggle for Recognition: The Moral Grammar of Social Conflicts*, trans. J. Anderson [Cambridge: Polity Press, 1995], 99) refers to Winnicott's claim that in order to overcome the phase of absolute dependence, the mother needs to turn to third parties. See Donald Winnicott, "The theory of the parent-infant relationship," in Winnicott, *The Maturational Processes and the Facilitating Environment* (London: Karnac, 1990 [1960]), 52. Honneth himself states that "For the 'mother' . . . emancipatory shift begins at the moment in which she can once again expand her social field of attention, as her primary, bodily identification with the infant begins to disperse." (*Struggle*, 100). Jessica Benjamin has shown in her book *The Bonds of Love* that failures to establish equality perpetuate symbiotic relations of domination; (New York: Pantheon, 1988).

or reflections.[4] They have to assure each other that they will relegate primary, 'natural' freedoms to a third party, survive separation,[5] and be able to care for each other under conditions of separation. Individuation is either a collective achievement or a collective failure. It is the outcome of a complex cooperation.

Two insights of psychoanalytic thought, outlined in the preceding paragraphs, are central to the argument on the nature of recognition. According to the first, the firmer the inner and outer institution of the law, the safer individual autonomy. As a relation among individuals, love is thus legally mediated. The institutional frameworks of private and public love are defined in jural terms. Familial love, for example, is mediated by the legal structure of the family, which consists of juridical categories of kinship, property, privacy, and parental authority. Lacan's appropriation of Lévi-Strauss's theory of kinship underlies his assertion that the law, in the form of categories of kinship, mediates the most immediate relations. A similar claim was made by British anthropologists. As Fortes summarizes Radcliffe-Brown's and his own position, the jural categories of kinship "form . . . the inherent framework upon which the emotional relationships, the sentiments and activities, the cooperation of siblings, and the incest barrier between parent and child, must everywhere be built . . ."[6]

According to the second point, in the process of individuation the imaginary total object is not only displaced in order to give way to law,

---

[4] Benjamin describes the mother's side in the joint task of establishing separation: "The child is different from the mother's own mental fantasy, no longer *her* object . . . The mother has to be able both to set clear boundaries for her child and to recognize the child's will, both to insist on her own independence and to respect that of the child – in short, to balance assertion and recognition. If she cannot do this, omnipotence continues, attributed either to the mother or the self; in neither case can we say that the development of mutual recognition has been furthered," Jessica Benjamin, "Recognition and Destruction: An Outline of Intersubjectivity," in Benjamin, *Like Subjects, Love Objects: Essays on Recognition and Sexual Difference* (New Haven: Yale University Press, 1995), 27–48, at 38.

[5] The dependence of recognition and separation on confidence in the survival of the other has been stressed by Honneth on the basis of Winnicott's observations (Honneth, *Struggle*, 101).

[6] Fortes continues: "If a mother's sister is classified with the mother, this is not because of the adventitious conditioning experience of being partly brought up by her. Nor has it anything to do with the ultimate ends of cultural transmission. It follows from the kind of recognition accorded in the social structure at large to the equivalence that is an inherent property of the sibling relationship." (Meyer Fortes, *Kinship and the Social Order* [Chicago: Aldine, 1969], 68–9).

but somehow founds law's authority. This claim can be traced to several profusely commentated remarks Freud made in "The Ego and the Id." Freud describes the father not only as the source of the superego but also, in the pre-oedipal stage, as the object of *primary identification*, thus postulating a continuity between pre-oedipal and oedipal "identifications."[7] A few paragraphs later (p. 36), Freud writes: "What has belonged to the lowest part of the mental life of each of us is changed, through the formation of the ideal, into what is highest in the human mind." As we shall see, an analogous process takes place on the social level: the group's collective superego, its law-giving authority – for Freud, ancestral totemic authority – is formed through a transformation of communal oneness into a common law.

II. THE TRIPOLAR STRUCTURE OF LOVE

Insofar as love is an approximation to an impossible oneness, the law, as a descendant of the imaginary original object, is the first love object.[8] In its inner and institutional instances, the law not only mediates love relations but forms an object of love. It binds the subject by exercising the authority of love.[9] The love of law sets in motion the quest for enduring relations with concrete others. The idea that love objects are largely chosen by virtue of some sort of resemblance to a prototypical loved object is central to psychoanalytic and popular accounts of love.[10]

---

[7] Freud, "The Ego and the Id," in *SE*, Volume 19 (London: Hogarth, 1961) 3, at 31.

[8] On love's root in an "original experience of merging," see Honneth, *Struggle*, 105.

[9] According to Legendre, "...institutional systems both prey upon and manipulate their subjects by means of seduction." Pierre Legendre, *Law and the Unconscious: A Legendre Reader*, Peter Goodrich (ed.) (London: Macmillan, 1997), 81; see also 92, 161. For comprehensive and illuminating discussions of law and love, see Peter Goodrich, *Law in the Courts of Love* (London: Routledge, 1996), 29–71; "Epistolary Justice: The Love Letter as Law," in: *Yale Journal of Law and the Humanities* 9 (1997): 245–295. Frankfurt refers to the "authority of love" in order to explain the power of ethical ideals as opposed to the authority of law, which derives, for Frankfurt, from another source. See Harry G. Frankfurt, *Necessity, Volition and Love* (Cambridge: Cambridge University Press, 1999), 138.

[10] Through concrete others or abstract ideals that stand in the place of a prototypical object, the latter is, according to Freud's oft-quoted formulation, "refound." At the opening of "Mourning and Melancholia"(1917), Freud lists a few types of object that can stand in the place of the original object: "Mourning is regularly the reaction to the loss of a loved person, or to the loss of some abstraction which has taken the place of one, such as one's country, liberty, an ideal, and so on." *SE*, Vol. 14, (London, Hogarth, 1957), 243–258, 243. On the refinding of the object, see Freud,

The law is a prominent candidate for the role of the prototypical object because the superego – in its 'inner' and social instances – represents within time the total and timeless primary object. It ties desire to temporal, durable objects by positing itself as the prototypical object. As such, it looms behind objects of love as diverse as concrete individuals, ethical ideals, homelands, and works of art.

The prototypical object is not equated in psychoanalytic literature with the internalized image of one of the parents, or of any other single person. Rather, it is generally seen as a compound prototype integrating different objects – and, to use Klein's term, 'part objects' – layered upon each other in a series of successive incorporations of pre-oedipal, oedipal and later love objects.[11] In his work on love relations, Kernberg has pointed out that individuals in a couple internalize elements of each other's ideal object, forming a shared ideal object. In other words, the couple as a single entity forms its own superego, its own ultimate love object and ultimate source of law. According to Kernberg,

... the couple as an entity also activates both partners' conscious and unconscious superego functions, resulting in the couple's acquiring, over time, a superego system of its own in addition to its constituent ones.... both partners' ego ideals... combine to create a joint structure of values. A preconsciously adhered-to set of values is gradually mapped out, elaborated, and modified through the years, and provides a boundary function for the couple vis-à-vis the rest of the world. In short, the couple establishes its own superego. (pp. 97–98)[12]

"Three Essays on the Theory of Sexuality," in *SE*, Vol. 7 (London: Hogarth, 1953), 222. The pursuit of an original object through more or less concrete objects of love found expression in central positions in the philosophy of love, such as Plato's and Rousseau's, according to which individuals are loved by virtue of approximating to abstract ideals. See, for example, Gregory Vlastos, "The Individual as Object of Love in Plato," in Vlastos, *Platonic Studies* (Princeton: Princeton University Press, 1981), 3, at 28–31. In political thought, the same idea appears in discussions of patriarchal and political authority, in the view of the prince as *Imago dei*, an image of God, a concrete object of love through which devotion to a superior object is expressed.

[11] The closing scene of Fellini's *Otto e mezzo* offers a visualization of the object's compound structure: the protagonist conjures up the various good objects assembled throughout his lifetime in the form of a hallucinated procession of past friends and relatives.

[12] Otto F. Kernberg, *Love Relations: Normality and Pathology* (New Haven: Yale University Press, 1995). On the couple's shared superego, see also Kernberg, *Love Relations*, 39, 42, 61.

Shared by the two members of the couple, the prototypical object can be regarded as a third party to the love relation. While multi-layered and complex, the shared object formed by couples acquires unity through the overarching category of ancestral authority – the mythical prototype on which all lesser objects of love and obedience, including parental and political authority, are arguably modelled. The couple is thus premised on the fiction of the shared descent of the two parties. Rules of endogamy guarantee that family members share their ultimate ancestral object.[13] Falling in love involves the identification or fabrication of indices of a shared object – a shared ancestry or myth. Common national or ethnic origin, shared political ideals, or love of art, for example, can denote a shared original object and establish a relation of love of lesser or greater intensity. The political bond unites individuals who share their original object – their genealogy and mythology, their law, their God – and find the original object reflected in each other. In the next section, the original object shared by parties to love relations, private or national, will be identified with the juridical concept of the corporate body.

Before turning to the corporation, it is worth recalling that the tripolar, juridical structure of love was clearly spelled out by Freud in his *Group Psychology and the Analysis of the Ego*. It is remarkable that Freud's finest remarks on love occur in his discussion of the group. Freud argues in *Group Psychology* that groups are held together by a libidinal bond mediated by common love for the leader, a horizontal bond of love that stems from a vertical one.[14] Freud's identification in *Group Psychology* of society's object with the leader is hardly consistent with earlier and later texts. Freud usually considers ancestral authority rather than the living leader as the shared love object of society and source of its law. In *Totem and Taboo*, Freud postulates a mythical absent ancestor who is at once the object of collective love and veneration and source of law. In *Moses and Monotheism*, Moses is depicted as the social superego for whose sake instinctual renunciation is made by successive generations. The leader can exercise superego functions only as the

---

[13] On endogamy, see Louis Dumont, *Affinity as a Value* (Chicago: University of Chicago Press, 1983), 39, 47–48.

[14] See the diagram in Freud, "Group Psychology," in: *SE*, Vol. 18, 65–143, at 116. Horizontal love among group members, writes Freud, was "originally made possible by their having the same relation to the object." Freud, "Group Psychology," 143.

representative of an absent legislator. Also the role of the ultimate 'ego ideal' – the ultimate love object – cannot be played by the leader, because the visible presence of such an object would precipitate social violence and merger.[15]

The leader is neither the ultimate law-giving authority nor the ultimate object of collective love but a representative of the group's ancestral authority: the ego-ideal and superego functions of political leaders respectively stage the mirroring and morally exacting aspects of ancestral authority. The picture that emerges from a juxtaposition of Freud's scattered references to ancestral authority and political leadership is that of a social order premised on the fictions of equal distribution of love and equal subjection of all members to a superimposed ancestral law. The burdens of separation, recognition, and social cooperation – burdens of finitude, scarcity, loneliness, and competition – can be undertaken by the individual only on the assumption of equality before the law and equal distribution of love. Groups, big and small, are held together by an idea of equality that combines equal concern with legal equality.

III. THE ORIGINAL OBJECT AS A CORPORATE BODY

Ancestral authority, as a third party in relations of recognition, can be identified with the corporate body of groups such as states and families. Vertical relations of recognition link corporate bodies, such as the state and the family, with their individual organs, situated in horizontal relations of recognition. The concept of the corporation played a central role in accounts of social structure given by anthropologists and historians of law from Maine to Fortes through Maitland and Kantorowicz. These theorists considered immortality as the most distinctive feature of corporations. The family and the crown served as the two paradigmatic, and closely related, instances of immortal corporations. The family preserves its identity across generations; it is not restricted to the life span of particular generations. Similarly, the crown, or in Kantorowicz's terms, the public body of the king, is indifferent to the death of individual kings and retains its identity across generations. The second characteristic of corporate bodies, according

---

[15] On Hitler as the ultimate love object of his subjects, see Helmut Ulshofer (ed.), *Liebesbriefe an Adolf Hitler – Briefe in den Tod* (Frankfurt am Main: VAS, 1994).

to Maine, Maitland, and Kantorowicz, is sovereignty. Kantorowicz's analysis of medieval kingship implies that sovereignty resides not in the private body of the king but in his corporate, public body. The king is obliged to defend and augment the inalienable possessions of the realm – they are not his own – an obligation that receives its clearest expression in the coronation oath. Maine made this point in his discussion of the Roman family: the *pater familias* embodies the abstract legal personality of the family and is in charge of its affairs. He can only act in the name of its immortal interests, not out of his own passing interests and desires.

I would like to supplement the classical account of the corporate body with several general suggestions, largely inspired by psychoanalytic views on the group.

The separate corporate personality of the family and the state is associated with the mythical person of its founding ancestors. The examples of the family and the state suggest that the corporation is identified with the person of the founding ancestor of a descent group, such as the mythical, heroic founder of a Roman family, the founder of a royal dynasty, or the founding fathers of modern nation states. This is plainly indicated by the names and symbols of descent groups, which often refer, directly or indirectly, to founding ancestors and circumstances.

The corporate-ancestral personality of the group is an absent, transcendent object of worship. Through its corporate personality, its mythical ancestors and their multiple totemic representations, the group articulates itself for itself. According to Hegel and Durkheim, notwithstanding the differences between their approaches to religion, society's self-representation is its object of worship. If the corporation is associated with ancestral authority and law, and constitutes the self-representation of the group, it cannot fail to be sacred. Like the Gods, corporations are transcendent: they are absent, invisible, external, and superior to the group, and act through representatives. The religious dimension of political systems and of families is inherent in their corporate structure. Civil and domestic religions worship the corporate bodies of the state and the family respectively.

The corporate body originates in the projection of sacredness outside of the group. Corporations come into being through the projection of sacredness from within the social onto a transcendent realm. Corporate-formation secularizes the social: once sacredness is projected outside the group, a temporal realm of pragmatic interaction can assert itself. When sacredness is immanent to the group, ancestral, corporate authority, and law are not recognized. Ultimate authority is then vested in the sacred private body of a divine king who is neither sanctioned nor constrained by a superimposed ancestral law. The passage from divine kingship to an authority that is grounded in law can be understood in terms of projection: the private body of the king is deconsecrated and its sacredness projected onto the transcendent domain of the ancestral-corporate body. From this moment onwards, sovereignty vests in the corporate – as opposed to the private – body of the king, in the dynasty or the realm as a whole. Kingship becomes hereditary: the king is seen as an ordinary mortal whose authority derives not from personal charisma but from a corporate constitutional order perceived as the expression of ancestral law.

It is the sacred communal body *that is projected outside the group and transformed into its corporate body.* By the notion of the *communal body*, I refer to the body of the group as a simple, inarticulate, immanent unity that results from the dissolution of interpersonal boundaries. The communal body is the sacred merger that occurs during rites of passage, carnivals, natural disasters, fascist regimes, wars, revolutions, referenda, elections, and other instances of *communitas*. In his essay on Canetti's *Crowds and Power*, Honneth described the group's enactment of its communal body: in the crowd, "the invisible barriers between strangers, which were erected around the individual's body in the maturational process, disappear suddenly."[16] Group psychologists such as Anzieu and Bion identified an unconscious image of the group as a single collective body.[17] This image constantly threatens to dissolve the individualistic body-image, which remains in tact only as long as the imaginary collective body is safely projected onto the corporate realm.[18] Communal oneness gives way to individual

---

[16] Axel Honneth, "The Perpetuation of the State of Nature: On the Cognitive Content of Elias Canetti's *Crowds and Power,*" in *Thesis Eleven* 45 (1996): 69–85, at 74.

[17] On the imaginary identification of the group with a single, all-embracing body, see, for example, Wifred Ruprecht Bion, *Experiences in Groups* (London: Tavistock, 1961), 162; Didier Anzieu, *The Group and the Unconscious* (London: Routledge, 1985), 120–124; Otto Kernberg, "Regression in Groups" in Kernberg, *Internal World and External Reality* (N.J.: Aronson, 1980), 211–234.

[18] There are various psychoanalytic theories of the "body-ego" and "body image." Notwithstanding differences between the different theories, it is widely assumed that the conscious and unconscious body image is a source of the self's fictional unity and

autonomy by being somehow condensed into the figure of ancestral, corporate authority. The projection of sacred communal fusion outside the group and its transformation into a transcendent corporate body attest to a social acceptance of absence and division. They allow for an enhanced degree of interpersonal separation and for the emergence of secular spheres of interaction.

Like the individual superego, ancestral law-giving authority – the social superego – comes into being through the transformation of primary imaginary oneness into an omnipotent external authority. The process through which mother and child establish their respective autonomy by submitting to a superimposed law and authority is analogous to the social construction of large-scale corporate entities. It is primarily through the legal institution of division that the communal body is projected. Juridification of social relations heightens their alienated, temporal character. In order to keep the communal body away from the group, and thereby deconsecrate the group, numerous divisions and subdivisions – between groups, classes, spheres of interaction, constitutional powers, individuals – are enforced by the law. The law commands and entrenches separation by laying down and enforcing individual rights and duties, confronting the expansionist attempts of the sacred communal body that abound on the level of the social.

The corporate body and the communal body correspond to social structure and communitas, *respectively.* In earlier work, I proposed to read into Turner's classical distinction between structure and *communitas* a few distinctions which Turner did not consider.[19] The first is the psychoanalytic distinction between relations of interpersonal separation and mutual recognition, on the one hand, and relations of violent fusion, on the other hand. Another distinction is the theological distinction between absence and presence. The combination of these two

---

separateness and an object of narcissistic love, and that it underlies higher capacities such as critical thought and autonomous judgment. The Lacanian concept of the *moi* designates the imaginary unity acquired by the self in the mirror stage through importation of the perceived unity of the body. "The Mirror Stage as Formative of the Function of the I" in Jacques Lacan, *Ecrits: A Selection*, trans. by Alan Sheridan (London: Tavistock, 1977).

[19] Lior Barshack, "Constituent Power as Body: Outline of a Constitutional Theology," *University of Toronto Law Journal* 57/1 (2007).

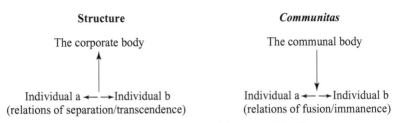

FIGURE 7.1. Corporate and Communal bodies.

characterizations entails an account of social structure as absence of fusion and of *communitas* as a presence of fusion, which I referred to earlier as the communal body.

The distinction between social structure and *communitas* corresponds to the distinction between the corporate and communal bodies (see Figure 7.1). The sacred communal body is formed during *communitas* through the dissolution of interpersonal boundaries, while under social structure it is projected outside the group, transformed into a corporate body, and worshiped from afar by firmly separated individual subjects. Interaction in social structure is mediated by normative social roles, a network of normative categories and boundaries through which differentiated individual identities are defined. Structures are articulate, divided. Clashes of interests, institutionalized competition over economic and political power, struggle over hegemony – these are inherent to social structure, whose greatest enemy is uniformity, and preserve a high level of individual autonomy within structure. In *communitas*, by contrast, division and difference are not tolerated. Every individual partakes in the communal body and is thereby consecrated. The absence and expectation that burden and animate ordinary social life give way to presence and immediacy.

Every social structure is occasionally interrupted by interludes of *communitas*. The firmer social structure, the more capable it is of integrating, instituting, and taming *communitas*. In his essay on Cannetti, Honneth succinctly describes the alternation of structure and *communitas* that governs social life: "...no social system, however advanced, has yet been able to reproduce itself without availing itself in the public sphere of mechanisms that are connected with deep-rooted needs of dissolving the body's boundaries."[20] Honneth offers at this point a

---

[20] Axel Honneth, "The Perpetuation of the State of Nature," 75.

critique of psychoanalytic group psychology which is at the same time instructive and overstated. Honneth writes:

> In his psychology of the crowd, Freud locates pathological mechanisms of compensatory identification in the subject at that point where, in Canetti's belief, just simple mechanisms of drive discharge prevail: individuals are, as we have seen, attracted to the crowd not because they are unconsciously searching for an enhancement of their ego ideals but because they are seeking a physical density in whose equalizing shelter they can act out elemental emotional impulses. Paradoxically, by means of this calculated reduction of the psychical, which robs the self of any inwardly directed depth, Canetti acquires the perspective on a multitude of crowd phenomena which could not even be noticed in the psychoanalytic tradition. Thus, in contradistinction to Freud's hypothesis, it becomes evident that in most cases it is not the compulsive identification with a figure in authority but the voluntary and riskless pleasure in the game of bodily fusion that enables a crowd to emerge in our daily life; and it becomes just as clear to what degree, even today, all collective forms of dealing with sorrow or joy make use of the simple mechanism that Canetti located in the mutual relinquishing of individual bodily boundaries. (Ibid., p. 77)

According to Honneth's critique of Freud, the phenomenon of the crowd cannot be fully understood in terms of identification with a leader and other group members. While Honneth's depiction of the crowd is convincing, the main purpose of Freud's group psychology is not the analysis of the crowd. Freud's model is devised to account for paradigmatic cases of social structure: his main examples are the army and the Church. Freud does not offer an elaborate theoretical account of *communitas*, though he recognizes its possibility in his discussion of collective panic. A state of collective panic, Freud suggests, can be precipitated by a sudden awareness of an oncoming disaster or an abrupt dissolution of the identificatory mechanisms that underpin social structure, for example, following the death of a leader. In other words, Freud does recognize the suspension of identificatory mechanisms – of love and law – in the state of panic. It is clear, however, that his analysis of the crowd remains far from complete. His group psychology needs to be supplemented by a fuller account of the resort to violent fusion with the breakdown of libidinal and normative ties.

Organs of corporate bodies are related to each other and to their corporate bodies in a bond of love, or 'refracted symbiosis.' Once projected, the communal body leaves behind separate individuals situated in relations of love and legal respect with each other and with their corporate body. In social as well as intimate contexts love is forged with the refraction of symbiosis through the projection of a collective body. The absent, prototypical object of love identified by psychoanalysis can be identified with the absent corporate-ancestral body. In familiar contexts it is the corporate body of the family, and in social contexts – the corporate body of the state, which function as ultimate objects for the members of the respective corporate groups. The universal belief in the benevolence of ancestral authority attests to the love of the corporate body. Ample anthropological evidence suggests that in stable social structures ancestral personifications of the corporate order are represented as predominantly benevolent, if also morally exacting.[21] Through the authority of benevolent ancestral figures the lawless violence of *communitas* is transformed into the life-affirming harshness of the law and is thereby humanized and domesticated.

Corporate sovereignty: The corporate object of ultimate love as a sovereign law-giver. In the passage from *communitas* to social structure, from an immanent communal body to a transcendent corporate body, the law comes into being. The law is always seen as prescribed by the corporate-ancestral authority of the group, and hence cannot be found in the course of *communitas* as the corporate body dissolves into a communal body. Law-giving is the predominant function of the corporate ancestral authority of a kin group: the more an authority is transcendent, the more its function is reduced to that of law-giving.

IV. PRIVATE AND PUBLIC RECOGNITION

The concept of the corporate body weaves together the two claims made at the outset about the nature of recognition: the coincidence of love and legal respect and their tripolar structure. Love and legal respect shape horizontal relations among organs of corporate bodies, such as the state and the family, as relations of refracted oneness. In relations of recognition, individuals identify each other as equal members of the same corporate body, the source and object of the love

---

[21] On ancestral benevolence, see Fortes, *Kinship and the Social Order*, 153, 159, 189, and his "Pietas in Ancestral Worship," in Fortes, *Time and Social Structure* (London: Athlone, 1970), 165–6.

and legal respect that govern their relationship.[22] Claims for recognition – for respect and care – invoke contested normative ideals of corporate membership. The third form of recognition that Honneth has analyzed and that has not been treated in the present discussion – ethical esteem – is embedded in corporate group membership, as are concern and respect for rights. Membership indicates adherence to the ethical standards of the group and bestows esteem upon individual members on the basis of their presumed contribution to the spiritual and material prosperity of the corporate group. The idea of corporate *dignity* of which members of families and states partake by virtue of their membership is a basic feature of corporate structures. Its place in medieval corporate theory has been reconstructed in Kantorowicz's study of medieval public law.[23] The three forms of recognition that Honneth describes – love and concern, legal respect, and esteem – illuminate the normative content of corporate membership.

Mutual recognition can be characterized as a relationship among kin because it is premised on the fictions of a shared body and ancestral authority. Recognition is operative through categories of kinship such as citizenship and other notions of membership.[24] Far from being the universalist contrast to particularist solidarity, the rule of law is characteristically taken to prevail among kin primarily – that is, within corporate groups.[25] The account of the state as an institution of kinship does not privilege fascist or communitarian conceptions of the political over liberal or republican ones. The object of proper political love is the corporate body, not the communal body. Communitarianism

---

[22] The fact that reconciliation between strangers and former enemies begins so often with a solemn evocation of a common real or fictional ancestor is highly suggestive. When common ancestors cannot be easily fabricated, the authorities heralded by the different sides arguably constitute a single amalgamated corporate-ancestral authority. This is one way through which relations of recognition are universalized. To avoid strife and fusion, the circle of corporate membership has to be constantly expanded, though the degree of love and respect reduces with the increase in corporate inclusiveness.

[23] Ernst Kantorowicz, *The King's Two Bodies,* (Princeton: Princeton University Press, 1957), 384–450.

[24] On citizenship as a category of kinship, see Lior Barshack, "The Holy Family and the Law," *International Journal of Law, Policy and the Family* 18/2 (2004), 222.

[25] Law can function as a symbol of group identity: the unity of a particular corporate group is often symbolized through the particularity of the law that defines and regulates it. On law and kinship, see Fortes, *Kinship and the Social Order*, 101–138.

and fascism, notwithstanding their differences, envisage society as an immanent communal body united through the type of political love that liberal and republican political thinkers such as Arendt were right to criticize.

While the elementary structure of private and public recognition is analogous, Honneth's account shows how a certain differentiation between forms of recognition is a mark of structural progress, and offers illuminating genealogies of the different spheres and forms of recognition.[26] According to Freud, the public realm is premised on the relegation of bodily immediacy and intimacy to the private realm.[27] Private and public spheres are differentiated through a reciprocal system of projections. While the communal body is banished from the public sphere to be experienced within the family in a relatively immediate manner, the private sphere relegates violence and negativity to the public realm. The latter represents law, limit, and objectivity for the private realm.[28] Corporate, juridical aspects are particularly pronounced in the state because of the relatively anonymous and abstract nature of membership in the state, its monopoly over violence, and its function as the anchor of division and guardian of objectivity.

The division of labour between different spheres of interaction is a condition for individuation. Recognition within any of the spheres depends on the subject's simultaneous participation in other spheres. As Hegel saw, freedom is realized through the uncoupling of different spheres. The simultaneous existence of different spheres prevents any single sphere from yielding to inner symbiotic aspirations and melting into a formless communal body. Whenever the corporate structure of either state or family founders, the disintegration of the other corporate sphere is imminent: none of the corporate groups can accomplish the projection of the communal body and the institution of autonomy on its own. The transcendence of the collective body

---

[26] Nancy Fraser and Axel Honneth, *Redistribution or Recognition? A Political-Philosophical Exchange* (London: Verso, 2003), 139, 140.

[27] "Group Psychology," in: *SE*, Vol. 18, 65–143, at 140.

[28] In his discussion of the relationship between the couple and the group in *Love Relations*, Kernberg describes the mutual dependence of the two spheres. "A truly isolated couple is endangered by a serious liberation of aggression that may destroy it or severely damage both partners." Kernberg, *Love Relations*, 181, see also 183. The group, for its part, needs the couple "because the couple enacts and maintains the group's hope for sexual union and love ..." (p. 182).

of any group depends on the participation of its members in other corporate bodies.

Without the family, the state would have been unable to expel the communal body and entrench subjectivity. The nation-state asserts the bond of kinship among all its organs *vis-à-vis* other nations and thereby provides citizens with an important component of their identity. However, by treating citizens as abstract legal subjects, the state fails to differentiate them from each other. Because of its generality, the legal system cannot provide citizens with differentiated identities. Such identities are drawn from other corporate memberships. The family asserts the exclusive unity of its organs in a way that differentiates them from other citizens, while instituting – together with politically enforced standards of autonomy – their separateness from each other.[29] In the absence of independent families, citizens seek to disappear into a single political body, and relations of mutual recognition are replaced by violent oneness. Fascism illustrates the correspondence between disempowerment of the family and dissolution of individual autonomy. Recognizing no superimposed law or limit, fascist regimes aspire to encompass the totality of human existence and eradicate competing spheres and commitments.[30] By denying the inherent value and corporate autonomy of the family, fascism precipitates an enactment of the communal body and collapses individual autonomy.

The dangers of a monopoly of a single sphere suggest that no dimension of individuation can be at any stage confined to one particular sphere. Individuation is a fractured, multi-focal process consisting in the simultaneous formation of relations of love and legal respect in different spheres. Contrary to the intersubjective dialogical paradigm underlying most accounts of recognition, individuation demands at

---

[29] Thus, Hegel conceived of the family as a bond of substantial unity on the level of immediate feeling, which nonetheless has an objective legal structure. Honneth acknowledges that legalization of domestic relations enhances individual autonomy within the family, while maintaining his strict distinction between different forms of recognition; see, *Redistribution or Recognition?* 188–189, and Honneth, "Between Justice and Affection: The Family as a Field of Moral Disputes" in Beate Rössler (ed.), *Privacies* (Stanford: Stanford University Press, 2004), 142.

[30] Honneth points out the unavoidable tensions between – and not only within – the different spheres of recognition: Axel Honneth, "Recognition and Moral Obligation," *Social Research* 64/1 (1997), 16–35, at 32–33.

any moment the involvement of multiple partners placed in rival arenas. The following concluding remarks consider the role of law and love in the political arena, in response to the recent debate between Fraser and Honneth on recognition and distributive justice.

V. POLITICAL LOVE

Political ideologies advocate a reform of horizontal relations of recognition and the reinstitution of vertical relations with the group's corporate authority. As struggles for recognition, political struggles orient themselves toward the realization of contested conceptions of corporate membership: conceptions of the scope of the corporate group and of the just relationship of group members to each other and to their corporate body. Rival conceptions of corporate membership are grounded in rival visions of the group's mythical-corporate body. One of the crucial factors that divide different claims for recognition is the position each accords to the corporate body in relation to society. Competing principles of justice reflect different perceptions of the degree of interpersonal and vertical separation. The degree of separation along the horizontal and vertical axes determines the moral content of corporate membership. The more a political stance is individualist and humanist, the more transcendent its image of the corporate body.

Greater distance between the group and its collective body advances the rule of law by subjecting mundane institutions to an increasingly impersonal law. Furthermore, the more abstract is corporate authority, the less ethnicist and exclusive is corporate membership. Finally, greater vertical separation fosters individual autonomy by enhancing horizontal separation. As a result of increasing separation from the collective body, self-realization derives less and less from active or passive participation in collective achievement, and consists instead in the fulfilment of personal choices and capacities. In his exchange with Fraser, Honneth points out that the developmental potential of recognition resides in the dimensions of *individuation* and *inclusiveness*. "Progress in the conditions of social recognition takes place ... along the two dimensions of individualization and social inclusion ... " (Fraser and Honneth, p. 186). Individuation and inclusion develop together with the separation of the group from its collective body.

The development of the rule of law and individual autonomy in advanced corporate structures need not reduce society's concern for the welfare of individual members. With the consolidation of autonomy, concern for the group's collective dignity and prosperity can be gradually, though never completely, shifted to the welfare and self-respect of fellow individuals. Despite differentiation, members of modern corporate structures identify with each other as organs/extensions of the same corporate body. They care about each other's well-being and dignity because they share the same corporate dignity and prosperity, even if these are now manifested primarily through individual differences rather than collective achievement.

Political ideologies can be ordered along a continuum according to the degree of transcendence that they preach. The continuum delineates a path of moral development, not dissimilar to the one postulated by Kohlberg: an increase of the distance between the group and its collective body amounts to moral progress. It is correlative to the development of a critical moral attitude, belief in human rights, a universalizing standpoint, and a sense of social justice.[31] Two political positions seem to lie outside the scope of this spectrum. Certain anarchistic positions deny the very existence of the collective body, while fascism denies the individual body any significant existence. Under fascism, the individual disappears in the political group as a boundless inarticulate whole, and political love deteriorates from a collective espousal of civic rights into total immersion in the communal body.

Honneth's account of social justice suffers from his denial of the role of love in political relations of recognition. According to Honneth, the forms of recognition that underlie practices of redistribution are mutual esteem and legal respect. Claims for greater resources can be read as demands for esteem of one's personal achievement or respect for one's legal rights. As Honneth writes,

On the one hand, up to a certain, politically negotiated threshold, it is possible to call for the application of social rights that guarantee every member of society a minimum of essential goods regardless of achievement. This approach follows the principle of legal equality insofar as, by argumentatively mobilizing the equality principle, normative grounds can be adduced for making

---

[31] On Kohlberg, anarchism, and fascism, see Lior Barshack, *Passions and Convictions in Matters Political* (Lanham: University Press of America, 2000), 97.

minimum economic welfare an imperative of legal recognition. On the other hand, however, in capitalism's everyday social reality there is also the possibility of appealing to one's achievements as something "different," since they do not receive sufficient consideration or social esteem under the prevailing hegemonic value structure.[32]

According to Honneth's theory, legal rights, as a distinct form of recognition, are designed to express, protect, and foster the equal moral autonomy of individuals. However, distributive justice is geared toward the enhancement of individual well-being in general, not exclusively toward the promotion of autonomy. Thus it cannot be fully derived from legal respect for autonomy. While a degree of material welfare conditions autonomy, a sweeping reduction of distributive claims to the interest in autonomy is often artificial, even when redistribution would in fact enhance autonomy, alongside other interests. Moreover, redistribution can be mandatory in many cases in which its contribution to the promotion of autonomy is improbable. It is regularly extended to individuals whose capacity for autonomy is deficient, and to individuals who seem to be fairly autonomous and fulfilled already, but reasonably demand a higher standard of living on the mere ground that society is affluent enough to provide it. Honneth points out that the principle of legal recognition can ground claims for redistribution "regardless of achievement," but it cannot ground demands for redistribution regardless of its contribution to the promotion of autonomy, according to Honneth's own classification of the forms of recognition.

Nor can distributive justice be fully grounded in the principle of *esteem* as interpreted by Honneth. Welfare systems are designed to promote the well-being and dignity of individual citizens irrespectively of the social appreciation of their uniqueness and achievement and regardless of a clear absence of achievement. However, redistribution can be grounded in that portion of social esteem that is secured by the mere fact of active membership in a corporate group and that is less sensitive to individual achievement. Group members share a sense of collective self-esteem and dignity, which is often invoked in demands for redistribution. Political theorists such as Brian Barry and David

---

[32] Fraser and Honneth, *Redistribution or Recognition*, 152–3.

Miller observed in recent years the mutual-dependence of redistributive practices and social feelings of solidarity and homogeneity.

An aspect of political recognition that is related to collective self-esteem and solidarity, and that bears on the justification of redistribution, is the principle of equal political love for all group members, which Freud regarded as a condition for social life. Political misrecognition is experienced not only as disrespect but also as desertion. Rooted in the refraction of oneness, the civic bond is a bond of love in which the welfare of all individual members and of the shared body are interdependent. Civic love is forged with the foundation of the body politic – that is, with the passage from *communitas* to structure through the projection of the sovereign communal body (constituent power) into the corporate realm.[33] It comes into being with legal rights and duties and must not be confused with the pre-legal experience of the communal body. Civic love would not have provided a sound ground for redistribution if it could not be instituted in the form of social rights. Political love properly understood is manifested *through* the law, not *beside* the law. It does not deny the antagonisms between the group and the individual and among different social groups. It uses the law to express equal concern for all group members under conditions of rivalry and animosity. A sentimental political discourse that assumes and extols an unqualified and blissful social harmony would be detrimental to individual welfare because it would undermine autonomy and plurality. On the other hand, the restriction of love to the confines of the private sphere produces a different type of tribalism.

If political love exists only under conditions of rivalry, it nevertheless transcends the realm of autonomy and difference, avowing the reality of the collective body – of a common social origin and a shared destiny. Political love turns individual destitution into a predicament of the entire body politic. It keeps reminding us that individual achievement is always in part a collective achievement from which the group as a whole should benefit. Corporate structures are perceived by their members as immortal households whose prosperity belongs

---

[33] The social contract, and the contractual justification of distributive justice, are secondary to the foundation of political love, because the autonomy of the contracting parties comes into being after, or with, the establishment of recognition.

to all members and thus depends on the well-being of each member, and that are capable of mitigating the arbitrariness of natural and economic allocations. As two corporate bodies premised on the principle of equal love, the state and the family engage, today more than ever before, in a flagrant competition over the power to promote individual welfare.

8

Recognition of Love's Labor

Considering Axel Honneth's Feminism

Iris Marion Young

PROLOGUE

Jean-Jacques Rousseau thought that the need for recognition was a big problem. The *Discourse on the Origin of Inequality* tells a story of human decline from a state of simplicity and self-sufficiency to the state of competition, war, domination, enslavement, and vice that is modern society. The desire for recognition from others, or what Rousseau calls *amour propre*, is the primary cause of this degradation. As soon as people ceased living independently and became sociable, they sought one another's praise.

Everyone began to look at everyone else and wish to be looked at himself, and public esteem acquired a price. The one who sang or danced the best; the handsomest, the strongest, the most skillful, or the most eloquent came to be the most highly regarded, and this was the first step at once toward inequality and vice; from these first preferences arose vanity and contempt on the one hand, shame and envy on the other; and the fermentation caused by these new leavens eventually produced compounds fatal to happiness and innocence.[1]

Living with others in society generates a struggle for recognition without limit. The self is never in possession of itself, but rather depends on the esteem of others. We compare ourselves with others,

---

[1] Jean-Jacques Rousseau, "Discourse on the Origin and Foundations of Inequality Among Men," in Rousseau, *'The Discourses' and Other Early Political Writings* (Cambridge: Cambridge University Press, 1997), 166.

and believe ourselves better, and demand acknowledgment of our superiority from them. This insults and dishonors them, however; they become angry, or demand a contest. To prove our worth before others, we accumulate fine clothes or extravagant furniture, or we become more learned, skillful, or witty; we develop our strength to defeat the others in combat or sport; we exalt ourselves before others without obsequious entourage. There is no limit to this process of competition and accumulation, because the others also engage in it. For Rousseau, this desire for recognition is in tension with a value of equal respect.

Society is a hall of mirrors for man. Standing in the center of his universe, he looks around him to see himself reflected and affirmed. Everywhere he turns, however, he finds his reflection mocked and distorted, going out to infinity in the bright lights of the desires and judgments of the others, who laugh at his awkward motions, themselves reflected without limit.

In *Emile*, Rousseau offers a solution to this problem: the love of a properly educated man for a properly educated woman. Love blocks the infinite dialectic in the desire for recognition. Love domesticates the social fun house where each time he turns around, a man sees himself distorted in the gaze of another, and creates a drawing room with just one smooth and flattering mirror, a woman.[2]

From his own point of view and that of many of his contemporaries, Rousseau challenged many traditional views about the proper relations between men and women. A man cannot very well have a fulfilling relationship with his soul mate in love if he aims to dominate her and make her servile. Nor can he derive pleasure from her company and enlist her aid in family projects if she is uneducated. Thus Rousseau counsels men against forcing themselves on unwilling wives, although he thinks that a little rough play and resistance increase sexual excitement for both. A woman should be well educated, though not in the abstract and speculative sciences, so that she can be a good companion, household manager, and mother. She should be physically active and trained in sport, engineering a natural beauty that

---

[2] I am using the mirror metaphor here in order to invoke Luce Irigaray's analysis of modern love, particularly in *Speculum of the Other Woman*, trans. Gillian C. Gill (Ithaca, NY: Cornell University Press, 1985). Late in this chapter, I will refer to Irigaray's analysis.

requires no makeup. She should make herself attractive and pleasing, for his sake, but in simple and modest attire. A man should respect his wife and earn her adoration rather than expect submission to his will.

Rousseau expresses a complementarity theory of gender relations. Man and woman are similar in many respects, and equally important, yet they differ in fundamental ways that mutually contribute to one another. There is not a perfect symmetry and reciprocity between them, however. A woman complements a man more than he does her; her function is to complete and please him:

In the union of the sexes each contributes equally to the common aim, but not in the same way. From this diversity arises the first assignable difference in the moral relations of the two sexes. One ought to be active and strong, the other passive and weak. One must necessarily will and be able; it suffices that the other put up little resistance. Once this principle is established, it follows that woman is made specially to please man. If man ought to please her in turn, it is due to a less direct necessity. His merit is his power; he pleases by the sole fact of his strength.[3]

This complementarity shows itself in a sexual division of labor. A woman should be well-trained in the arts of managing a household so that a man will have commodious surroundings and his needs will be taken care of without fanfare. She should devote herself to the care and upbringing of her children; she should be attentive to the society around her husband so as to help him interpret his friends and acquaintances and she should show herself to be a good nurse of the sick and injured. She takes satisfaction in serving as her husband's care giver, secretary, paramour, and sounding board. This is how she solves the problem of recognition for him: he relies on her for the affirmation of his self, and her role and desire is to provide this affirmation. What pleases her is to please him, and she pleases him by presenting him with an articulate reflection of his person, character, and station.

Thus the whole education of women ought to relate to men. To please men, to be useful to them, to make herself loved and honored by them, to raise them when young, to care for them when grown, to counsel them, to console

---

[3] Jean-Jacques Rousseau, *Emile* (New York: Basic Books, 1979), 358.

them, to make their lives agreeable and sweet – these are the duties of women at all times, and they ought to be taught from childhood.[4]

With an intelligent, sensitive, care giving, and faithful woman, a man attains recognition without having to worry about keeping up appearances or engaging in a competition for honor. Indeed, the man projects onto woman the anxieties associated with the scrutiny of society and the need to maintain a reputation. A woman must at all times maintain a reputation for modesty, chastity, intelligence, and caring. It is not sufficient that she do nothing against these virtues; she must at all costs also manage the social judgments of her that recognize her as upstanding and honorable. Her doing so assures the honor of her husband. He therefore does not need to be worried about the opinion of others about him. He can be independent while at the same time recognized by society's recognition of her.

When a man acts well, he depends only on himself and can brave public judgment; but when a woman acts well, she has accomplished only half her task, and what is thought of her is no less important than what she actually is. Since she is subject to the judgment of men, she ought to merit their esteem. She ought, above all, to obtain the esteem of her spouse. She ought to make him not only love her person but also approve her conduct. She ought to justify the choice he has made before the public and make her husband honored through the honor given to his wife.[5]

INTRODUCTION

Axel Honneth does not endorse Rousseau's theory of sexual complementarity and his idea that a woman exists to please man and deflect onto herself his *amour propre*. Indeed, Honneth takes special care to identify feminism as a social movement exemplary of a struggle for recognition. Especially in some of his most recent writing, Honneth gives explicit attention to issues of justice in the family and special problems of equality for women. He challenges a gender division of labor that denigrates women's work, and supports feminist calls for recognition of the unpaid work of domestic labor and for revaluation of typically female jobs of the paid workforce. In contrast to most

---

[4] Ibid., 365.
[5] Ibid., 383.

other theories of justice, moreover, Honneth makes relations of love and care constitutive for his conception of justice.

Honneth's theory of recognition, then, offers many resources for feminist social criticism. I will argue in this chapter,[6] however, that his conception of recognition of love and care is not specified enough fully to serve this purpose. In particular, Honneth does not offer a conception of reciprocity in sexual love to replace the complementarity ideology of the modern bourgeois conception of conjugal love I have quoted from Rousseau earlier, and that of Hegel after him. While Honneth calls for public recognition of unpaid housework and care work, moreover, he does not acknowledge the functional stubbornness of a gender division of labor that allocates care work primarily to women in the family. An alternative to the current gender division of labor requires conceptualizing the recognition of care work under some principle other than the achievement principle that Honneth argues dominates recognition as esteem in capitalist society. A full criticism of this gender division of labor, furthermore, requires softening the borders between esteem and care spheres of recognition, in Honneth's terms. The intent of my inquiry here is to follow Honneth's theory of recognition as far as it goes to support gender justice and equality, and to raise some questions about what else the theory of recognition requires to complete the task.

ON RECOGNITION

Recognition is central to social justice, according to Honneth, because we are reflectively self-conscious beings. A person's sense of dignity and worth derives from interaction with others who care for him or her, and acknowledge him or her as contributing to their own well being. The importance of recognition emerges from its absence or distortion in all too common experiences of degradation, violence, humiliation, exclusion, domination, and subordination. The difference between experiencing such sufferings as misfortune and calling them wrongs or injustices, Honneth argues, lies in the reflexive understanding that others actively deny one's intrinsic worth in these processes.

---

[6] My thanks to David Alexander, Christopher Zorn, Bert van den Brink, and David Owen for their comments on an earlier draft of this chapter.

An adequate theory of justice or moral rightness requires articulating three irreducible forms of recognition to account for the different possibilities of misrecognition and recognition typical of modern societies. Honneth adopts Hegel's distinction between moral spheres of family, civil society, and state to develop three principles of recognition: love, rights, and esteem. In the sphere of family and personal relations, particular others affirm the person in the specificity of his or her needs and personality. The sphere of rights recognizes individuals as bearers of rights promulgated by and enforced through law. The third principle of recognition concerns the esteem a person has in the eyes of others due to his or her contribution to production of the good life – his or her participation in collective projects and the exhibition of effort and ability in them.

Modernization consists in the progressive differentiation of each of these spheres of recognition. The sphere of state and law become institutionally differentiated from both the family and occupational networks, permitting a universalist recognition of one who has rights just because he or she is a person, and not by virtue of kinship or social station. The family and personal life specialize in care for the needs of the particular individual, and social contribution through skill and effort take on increasingly differentiated institutional forms in the modern occupational structure.

Modern history can be fruitfully interpreted as a progressive struggle over recognition in and between each of these institutionally differentiated spheres. Misrecognition, denigration, intolerance, exclusion from benefits, and hatred underlie most forms and experiences of injustice, according to Honneth. Social movements in the modern world have usually consisted in struggles to attain one or another of these forms of recognition. Emancipatory movements for civil and political rights first install the principle of equal citizen rights and then demand the extension of these rights to additional categories of people. Workers' movements demand respect for the laboring poor and recognition of their contribution to the social product in transformed systems of the allocation of material goods.[7] A major motive

---

[7] Part of the terms of the debate between Honneth and Nancy Fraser is about whether workers movements should be interpreted as emphasizing redistribution as distinct from a recognition principle, or whether worker demands for better pay and working

for participation in these struggles, according to Honneth, is anger and resentment at the denigration people suffer and their demand for dignity. Social progress, then, consists in a resolution of conflicts over recognition, and widening the extension of those included under its principles.

Love. Love is that form of recognition that affirms the person's physical and affective needs in intimate relations. Love or care are by their nature unconditional: the impulse to love arises from attraction or sympathy with vulnerability. Love and care are for the unique being of this individual. Love is the most fundamental form of recognition, because without the loving care of adults, the infant and child cannot grow into an autonomous and communicative person. "Because this relationship of recognition prepares the ground for a type of relation-to-self in which subjects mutually acquire basic confidence in themselves, it is both conceptually and genetically prior to every other form of reciprocal recognition."[8] While the sort of loving care that helps children survive and become socialized into the meanings and responsibilities of their societies is as old as humanity itself, the modern age makes this process more explicit by marking off childhood as a phase of life requiring special protections.

Only then could awareness develop within society of the special duties of care that parents (historically, of course, at first only the mother) have to assume with respect to the child in order to prepare the way from original helplessness to the development self-confidence. Parallel to this process, the recognition form of love similarly became independent: the relations between the sexes were gradually liberated from economic and social pressures and thus opened up to the feeling of mutual affection.... The recognition that individuals reciprocally bring to this kind of relationship is loving care for the other's well being in the light of his or her individual needs.[9]

Conjugal love thus represents another aspect of recognition in the family. In *The Struggle for Recognition*, Honneth closely follows Hegel's

---

conditions, even changes in property relations, form part of a complex system of claims for recognition. For Fraser's arguments, see "Social Justice in the Age of Identity Politics: Redistribution, Recognition and Participation," in Fraser & Honneth, *Redistribution or Recognition? A Political-Philosophical Exchange* (New York: Verso Publishers, 2003), 7–197.

[8] Axel Honneth, *The Struggle for Recognition: The Moral Grammar of Social Conflict*, (Cambridge, UK: Polity Press, 1995), 107.

[9] Honneth, "Redistribution as Recognition," in *Redistribution or Recognition?* 139.

discourse about conjugal love, without irony or revision. Modernity releases heterosexual love and marriage from economic imperatives and the constraints of social status, and allows women and men to choose one another for their own sakes. In conjugal love, then, the partners mutually recognize one another in their unique particularity, and each responds to the felt and expressed particular needs of the other. As we will see later, however, Hegel relies on a complementarity conception of conjugal love similar to Rousseau's in order to conceive love as mutual. I will argue that this claim of reciprocity is problematic.

Rights. Legal rights serve as a distinct form of recognition precisely because they are abstract. They do not refer to any particular attributes of a person, but instead express a recognition of the equality of all individuals as free beings and autonomous sources of ends. In contrast to previous social systems, the modern order of legal rights detaches this form of the recognition of equal formal personhood from reference to any role or status. Recognizing individuals as legal persons means granting them entitlements simply by virtue of being persons, and not due to family connection, occupation, or the satisfactory performance of activities. Rights acknowledge the person as a source of independent judgment: she or he can enter contracts, has the ability to consent or not, can deliberate and vote on leaders and legislation, and so on.

Esteem. It is not enough that individuals be recognized in the particularity of their needs and personality or the generality of their humanity apart from their attributes or achievements. In addition to these forms of the recognition of who the person *is*, there must be recognition for what he or she *does*. This is the general sphere of recognition Honneth calls esteem. In many societies, persons have social places that assign them status and the activities and skills appropriate to this status. Modern society progressively throws off such status recognition, according to Honneth, and increasingly rewards people according to their individual achievements in contributing to cooperative social life.

Thus social esteem is henceforth no longer linked to legal privileges of any sort, and does not constitutively include the designation of moral qualities of one's personality. Rather, 'prestige' or 'standing' signifies only the degree of social recognition the individual earns for his or her form of self-realization by thus contributing, to a certain extent, to the practical realization of society's abstractly defined goals.[10]

In industrial capitalist society, people most commonly show esteem for one another or denigrate one another according to the work they do – both the occupation they follow, how well they do it, and thus how much they are perceived to contribute to the social good. Premodern societies, by contrast, measure a person's status in terms of social honor. In this social system, persons occupy relatively unchangeable social positions in a hierarchy organized by a holistic ideology of how each position contributes to the social good. People are expected not simply to do their jobs well, but to follow customs and conventions of appropriate behavior and comportment for their station. In such a system, people within status groups esteem one another for properly performing their roles; esteem or lack of esteem for persons outside the groups is organized hierarchically. In modern social organization, by contrast, persons are esteemed according to the development of their own abilities and the accomplishments they make with them.

Modern capitalist society differentiates each of these forms of recognition into distinct institutional spheres, according to Honneth: love flourishes in the family, state and law recognize rights, and civil society and economic activity are the sphere of esteem. Each modern sphere of recognition, however, contains an internal conflict over the legitimate applications of its principle. Honneth argues that this theory of recognition is the best framework for interpreting social movements' claims that they are victims of injustice.

In intimate relationships this internal conflict typically takes the form of bringing forth newly developed or previously unconsidered needs by appeal to the mutually attested love in order to demand a different or expanded kind of care. In the sphere of modern law, it means including the excluded on terms of equal rights. In the esteem sphere, individuals bring forth neglected or underappreciated activities to demand social esteem.[11]

---

[10] *Struggle for Recognition,* 126.
[11] "Redistribution as Recognition," 144.

In his recent writing, Honneth pays more attention to the systematically distorted form of esteem dominant in capitalist society than he did in *The Struggle for Recognition*. In capitalist society, the distribution of goods and benefits is tied to control over capital resources and the operation of markets. Capital accumulation and market volatility generate inevitable inequalities, often severe inequality that gives to a wealthy few vast economic decision making power and deprives many others of the means of survival unless there is publicly funded welfare support. When a principle of social esteem has been separated from status hierarchy, however, it is difficult to justify this inequality. Honneth notes that "the achievement principle henceforth forms the backdrop of normative legitimation which, in case of doubt, has to provide rational grounds for publicly justifying the privileged appropriation of particular resources like money or credentials."[12] Within modern capitalist society, however, the achievement principle is one-sided and ideological, because it "is defined against a value standard whose normative reference point is the economic activity of the independent, middle-class, male bourgeois."[13]

Here is what I understand Honneth to mean by this. The achievement principle says that individuals will be esteemed and receive material compensation according to how they apply their talents to productive ends. The one-sided model, however, is that of the entrepreneur: he or she begins with capital, which he or she owns or borrows, uses the capital to invest in materials and labor power, makes a product that sells, and receives a reward for ingenuity, hard work, and a shrewd sense of what people want, in the form of high profits. While the achievement principle tries to view all distributions to both the rich and poor on this model of productive contribution, the model is distorted. Those without access to capital depend for their material well-being on the decisions and fortunes of those with capital than on their own ingenuity and hard work, and they are at the mercy of labor markets for employment opportunities. The standards according to which the productivity of employees will be measured, moreover, assume certain kinds of work and the measurability of quantities and quality of work done. A struggle for recognition of social contribution, then,

---

[12] Ibid., 148.
[13] Ibid., 141.

means not only recognizing the social value of more kinds of work and recognizing the skills and accomplishments of individuals instead of excluding them from equal compensation because of their group membership or unchangeable personal attributes. Recognition may entail de-coupling esteem from markets in capital and labor.[14]

HONNETH'S FEMINISM

Unlike many theorists articulating a general social theory and theory of justice, Honneth explicitly emphasizes issues of gender justice and concern for equality of women.[15] He applies his theory of recognition in several ways to issues of male supremacy and the devaluation and inequality of women. I rely primarily on two recent texts for his discussion of women's issues: "Redistribution as Recognition," which I have already referred to, and "Between Justice and Affection: The Family as a Field of Moral Disputes."[16]

Honneth is aware that the differentiation of a specific sphere of love where children and adults have their particular needs and personality cared for comes, at least initially, with special burdens for women. The individual's development calls attention to the special duties of parents, and especially mothers, to devote energy and intelligence to the individuation and socialization of children. By implication, this is time and intelligence diverted from other possible pursuits.

The specialization of the family in love relations that recognize the person in the individuality of her or his needs puts pressure on sexual relations and marriage to separate them from imperatives of economic or political alliance or simply domination over women by men, and

[14] I consider Honneth's claim that the achievement principle operates ideologically and is biased against less-advantaged people to resonate with arguments I have made against standard uses of ideas of qualification and productivity in job assignment. See Iris Marion Young, *Justice and the Politics of Difference* (Princeton: Princeton University Press, 1990), Chapter 7, "Affirmative Action and the Myth of Merit."

[15] For a useful interpretation of the ideas in *The Struggle for Recognition* for feminist ends, see Christopher F. Zurn, "The Normative Claims of Three Types of Feminist Struggles for Recognition," in *Philosophy Today*, Supplement 1997, 73–78; for a criticism of Honneth's ideas from a feminist point of view, see Kelly Oliver, *Witnessing: Beyond Recognition* (Minneapolis: University of Minnesota Press, 2001), 46–49.

[16] In *Privacies: Philosophical Evaluations*, edited by Beate Rössler (Stanford: Stanford University Press, 2004), 142–167.

to encourage the free choice of partners by women as well as men. Thereby a certain principle of equality between the sexes emerges. Insofar as women do not have legal rights as persons, however, such equality is only a promise. Thus a major form of the feminist struggle for equality consists in the legal recognition of women as full bearers of civil and political rights independently of their fathers or husbands.

Here, the central argument is that, in view of the structural domination of men in the private sphere, the preconditions for women's self-determination can only be secured when they take the form of contractually guaranteed rights, and hence are made an imperative of legal recognition.[17]

Honneth is particularly sensitive to the denigration of women's work, both inside the home and in more formal occupational settings. An aspect of the ideological application of the achievement principle, he says, is its judgment that the work women do is not a contribution as worthy of recognition as other kinds of work. Honneth attributes such devaluation of women's work to modernity's carrying over the traditional ideals of women's "nature" as fulfilling certain functions.

(T)he whole way of evaluating achievement was also influenced from the start by encompassing horizons of interpretation whose origins lie not in the evaluations of the capitalist elite, but in much older worldviews that nonetheless help determine what counts as an expression of individual effort. Naturalistic thinking, which attributes essentialist collective properties to social subgroups so that their practical efforts are not viewed as "achievement" or "work," but merely as the realization of an "innate nature, plays an especially big role here. Within the social-ontological horizon of this naturalism, the activities of the housewife or mother, for instance, are never viewed as a "productive" contribution to social reproduction that would justify any form of social esteem, while women's work in the formally organized sector is not believed to be as productive as that of men, since according to women's nature it involves less physical or mental exertion.[18]

This cultural disparagement of what is female, Honneth continues, is a holdover from a system of status hierarchy that conflicts with the achievement principle of social esteem; it explains the devaluation of most paid occupations that are dominated by or particularly associated with women. Nothing in the nature of these forms of work, nor the

---

[17] "Redistribution as Recognition," 189.
[18] "Redistribution as Recognition," 148.

skill and intelligence required to perform many typically women's jobs, accounts for this lack of recognition.

To summarize, Honneth understands that an important basis for the persistence of gender based inequality lies in a division of labor that assigns women primary responsibility for attending to the material and emotional needs of men and children. He criticizes the fact that these unpaid contributions of care workers to individual and social well-being are not properly recognized, and even denigrated by a public society oriented to achievement. He recognizes that this sexual division of labor limits the opportunities of many women to earn an independent living or pursue a career, and finds fault with the devaluation of paid occupations in which women predominate, and which are often associated with service or care work.

The main explanation that Honneth offers for this unequal recognition is a naturalistic thinking that believes housecleaning and care work are expressions of women's nature.

This seems a rather shallow explanation for a gender division of labor that persists long after women have obtained equal rights and admission to the achievement world. Despite his sensitivity to feminist analysis, Honneth does not sufficiently appreciate the extent to which the gender system he criticizes is integral to this particularly modern division between principles of affection and achievement.

Nor does Honneth raise enough questions about what struggles for recognition in the family mean. In his account, it appears that the sphere of love has a recognition dynamic different from that of the other two spheres. Whereas progress in the struggle for recognition in the spheres of rights or esteem involves extending these to more agents, moral progress in the sphere of affection concerns expanding an understanding of what needs of individual persons deserve attention. Honneth appears to assume that the affection in bourgeois marriage is indeed mutual, and that the struggle is over its content and quality. He seems not to find *equality* at issue in the family in the same way as in the public realms of rights and esteem.

In the concluding section of this chapter, I probe these issues. I will argue that the modern understanding of conjugal love operates in a biased or ideological way, just as Honneth argues that the achievement principle within capitalism tends to operate in a one-sided manner. I will suggest, further, that care work cannot easily be recognized as a social contribution within the dominant structures of esteem. Unjust gender divisions, then, require both reinterpretations of the practices of love and care, an alteration in the status accorded achievement, and a greater challenge to the division between the two spheres.

RECOGNITION OF LOVE'S LABOR

I began this chapter by quoting Rousseau in order to remind ourselves that inegalitarian gender structures have a specifically *modern* form and intention. Rousseau values an intelligent, educated woman, and he believes that marriage and sexual intercourse should have her consent. The modern Rousseauean woman has a mind of her own; her love satisfies a man's desire for recognition only if she is, and he thinks her to be, an autonomous person. At the same time, her role is confined to wife, mother, nurse, housekeeper, care giver, nurturer of a child's development. Rousseau's is a modern form of female subordination based in a principle of love: the need for children to develop as selves by means of an unconditional attentiveness from another; the need for a man who must face the world of competition for honor, status, money, power, to rely on an adoring and unquestioning recognition of his worth.[19] Rousseau theorizes love between a man and a woman as complementary; each fills a different kind of need for the other – he provides sustenance for her and she provides emotional support for him.

Hegel follows Rousseau in this account of conjugal love. The conjugal couple ideally reduces a self and other to the same. The differences between the sexes in marriage allows a complementarity in the union. The family and women's love give tranquility and feeling to the life of a man who enters a public world of struggle for "self-subsistent unity with himself."[20] Conjugal love, as articulated by Rousseau and Hegel,

[19] Even feminists of the eighteenth or nineteenth century were committed to this view of sentimental family and women's occupation. Neither Mary Wollstonecraft nor John Stuart Mill believed that marriage must be a woman's destiny, and both argued for equal rights for the individual woman even within marriage. With Rousseau they shared an important opinion, however. If a woman marries, her duty is to devote her intelligence and energy to the care of the household, the well-being and education of her children, and the support of her husband.

[20] G. W. F. Hegel, *Philosophy of Right*, transl. T. M. Knox (Oxford: Oxford University Press, 1967), §66.

involves a *mutual* recognition only if the woman in the pair makes no claims for independent recognition either in the family or in the sphere of esteem. In the modern conjugal circle, one party desires and ideally receives recognition from another subject able to be the source of her own ends and who chooses to take her husband's ends as her own.

Honneth theorizes the specifically modern character of gender relations in terms of the separation of marriage and family from political, social, and economic imperatives. Principles of love, affection, and care come to their own in the modern world when they constitute the only source of integration among family members. Love and care become distinct spheres of recognition when social practices and values require the cultivation and development of the person as an individual. Childhood emerges as a distinct and fragile stage of life, requiring of parents not simply that they maintain the child's physical being, but also provide support for development of his autonomous self and skills.

In earlier writing about love and the family, Honneth more or less uncritically adopted Hegel's views about the mutuality and complementarity of husband and wife, and the fulfillment of their union in the child.[21] In more recent writing, however, Honneth takes some distance from this harmonious image. Whereas Hegel finds that relations of love in the family properly recognize and sustain the particularity of all its members, Honneth now argues that bonds of affection are too fragile to sustain justice in the family. Left to itself, there is nothing to protect family members from the domination of kin who misrecognize their needs or have lost affection for them. To sustain justice, Honneth argues, taking his lesson from nineteenth- and twentieth-century feminist movements, particularistic relations between men and women in marriage must be nested in a universalistic legal system that guarantees equal rights for all individuals. The sphere of rights, that is, protects against abuses in the sphere of love.[22] Honneth properly argues that bringing rights to bear on relations between adults in the family mitigates some of the risks that separation of the principle of love from

---

[21] Cf. *The Struggle for Recognition*.

[22] Honneth, "Between Justice and Affection: The Family as a Field of Moral Disputes," op. cit., 1142–167.

social and economic imperatives creates. In this account, Honneth does not interrogate the Rousseauean-Hegelian idealization of conjugal love itself, however. Nor has he yet sufficiently attended to problems in the relation of the sphere of love to the sphere of esteem. I will close my analysis with an exploration of these two points.

(1) Conjugal Love as Ideology

The bourgeois ideal of conjugal love celebrated by Rousseau has living echoes in contemporary popular narratives of love, as well as in the desires and aspirations of many individuals. Is it possible that this ideal of love functions in a biased and one-sided manner in male-dominated modern society, much as Honneth argues that the achievement principle is biased and one-sided in capitalist society? Let me suggest how it might be so.

In her magisterial book, *Speculum of the Other Woman*, as well as in more recent writings, Luce Irigaray criticizes the sort of love that Rousseau extols. Apparently mutual, heterosexual love is more often a reduction of the other to the same. In the perfect conjugal relationship, one subject desires and receives recognition from another subject who reflects the first subject's projects and values back on to himself. The husband's recognition of the wife, in this configuration, consists in the recognition of his own reflection in another subject. The womanly lover plays an active role in this union. She herself, however, does not achieve recognition from him on the same terms. Relations between lovers in this conjugal model are essentially hierarchical because, as Irigaray analyzes it, this form of love seeks to reduce the other to the same. She supports his projects, she works for the enhancement of his public appearance. On this interpretation of the struggle for recognition in love, the lover who seeks to be recognized through love is more self-referential than reciprocating.[23]

The one-sidedness of this model of complementarity has been under attack for more than a century. In most societies today, larger or smaller segments agree that each partner in a love relationship should recognize the other as a free-standing individual with her own

---

[23] Irigaray, *Speculum of the Other Woman*, op. cit.

needs and projects, and not desire that the other person merge her self with his and serve his projects in ways that preclude having those of her own of equal importance which he recognizes. Honneth says that love consists in recognizing the needs of the individual, and that progress in love consists in expanding the scope of needs recognized. It is difficult to understand just how love can be mutual in an egalitarian way and at the same time expand its recognition. Each of us would like more attention, more understanding, and more soothing than we get. If there is a social or existential problem here, it may be with a desire for recognition itself. When a lover seeks recognition from the beloved in the form of a mirror of his or her self, he or she occupies the master position in Hegel's dialectic of recognition. Simone de Beauvoir recast this dialectic in gendered terms in her analysis of the position of woman as the Other to man's subjectivity, and Irigaray takes Beauvoir another step. If the desire for recognition in love retains this structure as a desire for a reflection of myself from the other person, but both partners assert an equal claim in such recognition, then a classic Hegelian struggle for recognition is likely to ensue. It would seem that only if desires and relations of subjects in love have a different dynamic can a destructive struggle be avoided.[24] I am not suggesting that Honneth's conception of love as recognition necessarily entails this mirroring structure. The point is that he had not specified what love as recognition might mean that avoids this problem with the modern conjugal ideal.

The model of conjugal love that traditionally assumed the man's subjectivity for which a woman's love served as mirror and complement has come into question, but retains many cultural and affective roots. I fear, however, that we have not replaced this conjugal model on a society-wide basis with realistic egalitarian free and mutual practices of sexual love. In the meantime, couples split in disappointment, or men beat and abuse women whom they find insubordinate, or they order brides from overseas whom they imagine will be self-effacing

[24] Patchen Markell analyzes the dialectic of recognition as having such a potentially destructive aspect, and proposes an alternative subject to subject relation, which he refers to as "acknowledgment." See Markell, *Bound by Recognition* (Princeton: Princeton University Press, 2003).

and adoring.[25] If we seek genuine mutuality and equality in love, then neither partner can expect mirroring of his or her subjectivity from the other. Perhaps this implies that our understanding of love should shift toward a model of care.

(2) Care Work

Care presents special difficulties, however, from the point of view of an interest in gender equality. Because care giving involves an asymmetrical relationship, it is difficult, though not impossible, for care givers and care receivers to live in terms of equality and mutuality. Care work, secondly, cannot be brought under a public achievement principle without losing its specific qualities. This complicates the feminist project of undermining the gender division of labor and giving recognition to the social contributions of domestic labor.

The principle of care, according to Honneth, involves recognizing the needs of individuals in their particularity. Moral progress in the sphere of care involves expanding the scope of individual needs that the caring one recognizes, and recognizing them in their individuality instead of as types or categories of neediness. The care principle is different both from principles of rights and esteem in this respect. Moral progress in the latter concern expanding the scope of persons and types of persons who deserve recognition under the principles. Ideally, the principles of rights and esteem should include everyone. Reciprocity in these spheres means equal standing, in the case of rights, or valuing the standards of excellence of diverse social contributions that persons make. Equality in the sphere of care is not homologous to these other two principles. Indeed, it is difficult to see what equality in care means, because care relations involve a kind of asymmetry inimical to the spheres of rights and esteem.

The invention of childhood, Honneth thinks, is crucial for the emergence of ideals of personal autonomy as the ability to contribute to social well-being from a choice among a range of opportunities. As a specific stage, childhood is more than years of dependency on others for physical security and the meeting of needs. It is also a period when

---

[25] See Nancy J. Hirschmann, *The Subject of Liberty: Toward a Feminist Theory of Freedom* (Princeton: Princeton University Press, 2003), 111–113.

care givers nurture in a person a stable sense of self, and the ability to reflect on one's own action and position in a complex social structure, to interact with others with cooperative generosity, and to develop intricate physical and cognitive skills. We should not forget that hundreds of millions of children in the world today are not afforded the opportunity for childhood in this sense, largely because the adults around them lack the material and experiential means to provide it. That all children should be cared for in this deep sense for a period of ten to twenty years is nevertheless a proper human rights aspiration.

The relationship of dependent and developing children to their care givers, however, is not reciprocal. The love with which children respond to care is unique in the world in its spontaneity, warmth, and loyalty. Even very young children, moreover, sometimes show care and concern for the needs of those they love. The relation between caring adult and child, however, is necessarily asymmetrical – because the care receiver depends on the care giver in a way that the giver does not depend on the receiver. Caring for children also involves a large amount of unreciprocated work – cleaning the child's environment and making it safe, getting, preparing and offering food, and teaching. This work has many satisfactions, including the gratitude those cared for sometimes express, but it is not work that is reciprocated.

Although the relation of adult care givers to dependent children most typifies these asymmetries of power, dependence, and unreciprocated labor, they structure to some extent all relations between care givers and receivers. Most of those who need care – sick and injured people, some people with physical and mental disabilities, frail old people, and all of us sometimes when we are stretched for time or emotionally wounded – are not in a position to care for the care givers, at least at the time they receive care. While care receivers are on the dependent end of a power relation with care givers, they also benefit from the labor of the care givers in ways they do not reciprocate.[26]

This asymmetrical character of care relations raises questions about what recognition means in the sphere of care. Looked at from the point of view of the one cared for, it is fairly clear what recognition means: the particular needs of the person are attended to by another. Of

---

[26] Joan Tronto discusses these dependencies and asymmetries of power in *Moral Boundaries* (New York: Routledge, 1992).

course there are issues of equality and dignity for the one cared for –
the asymmetry in caring often makes the care giver more powerful.
Presumably recognition is not extended in a care-giving relationship
when the asymmetrical power relation renders the one cared for dominated or demeaned. There would seem to be more to recognition
relations between care givers and care receivers, however, than merely
being treated with respect.

As so far developed by Honneth, recognition in the sphere of care
seems to assume this position of the subject cared for. But what of the
one doing the caring? She too has particular needs that deserve attention. Traditionally, the complementarity theory of gender difference
has applied to caring as well: the best care givers find their fulfillment
in care giving and do not themselves need to be cared for, and all they
need is adoring smiles of pleasure from their charges. If in fact everyone needs care in some respects some of the time, needs recognition
as a vulnerable person, then this sex-role theory was always suspect.
Increasing commitment to gender equality renders this complementarity view theoretically unsustainable today. In practice, however, society continues to rely to a significant degree on the implicit assumption
that there is always someone in the family who will take care of its
members when social services are inadequate.

Honneth's answer to the question "Who will care for the care
givers"? is to recommend a norm of reciprocity in the sphere of care.
If the relation of care giving and care receiving are asymmetrical, however, it is not apparent what this means. Reciprocity in the sphere
of esteem is easy to imagine. You and I start a conversation about a
philosophical problem, we exchange proposals and arguments, and we
criticize one another. We esteem one another reciprocally and simultaneously just to the degree that each of us pushes the other to think
harder. But caring is not like that. Reciprocity in caring is more like
taking turns: I care for you now in this respect, you care for me later in
that or another respect.[27] Certainly there are many love relationships
with that structure. The demands of both the sphere of esteem and
the sphere of care as currently structured in our societies, however,

---

[27] I read Eva Kittay as theorizing reciprocity in care giving as taking turns in this sort of
  way. See *Love's Labor: Essays on Women, Equality and Dependency* (New York: Routledge,
  1999).

make it very difficult for those who seek the recognition of esteem, especially as applied in the achievement principle, also to stand as care givers in a sustained way. This is the main reason that even in the most progressive of liberal and social democratic societies today that caring and achieving remain highly gender-segregated spheres.

Honneth is acutely aware of this continuing gender division of labor. His primary way of addressing it is to call for public recognition of care work in the sphere of esteem. Moral progress in the sphere of esteem consists in extending the scope of activities that count as making social contributions to include those unpaid activities that constitute socially necessary labor. In this formulation, nothing needs to change in the esteem or achievement principle, it just should be applied to new efforts and activities. It is not clear what it can mean to bring the work of caring under the esteem principle, however. To be sure, housework can be evaluated in its efficiency and effectiveness. Just because care work involves recognizing and attending to the particular needs of an individual in a personal and intimate manner, however, it cannot be generalized under standards of excellence without undermining its meaning.

The commodification of care work tends to lead to branding and marketing ploys that entice buyers without enhancing service, and often at the same time skimping on the service provision itself. For-profit child care centers, for example, often have glitzy decor to attract parents and children, but are insufficiently staffed to provide the kind of continuous quality care that includes individualized attention, educational programming, and outings. For-profit nursing homes for frail old people are notorious in the United States for providing poor care, largely because they are architecturally inadequate for elder privacy and comfort, and short staffed.[28]

When care work in non-profit or public settings is adequately resourced, it is likely to be of higher quality because it does not face the same marketing and profit imperatives. In our world, this is rarely true, of course, and is increasingly less true as welfare states all over the world cut back on support for social services, and privatize many

[28] See Iris Marion Young, "A Room of One's Own: Privacy and Old Age Residence," in *On Female Body Experience: 'Throwing Like a Girl' and Other Essays* (New York: Oxford University Press, 2004).

that were once state run. Even when adequately resourced, however, institutionalized and bureaucratic settings can rarely fully substitute for the way loving persons care for the needs of those with whom they are in long-term intimate relations; staff to whom care receivers have formed attachments leave and the rules of institutions impede the recognition of some of the particular needs or preferences of its wards. In this respect, Honneth is right to separate care as a principle of recognition distinct from rights and esteem.

What conclusions shall we draw about Honneth's recognition theory from these considerations? First, it is only minimally possible to recognize love's labor in a "wages for housework" strategy. We cannot get very far in recognizing the contribution of care workers by trying to convert that contribution into the currency of achievement in the public world of market and state. Properly to esteem those who do care work requires separating esteem from the achievement principle. Modern societies have always tried to find ways of publicly honoring wives and mothers, however, with medals and speeches and special holidays. Feminists find these gestures hollow and demeaning, because the achievement principle continues to define what counts as a "real" contribution. In his recent work, Honneth is right to point out that the primary allocation of the esteem principle in our society – achievement – operates as an ideology to legitimate inequality. In light of that argument, more needs to be said about what an alternative institutionalization of esteem could mean for us. Having such an account would help interpret what esteem for care work can mean. In filling out such an ideal of esteem, moreover, we might need to consider Rousseau's distrust of this particular desire for recognition. How can esteem be mutual, that is, instead of generating a competitive spiral?

A more specified theory and practice of esteem, however, would not yet address the problems with the gender division of labor. I have argued that this gender division does not derive primarily from outdated beliefs in women's natural attributes. It is, rather, functional for a social system that requires that much time, energy, and intelligence be devoted to caring at the same time that the society's primary economic rewards lie in market activity. The systematic assumption of a specialization in private care work, and the socialization of girls and boys in accordance with this assumption, allows the society to depend on care givers without noticing how much they do. A theory of recognition might probe the asymmetry of the caring relationship more, to theorize the satisfactions that care givers often obtain from their activities, which are not symmetrical with the recognition that care receivers obtain. Even with such satisfactions, however, families following the existing gender division of labor with women as care workers and men as achievers are now vulnerable to poverty; in the United States, it now takes a two income family to bring in a middle-level household income. The existing gender division of labor, moreover, limits the opportunities of primary care givers to develop skills and creative capacities in other recognized activities.

The proper way to address these problems is to encourage everyone – women and men – to participate in care work, and at the same time to make it possible for all care workers to have time and training for other socially valued activities. For all members of a society to have equal opportunity to be esteemed for their social contributions, that is, and at the same time not rendered vulnerable to poverty, the institutionalized borders between the esteem principle and the care principle should become more permeable without dissolving. It would seem as well that the dominance of achievement as the primary interpretation of esteem should be questioned. Through the achievement principle, people deserve esteem when they excel on productivity measures, when they attain to positions culturally coded as high status, or when they win out in a competition where most are losers. A theory of the recognition of love's labor can do more to envision a conception of esteem that does not measure people's achievements in these ways.

Axel Honneth's theory of recognition is rich because it divides recognition into three forms. This enables us both to see ways that one form can support another, and the potential tensions among them. So far, however, what recognition means historically and can mean is more developed for his theory in respect to rights and esteem than in respect to love. I have argued that the theory at least requires more specification about what mutual recognition can mean in relationships of love and care. These relationships typically involve asymmetries in modern societies that stand in some tension with goals of reciprocity and equality. Honneth pays more attention to the implications of the division of labor in the family for the ability of women to attain recognition in the sphere of esteem than do most theorists of justice. However, he underestimates the ease of bestowing esteem on unpaid care work. The theory then requires more reflection on the relationship and tensions between spheres of love and esteem. Pursuing these tasks of specifying the meaning of equal recognition in relationships of love and care may call for more fundamental revisions in the theory of recognition. For now I leave this as an open question.

PART III

RECOGNITION AND POWER
IN POLITICAL THEORY

9

"To Tolerate Means to Insult"

Toleration, Recognition, and Emancipation

Rainer Forst

1

In contemporary political discourse, the concept of toleration plays an important role, ranging from questions of the toleration of cultural and religious minorities within states to the alleged global "clash of civilisations." But while for some, toleration appears to be the magic word invoking a peaceful and cooperative way of living together in mutual *recognition* and political equality, for others it is a word signifying *power*, domination, and exclusion. And this ambivalence about the concept of toleration is not a recent phenomenon, for if we go back to the classic discussions of toleration in the Age of Enlightenment, the latter critique is what Goethe meant when he said: "Tolerance should be a temporary attitude only: it must lead to recognition. To tolerate means to insult."[1] And the former praise of toleration is expressed by

[1] "Toleranz sollte nur eine vorübergehende Gesinnung sein: sie muss zur Anerkennung führen. Dulden heißt beleidigen." Johann Wolfgang Goethe, "Maximen und Reflexionen," *Werke* 6 (Frankfurt am Main: Insel, 1981), 507.

For helpful comments, I thank the participants of the symposium "Recognition and Power" in Utrecht, the Seminar in Ethics and Public Affairs at the Center for Human Values in Princeton and the Colloquia in Political Theory at Columbia University, the New School for Social Research, and the University of Toronto. I am especially indebted to Bert van den Brink, Sankar Muthu, Jeremy Waldron and Melissa Williams for their profound and challenging written comments, as well as to Joel Anderson for a number of important suggestions. The chapter attempts to provide a short synopsis of central ideas and arguments of my study *Toleranz im Konflikt. Geschichte, Gehalt und Gegenwart eines umstrittenen Begriffs* (Frankfurt am Main: Suhrkamp, 2003), an English version of which is in preparation.

Voltaire, who spoke of toleration as *l'apanage de l'humanité*, as a sign of true humanity (though also as the fate of humankind).[2]

To gain a deeper understanding of this ambivalence, I want to tell two stories about toleration – a dark and pessimistic one and a bright and optimistic one – and I want to argue that from a sufficiently complex historical perspective, both of them are true. More than that, they are not just historically true; they still inform the contemporary meaning and practices of toleration. Toleration can be based on mutual *recognition* and respect, and it can also be an expression of disrespect and *domination*, which, however, also figures as a kind of "recognition" of minorities. *Emancipation*, to mention the third concept in my title, can then at the same time mean to fight for and to fight against toleration – that is, to fight for and against certain forms of recognition.

Ultimately, the discussion of my two stories leads to the following conclusions. First, to a critique of certain forms of "recognition" and their inherent power relations. Second, to some considerations as to what motivates those who fight against "false" recognition: Is there a desire for the "true" recognition of one's identity at work here, and if so, how is it to be understood? And third, I develop a normative justification for toleration that avoids the shortcomings of some interpretations of that concept and does justice to the struggles for justified forms of toleration and – as I will argue – equal respect.

2

But before I start with my two stories, a word about the general concept of toleration. Its core can be explained by the three components of *objection*, *acceptance*, and *rejection*.[3] First, a tolerated belief or

---

[2] Voltaire, *Dictionnaire Philosophique*, ed. by A. Pous (Paris: Gallimard, 1994), article entitled "Tolerance."

[3] With respect to the first two components, I follow Preston King, *Toleration* (New York: St. Martin's Press, 1976), ch 1. Glen Newey, *Virtue, Reason and Toleration* (Edinburgh: Edinburgh University Press, 1999), ch. 1, also distinguishes between three kinds of reasons in his structural analysis of toleration (which, however, differs from mine in the way these reasons are interpreted). For a more extensive discussion, see my "Toleration, Justice and Reason," in Catriona McKinnon and Dario Castiglione (eds.), *The Culture of Toleration in Diverse Societies* (Manchester: Manchester University Press, 2003), 71–85.

practice has to be judged as false or bad in order to be a candidate for toleration; second, apart from these reasons for objection, there have to be reasons why it would still be wrong not to tolerate these false or bad beliefs or practices – that is, reasons of acceptance. Such reasons do not eliminate the reasons of objection; rather, they trump them in a given context. And third, there have to be reasons for rejection that mark the limits of toleration. These limits lie where reasons of acceptance run out, so to speak.[4] All three of those reasons can be of the same kind – religious, for example – yet they can also be of different kinds (moral, religious, pragmatic, to mention a few possibilities).

Obviously, this definition is very general, and the problems begin once these components are fleshed out: What can or should be tolerated, for what reasons, and where are the limits of toleration? Toleration as such, it seems to me, is a *normatively dependent concept*, one that is in need of other, independent normative resources in order to gain a certain content and substance – and in order to be something good at all. Hence, an important aspect of every story about toleration is how the three components gain substantive content.

3

My first story about toleration and recognition starts in sixteenth-century France. In the course of the second half of that century, the party of the *politiques* gained and propagated the conviction that the principle of *une foi, une loi, un roi* could no longer be sustained, for the price to be paid for oppressing the Calvinist minority of the Huguenots was too high, economically, politically, and morally. Political unity could only be saved if the aim of religious unity was to a certain extent given up; *constituenda religione* and *constituenda republica* had to be separated and the monarch had to play not a perfectly "neutral" role, but a role of sovereign umpire and ruler. It took, however, until 1598 – and long and bloody fights, especially the St. Bartholomew's massacre in 1572 – before Henri IV, a former Protestant who had converted to Catholicism after becoming King – issued the famous Edict of Nantes. This Edict clearly *recognized* the Huguenots as French citizens, though as citizens of a second class. They were granted the

---

4 On this, see my "The Limits of Toleration," in *Constellations* 11 (2004): 312–325.

liberty to practice their religion only at specified places (not in Paris) and at certain times, and the Edict carefully explained which public offices they could hold, where and what kinds of schools and universities they could found, and where they could build "security zones" with armed forces. Hence, the Calvinist minority became recognized and was protected by law, but at the same time the law fixed their position in a situation of being "merely" tolerated, being dependent upon the goodwill of the authority and always taking second place after Catholics in everyday life. This kind of recognition/toleration, to be sure, was a great advantage compared with the prior situation (and later periods of oppression), yet it also meant a certain form of cultural and social stigmatization, political powerlessness, and dependency.

This is the kind of toleration that Goethe had in mind when he spoke of the insult of toleration, and also what Kant meant when he criticized the "presumptuous title of tolerant" (*hochmüthig*), and what lead Mirabeau to say that toleration is a sign of tyranny.[5] These quotations also show that the almost 200 years between the Edict of Nantes and the French Revolution had not altered the structure of this kind of toleration. For example, we also find it in the English Toleration Act of 1689, right after the "Glorious Revolution," which was declared to be "an Act for Exempting Their Majesties Protestant Subjects, Dissenting from the Church of England, from the Penalties of certain Laws,"[6] which shows that this act clearly defines which dissenters (Presbyterians, Independents, Baptists, and Quakers) fall under these *exemptions* from the – still valid – laws of uniformity and conformity with the Church of England and which do not (the unitarian Socinians, for example and, of course, atheists). Also, Catholics were excluded from toleration by the oath of allegiance that subjects of the king had to take. The result is a complex picture of inclusion and exclusion, of a majority and of various minorities, some of which were tolerated and some of which were not. Those who were tolerated were at the

---

5 Immanuel Kant, "An Answer to the Question: 'What is Enlightenment?'" in: *Political Writings*, ed. by H. Reiss, trans. by H. B. Nisbet (Cambridge: Cambridge University Press, 1991, 2nd. ed.), 58; Comte de Mirabeau, Speech in the National Assembly on August 22, 1789, discussing the *Declaration des droits de l'homme et du citoyen*.

6 See the text of the Act in Ole Grell, Jonathan I. Israel, and Nicholas Tyacke (eds.), *From Persecution to Toleration* (Oxford: Clarendon, 1991), 411–422.

same time *included and excluded*; they enjoyed a certain recognition and security that the others did not have, but they were dependent upon the protection of the monarch, and thus had to show extreme loyalty. A complex matrix of power had developed that worked with different forms of recognition.

The same holds true of another example, which I want to mention briefly, the so-called *Toleranzpatente* of the Hapsburg Emperor Joseph II in 1781 who – in contrast to his mother Maria Theresa who wanted to enforce religious unity – understood that in a time of intense religious strife, the most rational form of exercising political power was a kind of *discipline and peace through granting freedom*: this "enlightened monarch" was enlightened enough to know that toleration was the more effective policy towards powerful dissenters. Thus, he granted the liberty of the *Privat-Exercitium* of religious duties (not the public exercise of religion) to three minority confessions, the Lutherans, the Reformed, and the Greek Orthodox. It was exactly defined what they were allowed to do – for example, that their churches must not have bells and no entrances from the street. This form of liberty, Joseph was convinced, would produce good subjects out of religious dissenters who would automatically have become political opponents if no toleration were practiced. Toleration was the price to be paid for loyalty, and on the side of the subjects loyalty was the price to be paid for certain liberties and security: conformity in exchange for non-conformity.

4

Again, what we find here is the mixture of freedom and domination, of inclusion and exclusion, of recognition and disrespect that characterizes this conception of toleration, which I call the *permission conception*. According to it, toleration is a relation between an authority and a dissenting, "different" minority (or various minorities). Toleration means that the authority gives qualified permission to the members of the minority to live according to their beliefs on the condition that the minority accepts the dominant position of the authority. As long as the expression of their differences remains within limits and "private," and as long as these groups do not claim equal public and political status with the majority, they can be tolerated on both pragmatic and normative grounds – on pragmatic-strategic grounds because this form of toleration is regarded as the least costly of all possible alternatives and does not disturb civil peace and order as the dominant party defines it (but rather contributes to it), and on normative grounds because the authority may find it wrong (and in any case fruitless) to force people to give up their deep-seated beliefs or practices. In short, toleration means that the authority that has the power to interfere with the practices of the minority nevertheless tolerates it, while the minority accepts its dependent position. Thus, speaking in terms of the three components of toleration, all three of them are being defined by the authority alone.

As I said earlier, it is this conception that Kant, Mirabeau, and Goethe criticize; toleration appears to be a strategic, or at least a hierarchical, policy, and the form of recognition that is granted to minorities both gives them certain liberties *and* turns them into dependent subjects and second-class citizens. Not general and equal rights but specific permissions are granted, and they can always be revoked (as the Edict of Nantes was in 1685). Speaking in terms of recognition and power, this form of toleration had *liberating* as well as *repressive* and *disciplining* effects (the latter in Foucault's sense): liberating because it clearly was an advantage compared with the previous oppressive policies, repressive because to be tolerated meant to accept one's weak and underprivileged position, and disciplining because those policies of toleration "produced" stigmatized, non-normal identities that were at the same time socially included and excluded.[7] The "toleration" of the Jews from the Middle Ages to modern times is an obvious example of such forms of excluding inclusion; toleration always had to be paid for by stigmatization and by subservience.

5

If we look at the present discourses and practices of toleration through the lens of what I would call a *critical theory of toleration*, based on an analysis of repressive and disciplining forms of toleration, we see that

---

[7] On this point, see also Wendy Brown, "Reflections on Tolerance in the Age of Identity," in A. Botwinick and W. E. Connolly (eds.), *Democracy and Vision* (Princeton: Princeton University Press, 2001), 99–117.

the "dark" story is not yet over.[8] For contrary to what many believe, the end of absolutism was not the end of the permission conception; rather, it is still present in our societies, though now in a different, *democratic* form: the tolerating authority now appears as the authority of a democratic majority. Of course, the authorities I mentioned in my three examples were also backed by overwhelming religious and political majorities, but within a democratic regime things look different, for now it is part of the very self-understanding of the regime that it grants basic equal liberties to all citizens – and that the citizens recognize each other as free and equal. Yet in many contemporary practices of toleration, the permission conception still survives. I do not want to go into the many examples one could give for that, but only mention in passing that opponents of gay marriage laws often speak in favour of toleration but against equal rights in such cases (note the slogan of the Christian Democratic Union in Germany in the context of the debate about a certain form of gay marriage: "Tolerance yes, marriage no!"). In the famous German crucifix case – about whether the State of Bavaria may order crosses or crucifixes to hang in classrooms of public schools – many citizens, politicians, courts, and speakers for the churches found that to tolerate non-Christian minorities such that they are not forced to give up their beliefs is one thing, but to grant them equal public and symbolic status and remove the Christian symbols would be quite another: it would be anti-democratic and anti-religious and would jeopardize the very foundations of the Federal Republic.[9] Hence, the power structure of this form of

---

[8] See my *Toleranz im Konflikt*, ch. 12. I should note here that I use the term "repressive tolerance" in a way that differs from Herbert Marcuse's classic essay "Repressive Tolerance," in Robert Wolff, Barrington Moore and Herbert Marcuse, *A Critique of Pure Tolerance* (Boston: Beacon Press, 1965), 81–118. Whereas he calls a system of toleration "repressive" that veils unjust relations of power in an ideological way by neutralizing real opposition (in ideas and practice), I call forms of toleration "repressive" when they help to uphold unjustifiable relations of power by forcing those who are dominated to accept their inferior position. Critical political theory, as I envision it, would primarily be based on an analysis of existing "relations of justification" among members of a social and political basic structure. See also, in a different context, Rainer Forst, "Towards a Critical Theory of Transnational Justice," in Thomas Pogge (ed.), *Global Justice* (Oxford: Blackwell, 2001), 169–187.

[9] I have discussed this example in R. Forst, "A Tolerant Republic?" in Jan-Werner Müller (ed.), *German Ideologies Since 1945* (New York: Palgrave, 2003), 209–220.

toleration/recognition is still very much at work: inclusion and exclusion at the same time.

6

But here my second, more optimistic story starts. Following Foucault, we might say that where there is power – as opposed to domination – there is freedom and there is counter-power, resistance.[10] It is the very insight that modern power works through granting liberties and not through repression simply, thereby trying to *produce* "loyal" subjects, that questions the idea of fully "imposed" and "produced" identities of subjects who are nothing but "subjected." Identity construction does not work in just one direction: being subjected to certain institutions and practices of power forms its subjects not just in line with these practices but also *against* them; otherwise there are no demands for freedom or toleration in the first place and no need for more refined strategies of power.

My second story starts from the thesis that most of those religious groups whose identities were either not positively recognized at all and were persecuted, or were only partially recognized in policies of toleration, did form a certain *identity in and through struggle*. What made them question established forms of recognition (or misrecognition) was precisely the fact that they had generated the power *from within* to form an identity, as opposed to such regimes of toleration (though of course not one that was totally independent from their surrounding culture and society): the failure of recognition by the majority did *not* result in a loss of identity or the imposition of an externally constructed identity that was taken over (though this was partially possible),[11] but in the transformation of a primarily religious identity into a political identity of struggle and opposition, possibly even of warfare. Internal forms of recognition of this identity's generating sufficient self-esteem were the precondition of being able to fight at all; hence, what we find here is a struggle for recognition, which at the same time does

---

[10] See especially the essays in Michel Foucault, *The Politics of Truth*, ed. by S. Lotriner and L. Hochroth (New York: Semiotext(e), 1997). Foucault himself, however, did not analyse modern practices of toleration as forms of power.

[11] Still the *locus classicus* for such forms of "double-consciousness" is W. E. B. Du Bois, *The Souls of Black Folk* (New York: Signet, 1995).

not seem to be a struggle for the general social recognition or esteem of one's identity in a qualitative, Hegelian sense of *Sittlichkeit*. Rather, what was demanded was the freedom to keep one's identity as a communal one and to be recognized as equal legal and political citizens (as long as justifiable forms of toleration were the aim of these struggles, for sometimes they could of course turn into struggles for new forms of domination). A certain communal and personal identity was the precondition, not the aim of the struggle for recognition – and also of the struggle against recognition, i.e., against disciplining forms of recognition.

7

My second story about toleration also begins as a historical narrative – an extremely condensed, schematically constructed one – in the Netherlands of the sixteenth century. In the course of the battles of the primarily Protestant provinces in the north against Spanish rule and the enforcement of Catholicism, we find two important developments in the struggles for religious liberty, especially in the writings of the Calvinist monarchomachs such as Duplessis-Mornay.[12] First, a natural right to religious liberty – as God-given – was proclaimed as a basic political right, and second, a king who did not respect this basic right had to be resisted, out of a sense of political *and* religious duty. Such a tyrant had broken both the *foedus* with God and the *pactum* with the people; religious liberty accordingly was not something *granted* by the rulers; it was a natural *right* and thus a basic demand of political justice. The revolutionary result of that claim was the splitting off of the northern provinces in the "Union of Utrecht" in 1579, leading to the new republic that would become an example of toleration in the seventeenth century.

As the story goes on, the revolutionary claim of religious and political liberty as a "birthright" reappears in the context of the English Civil War.[13] The opposition to the king was justified by a "fundamental law" of justice that called for political and religious liberty; government was

---

[12] Cf. Quentin Skinner, *The Foundations of Modern Political Thought* 2 (Cambridge: Cambridge University Press, 1978), Part Three.

[13] On this period, see especially Richard Saage, *Herrschaft, Toleranz, Widerstand* (Frankfurt/M.: Suhrkamp, 1981).

no longer directly instituted by God but by men in order to safeguard the natural rights given by God to men as a special kind of "property." In the eyes of levellers such as Lilburne,[14] this kind of God-given liberty meant that any exercise of power, be it religious or political, had to be justified to the people who were "affected" (or better: "well-affected") by the laws. The right to freedom of conscience was justified with the Protestant argument that conscience was directly bound to obey and follow God and not men: a theory of the free and at the same time unfree conscience (as the "work of God," as Luther had said) that also figures prominently in Milton's thought and later in Locke's *Letter Concerning Toleration.* William Walwyn expressed this – in the debates between Independents and the Presbyterian majority in parliament – in a paradigmatic way:

> That which a man may not voluntarily binde himself to doe, or to forbear to doe, without sinne: That he cannot entrust or refer unto the ordering of any other: Whatsoever (be it Parliament, Generall Councels, or Nation-all Assemblies:) But all things concerning the worship and service of God, and of that nature; that a man cannot without wilfull sin, either binde him-selfe to doe any thing therein contrary to his understanding and conscience: not to forbeare to doe that which his understanding and conscience bindes him to performe: therefore no man can refer matters of Religion to any oth-ers regulation. And what cannot be given, cannot be received: and then as a particular man cannot be robbed of that which he never had; so neither can a Parliament, or any other just Authority be violated in, or deprived of a power which cannot be entrusted unto them.[15]

An early liberal argument of this sort for toleration is, however, highly ambiguous. On the one hand, the claim that there is a natural right to religious and political liberty does connect the demand for toleration with a radical demand for political justice – that is, the basic demand for the general justification of the exercise of political power. From this perspective, toleration is not merely an "exemption" being "granted" to some "non-normal" subjects, but a general rule

[14] See John Lilburne, *Englands Birth-Right Justified* (1645), in: *Tracts on Liberty in the Puritan Revolution* III, ed. by W. Haller (New York: Octagon, 1965), 257–308.

[15] William Walwyn, *A Helpe to the Right Understanding of a Discourse Concerning Independency* (1644/45), in *The Writings of William Walwyn*, ed. by J. R. McMichel and B. Taft (Athens: The University of Georgia Press, 1989), 136f.

of the way citizens treat each other within the confines of natural right. We see here the glimpse of a new, different conception of toleration – the *respect conception* – according to which democratic citizens respect each other as legal and political equals even though they differ greatly in their ethical-religious views about the good and true way of life. In this sense, toleration follows a logic of *emancipation rather than domination*.

On the other hand, the argument for freedom of conscience based on the theory of the "unfree free conscience" mentioned earlier is not only compatible with the permission conception of toleration; it is also potentially exclusive of those persons who do not have the right form of conscience: atheists and Catholics, for example, as Locke famously argued (and with him Milton, differing from the more tolerant Levellers and Baptists such as Roger Williams). In Locke's first *Letter*, for example, it is clear that there can be no justified claim to the freedom *not* to believe in God; indeed, we could call the fear that without a particular religious basis there could be no morality and no functioning state *Locke's fear*[16] (shared by many later Enlightenment thinkers such as Montesquieu, Rousseau, and Voltaire) – a fear, to be sure, still very much present in contemporary societies.

8

To continue our optimistic story about toleration, recognition, and emancipation, we must turn to a different voice in the historical discourse of toleration, one that questioned Locke's fear (though not as a direct reaction to Locke): the Huguenot philosopher Pierre Bayle (writing in exile in Rotterdam). In his *Pensées diverses sur la Comète* (1683), he introduced the later so-called "Bayle's paradox" by saying that religion was not necessary to support morality that rested on other motives (the desire for social recognition) and insights (of natural reason) independent of religious belief, and that religious fanaticism rather than atheism was the main danger for morality and the state. He even ventured the courageous idea that a "society of atheists"

---

[16] "The taking away of God, tho but even in thought, dissolves all." John Locke, *A Letter Concerning Toleration*, ed. by J. Tully (Indianapolis: Hackett, 1983), 51.

would be possible – and possibly be more peaceful than religious societies.

What is more, one of Bayle's decisive insights was that *mutual toleration* among persons with different religious beliefs could only be possible if there were an *independent,* generally shared moral basis of respect among human beings that would rule out the exercise of religious force. In his *Commentaire philosophique sur ces paroles de Jésus-Christ 'Contrain-les d'entrer'* (1686), Bayle provides such a justification of toleration that avoids the problems that Locke's defense of religious liberty faced. For from studying Augustine's famous arguments about the possibility and productivity of *terror* in freeing men from religious error and enabling them to see the truth "from the inside," so to speak, if properly informed,[17] Bayle already knew what Locke had to acknowledge after being confronted with Jonas Proast's critique: that although authentic and sincere beliefs could not be directly produced by outward force, there were many other, *indirect* ways to block men on a road of error and to make them turn around.

[. . .] I readily grant that Reason and Arguments are the only proper Means, whereby to induce the Mind to assent to any Truth, which is not evident by its own Light: and that Force is very improper to be used to that end *instead* of Reason and Arguments. [. . .] But notwithstanding this, if Force be used, not in stead of Reason and Arguments, i.e. not to convince by its own proper Efficacy (which it cannot do,) but onely to bring men to consider those Reasons and Arguments which are proper and sufficient to convince them, but which, without being forced, they would not consider: who can deny, but that *indirectly* and *at a distance*, it does some service toward the bringing men to embrace that Truth, which otherwise, either through Carelesness and Negligence they would never acquaint themselves with, or through Prejudice they would reject and condemn unheard, under the notion of Errour?[18]

---

[17] For Augustine's justification of the duty of intolerance, see especially his letter to Vincent, in Saint Augustine, *Letters,* Vol. II, trans. by W. Parsons (New York: Fathers of the Church, 1953), #93 (pp. 56–106).

[18] Cf. Jonas Proast, *The Argument of the Letter Concerning Toleration, Briefly Consider'd and Answer'd,* reprint of the edition of 1690 (New York and London: Garland, 1984), 4f. For a convincing critique of Locke on the basis of Proastian considerations, see especially Jeremy Waldron, "Locke, Toleration, and the Rationality of Persecution," in *Liberal Rights. Collected Papers 1981–1991* (Cambridge: Cambridge University Press, 1993), ch. 4. Where I disagree with Waldron, however, is on his claim that Locke did not find a plausible counterargument to Proast. For that, however, he had to change his position and move towards the epistemological-normative argument that we find

To avoid such counterarguments to a defense of the freedom of conscience, Bayle argued on normative grounds that every person had a moral duty to mutually justify any exercise of force – a duty that could be seen by the means of "natural reason"[19] – and he argued on epistemological grounds that in a case in which there was a standoff between one religious reason and another, there was no sufficient justification for using force on either side. And this was *not* because Bayle was a religious skeptic (as many have thought), but because Bayle insisted on faith being *faith* and not knowledge: as long as there was no reasonably non-rejectable proof as to the truth of one religion or confession, the duty of mutual justification called for tolerance (but not for skepticism, for knowing that one's faith ultimately is faith – based on "relative evidence"[20] – one has good reasons to regard it as true as long as it does not run against natural reason).[21] From that perspective, the claim of people like Bossuet[22] who believed that they were in possession of the truth and therefore could legitimately exercise force – according

---

in Bayle (in superior form). In his later letters on toleration, Locke argues that the use of religious-political force is in need of mutual justification, and that Proast's main assumption of the undeniable truth of the Church of England is unfounded. See especially Locke, "A Second Letter Concerning Toleration," in: *The Works of John Locke* VI (Aalen: Scientia, 1963), 111, where he asks Proast to put forth a mutually justifiable argument "without supposing all along your church in the right, and your religion the true; which can no more be allowed to you in this case, whatever your church or religion be, than it can to a papist or a Lutheran, a presbyterian or anana baptist; nay, no more to you, than it can be allowed to a Jew or a Mahometan."

19 See Pierre Bayle, *Philosophical Commentary*, trans. and ed. by Amie Godman Tannenbaum (New York: Peter Lang, 1987), 30: "[B]ut if it's possible to have certain limitations with respect to speculative truths, I don't believe there ought to be any with regard to those practical and general principles which concern morals. I mean that all moral laws without exception, must submit to that idea of natural equity, which, as well as metaphysical light, *enlightens every man coming into the world.* [. . .] I would like whoever aims at knowing distinctly this natural light with respect to morality to raise himself above his own private interest or the custom of his country, and to ask himself in general: *'Is such a practice just in itself? If it were a question of introducing it in a country where it would not be in use and where he would be free to take it up or not, would one see, upon examining it impartially, that it is reasonable enough to merit being adopted?'"* (Emphasis in original.)

20 Ibid., 93.

21 Hence, from a Baylean perspective, contrary to Brian Barry, *Justice as Impartiality* (Oxford: Oxford University Press, 1995), 179, it seems quite possible and reasonable in matters of religion that "certainty from the inside about some view can coherently be combined with the line that it is reasonable for others to reject that same view."

22 See Jacques-Benigne Bossuet, *Politics drawn from the Very Words of Holy Scripture*, trans. and ed. by Patrick Riley (Cambridge: Cambridge University Press, 1999).

to Augustine's interpretation of the saying *compelle intrare* (Luke 14, 15ff.) – would turn into nothing but a pure and illegitimate exercise of power. According to Bayle, in an argument about the norms and laws that are to regulate the common life to assume precisely what is contested – namely, the truth of one church rather than another – is "childish" and "ridiculous."[23] If such arguments were legitimate, "there would be no kind of crime which could not become an act of religion by this maxim."[24] As Bayle points out, a society can only exist peacefully if there is a generally accepted definition of right and wrong independent of struggles about the true church.[25]

In his famous *Dictionnaire historique and critique* (1696), Bayle carefully explained the distinction between knowledge and faith and the possibility of a form of "natural" practical reason that would lead to an insight into the duty of mutual justification. Faith was not seen, in a fideist sense, as being *against* reason but, as Bayle said, as being *beyond reason* (*dessus de la Raison*): faith was not irrational, but at the same time reason could not prove the true faith.[26] Human reason had to accept its own boundaries and finitude and the unavoidability of (what Rawls later called) "reasonable disagreement"[27] in matters of faith. According to Bayle, those who would give up their faith because of that – because they cannot prove its truth in a demonstrative way – and would become skeptics or atheists are no good believers:

Once again, a true Christian, well versed in the characteristics of supernatural truths and firm on the principles that are peculiar to the Gospel, will only laugh at the subtleties of the philosophers, and especially those of the Pyrrhonists. Faith will place him above the regions where the tempests of disputation reign. [. . .] Every Christian who allows himself to be disconcerted by the objections of the unbelievers, and to be scandalized by them, has one foot in the same grave as they do.[28]

---

[23] Bayle, *Philosophical Commentary*, 13.

[24] Ibid., 47.

[25] Ibid., 85.

[26] "[D]ifference in opinion seems to be man's inherent infelicity, as long as his understanding is so limited and his heart so inordinate." Ibid., 141.

[27] See John Rawls, *Political Liberalism* (New York: Columbia University Press, 1993), 54–66; Charles Larmore, "Pluralism and Reasonable Disagreement," in *The Morals of Modernity* (Cambridge: Cambridge University Press, 1996), Ch. 7.

[28] Pierre Bayle, *Historical and Critical Dictionary*, Selections, trans. by Richard H. Popkin (Indianapolis: Hackett, 1991), Third Clarification, 429.

9

For our story, Bayle's insights are essential. A justification of toleration such as his does avoid the pitfalls of a traditional argument for the liberty of conscience, which are (1) that the claim *credere non potest homo nisi volens* (Augustine) does not provide an argument against the suppression of religious "errors" because it is possible that "mild" force can bring about sincere beliefs, as the later Augustine and Proast argued, and (2) that such toleration could only extend to *authentic* religious beliefs (whereas a criterion for such beliefs seems to be lacking), and of course only to *religious* beliefs (and not to atheists). Bayle's alternative justification also avoids, if we look at the recent history of liberal thought, the problems of the view that religious liberty as part of a wider notion of political liberty is justified because personal autonomy is a precondition for the good life, for only the life "lived from the inside," on the basis of autonomously chosen values, could be good.[29] This is a plausible, though a non-generalizable conception of the good life, for it is not clear whether a life lived according to traditional values that are not chosen but simply taken over in a conventional, non-critical way would be worse (that is, subjectively less fulfilling and objectively of a lesser ethical value) than one that is autonomously chosen. The politically *free*, the personally *autonomous*, and the ethically *good* life may be three separate things. Also, such an argument would restrict the principled domain of the tolerable to ways of life that are "chosen" in a certain way, which is too narrow a view.

Of course, my alternative view also calls for a certain kind of respect for the autonomy of persons. Yet this kind of respect is not based on a particular *ethical* conception of the good, but on a *moral* notion of the person as a reasonable being with (what I call) a *right to justification*.[30] This basic right to justification is based on the *recursive* general

---

[29] See Will Kymlicka, *Multicultural Citizenship* (Oxford: Oxford University Press, 1995), 81. For a critique of Kymlicka's view, see R. Forst, "Foundations of a Theory of Multicultural Justice," in *Constellations* 4 (1997), 63–71 (with a reply by Kymlicka in the same issue).

[30] On this point, see R. Forst, "The Basic Right to Justification," in *Constellation* 6 (1999), 35–60, and R. Forst, "Die Rechtfertigung der Gerechtigkeit. Rawls' Politischer Liberalismus und Habermas' Diskurstheorie in der Diskussion," in Hauke Brunkhorst and Peter Niesen (eds.), *Das Recht der Republik* (Frankfurt/M.: Suhrkamp, 1999), 105–168.

principle that every norm that is to legitimize the use of force (or, more broadly speaking, a morally relevant interference with other's actions) claims to be reciprocally and generally valid and therefore needs to be justifiable by reciprocally and generally non-rejectable reasons. *Reciprocity* here means that neither party makes any claim to certain rights or resources that are denied to others (reciprocity of content) and that neither party projects its own reasons (values, interests, needs) onto others in arguing for its claims (reciprocity of reasons). One must be willing to argue for basic norms that are to be reciprocally and generally valid and binding with reasons that are not based on contested "higher" truths or on conceptions of the good that can reasonably be questioned and rejected. *Generality*, then, means that the reasons for such norms need to be shareable among all persons affected, not just dominant parties.[31]

I should emphasize the word "shareable" here, for the criteria of reciprocity and generality allow for judgments as to the justifiability of

---

[31] For a related view of democratic justification based on the principle of reciprocity, see Amy Gutmann and Dennis Thompson, *Democracy and Disagreement* (Cambridge, MA: Harvard University Press, 1996). However, they do not – at least not explicitly – apply their analysis to a view of toleration based on the respect conception; rather, for them toleration is an attitude below mutual respect. See ibid., 62 and 79, as well as Gutmann and Thompson, "Democratic Disagreement," in: Stephen Macedo (ed.), *Deliberative Politics* (Oxford: Oxford University Press, 1999), 251. Still, in their analysis of the famous case *Mozert v. Hawkins Board of Education*, Gutmann and Thompson do require the parents who were seeking an exemption from the general curriculum in order to make room for their religious views to accept that their arguments did fail the "test of reciprocity" (*Democracy and Disagreement*, 65) – and thus to be tolerant in the way I explain later.

The case raises important questions about how to apply the criteria of reciprocity and of "public justification" (see especially William Galston, "Diversity, Toleration, and Deliberative Democracy: Religious Minorities and Public Schooling," in: *Deliberative Politics*, 39–48, and Stephen Macedo, "Liberal Civic Education and Religious Fundamentalism: The Case of God v. John Rawls?" in *Ethics* 105 (1995), 468–496). For a number of reasons, I believe that the case of the parents did fail the threshold of reciprocity and generality: they did not accept the difference between making students familiar with certain views and advertising those views; their case would, if generalized, make public education and general curricula almost impossible and thus fail the task of educating students to become critical citizens and well-informed persons; and finally, it denies the difference between faith and science: not every view that conflicts with a religious comprehensive doctrine thereby turns into such a doctrine. Religious and scientific truths are of different kinds. Thus, it seems to me that Galston's as well as Macedo's (much more limited, see especially 475f.) suggestions for accommodation go too far.

claims even if – as is to be expected – no consensus is to be found.[32] A few brief examples: Those who argue for the equal legal recognition of intimate relationships between homosexuals may have, given the criterion of reciprocity, superior arguments compared with those who argue on the basis of a mutually contestable, religious understanding of "nature." Those who want to forbid persons from wearing headscarves in school (be they teachers or students) must be able to show how far the practice of wearing such symbols really violates basic rights and democratic principles. And those who want crucifixes to be put up in public classrooms by law need to show how far this is compatible with the equal rights of citizenship in a religiously pluralist political community. And it is questionable whether such arguments have been presented in the latter two cases. On the basis of the criteria of reciprocity and generality, then, some reasons seem to be "not reasonable to reject," to use Thomas Scanlon's formulation in a specific way.[33]

The normative ground for this conception of toleration is the moral demand to respect each other's moral autonomy as a reason-giving and reason-receiving being. Whether those who are respected in this way

---

[32] I agree with Jeremy Waldron, "Toleration and Reasonableness," in *The Culture of Toleration in Diverse Societies*, 13–37, that in a pluralist society, there will always be contestation about the "compossibility" of different ideals and practices of the good. And I do not want to suggest that I have developed what he radically doubts, a "Kantian algebraic liberalism" that would provide a general formula for solving such conflicts in a clearly non-rejectable way. Yet I want to claim that with the help of the criteria of reciprocity and generality, we can plausibly identify better and worse arguments for generally valid norms in many cases, looking at the claims and the reasons given. An argumentative "asymmetry" (ibid., 30) of claims and reasons then is important for such judgments. Is the claim, to use Waldron's Rushdie example, to be protected from blasphemous insult as strong as the claim to be protected from being threatened in life and liberty because of what you think and say? Can the first claim be generalized and supported with reciprocally valid reasons in the same way as the second? I doubt that it can. What seems to me undisputed, however, is that toleration is the attitude of those who are willing to engage in such arguments, who accept the criteria of reciprocity and generality, and who accept in a given case that their arguments do not suffice to be the basis of general law. Still, given Waldron's justified doubts, it is important to add another reason for toleration connected to this: the toleration of those who see that a debate remains in a standstill and that therefore no side can show its claims and reasons to be superior. In such a case, toleration means to accept that other grounds for the regulation of a conflict have to be found, by way of compromise.

[33] See Thomas Scanlon, *What We Owe to Each Other* (Cambridge, MA: Harvard University Press, 1998), Ch. 5.

will eventually lead an ethically better life can therefore be the subject of disagreement; there must be no disagreement, however, about the duty of justification and the criteria of reciprocity and generality. This is the *normative* component of that justification of toleration, while the *epistemological* component consists of an insight into the finitude of reason: that reason is not sufficient to provide us with the one and only, ultimate answer about the truth of the good life, which would show that all other ethical beliefs are false.

Most important in this context, however, is the insight that according to this conception of toleration, to be tolerant implies the willingness and the capacity to distinguish between one's *ethical* beliefs about the true and good life and the general *moral* norms and principles one thinks every person – regardless of his or her view of the good – has to accept (or, better: cannot reciprocally and generally reject).[34] Bayle's theory clearly implies such a distinction, and looking at the history of toleration, one may say that this differentiation, in theory as well as in practice, may be the greatest achievement within the discourse of toleration. It comes, however, at a certain cost, which makes tolerance (according to the respect conception as I sketched it) into a demanding *moral and political virtue*[35]: the cost is that in the case in which you cannot present reciprocally and generally non-rejectable arguments for your ethical judgments, you have to accept that you are not justified to make these judgments the basis for generally binding legal norms.[36]

10

Referring back to the three components of toleration, the main difference between the permission conception and the respect conception is that according to the former, all three components are determined by the ethical views of the dominant majority or authority, while in

---

[34] On this disctinction and the difference of various "contexts of justification" as well as of "contexts of recognition," see R. Forst, *Contexts of Justice*, trans. by J. Farrell (Berkeley and Los Angeles: University of California Press, 2002).

[35] On this point, see my "Tolerance as a Virtue of Justice," in *Philosophical Explorations* IV (2001), 193–206.

[36] Bayle himself, one needs to add, only saw this as a moral and civic virtue; politically, he stood in the tradition of the *politiques* arguing for a strong sovereign such as Henri IV.

the respect conception, things look different. The *objection* may be based on one's particular ethical (or religious) views; the *acceptance*, however, will be based on a moral consideration of whether the reasons for objection are good enough to be reasons for *rejection* – that is, whether they are reciprocally and generally justifiable. If they turn out to be sufficient for a negative *ethical* judgment, but not for a negative *moral* judgment, the case for toleration arises: for then one has to see that one's ethical judgment does not justify a moral condemnation and a rejection. This is the insight of toleration. The decisive difference, then, lies in the way the *limits of toleration* are being drawn: on the basis of particular ethical values or on the basis of mutually justifiable considerations and principles – principles that are open to critique as to their content and to the existing social and institutional "relations of justification" that constitute the framework for how they were arrived at.[37]

11

As I already indicated, our story would be far too optimistic if we thought that historically this became the dominant conception of toleration, which is neither true given the practice of toleration nor given the most important writings on toleration. Enlightenment thought before Kant hardly reached the height of Bayle's conception (though Kant also clung to the idea of the end of religious strife in a unified "reasonable religion" – which Bayle already had doubted). Therefore, the general idea that the Enlightenment marked the high point of thinking about toleration and then also made the step *beyond toleration* by positively institutionalizing the right to religious liberty in the American and French Revolutions is mistaken. No doubt the idea of a basic right to religious liberty does take a decisive step beyond the permission conception of toleration, but it is wrong to assume that this takes one "beyond toleration," for (1) toleration is still called for, as I said, but now on the horizontal level of citizens as authors and addressees

---

[37] This recursive, procedural aspect of the "terms of toleration," so to speak, is also highlighted by Onora O'Neill, "Practices of Toleration," in Judith Lichtenberg (ed.), *Democracy and the Mass Media* (Cambridge: Cambridge University Press, 1990), 155–185, and James Bohman, "Reflexive Toleration in a Deliberative Democracy," in *The Culture of Toleration in Diverse Societies*, 111–131.

of the law, and (2), from a critical perspective, the permission conception is still very much alive in the interpretations of what a right to
religious liberty means: Does it simply mean not being forced to give
up one's minority religious views, or does it entail equal public and
political status for minorities? In democratic states, the old absolutist
permission conception is gone, but there is still a constant struggle
going on between the democratic form of the permission conception
and the respect conception. Hence, if we want to develop a genealogy
of our idea and practice of toleration, both of my stories have to form
a *single* one.

1 2

What, finally, is the lesson of my two stories (or, rather, my general
story) about toleration in the context of a theory of recognition and
emancipation? This may be summarized in five points.

1. Toleration always implies, as I said, components of objection and
   of rejection. That is, there is an important normative negative
   judgment in place, and there is a limit to toleration. Toleration
   thus can never be a "complete" form of the positive recognition of the other's identity. And compared with such an ideal of
   recognition, toleration indeed implies an insult.

2. Toleration according to the permission conception is a form
   of the recognition of minorities by a majority or an authority
   protecting the minorities' basic security and liberty, yet at the
   same time it is a complex form of power in a repressive and
   a productive mode (which I do not see as mutually exclusive).
   To be recognized as a different and "non-normal" minority and
   to be awarded some kind of minority status is exactly that: a
   recognition as second class, as non-equal. To be tolerated and
   recognized in this way means to be dominated: it clearly is an
   insult.

3. The alternative, the respect conception of toleration, has a number of historical and normative roots, yet its most plausible justification is the one that takes recourse to a basic right to justification in combination with a theory of the difference between
   general knowledge, on the one hand, and ethical belief or

religious faith, on the other, the latter being subject to reasonable disagreement. This form of toleration entails a complex form of recognition and self-awareness: since one considers the others to be one's moral equals and fellow citizens, one knows that one owes them a fundamental form of respect and that one owes them certain reasons for norms and institutions to which they are subject. Hence the complexity resides in the fact that one has to be able to hold onto one's ethical beliefs and yet partially relativize them in situations of an ethical disagreement about the good – and be tolerant. What this means in practice will, of course, be heavily contested. But in principle, to mention the often made "schizophrenia argument" saying that such a conception of toleration implies a split self or split mind, one does not have to shed one's identity in order to be tolerant in this way. Why should one not, on the one hand, firmly believe that the cross is a symbol of the true faith and yet also, on the other hand, equally firmly believe that it would be wrong for it to be put up in classrooms of public schools by law?

4. Seen in this way, the guiding idea leading from the repressive, hierarchical to the horizontal, democratic form of toleration is the respect for the basic moral right to justification: one must have come to *see* oneself and the others as moral persons with such a right.

What this basic form of respect means in practice can only be determined by procedures of intersubjective reasoning with the help of the two criteria of reciprocity and generality – hence, without these two criteria, the normative insight into the right to justification has no content. From a normative point of view, there is an absolute priority of a *substantive* moral insight into the right to justification and the *procedural* criteria of reciprocity and generality over other conceptions of the good. In a political context of *justice*, there are no other, more substantive criteria in order to find out who owes to whom what kind of recognition. Practical, justificatory reason is autonomous in that respect.[38]

---

[38] See also my discussion of the relation between justification and recognition in *Contexts of Justice*, ch. 5, as well as my "Moral Autonomy and the Autonomy of Morality," in *Graduate Faculty Philosophy Journal* 26 (2005), 65–88.

5. But could it still be that the language of recognition does provide the resources necessary to explain the *motives* and *aims* of social actors in their political struggles? Do we reach here the limits of an abstract Kantian approach that cannot provide the basis for a critical theory of social conflicts?[39]

In order to answer this question, let us distinguish between the precondition and the aim of struggles for recognition such as the ones against intolerance and against false, condescending forms of tolerance. The *precondition* seems to be twofold: First, those engaging in such struggles must already possess a sense of themselves as being the moral equals of the majority that treats them wrongly – and they must have developed this sense before they enter into the struggle, for if that were not the case, they would remain in their subservient position. Second, they also must already have formed (as I indicated earlier) a certain sense of their religious and cultural identity as their own identity and as one worth having – again, before they fully engage in social struggles. They must have formed an identity before as well as in conflict in order to generate the resources for their fight for justice. Hence, neither on the basic moral level nor on the more concrete ethical-religious level does their sense of who they are seem dependent upon the recognition by the majority – the judgment that they are treated unjustly presupposes a developed form of moral and ethical identity (though not, of course, one developed in a totally independent way). In most cases I have mentioned, this has evolved through a certain form of *imagined* recognition: recognition by God – mediated by the social recognition internal to the religious community.

But what is the *aim* of such struggles for justice (that is, not struggles with the aim of simply reversing the power structure)? It is not, I believe, the aim to be esteemed in the eyes of those who one thinks are religiously and ethically deeply mistaken.[40] It is, rather, to be

---

[39] See especially the critique of such approaches by Axel Honneth, "Redistribution as Recognition," in Nancy Fraser and Axel Honneth, *Redistribution or Recognition. A Political-Philosophical Exchange*, trans. by J. Gelb and C. Wilke (London: Verso, 2003).

[40] I differ here from a number of authors who argue for "thicker" forms of mutual esteem (and more demanding forms of toleration) as the alternative to "mere toleration," though in very different ways. See, for example, Charles Taylor, "The Politics of Recognition," in Amy Gutmann (ed.) *Multiculturalism* (Princeton: Princeton University Press, 1994), 64; Joseph Raz, "Autonomy, Toleration, and the Harm Principle,"

respected as moral and political equals despite remaining, deep ethical differences: as persons with an effective right to justification. And the central aim, then, is to have the chance to live the life that one thinks the most worthy to live in the eyes of God and of one's community: negatively speaking, a desire for freedom, and positively speaking, a desire to be recognized as an equal and to be able to live a worthy life. The main motive, thus, for such struggles for fair toleration, is to be treated *justly* in one's dignity as a moral being. The primary language of critique was and is the language of power and of asking for justifying reasons for norms and institutions all are subject to,[41] not primarily the language of recognition in a more substantive sense.[42] Hence, both with respect to the motivational preconditions for and the aim of struggles for recognition and toleration, the general social recognition of one's identity as valuable such that only through *this* kind of esteem could one fully see or accept who one is does not seem to be in play. For the actors in these struggles know that such a *sittliche* – to use the Hegelian term – form of recognition is not attainable. But still they believe in the need for and the possibility of justice.

---

in Susan Mendus (ed.), *Justifying Toleration* (Cambridge: Cambridge University Press, 1988), 155–176; Michael Sandel, "Moral Argument and Liberal Toleration: Abortion and Homosexuality," in *California Law Review* 77 (1989), 521–538; Susan Mendus, *Toleration and the Limits of Liberalism* (Atlantic Highlands: Humanities Press, 1989). It seems to me that the (justified) move from a "permission conception," to a "respect conception"of toleration is not to be confused with the move towards an "esteem conception," according to which the tolerating parties tolerate each other on the basis of a general ethical agreement on the good, only tolerating variations of such "good" ways of life. For the distinction between these conceptions of toleration (plus a fourth one, the "coexistence conception"), see my "Toleration, Justice and Reason." For a position that lies somewhere in between a respect conception and an esteem conception, see the idea of a "public recognition of difference" by Anna Elisabetta Galeotti, *Toleration as Recognition* (Cambridge: Cambridge University Press, 2002).

[41] Close to Foucault's (in that sense, Kantian) notion of critique, see his "What is Critique?" 31: "And finally 'to not want to be governed' is of course not accepting as true [...] what an authority tells you is true, or at least not accepting it because an authority tells you that it is true, but rather accepting it only if one considers valid the reasons for doing so."

[42] This is where I differ from Axel Honneth, *The Struggle for Recognition*, trans. J. Anderson (Cambridge, MA: MIT Press, 1995).

10

Misrecognition, Power, and Democracy

Veit Bader

Critics of politics of 'identity' and 'recognition' who argue that 'material' or 'economic' inequalities have been neglected have presented a fairly dichotomous picture of two hierarchies.[1] Honneth has rightly questioned this dichotomy[2] and the accompanying mythical histories, which represent the 'old' labour movement as being only concerned with economic inequalities and equal rights and treat struggles for 'recognition of identities, cultures, and differences' as something 'new.'[3] His "turn toward recognition theory" claims to overcome these obstacles. Honneth presents his theory of recognition as a general, unifying, simple, and coherent conceptual and theoretical framework in order to describe, explain, and evaluate objective injustices as well as social experiences of injustice. He is "convinced that the terms of recognition *must* represent the unified framework for such a project."[4]

[1] Of material 'redistribution' and symbolic 'recognition'; Nancy Fraser, "From Redistribution to Recognition?" in *New Left Review* 212 (1995), 68–93; Will Kymlicka, *Contemporary Political Philosophy: An Introduction* (New York/Oxford: Oxford University Press, 2002), 332–4.

[2] Axel Honneth, "Redistribution as Recognition." in Nancy Fraser & Axel Honneth, *Redistribution or Recognition? A Political-Philosophical Exchange* (London: Verso, 2003), 113.

[3] Honneth, "Redistribution as Recognition." 122; see V. Bader, *Kollektives Handeln* (Opladen: Leske und Budrich, 1991), 30f, 254ff.

[4] Honneth, "Redistribution as Recognition." 113.

Thanks to participants of the Recognition and Power conference in Utrecht and to Bert van den Brink for suggestions and critical remarks.

"Even the 'material' inequalities . . . *must* be interpretable as expressing the violation of well-founded claims to recognition."[5]

In this chapter, I criticize these ambitious claims to internally link critical social sciences and political philosophy by means of a single monistic theory. I will argue that *multi-dimensional analysis* of structural power-asymmetries or serious inequalities in the social sciences, along with *pluralist accounts* of severe injustices in political philosophy,[6] provide a more adequate and productive basis on which to articulate the basic moral intuitions that we share about critical social science and political philosophy. In a pluralist approach, collective discrimination or misrecognition is conceived of as being based in predominant hierarchies of prestige, which are intimately linked to other power-asymmetries. For a long time, social sciences and political theory could not avoid the *double dangers of* making predominant prestige-rankings even more predominant than they actually are, and of underestimating the existence of counter-rankings and 'hidden transcripts' (the 'weapons of the weak'), thus drastically overestimating the stability of prestige-hierarchies (Section I).

Recently, political philosophers also have started to pay more attention to the impact of structural inequalities in general and misrecognition in particular. Some are focusing on the chances of negatively privileged groups to articulate their interests, organize, mobilize, and struggle, while others are looking closely at the psychic, moral, and cognitive capacities of agents.[7] Yet *theories of 'psychic and moral incapacitation'* often show an inherent tendency to 'victimize the victims' making them even more powerless than they actually are. Instead of assuming or prematurely concluding that the negatively privileged also lack

---

[5] Honneth, "Redistribution as Recognition." 134, emphases added; see 157 "moral-theoretical monism"; see also Axel Honneth, "Recognition as Moral Obligation," in *Social Research* 64/1 (1997), 19, 24.

[6] Recently, Fraser ("Socialist Justice in the Age of Identity Politics," in *Tanner Lectures XIX* [Salt Lake City: University of Utah Press, 1998], 1–67; "Social Justice in the Age of Identity Politics," in Fraser & Honneth, *Redistribution or Recognition?*) has been 're-inventing' a three-dimensional (Weberian) approach, adding 'representation' (power) to 'redistribution' (class) and 'recognition' (status).

[7] See J. Mansbridge & A. Morris (eds.), *The Subjective Roots of Social Protest* (Chicago: Chicago University Press, 2001); D. Allen, "Invisible Citizens: Political Exclusion and Domination," in M. Williams & S. Macedo (eds.), *Nomos* (New York: New York University Press, 2005); J. Tully, "Exclusion and Assimilation. in M. Williams & S. Macedo (eds.), *Nomos* (New York: New York University Press, 2005).

alternative cognitive and normative framing capacities, or even agency, critical theory has to scrutinize objective power-asymmetries and their impact on articulation, organization, mobilization, and strategies of collective action. In all these regards, pluralist frameworks provide more adequate tools, so I claim (Section II). The core intuition of my contribution is that wrongly conceived theories of incapacitation can tragically add to the incapacitation of the incapacitated, as they so often have done in the constructions of inescapable domination and closed monolithic worlds by 'critical theorists' and 'postmodernists.'

If – and to the degree that – entrenched inequalities, and in particular misrecognition, actually reduce capabilities and agency of 'powerless people' so that they not only lack resources and opportunities but also are unaware of injustices and unable to articulate their own objective needs and interests, critical social science and normative theories of democracy are in trouble. *Critical social sciences* have to elaborate theories of objective needs and objective interests – instead of taking the actual preferences of 'happy slaves' or 'contented house-wives' at face value – without falling prey to paternalism. *Normative theories of democracy* addressing the impact of power-asymmetries on democratic deliberation have responded by two strategies: first, by moral pedagogy and civic education, and second, by designing more apt institutions for deliberation and representation. Unfortunately, political theory is badly prepared for this latter task, and an institutional turn is urgently required (Section III).

I INEQUALITIES AND (MIS)RECOGNITION: PLURALIST OR MONIST FRAMES

Collective misrecognition is certainly amongst the most serious forms of structural inequalities. In a pluralist conceptual and theoretical framework,[8] however, collective misrecognition does not cover all forms of structural inequalities. More than fifteen years ago, I developed such a framework systematically linking the plurality of forms of

---

[8] Pluralist conceptual and theoretical approaches in social sciences and moral philosophy, as defended here, are loosely linked with ontological and epistemological pluralism, and with societal, political, cultural, and institutional pluralism: V. Bader, "Pluralism," in A. Harrington et al. (eds.), *Routledge Encyclopedia of Social Theory* (London: Routledge, 2004).

inequalities, misrecognition amongst them, with a plurality of experiences and articulations of injustice.[9] I will give a short summary of my main findings in order to clarify the relations between power and (mis)recognition (I.1). I will also mark the main topics distinguishing my approach from Honneth's and present a short summary of my main arguments in favour of a pluralist approach (I.2).

I.1. A Pluralist Frame

Amongst the many basic human needs is the contested *bundle of emotional needs* for love and care, for social recognition, and for distinction, power, and collective prestige.[10] Love, care, and social recognition do not need hierarchy and superiority but can, in principle, be satisfied without harming or disadvantaging others whereas 'my' distinction/power/glory and 'our' collective prestige "can only be satisfied at the expense of injuring yours."[11] Yet, individual distinction under conditions of fair competition – contrary to the individual will to power – however insatiable, does not block, but may even stimulate, the developmental powers of others (it may initiate a positive sum game), whereas both "love of power" and of "collective prestige" block the developmental powers of others (zero-sum games).[12]

---

[9] V. Bader, *Ungleichheiten*, together with A. Benschop, (Opladen: Leske und Budrich, 1989); Bader, *Kollektives Handeln.*

[10] Bader, *Kollektives Handeln*, 97ff.

[11] K. Soper, *On Human Needs. Open and Closed Theories in Marxist Perspectives* (Atlantic Highlands, NJ, Humanities Press, 1981), 157.

[12] All social relations that individuals are embedded in to fulfil these emotional needs can be analysed from the perspective of "recognition" as "recognitional relations" in order to analyse their divergent impact on 'the self' (Axel Honneth, *The Struggle for Recognition* [Cambridge: Polity, 1995], Chs. 5 and 6). My approach differs from Honneth's in three regards: (1) I treat them as fairly independent needs and relationships that can also be analysed from other perspectives. I would now hesitate to see the need for prestige as a specific, collectivist, asymmetrical variety of needs for social recognition, as I have earlier (*Ungleichheiten*, 142f). In-egalitarian 'prestige' is an independent 'object' to be distinguished from 'receptive recognition.' (2) I would not only distinguish clearly between 'egalitarian' or 'just' 'receptive' ones and principled *in-egalitarian* ones (power-relations, collective prestige) but also elaborate more clearly that relations of love, care, social recognition, and distinction, which may be more egalitarian (matters of degree), are empirically always embedded in asymmetrical power-relations. (3) The link of these relations to the self is, again, contingent: more egalitarian ones can still lead to defective, inauthentic selves, and relations of collective prestige or objective misrecognition need not incapacitate. Comments by Bert van den Brink stimulated me to clarify these points.

The nature of "collective *prestige*" is not – even after decades of research in the status-sociological tradition[13] – sufficiently clear. Whatever the objects of 'deferential judgements,' its evaluative rankings aim at "attribution of superiority/inferiority."[14] The hierarchically ranked objects are extremely varied and numerous.[15] The most important ones are material objects, credentials, occupations, high positions in organizations, wealth, high incomes, free time, social relations, membership in specific organizations; specific cultures and styles of work, consumption, life; specific habitus; and the various ascribed characteristics (see later). These objects do not satisfy prestige-needs in themselves, but they can be understood as signs, symbols, or markers of predominant societal rankings.

The *objectivity* of such predominant prestige-hierarchies is not easy to understand, because prestige-hierarchies are constituted by subjective evaluative judgements depending on "time t, space s, and perspective p."[16] In societies marked by deep class, elite, and ascriptive cleavages and by deep cultural diversity, there is no informational, cognitive, and evaluative consensus to be expected regarding specific partial (such as occupational, income, living-room) or total prestige-hierarchies[17]: When, and where (in public, in private, on-stage or off-stage) is it ranked and by whom? Prestige-hierarchies seem to resolve/collapse into a nearly unstructured chaos of completely arbitrary, unstable, private, heterogeneous, and conflicting subjective rankings. Two combined social mechanisms help explain the objectivity of predominant prestige-hierarchies. First, their *institutionalization*, or the fact that expectations and evaluations are not grounded in "actual agreement" but are successfully overstretched: prestige-hierarchies exist "as long as nearly all assume that nearly all agree;

---

[13] This tradition – like its monistic counterpart in political philosophy (Honneth's and David Miller's strategy) – has tried to reduce all forms of inequality into the presumedly uniform 'money of status' instead of measuring all inequalities, including status-inequalities, in terms of money as in monistic neo-classical economy and its sociological derivatives.

[14] E. Shils, "Reflections on Deference," in Shils, *Center and Periphery: Essays in Macrosociology* (Chicago, University of Chicago Press, 168), 319).

[15] See Bader, *Ungleichheiten*, 133, table 6, row 5.

[16] H. Nelson & T. Lasswell, "Status Indices, Social Stratification, and Social Class," in *Sociology and Social Research* 44 (1960), 412).

[17] Bader, *Ungleichheiten*, 145ff.

possibly even if nearly all assume that nearly all assume that nearly all agree."[18] Second, *mobilization of bias* or, stated simply, the fact that the prestige-hierarchies of the powerful, the positively privileged, and the 'majorities' have far better chances of becoming the predominant and institutionalized societal rankings: 'power into prestige.'[19]

Before summarizing my analysis of ascriptive categorization and discussing this relationship between structural power-asymmetries and prestige in more detail, let me draw some general methodological and substantive consequences. *Methodologically*, prestige- or status-research has to spell out exactly whose evaluations are at stake (and it has to focus on the evaluations of the different groups of actors themselves instead of those of sociologists or panel experts) and what exactly is evaluated. Particularly, it must distinguish very clearly between actual evaluations and rankings by respondents, their expectations and opinions with regard to evaluations by others, their expectations regarding predominant rankings in society, and their respective attitudes regarding these presumably predominant hierarchies. Only in this way can we stop using and reproducing fictions or producing sociological artefacts.[20]

Substantively, we should not overestimate the fragile objectivity and precarious predominance of prestige-hierarchies: the "assumption of the assumption" that nearly everybody shares the same rankings may collapse easily in "unleashed communication" if confronted with hard facts to the contrary. Moreover, the predominance of the rankings of the powerful may be due, firstly, to a restricted focus on 'on-stage' communications, neglecting off-stage opinions (James Scott), and secondly, to the lack of political resources (see later) instead of being the result of 'affective internalization,' 'identification with the aggressor,' of 'colonized conscience,' of a 'culture of poverty,' or simply of a lack of alternative ways of framing experiences of injustice.[21]

I present my analysis of *ascriptive criteria as bases of prestige-hierarchies* in a more detailed form because ascriptively categorized groups are at the core of recent theories of 'politics of identity and recognition.'

---

[18] N. Luhmann, *Rechtssoziologie* (Reinbeck: Rowohlt, 1972), 71, my translation.
[19] Bader, *Ungleichheiten*, 150ff.
[20] Bader, *Ungleichheiten*, 147f, 152.
[21] Bader, *Ungleichheiten*, p. 153, 321, and Bader, *Kollektives Handeln*, 191ff and notes 115, 119.

Ascriptive minorities are constituted by a specific process in which a whole range of real or imagined 'characteristics' are collectively ascribed to a category of people and negatively evaluated in terms of prestige[22] without any regard to real individual or collective performance. People are classified on the basis of socially defined 'natural' characteristics such as kinship/descent, sex, age, colour, and/or 'historical, socio-cultural' characteristics such as space, history, language, culture/lifestyle/habits (including gender, religion), social class, political culture, and state-membership.

In Table 10.1, the criteria of ascription, the practices of closure and exclusion, and the respective ideologies are separated for analytical purposes, but evidently they overlap: all existing ascriptive minorities are clusters (for example, 'ethnic' categories often are clusters of 'racialized' criteria of descent, colour, of history, language, culture, and religion, fairly independently from the question of whether these minorities perceive themselves at all as an 'ethnic group').

'Women,' 'races,' 'native,' 'ethnic,' 'national,' and 'gender'-minorities are defined and negatively evaluated by others and by the respective societal majorities. As in all other cases, it is to be expected that there is no informational, cognitive, and normative consensus regarding what is evaluated, how it is evaluated, and which of the conflicting rankings is predominant in society. But even though here this is more obvious and clear than in most other cases, it does not mean that there would not be a predominant and powerful prestige-hierarchy: the reference to sexist, ageist, racist, and ethnocentristic ideologies should be enough to indicate this predominance.

Any critical social theory has to explain the predominance of the prestige-hierarchies of the respective majorities as a result of other structural power-asymmetries (transformation of *'power into prestige'*). My own proposal (Table 10.2) is a specific mix of exploitation, oppression, exclusion, and overall marginalization.[23]

---

[22] See my analysis in Bader, *Ungleichheiten*; V. Bader, *Rassismus, Ethnizität und Bürgerschaft* (Münster, Verlag Westfälisches Dampfboot: 1995), and short summary in English in V. Bader, "Ethnicity and Class," in Wsevolod W. Isajiw (ed.), *Comparative Perspectives on Interethnic Relations and Social Incorporation* (Toronto: Canadian Scholars' Press, 1997), 103–128. Honneth recognizes that "receptive recognition" excludes ascription.

[23] Bader, *Ungleichheiten*, Chs. VI and VII; short English version: "Ethnicity and Class," p. 117ff.

TABLE 10.1. *Ascriptive Criteria of Allocation: Practices of Discrimination, Oppression, Exclusion: Typical Ascriptive Ideologies*

	Criteria of closure	Practices of closure	Typical ideologies of legitimation		
Socially defined biological physiological phenotypical "natural" characteristics	Kinship/descent	Clan domination, discrimination, and closure	Kinship ideologies	**BIOLOGISTIC**	**LEGENDS**
	Sex	Discrimination, oppression, and exclusion of women	Sexist ideologies		
	Age	Generational closure, gerontocracy, etc.	Ageism		
	Colour, etc.	Racist oppression, discrimination, and exclusion	Racist ideologies		
	Community/ belonging to:	**Exclusion, oppression, discrimination of:**			
Social historical ascriptive characteristics	Territorial space	Neighbourhoods/ regions, etc.	Urbanistic/ regionalistic ideologies	**ETHNOCENTRIC**	**LEGENDS**
	History	Established/ outsiders	Nativist ideologies		
	Language	Language groups	Language ideologies		
	Culture, habits, lifestyle, gender	Cultural minorities	Culturalistic ideologies		
	Religion	Religious groups	Religious ideologies		
	Social class	'Lower' or 'working' class	Class legends and ideologies		
	Political culture	Political communities	Liberal, republican ideologies	**CIVIC**	**LEGENDS**
	(Forced) membership of:				
	Hierocratic institutions (church) sects	Members of churches	Clerical, papist ideologies		
	Political units state membership	Foreign states, aliens	Statistic and imperialistic ideologies		
	Membership of (political) organizations	(Members) of political parties, unions, etc.	Political (e.g., anti-socialistic ideologies)		

NATIONALISTIC LEGENDS (spanning ETHNOCENTRIC and CIVIC sections)

TABLE 10.2. *Basic Types of Positional Inequality and Structural Asymmetries of Power*

Level of societal relations	Positional structure	Potential collectivity	Basic types of power
Relations of work	Class positions	Classes	Exploitation
Organization interactions	Elite positions	Elites	Domination/ oppression
	Interaction-positions	Selective associational groups	Selective association Discrimination
Relations of prestige	Positions in hierarchies of prestige	Prestige groups	
		Excluded groups marginalized	Exclusion marginalization

Changes in predominantly negative prestige of ascriptive minorities – their institutionalized social and, most often, legal and political *collective misrecognition* – are intimately linked to changing patterns of inequality in the distribution of natural and social resources and to changes in the class-structure elite-structure of societies, among other things.

Once predominant and institutionalized, however, positive prestige itself becomes an important resource (transformation of *'prestige into power'*). Prestige is – in my approach – a very important "indirect resource."[24] *Positive prestige*, in combination with other indirect resources, opens access to important societal arenas or 'markets' (for example, labour-, housing-, marriage-, education-, or 'political markets'), it increases the chances of promotion and power inside organizations, and reward-chances in all societal fields.[25] *Negative prestige – collective misrecognition of ascriptive minorities* in particular – more or less effectively closes access to all these arenas and organisations. If *closure* is not complete, it diminishes the chances of promotion and power in organizations, and it negatively affects all societal rewards such as income, free time, chances of work-satisfaction, esteem, social recognition by colleagues, health, and so on. Collective misrecognition can also be so harsh that it leads to more or less *all-encompassing exclusion and marginalization* (for examples, 'untouchables,' ethnic under-classes),

[24] See Bader, *Ungleichheiten*, 132 (Schema 6) for the other indirect resources.
[25] Bader, *Ungleichheiten*, 127, 141.

and even to genocide without any formalization into a second-class legal and citizenship status (the various 'apartheid' systems).

Ascriptive minorities are constituted by negative evaluations of others (*other-definitions*), however they themselves respond to such categorization. In cases of harsh collective misrecognition, it is nearly impossible not to be aware of such categorization (you may wish to ignore it, but 'they' make you aware of it). In their *self-definitions*, the ascriptively categorized (1) may wish to *ignore* other-definitions as far as possible. (2) They may *criticize* the presumption that there would be any real (for example, cultural) or imagined common characteristics. In this case, they develop what I call a purely *negative collective conflict-identity*: the only thing they share is being discriminated against. They define themselves and organize and mobilize as a collectivity on this basis, fighting against this specific or against all ascriptive categorization. (3) They may *criticize* the negative evaluation of selected real common characteristics (for example, some shared cultural practices) asking for equal recognition of their cultures. (4) They may try to *reverse* the predominant *ranking order* ('black is beautiful' and 'white is ugly'). (5) They may (be forced to) more or less fully *accept* the predominant ranking by making the negative evaluations of their 'characteristics,' 'personality,' and 'group' into their own.[26]

In the last case (5), the 'power of negative prestige' would be so harsh that ascriptive minorities – against their own objective interests – would be doomed to remain 'happy slaves,' 'contented untouchables,' and so on. In all other cases (1–5), they minimally protest against this socially, politically, culturally, and often also legally institutionalised collective misrecognition; and in order to be able to do this, they have to become aware of their objective situation, develop some kind of collective conflict-identity, organize, and mobilize.[27] The ways in which

---

[26] See Bader, *Rassismus, Ethnizität und Bürgerschaft*, 98ff; V. Bader, "Culture and Identity. Contesting constructivism," in *Ethnicities* 1/2 (2001), 260–6, for a more elaborate discussion of these options in the case of 'ethnic minorities.' Purely negative collective identities may lack comparative motivating power, but this does not mean that it would be necessary for the formation of self-respect of movements of resistance that they would have to reflect on "valuable properties they seek to have acknowledged by oppressors" (suggestion by Bert van den Brink). That they value these properties themselves is enough.

[27] Bader, *Kollektives Handeln*, Chs. III–VIII; Mansbridge & Morris, *The Subjective Roots of Social Protest*.

they want and can do this are numerous, but from this '*minima socio-logica,*' two things follow directly: (i) Their protest has also to address the other structural power-asymmetries responsible for the development and reproduction of predominant prestige-hierarchies; it cannot be only concerned with fighting collective misrecognition as such. (ii) Their chances to succeed are structured by (*changes* in) the existing distribution of societal resources and by their own 'mobilization-resources' and strategies.

I.2. A Monist Frame

That 'struggles for recognition' and 'for redistribution' cannot be separated is an insight Honneth and I certainly share. Whether we need a monist, unifying conceptual framework in critical social science and political philosophy, and if so, whether such a framework – a generalized theory of positive recognition – would be productive is the main point of contention. I first present some doubts concerning an ideal theory of recognition, staying inside the 'recognition'-framework. Then I present three main charges against the need for a unified and monist theory in critical social science and political philosophy.

First. 'Recognition' (or family-like categories such as respect, concern, esteem, approval, prestige, status, honour) can be analysed in two different ways, *negatively* or in a *positively*.[28] One can focus on *misrecognition* and discuss measures to prevent or minimize it, or one can focus on *recognition* and measures to achieve it. Two issues are at stake: the chances to reach agreement on positive ideals compared with the chances to reach agreement on serious harm, and the question of whether we have to spell out what recognition positively and fully means in order to be able to know, detect, and evaluate what misrecognition is.

(i) My claim is that the chances to reach agreement (in theory and in politics) are much better if we focus on serious misrecognition[29]

---

[28] Honneth, *Struggle*, 131ff; Axel Honneth, "Recognition as Moral Obligation," in *Social Research* 64/1 (1997), 16–35.
[29] On disrespect, disapproval, neglect of concern, esteem, status, honour, humiliation, moral injuries: Honneth, *Struggle*, 132, 135ff.

instead of positively spelling out what recognition requires: personal integrity, identity, positive self-relation (care/love, moral respect, solidarity/loyalty). A universal theory of positive recognition[30] would have to clarify the different objects of recognition, such as individual autonomy, individual integrity or authenticity, individual identity-claims, collective identity-claims, cultural practices, and differences. Defenders of a 'politics of identity, difference, or recognition' have not answered these questions unambiguously and convincingly.[31] The core of Honneth's own theory of recognition lies in (the conditions of) positive self-relation. His three stages of positive self-relation may illustrate the increasing disagreements among social scientists and political philosophers:

(a) We know fairly well what physical injuries are and why 'murder, abuse, torture, and rape' are bad,[32] but we are severely divided when it comes to the corresponding forms of positive recognition of 'unconditional concern': how much and what kind of care and love are (minimally or optimally) needed for self-confidence?

(b) We know what individual deceit and fraud are, and what collective discrimination is, and we know fairly well what is needed to achieve legal equality as a minimal basis for self-respect (Kantian 'moral respect'), but we are more seriously divided when the issue is how (by which means) to fight persisting social discrimination effectively and how far such a struggle has to go.[33]

---

[30] Axel Honneth, "Recognition as Moral Obligation," 27ff.

[31] See criticism by J. Waldron, "Cultural Identity and Civic Responsibility," in W. Kymlicka & W. Norman (eds.), *Citizenship in Diverse Societies* (Oxford: Oxford University Press, 2000), 155–174 and B. Barry, *Culture and Equality* (Cambridge: Polity Press, 2001), amongst others. Both, however, tend to neglect cultural inequalities (see V. Bader, "Defending Differentiated Policies of Multiculturalism," Portuguese translation: "Em Defesa de Políticas Multiculturais Diferenciadas," in J. C. Rosas [ed], *Ideias e Políticas para o Nosso Tempo* [Braga: Universidade Do Minho; Hespérides/Filosofia 4, 2004(2002)], 207–240).

[32] Honneth, *Struggle*, 132f; Honneth, "Recognition as Moral Obligation," 26.

[33] Van den Berg ("Be prestige-resilient!" in *Ethical Theory and Moral Practice* 6/2 [2004], 197–214) tries to steer a balance midway between exaggerated "prestige-sensitivity" and "prestige aversity" in his plea for "prestige-resilience" (see also N. Chavkin & J. Gonzalez, *Mexican Immigrant Youth and Resiliency* [Charleston, WV: AEL Inc., 2000]).

(c) We have some knowledge of cases "in which it is made known
to one ore more persons through humiliation and disrespect that their capabilities do not enjoy any recognition:
such acts harm the feeling of being socially significant within
a concrete community,"[34] but we seriously disagree about
possible measures – apart from general anti-discrimination
law and policies – to impose 'solidarity' and 'loyalty' upon
such 'communities.'[35]

In my view, attempts to "economize moral disagreement"[36] are a
virtue not only in practical politics but also in political philosophy.[37]
In recent discussions of what justice or equality requires, one finds a
remarkable shift from ideal theories towards more minimalist ones
mainly motivated by the fact that disagreement amongst philosophers
constructing ideal theories is endless and even rising.[38] My guess is
that reasoned disagreement might be even tougher and deeper when
it comes to ideal theories of recognition.

(ii) Do we need an ideal theory of positive recognition in order to
know, detect, and evaluate what misrecognition is, or is a rough
notion of minimal recognition – implicit in all judgments of
serious misrecognition – enough? Again, it depends upon our

---

34 Honneth, "Recognition as Moral Obligation," 27.

35 Even this short summary suggests that – contrary to H.'s claim – the "three moral
attitudes" can be "ranked from some superior vantage point" ("Recognition as Moral
Obligation," 33), and that this is exactly the second, 'narrow' Kantian one. I fully
agree with Fraser's third point of criticism: one has to "avoid the view that everyone
has an equal right to social esteem. That view is patently untenable" (Nancy Fraser,
"Social Justice in the Age of Identity Politics," in Nancy Fraser & Axel Honneth, *Redistribution or Recognition? A Political-Philosophical Exchange* (London: Verso, 2003), 32).

36 Amy Gutmann & Dennis Thompson, *Democracy and Disagreement* (Cambridge, MA:
Harvard University Press, 1996).

37 My disagreement with Honneth is not a matter of the strategic application of his theory of recognition but a matter of theoretical strategy: whether we should develop
'ideal theories' or be content with more minimalist 'satisfying' or even more minimalist threshold theories.

38 See my own shift from the idea of "complex, rough equality" (V. Bader, "Egalitarian Multiculturalism: Institutional Separation and Cultural Pluralism," in Rainer
Bauböck & John Rundell (eds.), *Blurred Boundaries* [Aldershot: Ashgate, 1998], 189f)
to a more minimalist concept (V. Bader, "Immigration," forthcoming in S. Caney &
Lehning [eds], *International Distributive Justice* [London/New York: Routledge,
2006]). See I. Shapiro, *Democratic Justice* (New Haven: Yale University Press, 1999);
C. Hacker-Cordon, *Our Deliberative Situation* (PhD unpublished manuscript, 2003),
Chapter 2.

TABLE 10.3. *Pluralist Versus Monist Strategies**

Pluralist		Monist	
(Ob)jective injustices, (in)equalities, structural (po)wer asymmetries)	Subjective injustices, motivational bases of collective action (experience, feeling, claim to be):	Unifying motivational bases of collective action (if any) Feeling treated:	Unifying concepts of justice/injustice (if any)
(Ex)ploitation	Exploited	Misrecognized / Dominated / Unequal / Unfair / Unjust	Recognition / Non-domination / Equality / Reciprocity / Fairness
(Do)mination/Oppression	Dominated/oppressed		
(Di)scrimination	Discriminated		
(Ex)clusion	Excluded		
(Ma)rginalization	Marginalized		

*(Su)bheadings here are set perpendicular to those under Pluralist strategies to avoid the impression (t)hat the unifying motivational bases of collective action within Monist strategies are the same as in (t)he first two columns.

aims: if we are satisfied with detecting, analysing, and evaluating serious misrecognition, such a minimalist notion of 'malfare' will do. If we aim at a more emphatic theory of full recognition, then we have to do more than to draw a minimum limit of conditions preventing malfare: we have to define 'welfare' and spell out its full conditions and policies but, again, the dangers of a heavy and unavoidable culturalist bias are paramount.[39]

Second. Honneth develops (Table 10.3) an explicitly *monist social theory* attempting to describe, analyze, and evaluate objective injustices,

[39] Honneth may agree that a minimalist, negative approach is enough in order to know and detect misrecognition as his privileged basis for 'struggles for recogniton' (*Struggle*, 16off; methodologically and ontologically, so to speak) but insists that a positive approach is needed to spell out the evaluative standards of a 'morality of recognition' (*Struggle*, 171ff). Honneth's positive theory of recognition claims to develop a formal conception of ethical life (*Sittlichkeit*) which goes way beyond the reach of 'Kantian' morality but is still faithful to the idea that the evaluative standards would be non-contingent and ethically uncontroversial. Whether such a theory of the good, which may be thicker and more perfectionist than Honneth wants to admit (see Bert van den Brink, *The Tragedy of Liberalism* [Albany: SUNY, 2000], 151–61) can be articulated in a universalist and non-controversial way, is contested (see also Fraser's first point of critique ["Social Justice," 30f]). Even a much thinner version, a theory of capabilities (like Sen's or Nussbaum's) could not effectively refute charges of particularist cultural bias.

subjective experiences of injustices, and motivational bases of collective action in terms of one unifying concept of justice/injustice.

Honneth rightly insists that an important task of any critical social theory is to detect "unthematized" forms of everyday suffering and moral injustice[40] instead of only reproducing already publicly articulated claims of different groups or movements. To make this possible, critical social theory has to present an elaborate set of *concepts and strategies to detect objective injustices*. One consequence of a monist approach is that all different forms or types of injustices (for example, exploitation, domination/oppression, discrimination, exclusion, marginalization) have to be re-described and conceptualized as 'misrecognition' (or as 'domination/oppression,' or as 'exclusion').[41] Consequently, this would mean that one has to analyse exploitation, domination/oppression, exclusion, and marginalisation as social bases of discrimination/misrecognition. It would mean that struggles against discrimination/misrecognition would also have to address the processes of ongoing exploitation, domination/oppression, exclusion, and marginalisation (in catchwords: 'struggles for recognition' would include 'redistribution'). But it would also mean that Honneth himself would have to re-describe exploitation, domination/oppression, exclusion, and marginalisation itself as forms of misrecognition. And in fact he explicitly makes this claim in his works.[42]

I want to argue that if he were to try to do this – I could not find any serious attempt in his writings so far – this would have two quite unfortunate and counterproductive consequences. First: Misrecognition would play a double role in such a theory: it would serve as a roof-concept (Misrecognition 1) covering all forms of injustice and, at the same time, it would designate a specific type of injustice (Misrecognition 2), which would be analytically separate from, but empirically overlapping with, the other forms. In such a way, one would introduce and reproduce much terminological ambiguity, and one would have to reintroduce the plurality of forms of injustice via the back door to avoid

---

40 Honneth, "Redistribution as Recognition," 114–16, "unexpressed and often inexpressible malaises" (119, quoting Bourdieu).

41 See my criticism of Young, Pettit, Parkin, and others: V. Bader, "Against Monism: Pluralist critical comments on D. Allen and Pettit," in M. Williams & S. Macedo (eds.), *Nomos* (New York: New York University Press, 2005).

42 Honneth, "Redistribution as Recognition," 113, 134 quoted earlier.

outright reductionisms such as declaring other types only as 'epiphe-nomena' of 'exploitation' (vulgar 'Marxism'), 'oppression' (Young, Pettit), 'exclusion' (Frank Parkin's vulgar Weberianism) or 'discrimi-nation' (vulgar 'status sociology' or reductionist 'equality of status' in political theory).[43] Second, this conceptualization would be at odds with the hard core of terminological and research traditions in recent social sciences (such as Peter Berger or Stefan Hradil). I believe that a monist conceptual and theoretical strategy is a formidable obstacle preventing a detailed and empirically rich analysis of objective injus-tices.

Third, Honneth's claim that the language *of misrecognition covers all different kinds of subjective, social experiences of injustice* seems, prima facie, more plausible if recognition is understood in a very fundamental and simple sense: as a basis for the general minimalist capability of having experiences, making judgments, and undertaking agency with-out which human beings would be cultural dupes and not agents in any meaningful sense who can feel unjustly treated and complain/act against all different kinds of injustices.[44] Given such minimalist agency, however, two issues are contested: first, the linguistic framing of the diversity of experiences of injustice, and, second, the claim that feeling misrecognized is the most important or even the only strong motiva-tional basis of collective action.

(i) In my view, negatively privileged people use a whole array of everyday notions – exploitation, oppression, exclusion amongst them – to articulate their experiences of injustice.[45] A theo-retical re-description of these experiences in terms of recogni-tion/misrecognition is not just a 'natural' extension of every-day language. Quite to the contrary, it would be an attempt to

---

[43] James Scott reduces structural inequalities in a more ambiguous, less systematic way to exploitation and domination: J. Scott, *Domination and the Arts of Resistance* (New Haven: Yale University Press, 1990).

[44] Besides some minimalist care/love, however, we certainly also need some minimal satisfaction of a bundle of basic needs as preconditions for this kind of minimally autonomous agency.

[45] According to Honneth's dichotomy of two 'logics' of conflicts – collective interests versus recognition (*Struggle*, 164ff) – these experiences cannot be experiences of injustice. Everyday concepts, by the way, may also be influenced by prominent theo-retical traditions: Consider Marx's concept of exploitation in addition to the socialist labour movement and everyday framing of workers.

impose a theoretically inspired 'imperialist' concept, linked to a much more narrowly used everyday notion of misrecognition as the only 'adequate' one on the life-world of negatively privileged people. Honneth's claim that "what is called 'injustice' in *theoretical* language is experienced by those affected as social injury to well-founded claims to recognition"[46] lacks theoretical plausibility and empirical validity. Contrary to his claim, not only are 'exploit/being exploited,' 'oppress/being oppressed,' and 'exclude/being excluded' concepts of both everyday language and theoretical language, but this is obviously also true for 'just/unjust.'

(ii) Even if people use a variety of everyday notions to articulate their experiences and feelings of unjust treatment, it might still be the case that being discriminated and feeling misrecognized is the strongest, or even the only, motivational basis of collective action. Such a monist account of motivation for struggles would be the most moderate interpretation of Honneth's claims. At the same time, it would be the most plausible one. This intuition seems to be shared by E. P. Thompson, Barrington Moore, and James Scott[47] though they do not try to develop a monist 'theory' of recognition/misrecognition. Still Honneth would have to give a plausible account of why the feeling of being exploited, oppressed, excluded, or marginalized would have to be somehow translated into the feeling of being misrecognized before gaining motivational force. Suppose that exploitation would not – as it historically always did – spill over into societal prestige-hierarchies (exploited classes also lacking societal recognition), the experience of being exploited (being forced to deliver surplus labour in modern capitalist forms) would then most likely not be articulated as being misrecognized. It would most likely be articulated as being forced to illegitimately work for others even under conditions of full societal and legal recognition as

---

46 Honneth, "Redistribution as Recognition," 114, emphasis added; see *Struggle*, 164f.
47 E. P. Thompson, *The Making of the English Working Class* (London: Victor Gollancz, 1963); B. Moore, *Injustice. The Social Bases of Obedience and Revolt* (London: Random House, 1978); J. Scott, *Weapons of the Weak* (New Haven: Yale University Press, 1985; and *Domination and the Arts of Resistance* (New Haven: Yale University Press, 1990), XIf, 7 et pass.

equals in all other regards).[48] It is also not plausible why such experience and articulation of exploitation would lack motivational force.

Finally, Honneth might respond that conceptual and theoretical monism in the social sciences may – after due consideration – indeed not be such a good idea as he thought (after all, we can combine conceptual and theoretical pluralism in the social sciences with monism in philosophy[49] but at least we should choose a *monist theoretical strategy in moral and political philosophy* where we have the task to make our evaluative standards – often neglected or left implicit in social sciences – explicit, explain and justify them by giving reasons, make them coherent or consistent, and possibly find deep foundations for them. Obviously here I can only touch on these contested issues, demarcating my own position, and raising some worries for Honneth's recognition-theory.

(i) Why would there be, apart from parsimony, a theoretical need for one unifying concept? The main argument for this position is that only moral monism (one unifying and overarching moral principle only) can really avoid the danger of moral relativism. Yet moral pluralists such as Berlin and Galston have convincingly shown that moral pluralism (we have independent, good reasons to defend a plurality of often conflicting moral principles) is a viable alternative to moral relativism, and that pluralism enters into monist frames as soon as we interpret and apply the respective supreme principle.[50]

[48] This would be the ideal-typical case of modern capitalist exploitation. The historically more common, reverse case is that of 'middle-men minorities' (being legally discriminated and socially excluded and misrecognized but not exploited). Needless to say, the overlap and reinforcement (Matthew-effect) of exploitation, oppression, discrimination and exclusion, characteristic for negatively privileged classes or groups, together with the respective feelings and articulations, also normally produces the strongest motivational force for collective action.

[49] See V. Bader, "Against Monism: Pluralist critical comments on D. Allen and Pettit," in M. Williams & S. Macedo (eds.), *Nomos* (New York: New York University Press, 2005).

[50] V. Bader & E. Engelen, "Taking Pluralism Seriously. Arguing For an Institutional Turn in Political Philosophy," in *Philosophy and Social Criticism* 29/4 (2003), 379f.; V. Bader & S. Saharso, "Introduction: Contextualized Morality and Ethno-Religious Diversity," in *Ethical Theory and Moral Practice* 7/2 (2004), 107–115.

(ii) If we choose a monist theoretical strategy,[51] then why not opt for 'justice' or 'fairness' or 'reciprocity' or 'equality' instead of 'recognition'? The concept of justice/injustice has traditionally served as a basic or roof-concept in moral theories, and allows quite naturally the detection and evaluation of different types of objective injustices and corresponding subjective claims. The same is true for fairness, reciprocity, and equality.[52] It is understandable that Honneth does not choose 'justice' and 'equality,' which are the core concepts in Kantian 'moral' theories in the strict sense (theories of the Right, not the Good), since his main aim is the development of a richer and thicker 'ethical' theory in the Hegelian tradition. Yet the concepts of 'fairness' and 'reciprocity' would also allow this. They would also articulate the minimal egalitarian threshold required to "elaborate the normative content of morality" or "the 'moral point of view'"[53] more directly and clearly. The disadvantage of 'recognition' in this regard is that all historically known forms of recognition have been deeply inegalitarian, as Honneth himself acknowledges.[54] Respect and concern have clearly not been 'equal respect and concern' – often not even 'decent' – and it is no accident that Honneth has to qualify his basic notion of recognition as "reciprocal" or "mutual recognition."[55]

---

[51] Honneth, "Recognition as Moral Obligation," 19, 24.

[52] See, for justice and fairness: Kant, Rawls; for reciprocity and equality: Moore, *Injustice*; C. Sigrist, *Regulierte Anarchie* (Frankfurt am Main: Suhrkamp, 1967): Scott, *Domination and the Arts*; see also Max Weber's "anthropologisch tiefsitzendes Legitimationsbedürfnis"; M. Walzer, "Response," in D. Miller & M. Walzer (eds), *Pluralism, Justice, and Equality* (Oxford: Oxford University Press, 1995), 288. The language of equality easily and naturally covers all 'resources and rewards,' all 'fields' or 'spheres,' 'status,' 'capabilities,' 'access,' 'chances,' 'opportunities,' 'basic goods,' 'rights and liberties,' and so on.

[53] Honneth, "Recognition as Moral Obligation," p.17.

[54] See Forst: pro 'reciprocity' versus 'false recognition' (2003, in this volume). Young: 'rigged mutuality'. See Fraser, "Social Justice in the Age of Identity Politics," 37ff: "Justifying claims for recognition."

[55] Honneth, "Redistribution as Recognition," 157, 158; "Recognition as Moral Obligation," 17). "Non-domination" is a better candidate than recognition (Pettit) because it is more difficult to clearly distinguish fair recognition (or "receptive recognition") from power-entrenched recognition ('ascriptive,' ideological, or repressive recognition).

(iv) In a monist moral philosophy, our evaluative standards refer to one supreme concept (of recognition or non-domination), and this process may be extended to deep-foundations: the reasons why we should treat people justly, fairly, equally, respectfully, and so on refer to 'our common nature' as sentient beings with basic needs, as linguistic animals, as autonomous beings, as recognition-seeking animals, as '*zoon politikon,*' and so on, and so on. Non-foundationalists and pluralists choose another strategy in order to find reasoned criteria to distinguish power-based categories of evaluation from ones that can be morally defended.

(a) They do not claim that it would have to be the same evaluative standards covering all injustices: they try to elaborate the positive evaluative standards inherent in our respective judgments of injustices.[56] If exploitation is defined by a critical concept of surplus-labour,[57] then non-exploitation as a standard is the absence of being forced to work for others. If domination/oppression is defined as forced or democratically illegitimate subjection (p. 193, not all hierarchical relations are morally illegitimate and count as domination/oppression), then non-domination as a standard again is the absence of such relationships. If discrimination is defined as the process through which equal rights and/or chances of social recognition of the collectively discriminated are reduced or blocked, recognition as a standard is the absence of such patterns. If morally illegitimate closure and exclusion is defined as the process through which people are prevented from entering positively privileged societal positions or relations by irrelevant criteria, then the positive standard of inclusion means that all those who fulfil the respectively relevant criteria should have access. These positive standards also allow for an evaluation of practices as a matter of degree.

(b) They do not claim that we would have to have the same reasons in justifying such different standards or, more

---

[56] See also Shapiro, *Democratic Justice.*

[57] Bader/Benschop, *Ungleichheiten,* 198ff: not all labour 'for others' is morally illegitimate or counts as surplus-labour.

modestly, that our reasons may refer to very general concepts of fairness or reciprocity (in order to explain the differences between morally legitimate and illegitimate surplus-labour, domination, exclusion). But they have to be specified regarding the respective processes and mechanisms by which structural power-asymmetries are produced and reproduced.

(c) Such specified standards and reasons serve as a basis for evaluating whether subjective claims to be exploited, oppressed, discriminated, or excluded actually are justified. Clearly, not all such claims can be taken to be so at face value. A monist theory of recognition has the double disadvantage that it has to transform all such claims into claims to be misrecognized (moral injuries of individual autonomy or, more often, of individual integrity or identity). But the claims of misrecognition are particularly difficult to evaluate: it is so difficult to draw a line between legitimate and illegitimate complaints, because they are so heavily moulded by power-asymmetries. This is also the case because all former slave-holders, upper castes, estates, and classes – in short all positively privileged – claim to be morally injured, particularly not treated 'with due respect,' and because identity-, authenticity-, and integrity-claims are so malleable and strategically manipulated.[58]

II MISRECOGNITION, POWER, AND INCAPACITATION

Having challenged Honneth's monist theory of recognition, I now turn to the broader question of whether, and if so, how, are people psychically or morally incapacitated by entrenched power-asymmetries and by severe and longstanding collective misrecognition in particular. Again, two diametrically opposed dangers have to be avoided. First, we should avoid victimizing the victims more than they actually are and, second, we should not neglect or underestimate the impact of inequalities on agency and capability. It seems difficult to find a

---

[58] This seems to be a serious problem for all fashionable theories of 'integrity.' It is often not properly addressed at all. For example, see C. Menke (2002) "Grenzen der Gleichheit," in *Deutsche Zeitschrift für Philosophie* 50/6 (2002), 897–906.

balanced answer to the old quarrels of 'structure versus agency.'[59] In this section, I will argue that ideal theories of full and positive recognition as a necessary condition of emphatic concepts of agency (Pippin), moral capacity, developmental powers, and of emphatic "autonomous self-realization," (Honneth) have more trouble avoiding the first danger compared with low-threshold or base-line conceptions,[60] and that structuralist approaches in psychology and sociology are much more prone to victimize the victims compared with methodologically more agent-centred approaches, which are more common in (political) anthropology. The combination of both of these by critical theorists such as Adorno[61] and Marcuse but also Frantz Fanon, and by 'postmodernists' such as Foucault, is particularly dubious.

Theories of 'colonized' or 'submissive conscience' commonly assume that the self-conceptions, self-perceptions, and the self-worth of colonized people, are seriously damaged. They try to explain these restricted capacities by mechanisms such as 'internalization of the aggressor' known from traditional *psychoanalysis*. Traditional PA, and also 'object-relations' PA, have lost much of their credibility in recent social psychology, particularly amongst cognitive social psychologists, who rightly stress the neglected conditions and processes of cognitive and normative framing and the working of power-asymmetries.[62] When we bracket these conditions (see later) and focus on the development of psychic capacities as such, *low-threshold assumptions of incapacitation* seem to be more plausible. We may have trouble reaching agreement on what psychic 'health' or 'autonomy' require (contested, culturally, and elite-biased perfectionist arguments loom large),[63] but

---

[59] V. Bader, "Culture and Identity. Contesting constructivism," in *Ethnicities* 1/2 (2001), 283f.

[60] The difficulty of avoiding the incapacitation trap obviously does not mean that authors would be doomed to fall into it. Honneth explicitly tries to avoid this (*Struggle*, 136–39 on 'emotion' – 'action' – conditions for self-organization) but his monist reconstruction of the motivational structure of 'struggles' (*Struggle*, 163, 165), together with his concept of autonomous self-realization, makes this more difficult (see 134, "typically brings with it" a loss of self-respect and of personal self-esteem). This is the second point of criticism that I share with Fraser ("Social Justice," 31f).

[61] See examples for Adorno in van Den Brink's chapter in this volume. See excellent and detailed criticism: J. Baars, *De mythe van de totale beheersing* (Amsterdam, SUA: 1987).

[62] See Bader, *Rassismus*, 16f and notes.

[63] See W. Galston, *Liberal Pluralism* (Cambridge: Cambridge University Press, 2002); D. Weinstock, "Group Rights: Reframing the Debate," in J. Spinner & A. Eisenberg

most of us agree that serious physical violence such as child beating, incest, or serious psychic neglect of babies and young kids by (natural or social) parents seriously damage the development of agency. Whether serious collective misrecognition – if it does not result in such violence or neglect – also would have such consequences is much more dubious. Above such thresholds, people eventually achieve the minimally needed psychic capacities for agency and judgment, however 'damaged' they may be declared by psychologists, therapists, post-conflict development experts,[64] judges of constitutional courts,[65] and moral philosophers. Whether they are able to resist negative self-worth does not, or at least not primarily, depend on psychic capacities but on *social conditions of framing and action.*

Structuralist *sociology* claims that accumulation of negative privileges leads to *"cultures of poverty."* Cultures of poverty as a theoretical tool has to explain why the 'poor' internalise the negative evaluation of their culture and person predominant in society, thereby losing the individual and collective "capacity to cope with harmful depreciation of cultural beliefs, values and lifestyles."[66] They are said to do so on three levels: Cultures of poverty, on the level of *individuals,* imply "a strong feeling of marginality, of helplessness, of dependence and of inferiority, a lack of impulse control, a strong present-time orientation., a sense of resignation and of fatalism." On the *family*-level: "absence of childhood, early initiation into sex, free unions, high incidence

---

(eds.), *Minorities within Minorities* (Cambridge: Cambridge University Press, 2005); Williams, M. (1998) *Voice, Trust, and Memory.* New Haven: Yale University Press); V. Bader, "Associative Democracy and Minorities within Minorities," in J. Spinner & A. Eisenberg (eds.), *Minorities within Minorities* (Cambridge: Cambridge University Press, 2005). See S. Saharso, "Female Autonomy and Cultural Imperative," in W. Kymlicka & W. Norman (eds.), *Citizenship in Diverse Societies* (Oxford: Oxford University Press, 2000), for a trans-culturally sensitive defence of a minimalist concept of autonomy.

[64] See Berghoefer (*An Examination of Beneficiary Participation in Post-Conflict Development Assistance,* master's thesis, ISHSS [Amsterdam: Universiteit van Amsterdam, 2003], 45ff) for an excellent criticism of the 'Traumatized by Violence' paradigm.

[65] See Rogers Smith ("Law's Races," paper presented at the conference on *Identities, Affiliations, Allegiances* [Yale, October 2003]) for an excellent criticism of both Earl Warren's "damaged race" or incapacitation talk and Clarence Thomas's "racial irrelevance" model of colour blindness (assuming no impact whatsoever of deep seated racism on capacities), and for a convincing outline of Smith's "distinct racial damage" approach.

[66] Berg, "Be prestige-resilient!" 207f; I follow van den Berg's short summary of Boxill's presentation of Oscar Lewis' approach.

of the abandonment of wives and children, mother-centred families, authoritarianism." The absence of substantial and stable voluntary organizations at the *community* level also leads to a failure to participate in the positively valued *institutions of society.*

Criticism that Lewis would align with the ideology of the 'idle' and hence 'deserving' poor is clearly misguided. The real debate is centred, firstly, on the issue whether such cultures of poverty exist at all and, if so, which cases qualify as cultures of poverty, what degree of poverty constitutes cultures of poverty. Secondly, the debate is centred on adequate methods of research both in a descriptive and explanatory perspective. In this regard, there are two critical *objections*:

(i) When using an appropriate pluralist conceptual and theoretical framework and appropriate methods of describing the experiences and off-stage articulations of entrenched ethnic under-classes, it is difficult to find cases in which the powerless passively reproduce hierarchical, monolithic prestige-rankings or fully internalise and *habitualise*[67] the negative stereotypes.

(ii) Practices of serious collective injustice such as severe exploitation, domination/oppression, misrecognition, exclusion, and marginalisation – far from being only quasi-passively and 'voicelessly' experienced – more or less inevitably also provide "the social conditions under which a hidden transcript might be generated,"[68] allowing to articulate these experiences. I fully agree with James Scott's thesis that "the large historical forms of domination . . . are . . . unable to prevent the creation of an independent social space in which subordinates can talk in comparative safety."[69] The basic argument is that the powerless need fairly secure and shielded *social sites* (in houses, factories, fields, alehouses, pubs, taverns, inns, cabarets, beer cellars, gin mills, and in markets, coffeehouses, barber shops, club-rooms, in jails)[70] to talk with different audiences (family,

[67] Bourdieu's theory of habitus, from which I learned a lot, also suffers from structuralist remnants (see my criticism: Bader, *Kollektives Handeln*, 96ff).

[68] Scott, *Domination*, 83.

[69] Scott, *Domination*, 85.

[70] Scott, *Domination*, 120f; see Bader, *Kollektives Handeln*, 218ff: "soziale Organisiertheit" and social spaces.

friends, neighbours, co-workers, peers, and so on) and give meaning to their experiences. Only if the powerful would be able to realize "totalitarian fantasies" in order not only to prevent public communication more or less effectively, but also any hidden communication – by more or less completely atomising the powerless and keeping them under close observation – would they be able to abolish "any social realm of relative discursive freedom."[71] They would then have to transform the conditions of everyday life into those of Benthamite jails or POW brainwashing camps. The more these totalitarian fantasies are realized, the more difficult it will be for the powerless to compare their experiences, articulate their individual experiences as collective ones, and develop counter-languages.[72]

(iii) The powerless, obviously, need not only social sites to articulate their experiences but also cognitive and normative *frames and languages* allowing them to distance themselves from predominant views of world, society, and predominant prestige-hierarchies. In this regard, any critical theory, in my view, should start from three assumptions: *firstly*, that the practices of serious injustices provide incentives/motivation and abundant evidence (the 'material stuff') for such critical articulations; *secondly*, that these experiences are not completely "malleable" – some articulations clearly "fit" better than others – and, *thirdly*, that alternative framing is much easier and more widespread than theories of incapacitation assume. One has only to look for and examine all varieties of 'hidden transcripts' instead of focusing on 'public transcripts' and on elaborate 'discourse.'

Let me, first, address some *substantive* issues:

Every subordinate group creates, out of its ordeal, a 'hidden transcript' that represents a critique of power spoken behind the back of the dominant."[73] The *forms of this critique are numerous* and should not be reduced to 'linguistic'

---

[71] Scott, *Domination*, 83.

[72] See Bader, *Kollektives Handeln*, 168 – 183, for such a critical concept of experience and the different levels of languages and criticism of constructivism and discourse-talk. Fraser rightly stresses the importance of 'folk paradigms' ("Social Justice," 11; "Distorted Beyond All Recognition: A Rejoinder to Axel Honneth," in Nancy Fraser & Axel Honneth, *Redistribution or Recognition? A Political-Philosophical Exchange* (London: Verso, 2003), pp).

[73] Scott, *Domination*, Scott XII.

ones: gestures, songs, the theatre of the powerless, rumours, gossip, folk-tales, jokes, codes, euphemisms, rituals (of reversal, carnival, and fêtes) and practices of resistance (poaching, pilfering, tax evasion, shabby work, go-slow, etc.). Next, the *linguistic articulations* should not be reduced to fully elaborate counter-discourses or 'utopias.' They take place on four different levels: 'pre-theoretical everyday speech,' rudimentary everyday theories, field-specific languages and theories and, eventually, symbolic universes. In addition, criticism does not require fully articulated or elaborated counter-utopias all the way up,[74] it very often, and very effectively, uses symbolic inversion and alternative critical interpretation of 'the discourse of the dominant.'[75] "The obstacles to resistance, which are many, are simply not attributable to the inability of subordinate groups to *imagine* a counterfactual social order.[76]

Even if transcripts are hidden, they are expressed openly somewhere and somehow. The degrees of their *visibility* and *audibility* depend on factors such as the seriousness of entrenched, overall power-asymmetries, the degrees in which different social sites are fairly secure from patrolling by the powerful. Whether the hidden transcripts can find *public expression*, whether off-stage articulations can "storm the stage"[77] depends (1) upon individual courage: 'speaking truth to power' under conditions of serious power-asymmetries is an act of heroism: the "first open statement of a hidden transcript" is "a dec-laration that breaches the etiquette of power relations . . . a symbolic declaration of war."[78] It also depends (2) on significant changes in the power-relations, (3) on organization and mobilization, (4) on changes in the political opportunity structure and, last but not least, (5) on con-tingent events like crises and revolutions.[79]

Secondly, I want to make three short remarks on *methods:*

(i) It is "impossible to know from the *public transcript alone* how much of the appeal to hegemonic values is prudence and

---

[74] "An elaborate riposte, one that goes beyond fragmentary practices of resis-tance . . . resistance to ideological domination requires a counter-ideology" (Scott, *Domination*, 120; see more in detail: Bader, *Kollektives Handeln*, 191ff).

[75] See Bader, *Kollektives Handeln*, 182f, 191f and note 115; Scott, *Weapons of the Weak*; Scott, *Domination*, 77ff, criticizing all varieties of 'ideological hegemony,' 'false con-sciousness.'

[76] Scott, *Domination*, 81.

[77] Scott, *Domination*, 16.

[78] Scott, *Domination*, 8.

[79] See Bader, *Kollektives Handeln*, Figure 7, 221.

formula, and how much is ethical submission"[80] Most importantly, researchers and political theorists should not be deceived by strategies and patterns of disguising ideological insubordination and by the "infra-politics of the powerless,"[81] particularly by public acts of deference in on-stage encounters.

(ii) One first has to extensively analyse actual hidden transcripts before one prematurely makes any assumptions and draws any hasty conclusions about psychic and moral incapacitation, on "ethical submission," "psychological mechanisms of self-exclusion," a "lack of self-confident assertiveness," or a "distorted pattern of preference formation,"[82] or a deep-seated inability to resist 'internalisation' to cope with negative prestige, to criticize '*amor fati*,'and so on. If one has to make assumptions about the relationship between agency and constraining structures at all, then it seems a better idea to start from agency and capability to do anything in order not to overlook hidden transcripts. Before claiming internalisation or habitualised subordination, it seems advisable to exactly analyse the social, cultural, and political conditions preventing the more or less public expressions of hidden transcripts. Historical evidence shows again and again that so-called internalised submission melts like snow in the sun if windows of opportunity to communicate and act are (left) open. If researchers do not want to wait for crises and revolutions to teach this lesson, they have "little choice but to explore the realm of the hidden transcript."[83] Clearly, incapacitation is not so deeply ingrained and insurmountable as some misguided psychological, cultural, and sociological structuralists make us think. The test is always practical, and practice is hard to predict. If we cannot exactly know in advance what really is possible, then the old formula of utopian socialists, "be realistic, ask for the impossible," becomes more attractive.[84]

---

[80] Scott, *Domination*, 92.

[81] XIII, "conformity is a tactical art of manipulation" (Scott, *Domination*, 33).

[82] Berg, "Be prestige-resilient!"

[83] Scott, *Domination*, 16.

[84] See Scott, *Domination*, 16. For elaboration on crises, see Bader, *Kollektives Handeln*, 334f. Examples such as the breakdown of the Shah's regime show that the loopholes and the velocity of practical learning by doing are drastically underestimated by most theories.

(iii) Even if the powerless are fully aware of objective injustices, define their interests in a clearly oppositional way and command a more or less fully elaborate utopia and program of action, the way to organization, mobilization, and successful collective action is long and thorny. Instead of taking the absence of open protest as a sign of psychic and normative incapacitation or of a lack of imagination of alternatives, one should soberly analyse the conditions for successful collective action of "poor peoples": their direct power-resources are grossly inferior, their organization and mobilization is countered, difficult, and costly, and they are confronted with specific strategic dilemma's of poor protesters.[85]

III DEMOCRACY AND INCAPACITATION

The degree to which entrenched inequalities and power-asymmetries actually affect capabilities and articulations of long-term negatively privileged groups depend on the effectiveness of the patrolling of their social sites of articulation and the harshness of social control and political oppression, and so on. The relevant cases would be slavery, serfdom, lower castes, indigenous peoples, and entrenched ethnic under-classes – all fully marginalized categories. Even partial incapacitation generates serious methodological problems for *critical social sciences* and even more serious troubles for *democratic theory and politics*.

Powerless people, then, are partially unable to articulate their own '*objective needs and interests,*' and it seems that *social science*, if it were not to fall prey to indefensible paternalism, would have to accept their 'preferences' at face value. Along with many others, I am convinced that social science and moral philosophy would lose its critical sting if it were to abandon the distinctions between 'needs and wants' and 'objective and subjective interests' or between 'informed, second order preferences' and 'subjective preferences.'[86] In addition, I'm convinced that critical theories can refute paternalism charges.

---

[85] See Bader, *Kollektives Handeln*, 294ff.

[86] Critical social science needs a detached analysis of objective interest-positions and objective inequalities/power asymmetries in order to adequately describe and explain life-chances and collective action. Critical moral theory needs such an analysis in order to be able to critically judge and evaluate actual claims of being unjustly treated.

Subjective definitions may be more or less systematically distorted under conditions of serious inequalities for four reasons: (1) the predominant cognitive and normative frames and interpretations are biased and the chances of alternative framing are unequal; (2) information may be systematically distorted and information chances are unequal; (3) conditions of communication are distorted and unequal; (4) the powerless may be, to a certain degree, psychically incapacitated.[87] Accepting the 'subjective preferences' of 'happy slaves' or 'contented housewives' would mean neglecting these structural distortions.[88]

Democratically illegitimate paternalism, distinct from legitimate paternalism, can be *prevented* if 'mature' people – however distorted their definitions may be according to the judgement of parents, teachers, priests, politicians, sociologists, utilitarian welfare-economists, psychiatrists, development-experts, moral and political philosophers – having heard their criticism, are left free to define and decide for themselves 'in the last instance' – that is, whenever it comes to actual decisions.

The guarantee and protection of this actual, legal, and political autonomy – which is always to a certain degree counterfactual – is the cornerstone of morally defensible versions of *democracy*.

Political philosophy,[89] for quite a while, focused on the construction of *ideal models* of democracy and deliberation under Habermasian

---

[87] See Bader, *Kollektives Handeln*, 140–151.

[88] See, for a short summary in political philosophy, Will Kymlicka, *Politics in the Vernacular* (New York/Oxford: Oxford University Press 2001), 15ff (absent from the 1st edition).

[89] Political theorists and philosophers, in general, should draw at least two important lessons from the 'minima sociologica' summarized in Section II: (a) Their working concepts of public reason should be freed from monism in moral philosophy and from consensualist, cognitivist, rationalist assumptions predominant in Rawlsian and Habermasian philosophy. This is increasingly done during the last decade or so (for example, I. M. Young, "Communication and the Other," in S. Benhabib [ed.], *Democracy and Difference* [Princeton: Princeton University Press, 1996], 120–35; I. M. Young, "Difference as a Resource for Democratic Communication," in James Bohman & William Rehg [eds.], *Deliberative Democracy* [Cambridge, MA: MIT Press, 1997], 383–406; S. Benhabib, "Toward a Deliberative Model of Democratic Legitimacy," in S. Behabib [ed.], *Democracy and Difference* [Princeton: PUP, 1996], 67–94; J. Tully, "The Agonic Freedom of Citizens," in *Economy and Society* 28/2 [1999], 161–82; J. Tully, "Exclusion and Assimilation," in M. Williams & S. Macedo [eds.], *Nomos* (New York: New York University Press, 2005); J. Valadez, *Deliberative Democracy, Political Legitimacy, and Self-determination in Multicultural Societies* [Boulder: Westview Press, 2001]; V. Bader, "Religious Pluralism. Secularism or Priority for Democracy?" in *Political Theory* 27/5 [1999], 597–633; V. Bader, "Taking Religious Pluralism Seriously:

conditions of "*Herrschaftsfreiheit.*" It assumes equal chances for all to start cognitive or normative discourses, equal chances of all in these discourses, and no power-asymmetries between participants and truthfulness. Such normative standards are useful in efforts to detect actual inequalities. Recently, deliberative democrats slowly descended from Mount Olympus in order to address conditions of democracy in the '*muddy*' *world* of inequalities, power-asymmetries, distorted definitions, and even psychic and moral incapacitation. They increasingly discuss the spill over of exploitation, domination/oppression, misrecognition, exclusion, and marginalisation – and of seriously unequal command of relevant political resources – into drastic unequal political chances in general and the *consequences of these power-asymmetries for public deliberation* in particular, even without assuming any psychic or moral incapacitation of the powerless.[90] The main challenge then lies in designing institutions and policies to tackle serious background inequalities, and proponents of both 'deliberative democracy' and 'associative democracy' still have a hard time doing this in a plausible way.[91] If inequalities and state-repression are so harsh that the

---

Introduction," in *Religious Pluralism, Politics, and the State. Special Volume of Ethical Theory and Moral Practice* 6 / 1 [2003], 3–22; B. Parekh, *Rethinking Multiculturalism* [Houndsmill: Macmillan Press, 2000]; M. Williams, *Voice, Trust, and Memory* [New Haven: Yale University Press, 1998]; D. Archard, "Political Disagreement, Legitimacy, and Civility," in *Philosophical Explorations* IV/3 [2001], 207–23; Bert van den Brink, "Political Liberalism's Conception of Citizenship," German version in *Deutsche Zeitschrift für Philosophie* 50/6 [2002]: 907–24; M. Deveaux, "A Deliberative Approach to Conflicts of Culture," in J. Spinner & A. Eisenberg [eds.] *Minorities within Minorities* [Cambridge: Cambridge University Press, 2005]). In addition, they should work with highly diversified and pluralized notions of 'discourse' or 'practices of reasoning' presented and discussed in detail by James Tully ("Exclusion and Assimilation," 31). (b) They should shift their attention to the detailed study of old and new "practices of freedom" (p. 36), which may also help to avoid the risk of theoretical incapacitation and of practical incapacitation by experts, advisors, and helpless helpers informed by working paradigms of incapacitation.

90 E. Schattschneider, *The Semisovereign People* (New York: Holt, Rinehart, and Winston, 1960); J. Elster, "The Market and the Forum," in James Bohman & William Rehg (eds.), *Deliberative Democracy* (Cambridge, MA: MIT Press, 1997), 3 – 34; J. Bohman, "Deliberative democracy and effective social freedom," in James Bohman & William Rehg (eds.), *Deliberative Democracy* (Cambridge, MA: MIT Press, 1997); Williams, *Voice, Trust, and Memory*, 75ff; Shapiro, *Democratic Justice*; Deveaux, "A Deliberative Approach".

91 See V. Bader, "Problems and Prospects of Associative Democracy," in Hirst & Bader (eds.), *Associative Democracy – The Real Third Way?* (London: Frank Cass, 2001), 45ff.

'worst off' also lack 'motivational sources' and alternative framing capabilities to express their objective interests – as is assumed by for example Knight/Johnson and Valadez[92] – then the problem is even more intractable.

In my view, *two* – analytically and also, to a certain degree, practically – *different ways* to address the problem can be distinguished. Both share more or less detailed and concrete proposals to make the institutional setting of the political process as open and equal, and as culturally sensitive as possible. The *first* approach tries to "cultivate motivation for political participation" and to build political capacities by moral pedagogy and by education.[93] One could call it "a politics of more or less *direct capacitation*." This strategy is vulnerable to paternalism charges: who educates the educators? In addition, it is fairly ineffective if not combined with institutional re-design and increasing opportunities for actual and meaningful participation (learning by doing). The *good news* is that, happily, the 'worst off' are commonly not as worse off in terms of capabilities, as Valadez and others assume.

The *second* approach acknowledges that – as a price for non-elitist and non-paternalist forms of democracy – 'the powerless' have to overcome existing thresholds of self-definition and agency even if this is objectively unjust given the long-term and entrenched inequalities they had to cope with.[94] It focuses on a mid-term strategy of changing political institutions and policies creating opportunities for participation and representation. It could be called "a strategy of *indirect capacitation* trusting more on learning by doing than on moral pedagogy and civic education." The *bad news* is that this needs more time and a lot of political power. The *worst news* is that proposals for increased participation and institutional representation of minorities in the political process, particularly purely procedural ones, are unable to undo deep power-asymmetries grounded in history and in the structure of recent

---

[92] J. Knight & J. Johnson, "What sort of equality does deliberative democracy require?" in J. Bohman & W. Rehg (eds.), *Deliberative Democracy: Essays on Reason and Politics* (Cambridge, MA: MIT Press, 1997) and J. Valadez (*Deliberative Democracy*, Ch. III)

[93] Valadez, *Deliberative Democracy*, 8off.

[94] Williams (*Voice, Trust, and Memory*, 196ff) defends the "intuition that recognition should not be extended to a group that lacks a sense of shared identity." "Memory," the subjective aspect of group definition, is just such a minimalist expression of agency.

societies. They have to be complemented by institutional designs and policies to redress these entrenched background inequalities needing even more time and political power than changing polities. Recent political theory is badly prepared for such a task – an institutional turn is urgently required – and, politically speaking, such long-term building of political counter-power requires more *"geduldiges Bohren dicker Bretter"* than even Max Weber would have imagined.

11

Reasonable Deliberation, Constructive Power, and the Struggle for Recognition

Anthony Simon Laden

Dusk falls on Europe and North America at somewhat different times, and so it should not surprise us if the owl of Minerva adopts different flight paths in the two places. In the work of Axel Honneth, Hegel's long shadow is unmistakable. In Honneth's continental context, it takes the form of a focus on social struggles and conflict, on oppositional social movements and other extra-government social actors. In the work of John Rawls, Hegel's shadow is no less present, though perhaps less noticed.[1] There, however, it takes the form of a focus on social institutions, and in particular, the institutions of government and its agents.

Once we see that these seemingly very different theories have a common root, a possible project of reconciliation, or at least cross-fertilization, presents itself. We can ask how political institutions might be set up so as to be responsive to struggles for recognition, and how such struggles might appeal to such responsiveness. Such questions

---

[1] It is perhaps more noticed by writers on Hegel than writers on Rawls. See, for instance, Frederick Neuhouser, *Foundations of Hegel's Social Philosophy: Actualizing Freedom* (Cambridge: Harvard University Press, 2000), esp. 227–229, 266–270. For discussion of Rawls that brings out his Hegelian roots, see Sybil Schwarzenbach, "Rawls, Hegel, and Communitarianism," in *Political Theory* 19 (1991): 539–71, and my *Reasonably Radical: Deliberative Liberalism and the Politics of Identity* (Ithaca, NY: Cornell University Press, 2001), especially 70–72. For Rawls's own view of Hegel, and the relationship of Hegel's work to his own, see his *Lectures on the History of Moral Philosophy* (Cambridge: Harvard University Press, 2000), esp. 365–369, though the whole second lecture on Hegel is instructive.

become particularly urgent in cases where the group struggling for recognition has achieved what I will call "basic respect," in the form of legal status, and even a measure of social esteem, but are nonetheless still denied what I will call "fully equal respect." That is, they fail to be recognized by those who maintain power over them as fully co-equal authors of the contours of their mutual relationship. As a result of this misrecognition, those who maintain that power may fail to see demands that they give up this power as demands of justice, and so be less open to them. Examples of this oppressive dynamic include the failure of whites to give up their privilege in white supremacist but not overtly racist societies, and the failure of men to give up their male privilege in patriarchal but not overtly sexist societies. Because such misrecognition can take place even within the confines of legal equality and social esteem, it is often overlooked in an exclusive focus on oppositional struggles for respect and esteem or on just and legitimate political institutions. By bringing these two approaches together, however, we can better understand this problem and work out possible routes to its solution.

In the course of my argument, I rely on my own Rawls-inspired work on reasonable deliberation, rather than discussing Rawls directly. Nothing of that work, I take it, is incompatible with Rawls's work, although it sometimes goes beyond what he says. The chapter unfolds across three main sections. First, I set out the main components of Honneth's theory of recognition, paying special attention to the role of hierarchical relations of power in disrupting such recognition, and thus prompting the resistance expressed through social movements. Then I turn to an account of reasonable deliberation, with the aim of showing that it provides a kind of model of relations of recognition. Situating Honneth's theory within the context of reasonable deliberation brings out interesting features of both accounts. In particular, it highlights a republican idea of seeing citizens as engaged in the co-authorship of their shared identity that runs through both theories. Focusing on this aspect of each theory leads me, in the final section, to suggest how we might conceive of struggles for fully equal respect as moves within a deliberative process, and the sorts of institutional structures that might hear such struggles as reasonable and thus be responsive to them.

RECOGNITION AND POWER: A THEORY AND A PROBLEM

In *The Struggle for Recognition* and the various essays that build on it, Honneth provides a rich updating of Hegel's early work on recognition. For my purposes, three main features of Honneth's work need to be recalled. First, the theory rests on a social-psychologically based understanding of the human self, such that it forms and maintains itself through relations of recognition.[2] In such relationships, each person is confirmed in her understanding of her own identity and value through the recognition of that identity and value by others. As was noted already by Rousseau, and more famously by Hegel, such relations must be mutual and reciprocal for the following reason: The recognition of the other can serve to sustain my own self-conception only if I regard the other as having the identity and value of someone capable of conferring proper recognition. The master represents a developmental dead-end for Hegel precisely because he has left himself dependent on the recognition of his slave, a being whom he must also regard as unworthy of conferring adequate recognition on him.[3]

Second, relations of recognition can be divided into three subgroups: relations of love, respect, and solidarity. Very roughly, love involves the recognition of a specific other's particular needs as worthy of satisfaction, and is exemplified in the love of parents for children, and of lovers and friends for each other.[4] It also involves an emotional tie that balances recognition of the loved one's independence with an

---

[2] Honneth stresses that his updating of Hegel is done "in the light of empirical social psychology," *The Struggle for Recognition*, transl. by Joel Anderson (Cambridge: MIT Press, 1996), 68.

[3] Rousseau makes this point most clearly in his "Discourse on the Origins of Inequality," part II, par. 27, in *The Discourses and other early political writings*, transl. by Victor Gourevitch (Cambridge: Cambridge University Press, 1997), 170. For Hegel, see his *Phenomenology of Spirit*, transl. by A. V. Miller (Oxford: Oxford University Press, 1977), §190–192.

[4] Honneth tends to treat the love of parents for children as structurally similar to the love between adults, ignoring the degree to which one is of necessity asymmetrical. Given what I say about the difference between two forms of respect later, it is also conceivable that attention to issues of power would require dividing the category of love into two: love of someone who is wholly dependent on you and the love for someone with whom you share an interdependent relationship. See Iris Young's contribution to this volume for further reflections on this point.

orientation of continuing care. It is thus limited in scope, focused on particular features, and inextricably emotional.

Respect involves the recognition of the other's generalized status as an equal subject of dignity. It is exemplified in legal relations and those captured in Kantian morality. It is fundamentally cognitive and general: I respect others as, say, legal persons who are bearers of rights, or autonomous agents in light of their being members of a general class, rather than in light of their particular qualities. Part of the value of respect, then, is that through respect we affirm to one another that our value and place is not dependent on our particular talents, traits, or affective ties. In the course of discussing respect, Honneth does not make a distinction on which I will place a great deal of weight: between merely basic respect and fully equal respect. Merely basic respect involves recognizing another as a member of a rights-bearing category of persons. It thus only requires a level of formal equality. Fully equal respect, on the other hand, involves recognizing the other as a fully equal participant in the construction of your shared relationship. As I will suggest later, fully equal respect requires reciprocal levels of what I will call "constructive power." There are at least two reasons why Honneth does not insist on this distinction. First, he is concerned to mark the differentiation of respect from esteem, and thus highlights those aspects of respect that are independent of the substantive relationships in which the respecting parties stand. This concern pushes him to describe respect in terms that suggest the idea of merely basic respect, even when it appears that he has fully equal respect in mind. Second, he argues that there is a kind of rational historical progression that leads merely basic respect to, ultimately, fully equal respect. He sees this historical progression as working out the logic of respect rather than moving us from one species of respect to another.[5]

Finally, solidarity, like love, is tied to particular features of the other, while like respect, it is fundamentally cognitive. Relations of solidarity involve esteem: the recognition that we each make a positive individual contribution within some collective value-horizon. Esteem can take either a corporatized form or an individualized form. Others may

---

[5] Honneth discusses respect in *Struggle* at 107–121. The historical progression is laid out most explicitly at 115–118.

esteem me as a member of a group that is considered valuable in its particular features. So, for instance, if I am esteemed as a Jew or as a philosopher, this involves not merely the grudging acknowledgement that Jews or philosophers are, after all, human (and thus deserving of basic respect), but a positive recognition that Jews as Jews or philosophers as philosophers contribute something of value to the society at large, that the society would be poorer for their absence (perhaps merely in being less diverse and thus less interesting). Others may also esteem me for my own individual achievements, and their value either within a local context, or more widely: for my contribution to the life of the department or the congregation or to the wider community.

Third, the absence of any of these forms of recognition constitutes a harm, and thus a motivation for a struggle for recognition. In particular, we can understand many social struggles of the past and present as being motivated by a lack of respect or esteem from the wider society, and thus directed at securing adequate recognition. In the case of esteem, the struggle for recognition can achieve its purpose in several ways: In struggling for forms of corporative esteem for members of our group, we may come to esteem each other individually for our contributions to the struggle. We may also come to see more clearly that we are worthy of corporative esteem via our membership in this group: The struggle itself is an act of self-assertion on the part of our group. Finally, others who have previously failed to esteem us as members of the group may be moved to do so, either because they come to be convinced of our distinctive value, or merely in virtue of the fact that we stand up for ourselves. ("You've got to admire those people, they really stand up for themselves.")

It is in the analysis of the harm that misrecognition inflicts that the question of power plays a key role. If misrecognition is to be a harm, it must matter to the one misrecognized. Misrecognition can matter in one of two ways. First, it can cause psychological harm to an individual by depriving her of a source of identity and value. But note that we are only vulnerable to such psychological harm at the hands of those we recognize as being in a position to confer value on us through their recognition.[6] Moreover, in many cases, a sufficiently

---

[6] The recognition that another has the ability to confer value on me need not be accompanied by my esteem for that person. G. A. Cohen provides a nice example of

strongly entrenched institutional recognition will give me the psychological wherewithal to dismiss those who misrecognize me as thereby unworthy. Faced with someone's failure to recognize me adequately, I may be able to dismiss her failure as saying more about her than about me. It is interesting to note in this regard that the sorts of actions that Honneth counts as paradigmatic of disrespect are denials of rights and exclusion, but not the more individualized failure of recognition found in crime. The thief clearly fails to respect my rights to my property, but this need not undermine my self-respect as long as the state continues to recognize my status. Upon being robbed, I may feel invaded or violated, but I am unlikely to suffer harm to my self-respect, unless and until no legal authorities come to my aid.

Second, misrecognition can play a role in more material harms. As the discussion chapter suggests, I rely on the recognition of established social attitudes and structures not only for my sense of my psychological well-being, but also because of the varied and indirect effects it has on my ability to live my life. This benefit from recognition does not require that I value its source positively, however. Thus, someone's failure to recognize me can still harm me if, regardless of my view of her, she is in a position to make her view of me socially effective or if her perception of me is guided by socially entrenched attitudes and stereotypes. I might personally think that anti-Semitism is an indefensible, unreasonable, and ultimately stupid attitude for anyone to have. On its own, this view of mine will help to insulate me from psychological harm at the hands of anti-Semites. If, however, those anti-Semites either occupy positions of authority where they are allowed to give their anti-Semitism free reign, or are supported in their attitudes by socially entrenched and thus authoritative attitudes, their anti-Semitism will harm me regardless of what I think of it. Their misrecognition of me will harm me insofar as the society in which I live will take my Judaism to tell against my humanity in a whole myriad of possibly small but tangible ways. It is this social form of misrecognition and its harms that will be my primary concern in what follows.

---

this vulnerability in his *If You're an Egalitarian, How Come You're So Rich?* (Cambridge: Harvard University Press, 2000), 34–37. He describes the effect of his high school English teacher's anti-Semitism on him, an effect that was no less harmful for the fact that Cohen had ample evidence, which he believed, that the man was "an empty windbag."

To understand the nature of this harm, it will help to introduce and define some terminology. I use the term "identity" in a way that is now familiar from what has come to be known as "the politics of identity," but understand it through the lens of Christine Korsgaard's discussion of "practical identity."[7] An identity is a particular social self-conception that a person has, as, say, a member of a particular race or gender or ethnic group. Having a given identity places you in a particular social category, and in a variety of relationships with people with whom you share the identity, and with those who have complementary identities (for example, man/woman, white/black). Sometimes I have an identity because I identify myself as a member of the group in question. In other cases, my membership in the social category marked out by a given group is the result of others' identifying me that way. Of course, given the intersubjective nature of recognition, these two paths to identity-formation are by no means exclusive. Nevertheless, we can use the conceptual distinction between them to introduce the idea of "constructive social power." A group has constructive social power insofar as they have the capacity to set out the boundaries, relevance, and status of certain identities. That is, constructive social power is the power to determine what characteristics are marked as socially significant, and what the social consequences are for finding yourself with those characteristics. It is the capacity, for instance, to determine that sex or skin color mark you as a member of a social group with a certain status, while finger length and whether your earlobe is attached or not do not. Put more succinctly, it is the power to construct an identity. Constructive social power can then be distributed reciprocally or asymmetrically with respect to the capacity to determine the boundary, relevance, and status of a given category. When it is distributed reciprocally, then to the extent that others have power over your identity, you have power over theirs. When it is distributed asymmetrically,

---

7 To the extent that one makes a distinction, as Iris Young does, between the politics of difference and the politics of identity, my use of the term "identity" is that made by Young in her discussions of the politics of difference. See Young, *Justice and the Politics of Difference* (Princeton: Princeton University Press, 1990) and "Difference as a Resource for Democratic Communication" in *Deliberative Democracy*, ed. by James Bohman and William Rehg (Cambridge: MIT Press, 1997). For Korsgaard's discussion of practical identity, see her *Sources of Normativity* (Cambridge: Cambridge University Press, 1996), 100–102.

then one group of people has the power to construct the identity of another group of people, who in turn have no power to effectively resist or contest that construction of their identity. When power is thus distributed, we can say that some people have the capacity to impose identities on others. I will describe people or groups with this capacity as powerful and those who have particular identities imposed on them as powerless. Since everyone has many identities, it is possible to be powerful with regard to some of your identities while being powerless with regard to others.[8]

With this machinery in place, then, we can describe the sort of social relationship outlined earlier that supports socially entrenched misrecogniton as one where constructive power is distributed asymmetrically. Note that according to this analysis, unequal relations of power generate the harm of misrecognition even if the powerful either positively or accurately identify the powerless. That is, the imposition of an identity is a form of misrecognition even if the identity imposed would be endorsed by the powerless group. Even such positive and accurate imposition involves a failure of respect owed to the powerless as self-determining agents capable of forging their own identities and affiliations and their relations to them precisely because it is an imposition. It helps to locate this form of misrecognition within Honneth's system by calling it a lack of fully equal respect. Since fully equal respect is a form of respect that recognizes others as fully equal partners in our mutual construction of our relationship via reciprocal recognition, it is only possible in the context of reciprocal distributions of constructive power, since it is only in that context that neither side can impose an identity on the other. By contrast, mere basic respect involves the extension of formal legal recognition in the form of rights, and this can be achieved even in the context of asymmetrical distributions of

---

[8] This paragraph draws heavily on other work of mine, where the ideas sketched here are more fully developed. See, in particular, *Reasonably Radical*, 73–98 and 131–58, and "Reasonable Liberals, Radical Feminists," in *Journal of Political Philosophy* 11 (2003): 133–52. The general idea of power laid out here is indebted to the work of Catharine MacKinnon and Michel Foucault. See, for instance, Catharine MacKinnon, "Difference and Dominance: On Sex Discrimination," in MacKinnon, *Feminism Unmodified* (Cambridge: Harvard University Press, 1987), and Michel Foucault, "The Subject and Power," in *Michel Foucault: Beyond Structuralism and Hermeneutics*, 2nd ed., ed. by Herbert Dreyfus and Paul Rabinow (Chicago: University of Chicago Press, 1983), and Foucault, *Discipline and Punish*, transl. by Alan Sheridan (New York: Vintage, 1979).

constructive power. The powerful can impose the identity of rights-bearer on the powerless without thereby yielding their constructive power over the powerless.

That the mere presence of asymmetrical relations of constructive power constitutes a kind of misrecognition opens up a possibility that Honneth does not always emphasize. Whereas Honneth discusses struggles for basic respect on behalf of groups who are excluded from the legal system, and struggles for esteem on behalf of groups that are included in the legal system but degraded or despised by the dominant culture, he is less clear about struggles for fully equal respect that involve a demand for a redistribution of power.

Such struggles present a problem for Honneth's view that is tied to its focus on social movements and its lack of attention to institutional issues. The problem involves the likely response of the powerful to such struggles, even after the basis of the struggle has been clearly articulated via Honneth's theory. In the case of struggles for basic respect and esteem, the mere articulation of the demand may go a long way toward moving others to accept it. The struggle for basic respect claims that those excluded are generically similar to those included, and so there is no basis for their exclusion. Once those on the inside are made to see that those they are excluding are human, too, they have compelling grounds to broaden the scope of their respect. The basic struggle for esteem involves making clear why the contributions of the disesteemed group are valuable: why they count as art or culture, for instance. Once again, a conceptual shift on the part of the dominant group suffices to provide them with compelling grounds for broadening the scope of their recognition. In neither case is there a direct cost to the dominant group for greater inclusion.[9] When, however, the

---

[9] Things are, of course, messier in real life. First of all, the extension of humanity or citizenship to those formerly excluded from the category may be thought to rob the identity of some of its status. In such situations, however, I would suggest that there is a mixture of two sorts of cases: exclusion from a universal category tied together with a resistance to a redistribution of power. Second, in the case of granting esteem to the cultural products of heretofore disesteemed groups, there may be costs involved: If jazz concerts are scheduled at Carnegie Hall, then there will be fewer classical concerts there. If we include female authors in our syllabi, we cut down the time devoted to reading male authors. Without dismissing these problems as unimportant, I do think they are different in kind from the sorts of costs involved in explicitly yielding constructive power.

powerless struggle for fully equal respect, they demand that the powerful give something up: in particular, the ability to impose identities on others. As a result, it is much less clear that the mere articulation of the demand will motivate the powerful to accede.

Honneth's theory provides some of the resources for addressing this problem. For now, however, I merely want to note that his general orientation has meant that he has failed to pay attention to it. That is, by focusing on social movements and their demands, he has been drawn away from asking how those demands are received. This lack of attention may not matter in the first two types of struggle, as the mere clarification of the demand may serve to motivate its acceptance. In the third type of struggle – for fully equal respect – more needs to be said.

Furthermore, if we want not only to provide a framework for analyzing struggles of the past that we now regard as unproblematically worthy of positive response, but to provide a framework for thinking about future struggles that may initially appear not so obviously reasonable, we will need to pay more attention to how struggles for recognition in general are met and understood by the powerful. Asking about how struggles for recognition will be taken up by the powerful is an institutional question. It focuses not only on the motivational structure of the powerful (why should the struggles of the powerless move them to change?), but also on the institutional pathways by which, within an existing and ongoing society, such struggles can stake an undismissable claim to legitimacy. We need, then, an institutionally oriented theory that captures the essential insights and details of Honneth's account. A theory of reasonable deliberation, I argue, will do the trick.

REASONABLE DELIBERATION: A MODEL OF RECOGNITION

In this section, I highlight three essential components of reasonable deliberation in order to show that in reasonable deliberation, all the previously discussed aspects of recognition are to be found.[10] First, I

---

[10] These remarks draw on my "Outline of a Theory of Reasonable Deliberation," in *Canadian Journal of Philosophy*, 30 (2000): 551–580, where they are developed in more detail. See also, *Reasonably Radical*, 73–130, and John Rawls, *Political Liberalism* (New York: Columbia University Press, 1993, paperback ed., 1996). My "Radical Liberals,

distinguish deliberation from negotiation. Negotiated agreements are compromises amongst parties who have different pre-existing interests they are trying to satisfy. They engage in bargaining as a means of maximizing the satisfaction of these interests, because they realize that the presence of other agents with different interests places an obstacle in their way. Deliberation, on the other hand, involves an exchange among people who regard themselves as partners trying to work out together a shared solution to a shared problem.[11]

The aim of deliberation is not merely a mutually acceptable compromise, but rather a shared solution that each of the parties can regard as expressing her investment in the issue under discussion. It aims, to put this in Rawls's terms, at something like an overlapping consensus and not merely a *modus vivendi.* Nevertheless, even if it aims at a kind of agreement, deliberation can be ongoing without this being a sign that it has failed.[12] The very act of deliberation reflects a kind of agreement among the parties to resolve their differences cooperatively and on mutually acceptable terms. Despite this common aim, deliberators come to deliberation with different perspectives, and thus see the problem they are working through differently. Because of their diversity, parties engaged in deliberation must strive to offer up reasons for their proposed solutions that can rest on a shared, or potentially shared, identity.

We can thus understand deliberation as involving the exchange of purported "we"-reasons: claims whose authority as reasons derive from the nature of the identity the deliberators do or might come to share: the "we" they form. Reasons so understood are intersubjective and rely for their authority on the shared warranted understanding that the deliberators have of their relationships to one another. Because reasons are thus tied to particular shared identities, they can serve

---

Reasonable Feminists," argues that Rawls is best read as a theorist of reasonable deliberation. See especially 143–148.

[11] Examples of writers who work within what might be called "the logic of negotiation" are David Gauthier, *Morals by Agreement* (Oxford: Oxford University Press, 1983), and bargaining theory more generally. Much, though not all, work in "deliberative democracy" works with a logic of deliberation. See for example, Bohman and Rehg, *Deliberative Democracy*; James Tully, *Strange Multiplicity* (Cambridge: Cambridge University Press, 1995), and my *Reasonably Radical.*

[12] James Tully stresses this aspect of deliberation (though he calls it negotiation) in *Strange Multiplicity,* 135–36. See also *Reasonably Radical,* 127.

as vehicles of both the general and the particular aspects of recognition that Honneth highlights. In offering a deliberative reason to you, I express my basic respect for you as someone capable of evaluating reasons and deserving of the chance to do so. At the same time, in offering this specific reason to you, I express my sense of your individual character, as someone who will find this claim compelling. The sense in which deliberation involves fully equal respect becomes clear when we turn to the second and third features of deliberation.

Since the authority of deliberative reasons rests on their shared acknowledgement, an offered claim can only count as a reason if it meets with proper acknowledgement that it is indeed a reason. This requires some qualification to distinguish between cases where a failure of acknowledgement casts doubt on the original claim, and cases where it casts doubt on the good faith of our deliberative partner. An aspect of that qualification will come in the third feature of reasonable deliberation. Note, however, that by making the force of my claim depend on your acknowledgement of it as a reason, I further demonstrate my fully equal respect for your general capacity for reflection, your autonomy, and your status as a co-author with me (and perhaps others) of the nature and character of our relationship.

Finally, deliberation is reasonable only when the reasonable rejection of a claim by one deliberator matters in the sense that it will significantly affect the future course of the deliberation. Deliberation can, of course, fail this way, if one party or the other is willfully obtuse, and fails to take heed of his partner's rejection of his claims or the reasons offered to justify those rejections. But it can also happen on structural grounds. In this case, what prevents my rejection from mattering is your failure to see it as reasonable, because you understand the identity that supports my rejection differently from the way I do, and it is your understanding rather than mine that is effective in dictating the future course of the deliberation. In other words, it can happen if you have imposed an identity on me. Notice that this can happen even if we are both deliberating in good faith. You may honestly think that what I have said is unreasonable, mere special pleading, or whining, and you are supported in your belief by all sorts of social attitudes and practices. In this case, what distorts our deliberation is an unequal distribution of constructive power. Note that what goes wrong here is that we are prevented from forming a relationship of mutual recognition in Honneth's sense. While you may esteem me insofar as I have the identity you impose on me, by imposing that identity on me, you fail to show me fully equal respect as a self-determining co-author of our relationship.

Furthermore, our deliberation will fail to be reasonable in the presence of such an unequal distribution of power even if it does not run into the problems mentioned earlier. We can trace this sort of failure to your unwillingness to relinquish your power over me, even if you do not consciously rely on it in our interaction. Imagine, for instance, that we both not only deliberate in good faith, but are of what is often called "good will." Though you have power over me, and so have the resources to impose an identity on me, you very much wish not to do so. You thus go out of your way to take heed of what I say, to treat it as reasonable. Nevertheless, the choice of whether to do so remains always in your hands, and despite your good will, you do not take any steps to give up your power. Here, too, our deliberation is not reasonable, and precisely because it is not a form of genuine recognition. Your basic respect and esteem for me are, in an important sense, at your own whim, and so your taking up these attitudes towards me does not show me fully equal respect. Your willingness to accept my reasons combined with your unwillingness to give up the power to choose to do so demonstrates that you do not regard me as a valid source of claims on you, as a co-equal author of the nature of our relationship.[13] As we will see later, this requirement – that in order to deliberate reasonably with you, I must fully respect you as a co-author of our relationship – provides the key to understanding how struggles for fully equal respect can find a hearing. It is thus here that a theory of reasonable deliberation makes its greatest contribution to Honneth's theory of recognition.

---

[13] There is a parallel here with republican arguments about the threat to one's liberty created by dependence on another. See Philip Pettit, *Republicanism: A Theory of Freedom and Government*, paperback ed. (Oxford: Oxford University Press, 1999); Quentin Skinner, "The Republican Ideal of Political Liberty," in *Machiavelli and Republicanism*, ed. by Gisela Bock; Quentin Skinner and Maurizio Viroli. (Cambridge: Cambridge University Press, 1990), 293–309, and Skinner, *Liberty before Liberalism* (Cambridge: Cambridge University Press, 1998).

REASONABLE STRUGGLES AMID INSTITUTIONS
OF RECOGNITION

If we think of struggles for recognition in terms of reasonable deliberation, we can then ask what sort of deliberative moves are open to social movements struggling for recognition, and what sorts of institutional structures might insist that these deliberative moves be granted a hearing. In particular, we can ask about the nature of the reasons that a social movement struggling for recognition might urge on the wider society. One possible source of their claim, we have seen, is that under current conditions (including the unequal distribution of constructive power), they are not in a position to deliberate reasonably with the powerful. We can then ask why the powerful should respond to such a claim. In the context of a theory of reasonable deliberation, this means asking why they have grounds for treating this claim as a reason, as having authority for them.

Two common responses to this question aim to show that it is in the interests of the powerful to relinquish their dominant position, or, alternatively, to show why they are under a moral imperative to do so, even if they might not be otherwise motivated to do so.[14] The theories I have been discussing highlight a third type of consideration, however. According to the theory of reasonable deliberation, a claim becomes a reason when it appeals to a feature of the relationship that binds the reasoners together. We can thus appeal to a feature of the identity of the powerful, perhaps independently of their interests, but nevertheless not external to them in the way that a moral imperative may appear to be. There are, I think, two different strategies for doing this, the first to be found in Rawls's political liberalism and the second in Honneth's work.

First, we might look to a separate identity that the powerful and powerless share, and via which each side already acknowledges the other as equal. The powerless could then appeal to this aspect of the identity of the powerful in making their case and thereby gain some authority over their oppressors. Thus, for instance, if we understand

---

[14] The first of these options is preferred by writers such as Gauthier working in a broadly Hobbesian tradition. The second is found among some Kantian and Utilitarian writers.

democratic citizenship as a political relationship amongst free and equal co-legislators, then a misrecognized group could appeal to their common citizenship to challenge the dominant group to change. To take an example, the presence of white supremacist attitudes and social structures in United States society serves to leave non-whites socially invisible and thus not fully recognized. As a result, reasonable deliberation between non-whites and whites is impossible. If, however, both whites and non-whites regard themselves and each other as democratic citizens, then non-whites can appeal to whites in the name of their common citizenship to heed their call for recognition and act to redistribute power to bring it about. In such a case, whites are appealed to on the basis of their identity as citizens, an identity they regard as racially neutral. Non-whites argue that unless whites give up their power over non-whites, they cannot be democratic citizens in the way that they take themselves to be. Such an appeal will work to the extent that whites are more fully attached to their self-conception as non-racialized democratic citizens than their self-conceptions as racially superior. There are, of course, a number of crucial "if"s in this argument, and in actual cases, it may run aground on any or all of them. In the final analysis, we may find that the struggles for basic respect and esteem may not have succeeded, that whites do not, in fact, see non-whites as fellow citizens or do not esteem them enough to accept them as fellow citizens on their own terms. My point here is merely that the logic of the struggle for fully equal respect suggests that an appeal to a shared non-racialized citizenship might be effective (and that its failure to be effective might highlight other, more basic failures). To see that potential force, imagine examining the details of the lives of the disempowered in any Western democracy and asking, "Are these people being treated consistently with their status as rulers of their country?" As we have seen, only the recognition of all of our fellow citizens as rulers, as co-authors of their relationships, will grant them fully equal respect.

Honneth's theory points to a slightly different way of articulating the claim made by the powerless. As we saw earlier, recognition must be mutual. I cannot receive the benefits of recognition from someone on whom I am unwilling to bestow recognition. Thus, a claim of misrecognition will serve as a reasonable deliberative move if it points out to the person with power that in failing to recognize me, he is depriving himself of the value of my recognition of him. Here, rather than appealing to a separate identity we both share, we point to the very identity that is the source of the problem, and show that the fact that the identity is wrapped up in taking a dominant position makes it ultimately defective as an identity for someone who needs recognition. To clarify the difference this makes, let us return to the case of racial inequality in the United States Non-whites, following this second path, point not to claims of a shared citizenship, but rather to problems inherent for whites if they rely on a self-conception as racially superior. In particular, they point out that such an identity is a recognitional dead end. That is, insofar as whites conceive, whether explicitly or not, their racial identity as whites through the framework of white supremacy, they cut themselves off from the possibility of receiving recognition from many other members of their society, and thus leave their ability to receive recognition unnecessarily precarious. A deliberative move of this sort does not call on the powerful to live up to the demands of a different identity they already have, but invites them to transform the identity in virtue of which they are powerful in the name of securing an otherwise unavailable form of recognition. Rather than being told that their whiteness is incompatible with their already affirmed democratic citizenship, they are told that it presents a bar to their as yet unclaimed humanity. An example of such an appeal can be found in the slogan of the radical journal *Race Traitor*: "Treason to whiteness is loyalty to humanity," and the claims of many feminists and race-theorists that white privilege and male privilege serve to distort the humanity of their possessors.[15] Once again, however, the success of such a deliberative move in motivating the powerful to give up their power will depend on the relative depth of the various self-conceptions the powerful have. Here, however, the problem turns not on the relative strength of particular identities but on their wider understanding of the source of the authority of reasons. If the powerful assess deliberative claims on them in terms of their pre-existing interests, seeing themselves as primarily self-interest maximizers, then claims that point the way to wider and more secure forms of recognition will not appeal to them. If, however,

---

[15] See, for instance, Peggy McIntosh, "White Privilege and Male Privilege," in *Race, Class, and Gender*, ed. by Margaret Atherton and Patricia Hill Collins (New York: Wadsworth, 1995), and Charles Mills, *Blackness Visible* (Ithaca: Cornell University Press, 1997).

they see themselves as intersubjectively constructed beings dependent on the recognition of others, then such claims are likely to have an impact. This points to a different kind of value of Honneth's work, insofar as he helps us to see ourselves as Hegelian rather than Hobbesian selves.[16]

In describing the pathways by which social movements can raise reasonable deliberative challenges to the existing order, we have also highlighted some of the central features that will contribute to the positive uptake of their demands by the powerful. I will mention and reflect on two of them. First, we have seen that insofar as the powerful conceive of themselves as deliberative democratic citizens, and as beings dependent on the recognition of others, they will be more open to the variety of deliberative challenges posed to their position by social movements struggling for fully equal respect via the redistribution of constructive power. We can thus ask about the social institutional forms that are likely to promote and maintain such self-conceptions.[17] Second, we have seen a general form that reasonable deliberative challenges of this sort will take. We can thus ask about institutional structures that would keep a society continually open to recognizing such challenges as reasonable. Full-blown developments of either of these points are far beyond the scope of this chapter. Rather than offering such development, I close with two brief proposals and three general remarks.

In recent years, there has been much discussion of political deliberation as the source of democratic legitimacy. Less has been written, however, on the role of political deliberation in fostering both a sense of shared citizenship and the deliberative skills and attitudes that go with it. Nevertheless, a good case can be made that citizens who participate in political deliberation, and who see that participation as having an impact, will come to identify themselves more thoroughly as deliberative citizens. Such identification will be further enhanced if that deliberation provides a means by which they are also recognized in all their particularity and difference.[18] Rather than argue for that claim here, I want to point out what might follow from it if we are interested

---

[16] See, for instance, Honneth, *Struggle*, 5.
[17] Note once again the parallel with the central concerns of civic republican theorists.
[18] For an argument in support of this claim, see my *Reasonably Radical*, chapter 8. See also Tully, *Strange Multiplicity*, 204–209.

in developing institutions that serve to develop people who identify themselves as deliberative citizens. In particular, I think we need to think of ways to multiply the number of opportunities that citizens have for taking part in such deliberations. One standard opportunity we have to deliberate with our fellow citizens and to see that deliberation as having an impact is when we sit on juries. My argument thus suggests finding other avenues for such participation. One could imagine citizen oversight boards in all sorts of public institutions, from hospitals and prisons to regulatory agencies and park administrations, where citizens were chosen for short terms by lot and given oversight authority over issues of political or social relevance. The point of multiplying such boards would not be directly to increase the society's recognition of those otherwise excluded or rendered invisible, but to support and deepen citizen's self-conceptions as deliberative citizens so as to make them more responsive to the claims of those struggling for recognition.

My second proposal focuses more specifically on pathways by which social movements can be heard. As I have argued, a great deal of the harm of structural misrecognition relies on unequal relations of power. Many struggles for fully equal respect, then, will be aimed at restructuring such relationships, whether or not they are legally or politically entrenched. One way in which such struggles are likely to be heard is if they can appeal to constitutional principles of equality that mandate restructuring unequal relations of power. In such a case, relief could be sought by appeal to a supreme judicial body if all other appeals failed, and it would also increase the likelihood that not all other appeals would fail. An example of this in the American context is Cass Sunstein's proposal that the equality clause of the Fourteenth Amendment to the U.S. Constitution be read as an "anti-caste" principle rather than a principle of formal equality or difference-blindness.[19] However the principle is worded, the point is that analysis of this proposal gives us reason for insisting that any principle of equality at the heart of a just legal order should address unequal relations of power.

Moving from specific proposals to general remarks, then, note first that institutions with the features highlighted earlier will be what Rawls

---

[19] Cass Sunstein, *The Partial Constitution* (Cambridge: Harvard University Press, 1993), 338–345.

describes as "stable for the right reasons."[20] That is, they will reproduce themselves in two senses. First, they will be characterized by a
general harmony between their members' roles and their members'
self-conceptions. It will thus be through playing their designated roles
in society that members of these institutions will best realize their self-
conceptions. This, of course, is also a central feature of the institutions
of what Hegel called "ethical life."[21] A form of deliberative democracy
will thus be stable in this regard insofar as its citizens see themselves
as deliberative co-authors of the laws and principles that structure and
govern their society. The second form of reproduction takes place
over time. As people grow up within these institutions, they come to
develop identities as members of these institutions, and thus to value
themselves insofar as their lives are structured by them. A society that is
stable for the right reasons, then, is not a hegemonic and static society
that leaves no room for the politics of struggle. It is, rather, a society
whose institutions foster responsiveness to the reasonable deliberative
challenges raised by social movements struggling for recognition.

Second, a focus on the responsiveness of institutions and their members builds a kind of future-oriented open-endedness into our social
and political theory, thus leaving it truly mindful of the pluralism of
our social world.[22] As we have seen, Honneth's theory of recognition
provides a rich taxonomy of the kinds of claims social movements have
made, and its power is perhaps further evident in its ability to characterize struggles for redistributions of power to which he has been less
explicitly attentive. Nevertheless, by providing a kind of script, or perhaps more precisely, a language in which to articulate social struggles,
he may inadvertently blind himself to social struggles that not only
speak in other languages and use other scripts, but whose demands
are, as it were, untranslatable. In contrast, a focus on the institutional

---

[20] Rawls uses this phrase in his 'Reply to Habermas," reprinted in the paperback edition
of *Political Liberalism*, 390, 392. Though the term does not appear earlier, the idea
has been central to Rawls's work on justice and legitimacy for a long time. See, for
instance, Rawls, *Political Liberalism*, 143ff; John Rawls, *A Theory of Justice*, revised ed.
(Cambridge: Harvard University Press, 2000).

[21] See, for instance, G. W. F. Hegel, *Elements of the Philosophy of Right*, transl. by H. B.
Nisbet (Cambridge: Cambridge University Press, 1991), §147.

[22] For a discussion of responsiveness that shares many of the concerns of this paper,
see David Owen and Russell Bentley, "Ethical Loyalties, Civic Virtue and the Circumstances of Politics," in *Philosophical Explorations* 4 (2001).

conditions of responsiveness to deliberative challenges need not have this feature. If we characterize reasonableness in a suitably broad way, as I have tried to do here, in terms of an openness to deliberative challenges, it need not rule out alternative scripts and languages of struggle, and thus can be more inclusive.

Finally, the effort to work out an institutional structure that would be appropriately responsive to social movements that struggle for recognition is not, it should now be clear, an effort to eliminate such struggle or marginalize it as beyond the bounds of properly polite and domesticated politics. It is, rather, in the Hegelian spirit that animates both Rawls and Honneth, to give such struggles a home.

12

Self-Government and 'Democracy as Reflexive Co-operation'

Reflections on Honneth's Social and Political Ideal

David Owen

This chapter approaches the political significance of Honneth's theory of recognition by way of his articulation of an ideal of (radical) democracy as reflexive co-operation drawn, in large part, from the work of Dewey. The opening two sections of the chapter sketch the main features of this ideal and its apparent advantages with respect to competing proceduralist and republican ideals. It then proceeds to demonstrate the relationship between this ideal and the formal ethical account of the good that Honneth proposes in *The Struggle for Recognition*, before turning critically to evaluate the naturalistic moral psychology and theory of recognition that underpins Honneth's articulation of this ideal. The chapter concludes by drawing attention to a number of problems that this account identifies with Honneth's research project.

I

Honneth's argument for 'democracy as reflexive co-operation' is articulated by way of the claim that Dewey's mature democratic theory combines two elements: (1) a theory of human socialization that links self-realization to membership of a community of co-operation, and (2) an epistemological argument for democracy that emphasizes the rational value of democratic procedures for problem-solving. Let us address each in turn.

Honneth glosses Dewey's theory of human socialization thus:

From their completely open drives, which at first consist of nothing other than a multitude of undirected and thus formable impulses, human beings can develop only those capabilities and needs as stable habits of action which have met the approval and esteem of their particular reference group; the satisfaction that a subject has in realizing certain action impulses increases to the degree to which it can be sure of the recognition of its partners in interaction. Insofar as every member of society always belongs to various reference groups, the superimposed layers of expectations see to it that, in the course of the development of a personality, only socially useful habits of action are formed.[1]

In the context of Dewey's concern with democracy, Honneth argues that this theory of socialization 'assumes the function of bringing out the connection between the individual development of personality and a democratic community, which is presented as free relation of co-operating groups'.[2] The basic idea is this: while membership of any particular group develops those habits of action that are socially useful *qua* membership of that group and, thus, facilitates a realization of a particular aspect of oneself, it is only in a democratic community, as a free relation of co-operating groups, that one can realize the plurality of aspects of oneself *in a way which is mutually enriching*:

A member of a robber band may express his powers in a way consonant with belonging to that group and be directed by the interest common to its members. But he does so only at the cost of repression of those of his potentialities which can be realized only through membership in other groups. The robber band cannot interact flexibly with other groups; it can only act through isolating itself. But a good citizen finds his conduct as a member of a political group enriching and enriched by his participation in family life, industry, scientific and artistic associations. There is a free give-and-take: fullness of integrated personality is therefore possible of achievement, since the pulls and responses of different groups reinforce one another and their values accord.[3]

At the same time, and as a corollary to this argument, Dewey claims that democracy is a 'tendency' of all forms of human association (for

---

[1] Axel Honneth, "Democracy as Reflexive Co-operation: John Dewey and Democratic Theory Today," in *Political Theory* 26/6 (1998), 771–2.

[2] Honneth, "Democracy as Reflexive Co-operation," 772.

[3] John Dewey, *The Public and its Problems* (Chicago: Gateway Books, 1946), 147–48, cited in Honneth, "Democracy as Reflexive Co-operation," 772.

example, the family, the workplace, etc.) precisely because it is the form of association that most effectively cultivates both the personality of individuals and the common good of groups.[4]

Now, reflecting on the role of this theory of socialization with respect to Dewey's argument for democracy, we should note that Dewey's characterization of the member of the robber band as suffering the cost of the repression of potentialities is only intelligible if we understand human beings as having a general second order interest in the realization of their own individuality as the 'fullness of integrated personality,' which is obstructed by non-co-operative ways of life such as membership of a robber band. Matthew Festenstein has argued that without such a presupposition, four points tell against Dewey's argument:

First, the repression of potentialities is not itself necessarily a 'cost': an agent's repression of the potential to torture, or to succumb to suicide or alcoholism does not obviously impose a cost on the agent or others. Second, it seems plausible that repression of some potentialities may be a precondition of fully achieving others: limits on my time and energy mean that I cannot both be a virtuoso violinist and a champion boxer. Third, the fulfilment of some potentialities is logically incompatible with the fulfilment of others: monasticism is incompatible with libertinism, yet the novice in one or other pursuit might well contain the potentialities for both, and have to suppress one set. Fourth, given the first three points, the assumption that the integrated personality is the one which expresses itself across a wider range of social domains is ungrounded: why is the company of thieves, and the goods brought about by this life, not sufficient?[5]

As Festenstein points out, only if the potentialities 'at issue are potentialities for *growth* – that is, they are ethical potentialities' – can we grasp the connection between individual self-realization and democracy:

It is not, then, the repression of just any potentialities which imposes a cost on the thief, but the repression of those potentialities which are constitutive of his growth, or the fullness of integrated personality.[6]

So the connection between individual self-realization and democracy to which Honneth directs our attention is coherent only if we

---

[4] Dewey, *The Public and its Problems*, 325–6.
[5] M. Festenstein, *Pragmatism and Political Theory* (Cambridge: Polity, 1997), 92.
[6] Ibid.

situate it in relation to a naturalistic moral psychology that posits a general second order interest in the fullness of integrated personality. But, given this general second order interest, why do robber bands exist at all? Dewey's response to this sort of objection is straightforward: while human beings have a general second order interest in growth, recognizing and acting on the first order desires and interests that foster growth depends on one's capacity for practical deliberation, and this capacity develops through free communication with a plurality of others. In other words, the more co-operative the ways of life one leads, the more flexible the groups of which one is a member, then the more one develops the capacity for practical deliberation requisite to the achievement of fullness of integrated personality. This point also directs us to the second element of Dewey's mature political theory – namely, his epistemological argument for democracy.

This argument is presented by Honneth as a development of the pragmatist thesis that 'we have to be able to grasp every kind of scientific practice as a methodologically organized extension of those intellectual abilities with which we, in our everyday action, attempt to investigate and solve the problem causing a disruption.'[7] Guided by the example of experimental research in the natural sciences, Dewey argues that the chances of intelligent problem-solving rise in relation to two factors: first, the number of researchers co-operating and, second, the degree of freedom of communication:

It is this conclusion that Dewey then began gradually to transfer over to social learning processes as a whole. In social co-operation ... the intelligence of the solution to emerging problems increases to the degree to which all those involved could, without constraint and with equal rights, exchange information and introduce reflections.[8]

As Honneth notes, this argument not only provides an epistemological argument for democracy, it also stresses 'the rational value of democratic procedures' that secure the conditions of free communication.[9]

The question that arises at this stage is this: how is Dewey to reconcile his two arguments? We have already noted a relationship between the

[7] Honneth, "Democracy as Reflexive Co-operation," 772.
[8] Ibid., 772–773.
[9] Ibid., 773.

two arguments via the significance of practical deliberation for Dewey's thought, but this is not by itself sufficient to unite what appear to be an argument for democracy as a political community of co-operation and an argument for democracy as a set of rational procedures for solving social problems. Honneth argues that Dewey provides a two-part reconciliation of these arguments.

First, Dewey starts from the simple (and undeniable) point that social actions often have intended or unintended effects on individuals or groups other than those immediately engaged in this action:

> When A and B carry on a conversation together the action is a trans-action.... One or other or both may be helped or harmed thereby. But presumably the consequences of advantage or injury do not extend beyond A and B; the activity lies between them; it is private. Yet if it is found out that the consequences of conversation extend beyond the two directly concerned, that they affect the welfare of many others, the act acquires a public capacity, whether the conversation be carried on by a king and his prime minister or by Catiline and a fellow conspirator or by merchants planning to monopolize a market.[10]

Where the consequences of such (trans)actions are extensive, enduring or serious, they give rise to demands by those who are affected for the joint regulation of such actions:

> The public, *qua* group, is constituted when some association perceives a common interest in the regulation of some set of indirect consequences. The public, then, is created through an act of shared practical judgement. It consists of 'all those who are affected by the indirect consequences of transactions to such an extent that it is deemed necessary to have these consequences systematically cared for.'[11]

As Honneth argues, this gives rise to a conception of the state as a secondary form of association though 'which connected publics attempt to solve rationally encroaching problems of the co-ordination of social action.'[12] However, following Dewey's epistemological argument for democracy, the state 'also has, vis-à-vis co-operating society as the sovereign, the function of securing with the help of legal norms the social conditions under which all citizens can articulate their interests

---

[10] Dewey, *The Public and its Problems*, 244, cited in Festenstein, *Pragmatism*, 85.
[11] Festenstein, *Pragmatism*, 85.
[12] Honneth, "Democracy as Reflexive Co-operation," 775.

without constraint and with equal opportunity'[13] in order to maximize the rationality of its problem-solving activity. Thus, in this initial stage in his argument, Dewey presents the political sphere as 'the cognitive medium with whose help society attempts, experimentally, to explore, process, and solve its own problems with the co-ordination of social action' and because 'the rationality of such problem solving increases to the degree to which all whose affected are equally included in the "research process," it is beyond question for Dewey that the political self-steering of society has to be democratically organized.'[14]

The second part of Dewey's argument, on Honneth's account, concerns how this procedural conception of the democratic public sphere is linked to the idea of political community. Honneth suggests, under contemporary conditions of industrialization, complexity, and individualization, that Dewey recognizes that 'for all citizens to take their orientation from democratic procedures of political problem solving, a form of prepolitical association must be presupposed, such as those that originally existed only in the small, easily observed communities of American townships':[15]

To that extent... the "great society" must first be transformed into a "great community" before democratic procedures can be comprehended generally as a function of co-operative problem solving. Therefore, under conditions of complex, industrialized societies, the revival of democratic publics presupposes a reintegration of society that can only consist in the development of a common consciousness for the *prepolitical association* of all citizens.[16]

In other words, if citizens are to be motivated to engage in the democratic public sphere as co-operating members of a political community – that is, as agents engaged in activity of deliberating on common affairs and pursuing common goals – they must already understand themselves as having common affairs and common goals – and this common consciousness can only be grounded in the social association of individuals. Dewey's claim is that 'only a fair and just form of a division of labor can give each individual member of society a consciousness of co-operatively contributing with all others to the

[13] Ibid.
[14] Ibid.
[15] Ibid.
[16] Honneth, "Democracy as Reflexive Co-operation," 776.

realization of common goals. Taking one's orientation from democratic procedures presupposes a form of democratic ethical life that is anchored not in political virtues but in the consciousness of social co-operation.'[17]

So Honneth's claim, in endorsing Dewey's position, is that a just form of the division of labour acts to produce a common consciousness of ourselves as engaged in a co-operating society oriented to the freedom and welfare of all its members, and that this grounds a common civic consciousness in which we understand ourselves as members of a political community oriented to co-operatively solving social and political problems through engagement in the democratic public sphere. For Honneth, as for Dewey, this is a political ideal:

> Yet it is not 'ideal' in the sense of being visionary and utopian; for it simply projects to their logical and practical limit forces inherent in human nature and already embodied to some extent in human nature. It serves accordingly as basis for criticism of institutions as they exist and of plans of betterment.[18]

This claim, of course, hangs on the plausibility of the naturalistic account of moral psychology that underpins this political ideal, but it also places considerable weight on the role of the social division of labor – and I will return to these issues later in this chapter.

II

How does this ideal stand with respect to its republican and procedural competitors? Do we have good reasons to endorse Honneth's Deweyan ideal to these competitors, which Honneth associates with the radical democratic theories of Jurgen Habermas and Hannah Arendt, respectively. I will begin by reviewing these competitors, before turning to consider the reasons that Honneth offers in support of his own proposal.

Let us begin, then, by noting two similarities and two differences between proceduralism and republicanism as theories of radical democracy. On the one hand, both theories take themselves to offer critiques of political liberalism in the sense that (1) they seek to

---

[17] Ibid., 776.
[18] Dewey, *The Public and its Problems*, 145.

give a fundamental role to processes of democratic will formation, and (2) they understand democratic will formation in terms of the model of communicative consultation. On the other hand, these theories offer distinct conceptualizations of the democratic public sphere in the sense that (3) whereas proceduralism regards it in terms of morally justified rules, republicanism grasps it in terms of civic virtues, and (4) whereas proceduralism sees it as 'the procedure with whose help society attempts to solve political problems rationally in a legitimate manner,' republicanism views it as 'the medium of a self-governing political community.'[19] These differences between the two models are clearly exhibited in their conceptions of law:

> Political republicanism by nature has a certain tendency to understand legal norms as the social instrument through which the political community attempts to preserve its own identity. According the proceduralist conviction, basic rights represent a kind of guarantee for the continued existence of the interplay of the democratic public sphere and political administration. For the former, law is the crystallized expression of the particular self-understanding of a solidary citizenry, for the latter it represents state-sanctioned but morally legitimated precautionary measures to protect the democratic procedure in its entire complexity.[20]

Each of these models has significant strengths. The republican theory offers a rich account of political community in which self-government is integrally interwoven with participation in the collective activity of articulating the common good. The proceduralist theory provides a robust account of procedures for the rational resolution of political problems in which the equiprimordiality of private and public autonomy is asserted and maintained. However, each model also has certain weaknesses, and it is by focusing on these that we can begin to grasp Honneth's case for democracy as reflexive co-operation.

With respect to the republican model, Honneth notes two problems. The first is the criticism often advanced by political liberals such as Rawls that because this form of classical republicanism identifies the political sphere as the locus of the good life, it is incompatible with the value pluralism characteristic of modern societies. In other words, the privileging of political activity as the highest form of human

---

[19] Honneth, "Democracy as Reflexive Co-operation," 763.
[20] Ibid., 764.

activity requires that this form of republicanism be intolerant of those comprehensive conceptions of the good that do not assign priority to political activity. The second problem with republicanism is that 'it is never entirely clear according to what standard the institutional form of intersubjective opinion formation is to be precisely measured since it is an end in itself.'[21] I take it that the point of this remark is to suggest that because this strong form of civic republicanism values political participation in and of itself, it lacks criteria in terms of which to differentiate the institutional forms in and through which this activity is articulated. Now, if it were the case that this form of republicanism *only* valued political participation as an end in itself, this criticism would be valid. However, it is not clear that this is in fact the case.

Consider, for example, Honneth's own description of this form of republicanism as one in which citizens engage in 'the intersubjective negotiation of common affairs' such that law is 'the crystallized expression of the particular self-understanding of a solidary citizenry.'[22] This description already points to one criterion in virtue of which the institutional form of intersubjective opinion formation can be judged: namely, its capacity to sustain and reproduce the identification of citizens with the political community of which they are members – that is, ultimately, the capacity of the institutions of democratic will formation to sustain and reproduce the republic. We can put this response to Honneth another way by recalling that a central concern of all forms of republicanism is the problem of corruption, where 'corruption' refers to the condition under which the political deliberation and actions of individuals are oriented to self-interest rather than the common good. Consequently, for republicans, it is precisely the capacity of particular institutional forms to avoid or minimize the corruption of the citizenry that provides criteria on which to differentiate and evaluate institutional forms. It seems, then, that the rationality of the institutional forms of intersubjective opinion formation can be adjudicated by reference to their capacity to maintain the effective orientation of citizens to the common good. Consequently, while Honneth is no doubt right to point to the problem posed by the privileging of political activity

[21] Ibid., 778.
[22] Ibid., 764.

in Arendt's somewhat idealized version of ancient republicanism, it is not at all clear that his second criticism holds up to scrutiny.

With respect to the proceduralist model, as it is elaborated by Jürgen Habermas, Honneth also points to a significant problem – namely, that the 'idea of the democratic public sphere lives off social presuppositions that can be secured only outside this idea itself.'[23] In other words, while the procedural model secures the legal conditions of participation in public opinion formation, it 'can function only on the tacit premise of an inclusion of all members of society in the social reproduction process'[24] and it is precisely because it cannot articulate this premise itself that proceduralism is incapable of addressing the issue of how democratic habits are to be formed and sustained. This point is effectively acknowledged by Habermas when, in a 1996 response to reflections on *Between Fact and Norm*,[25] he notes that the basic rights necessary to secure the public use of communicative freedom only make the exercise of communicative freedom possible; they do not guarantee that these rights can be exercised *as* communicative liberties for the purpose of a "public use of reason." Rather such assurance requires that citizens "take the perspective of participants who are engaged in the process of reaching understanding about the rules for their life in common"[26] – and this assurance cannot be given within the terms of the procedural account of democracy but depends precisely on social presuppositions that can be secured only outside this idea itself.

To this extent, Honneth's criticism is entirely cogent; as he remarks, 'because Habermas is afraid that such an idea of democratic ethical life could lead him on the track of an ethical understanding of politics, he shifts the problems emerging here into the domain of sociological functionalism.'[27] However, all that this criticism entails by itself is that the cogency of Habermas' procedural account of democracy cannot be separated from his account of modern society and, in particular, his claim that new social movements both emerge as forms of resistance

---

[23] Ibid., 779.
[24] Ibid.
[25] Jürgen Habermas, *Between Fact and Norm*, trans. W. Rehg (Cambridge: Polity, 1996)
[26] Jürgen Habermas, "Afterword," in M. Deflem (ed.) *Habermas, Modernity and Law* (London: Sage, 1996), 147.
[27] Honneth, "Democracy as Reflexive Co-operation," 779.

to the colonization of the lifeworld by the system and act as carriers
of the democratic ethos that is required as a supplement to his proceduralist account of democracy.[28] Yet, despite the fact that Honneth's
criticism of Habermas' proceduralist account of democracy is subject
to this limitation, he has already provided the resources for the requisite expansion of this criticism in *The Critique of Power*. He demonstrates
there that Habermas' theorization of modern society in terms of system
and lifeworld is incoherent. Without repeating this argument here, let
us simply recall Honneth's conclusion:

> If capitalist societies are conceived in this way as social orders in which system
> and lifeworld stand over against each other as autonomous spheres of action,
> two complementary fictions emerge: We then suppose (1) the existence of
> norm-free organizations of action and (2) the existence of power-free spheres
> of communication.[29]

Insofar as this conclusion is valid, the claim that Habermas' proceduralist account of democracy can be rescued from Honneth's criticism by recourse to the general account of modern society in which
it is embedded only leads to a demonstration of deeper problems in
Habermas' theory of communicative action. We should note, however,
that this point can be generalized to other procedural accounts of
democracy if, and only if, we have good reasons to think that the theoretical presuppositions of procedural accounts of democracy entail an
inadequate theory of society – that is, if the type of account of human
agency exhibited in the former cannot be adequate to the latter. (This
is, I take it, the claim that Honneth effectively advances in *The Struggle
for Recognition*, and so we will leave this question open until we consider the argument presented there.) We may, however, conclude that
Honneth has identified a cogent criticism of procedural accounts of
democracy to the extent that he can provide an account of democracy
that does not exhibit this limitation or need for supplemental recourse
to a theory of society.

Now the criticisms that Honneth advances provide criteria on
which to evaluate his own proposal. They must be (1) compatible with

---

[28] Habermas, *Between Fact and Norm*, 368–73, cf. also J. Cohen & A. Arato, *Civil Society
and Political Theory* (Cambridge, MA: The MIT Press, 1994).

[29] Axel Honneth, *The Critique of Power*, trans. K. Baynes (Cambridge, MA: The MIT Press,
1991), 298.

value-pluralism, (2) able to specify criteria on the basis of which institutional forms of intersubjective opinion formation can be judged, and (3) capable of giving an account of how democratic habits are formed and maintained. Let us consider 'democracy as reflexive co-operation' with respect to each in turn.

First, the ideal that Honneth proposes is compatible with value-pluralism because it does not privilege political activity or any other specific form of human activity as the locus of the good life. One can choose to engage in or exit from the plurality of groups or associations that make up the society of which one is a member. Second, the Deweyan ideal can specify criteria according to which to evaluate institutional forms of democratic will formation:

Because the democratic public sphere constitutes the medium through which society attempts to process and solve its own problems, its establishment and composition depend entirely upon criteria of rational problem solving. Indeed, Dewey goes so far as to make the differentiation of state institutions as a whole dependent upon an experimental process in which, according to the criteria of the rationality of past decisions, we continually decide anew how state institutions are to be specifically organized and how they are to relate to one another in terms of their jurisdiction.[30]

Third, Honneth's proposal can also give an account of how democratic habits are formed and maintained because it grounds the motivation to engage in the democratic sphere in a consciousness of social co-operation that is instantiated through a just division of labour. The great advantage of this proposal is thus that it is able to reconcile the two elements of rational deliberation and democratic community that have been separated into opposing positions in recent democratic theory, and so overcome the limitations of these positions.

III

In Section I, we noted that Honneth's proposal presupposes a naturalistic moral psychology that posits a general second order interest of human beings in the 'fullness of integrated personality' (as Dewey's phrase has it). Consequently, this section will begin the task

---

[30] Honneth, "Democracy as Reflexive Co-operation," 778.

of addressing the plausibility of Honneth's proposal by sketching how this proposal is related to the formal conception of ethical life that Honneth advances in *The Struggle for Recognition* and thus to the naturalistic account of moral psychology on which this conception of ethical life is predicated.

In concluding *The Struggle for Recognition*, Honneth sketches a formal conception of ethical life that is 'meant to include the entirety of intersubjective conditions that can be shown to serve as necessary preconditions for individual self-realization.'[31] Honneth's argument is that there are three necessary preconditions for individual self-realization – self-confidence, self-respect, and self-esteem – which are constituted in and through intersubjective conditions that secure the experience of three patterns of recognition – namely, love, rights and solidarity. He writes:

> The connection between the experience of recognition and one's relation-to-self stems from the intersubjective structure of personal identity. The only way in which individuals are constituted as persons is by learning to refer to themselves, from the perspective of an approving or encouraging other, as being with certain positive traits and abilities. The scope of such traits – and hence the extent of one's positive relation-to-self – increases with each new form of recognition that individuals are able to apply to themselves as subjects. In this way, the prospect of basic self-confidence is inherent in the experience of love; the prospect of self-respect, in the experience of legal recognition; and finally the prospect of self-esteem, in the experience of solidarity.[32]

Honneth's claim is that this account provides the basis for a specification of a *formal* conception of ethical life because '[on] the one hand, the three patterns of recognition...are defined in a sufficiently abstract, formal manner to avoid raising the suspicion that they embody particular visions of the good life. On the other hand, from the perspective of their content, the explication of these conditions is detailed enough to say more about the general structures of a successful life than is entailed by general references to individual self-determination.'[33] Now, for the purposes of this section, I want

---

[31] Axel Honneth, *The Struggle for Recognition*, trans. J. Anderson (Cambridge: Polity, 1995), 173.
[32] Honneth, *Struggle*, 173.
[33] Ibid., 174.

to draw attention to three features of Honneth's account. First, like Dewey's ethical theory on which Honneth draws,[34] it is based on an account of moral psychology that is both intersubjectivist and focused on self-realization. Second, basic self-confidence or trust in oneself – the capacity to articulate one's needs and exercise one's abilities – is taken by Honneth both to be 'the basic pre-requisite for every type of self-realization'[35] and, insofar as this capability is formed through the experience of love-recognition, to be situated in the sphere of familial/intimate relations. Third, and relatedly, while 'none of the three fields of experience can be adequately described without reference to an inherent conflict,' the forms of recognition associated with self-respect and self-esteem provide the moral contexts of social struggles:

The forms of recognition associated with rights and social esteem . . . do represent a moral context for societal conflict, if only because they rely on socially generalized criteria in order to function. In lights of norms of the sort constituted by the principle of moral responsibility or the values of society, personal experiences of disrespect can be interpreted and represented as something that can potentially affect other subjects.[36]

From these three points, we can draw the following conclusions with respect to a political ideal of the type with which we are concerned. While self-confidence is the basic pre-requisite for every type of self-realization, it is not the concern of a social and political ideal except in the indirect sense that 'it is possible that the development of [love's] invariant structures will be all the freer from distortion and coercion, the more rights come to be shared by partners in a friendship or love relationship' (1995: 176). Rather such an ideal must be structured in terms of maximizing the developmental potentials of self-respect and self-esteem. (Although Honneth has now revised the view expressed in *The Struggle for Recognition* that the love axis of recognition lacks developmental potential, and now holds that this axis does have such potential in terms of the perception of new needs of the other, it seems

---

[34] Ibid., 136–7.
[35] Ibid., 176.
[36] Ibid., 162.

clear that he still holds this to be a matter largely for the private rather than the public sphere of society.)[37]

In the case of self-respect, which Honneth associates with legal-recognition (rights), this developmental potential refers to both the generalization of rights (to the point that all human beings enjoy equal rights) and the de-formalization of rights – that is, the progressive movement from formal to substantive rights as, for example, described by Marshall and, more recently, Habermas (to the point where all human beings enjoy conditions of social and economic well-being as well as civil and political freedoms). In the case of self-esteem, which Honneth associates with recognition by a community of value, the developmental potential refers to both the individualization of social esteem, (to the point where each individual is seen as equally unique) and the equalization of social esteem (to the point where each individual is equally recognized for his traits and abilities, and is equally free from denigration). Now it is fairly straightforward to indicate the relationship between this formal conception of the good life in its ideal form and Honneth's advocacy of democracy as reflexive co-operation. Consideration of the following two points should suffice.

First, we can adduce some negative evidence for this claim by noting that a distinction between the grammar of 'respect' and that of 'esteem' – or between what analytic moral philosophers refer to as recognition-respect and appraisive respect.[38] The distinction is this: 'respect' denotes a normative non-appraisive attitude towards an individual *qua* personhood, whereas 'esteem' denotes a normative appraisive attitude towards an individual *qua* character. In Honneth's terms, 'respect' refers to an individual as a being capable of making claims, whereas 'esteem' refers to an individual as a being composed of various abilities and traits. The significance of this grammatical distinction between the concepts of respect and esteem becomes apparent if we bracket each in turn and ask what form of polity would secure the intersubjective conditions of each taken by itself. In the case of '(self-)

---

[37] See Axel Honneth, "Redistribution as Recognition," in Nancy Fraser & Axel Honneth, *Redistribution or Recognition?* (London: Verso, 2003), 110–197; especially 138–150.

[38] S. L. Darwall, "Two Kinds of Respect," in R. Dillion (ed.), *Dignity, Character and Self-Regard* (London: Routledge, 1995), 181–97.

respect,' Honneth's argument directs us to a *proceduralist* conception of the democratic polity in which individuals are recognized as equal persons – as both subjects and co-authors of law – in a sovereign association. In the case of '(self-) esteem,' Honneth's argument points us to a (classical) *republican* conception of the democratic polity in which individuals are recognized as equal members of a self-governing political community who are bound to the collective determination of the common good and whose political identities are forged by participating in this collective activity.

Noting this implication of the formal conception of the good life predicated on Honneth's account of moral psychology indicates why Honneth must argue that neither proceduralist nor republican accounts of democracy can be adequate insofar as both the requirements of self-respect and self-esteem must be met. Only a political ideal of radical democracy that combines a commitment to securing democratic procedures of rational deliberation (that is, the maximal conditions of the experience of respect-recognition) with a commitment to democratic political community (that is, the maximal conditions of the experience of esteem-recognition) is capable of satisfying both fundamental human needs. (Note that this argument also provides the basis for the claim that any account of human agency that is expressed as a proceduralist account of democracy cannot provide a basis for an adequate theory of society.) At the same time, Honneth may also suggest that the prevalence of the procedural and the republican accounts – as well as the long-standing debate between them – provides incidental support for the claim that the enjoyment of self-respect and self-esteem are basic human needs.

Second, we can adduce positive support for our claim by noting that Honneth's proposed ideal not only recognizes and articulates the need for self-respect and for self-esteem, but precisely because it is a social and political ideal, specifies the conditions of their maximal developmental potential. If we consider self-respect, we can note that Dewey's ideal, via the epistemological argument for democracy, requires both that rights are generalized (this corresponds to Dewey's claim that the intelligence of solutions to problems increases as the number of researchers increases) and that rights are de-formalized (this corresponds to Dewey's claim that the intelligence of solutions increases to the degree that freedom of communication is not constrained by political, social, economic or any other extraneous factors as well as to his emphasis on a just and fair division of labour). If we consider self-esteem, we can note that Dewey's ideal, via the argument that democratic political community is grounded on the experience of social co-operation, requires both that social esteem is individualized (because political community is conceptualized as a reflexive co-operative endeavour in which each individual deploys his particular traits, abilities, and life-experience in making his unique contribution to the common goal of solving social problems and maximizing the common good) and that it is equalized (because individuals are conceptualized as deploying their particular abilities and traits in co-operatively seeking to articulate and achieve the common goals of the political community).

Given these two points, we can see that Honneth's turn to Dewey's account of democracy as reflexive co-operation is consonant with the formal conception of ethical life sketched in the conclusion to *The Struggle for Recognition* and indeed is a way of giving expression to this formal conception of ethical life as a social and political ideal. This is significant for the purposes of this chapter because it enables us to conclude that the plausibility of this social and political ideal is bound up with the plausibility of the moral psychological account of recognition that underpins this formal conception of ethical life. Consequently, in the remaining two sections, I will focus on this account of recognition: in the next section, I offer a critical overview of the three forms of recognition, and in the following section, I draw out the implications of these criticisms for Honneth's democratic ideal. Let us then turn to this account of recognition.

IV

This section will proceed to analyse Honneth's moral psychological account of recognition by offering internal critical reflections on each of the axes of recognition that Honneth demarcates. For reasons that will become apparent, this discussion will include references to self-confidence as well as self-respect and self-esteem.

Let us begin then with Honneth's account of *self-confidence*. Here I argue that while Honneth has drawn our attention to an important aspect of basic self-confidence, he has underestimated both the dimensions and significance of this feature of human beings. An initial point of entry into this topic is to ask why Honneth claims that the forms of disrespect that correspond to basic self-confidence are 'abuse and rape' and, relatedly, why he identifies the threatened component of personality as 'physical integrity.' I do not, of course, wish to deny that abuse and rape are forms of love-disrespect nor that they threaten physical integrity, but I do want to ask why Honneth limits his account of basic self-confidence to these forms of disrespect and this component of personality. I ask this question precisely because Honneth's own characterization of love-recognition as 'an affirmation of independence that is guided – indeed, supported – by care' points to a wider range of forms of love-disrespect and of threatened personality components. Consider, for example, the experience of the breakdown of love-recognition that occurs when one discovers that one's lover has secretly been pursuing an adulterous relationship with another person. This experience involves feelings of rage, helplessness, and grief, a breakdown of trust in the other that easily becomes a breakdown of basic confidence in oneself – and is often described in language that refers to a loss of physical integrity: 'I felt like my guts had been ripped out.' Moreover, such experiences cannot be willed away; on the contrary, coming to terms with such an experience (as with the related experience of grief for the death of a loved one) is likely to be a protracted and painful business, not least because one's trust in others has been disrupted by the traumatic effects of this event. Now I take it that Honneth's general account is supported by the fact that descriptions of this sort of experience can and do use the language of physical violence in order to express the pain involved – but it is thus odd that, given Honneth's emphasis on care, he neglects what seems fairly straightforwardly to be a form of love-disrespect. With this first critical reflection, then, I want to plant an initial seed of doubt concerning Honneth's claim that basic self-confidence (as a practical relation-to-self) simply corresponds to physical integrity (as the threatened component of personality).

Turning to a second critical reflection, what I want to do here is generate some scepticism towards another feature of Honneth's account of basic self-confidence. In order to engender doubt here, let us consider a variety of forms of losses of physical integrity. Consider the following examples of losses of physical integrity:

1. One is mugged by a stranger and left bleeding on the pavement.
2. One is entirely unexpectedly caught in an earthquake and hit by flying household objects.
3. Out of the blue, one experiences impotency.

I want to suggest (somewhat pedantically) that each of these examples can be taken, at least potentially, to problematize the maintenance of basic self-confidence precisely because each is experienced as a breakdown of different basic features of trust that structure and facilitate our experience of ourselves as agents.

1. The experience of being mugged can problematize basic self-confidence because it forces reflection on our vulnerability to unknown and hostile others; it draws our attention to the fact that, for the most part (and unless we have specific reasons in a given context to expect otherwise), we exist in a social world in which we trust (more or less unreflectively) that the world of strangers is not warlike and aggressive towards us, and it problematizes this unreflective trust.
2. The experience of being caught in a natural disaster can problematize basic self-confidence because it impels reflection on our vulnerability to the physical world; it points out to us the fact that, for the most part (and unless we have specific reasons in a given context to expect otherwise), we trust in the regularity of nature, the continuity of basic features of our relationship to our physical environment, and it problematizes this unreflective trust.
3. The experience of impotence can problematize basic self-confidence because it constrains one to reflect on one's vulnerability to breakdown in the functioning of one's own body; it draws one to the recognition that, for the most part (and unless one has specific reasons in a given context to expect otherwise), one trusts in the functioning of one's body and it problematizes this unreflective trust.

Now the point that I want to draw from this discussion is the suggestion that what ties physical integrity to basic self-confidence is that our experience of our physical integrity is interwoven with – or, if you prefer, structured through – relations of trust with respect to our bodies, the physical world and the social world (including primary relationships), which are integral to the maintenance of our ongoing experience of ourselves as agents. Trauma, in whatever form it arises (and some forms may be more easily coped with than others) disrupts the basic dispositional expectation that we experience ourselves as agents. So, put bluntly, my claim is this: while basic self-confidence as a practical relation-to-self is initially formed through the experience of love, the maintenance of self-confidence is interwoven into each and every trust relationship in and through which we experience ourselves as agents – and, while only the first of these examples may be experienced as a form of disrespect, each case exhibits the problematization of basic self-confidence.[39]

Thus far, then, I have tried to suggest (1) that basic self-confidence as a practical relation-to-self need not be conceptualized simply in relation to abuse and rape as forms of disrespect and to physical integrity as the threatened component of personality, and (2) that it need not be conceptualized wholly in relation to primary relationships but extends into any relationship of which trust is an integral component. The final critical reflection builds on these sceptical thoughts by reflecting on basic self-confidence in relation to what we might call 'linguistic integrity.' The initial point to note is that just as bodily integrity is experienced as a taken for granted feature of our experience of ourselves as agents, so too is linguistic integrity; this point becomes clear when we reflect on the fact that, in our everyday goings on, we are not normally constrained to reflect on the vocabulary (or system of judgments) in terms of which we offer descriptions, evaluations, arguments, and so on. But this normal condition can be disrupted such that certain of our ways of describing, evaluating, arguing, and so on themselves become constituted as problems for us – and, indeed, Bernard Williams has argued that it is a feature of our modernity that the issue of confidence in our thick ethical vocabularies can easily be problematic in the sense that we, as reflective beings, are aware that there are plural

[39] Note that in each case, the capacity to re-establish basic self-confidence hangs on the capacity to identify the event in question – at both cognitive and affective levels – as an exception to the norm.

thick ethical vocabularies that are *real* and not simply *notional* options for us. Insofar as basic self-confidence is tied to experiencing ourselves as agents, the loss of confidence in our thick ethical understandings of ourselves as agents can issue in a loss of self-confidence.[40] I will take up the significance of these points in the second part of the section; for the moment, however, let us turn to the second of Honneth's axes of recognition: respect.

Honneth's argument with regard to *self-respect* claims that this practical relation-to-self is grounded in legal relations as a form of recognition – that is, in our reciprocal recognition of ourselves and others as morally responsible agents capable of raising and defending socially accepted claims that is instituted in our status as rights-bearers. As Joel Anderson glosses this point:

> The object of respect (including self-respect) is an agent's capacity to raise and defend claims discursively or, more generally, an agent's status as responsible. But this capacity can only become a basis for 'self-respect' if it can be exercised. Indeed, in this context it is unclear what it could mean to have a capacity one cannot exercise. Hence the importance of rights in connection with self-respect lies in the fact that rights ensure the real opportunity to exercise the universal capacities constitutive of personhood. This is not to say that a person without rights cannot have self-respect, only that the *fullest* form of self-respecting autonomous agency could only be realized when one is recognized as possessing the capacities of 'legal persons', that is, of morally responsible agents.[41]

In the following discussion, I will suggest two ways in which this account is inadequate.

We can begin by noting that apparent support for this account can be adduced by reflecting on the self-expressions of groups engaged in claiming rights. Consider, for example, the arguments of Frederick Douglass and W. E. B. Dubois *contra* Booker T. Washington, that protest by black Americans aimed at claiming rights, even when it had no effective chance of success, was central to the experience of self-respect.[42] But, in reflecting on this support for Honneth's argument, we should

---

[40] Bernard Williams, *Ethics and the Limits of Philosophy* (London: Fontana Press, 1985).

[41] Joel Anderson, "Translator's Introduction," in Axel Honneth, *The Struggle for Recognition* (Cambridge: Polity, 1995), xv.

[42] B. R. Boxhill, "Self-Respect and Protest," in R. Dillion (ed.) *Dignity, Character and Self-Regard* (London: Routledge, 1995), 93–104.

also note a feature integral to struggles for rights-recognition and, indeed, that acts as a condition of being motivated to engage in such struggles. This feature is picked out by the activity that has become known as 'consciousness-raising,'[43] and it is worth paying attention to the features of this activity.

Consider the slogan advanced by Steve Biko in the context of apartheid South Africa: 'Black is Beautiful.' The rationale for this form of discourse is provided by the context of denigration of black South Africans (and, indeed, black people in general) in which both their dignity and (non-instrumental) value are denied. The point raised by this slogan is that it does not simply address the issue of the equal moral dignity of persons but, on the contrary, and partly to motivate its black audience to claim this status, it focuses on the conditions of self-confidence and self-esteem. Is this just a mistake? I don't think so. The pertinence of Biko's slogan is its recognition that, under conditions of apartheid, the experience of (many) black South Africans is not simply an experience of disrespect but an experience of powerlessness and of lack of self-esteem. Hence a precondition of motivating black South Africans to claim rights, to assert their entitlement to the status of equal citizens, is to cultivate an awareness of themselves as, on the one hand, agents (basic self-confidence) – that is, as beings with powers to act in respect of their situation – and, on the other hand, non-instrumentally valuable members of society (self-esteem) – that is, as beings with ethical worth whose cares and commitments matter. My hypothesis – which must here remain a speculation – is that the significance of the activity of 'consciousness-raising' in struggles for recognition discloses an important sense in which basic self-confidence and some basic level of self-esteem are preconditions of struggles for rights.

The second critical issue I will raise involves the claim that there is an important form or dimension of self-respect that is not captured by the status of being a rights-holder. This point has been developed, although not specifically in relation to Honneth, by Thomas Hill Jr.,

---

[43] This was a major focus of feminist practice after the publication of Betty Friedan's *The Feminine Mystique*, and also structured the political practice of Steve Biko's black consciousness movement in South Africa as well as the political thought of Malcolm X and other radical black American writers.

through an example of 'two neighbours who are quite ordinary in their abilities and aspirations':

> I respect both the human and special rights of each and yet, in another sense, I respect one much more than the other. Neither is doing anything illegal or morally wrong, but one, unlike the other, has a clear sense of what he values and counts important and he lives accordingly. It is not that he has exceptionally high ideals. Rather he has a sense, quite aside from matters of moral right and wrong, that certain ways of behaving are beneath him, and his acts, both deliberate and impulsive, never go past this line.... Though he holds them [his ideals] deeply, he does not universalize his basic non-moral standards (except in a trivial sense).... He says that he just has certain standards for himself and would lower himself in his own eyes if he did not stick by them.... The other neighbour, let us say, lives equally well within the bounds of the law and basic moral requirements...but otherwise seems to have no personal standards.... He would feel *regret* if he acted, impulsively or deliberately, in ways that failed to have the consequences that he wanted; but he would never feel *self-contempt*.[44]

The point of these examples is to suggest a form of self-respect that is not tied to appreciating one's rights or one's status as a moral-legal person and yet where we have a clear sense that, other things being equal, it is better to have this form of self-respect than to lack it, either in the sense of having the related form of self-contempt through failing to live according to one's non-moral standards or in the sense of cutting oneself off from the possibility of experiencing these forms of self-respect and self-contempt by having no personal (nonmoral) standards at all. This notion of self-respect, as Hill points out, is linked to the sense in which we talk of people who display a 'sense of their own worth,' where this is neither 'worth *to* others' nor 'a belief that one has...an equal status in a system of moral rights,' rather 'at least part of a sense of one's own worth is having, and living by, personal standards or ideals that one sees...as an important part of oneself.'[45] One should note further that this notion of self-respect is not only distinct from an appreciation of one's rights but also entirely independent of an acknowledging of one's merits, which is to say that it cannot be cashed out in terms of either respect or esteem in Honneth's uses of these terms.

44 Thomas E. Hill Jr., "Self-respect reconsidered," in Hill Jr., *Autonomy and Self-Respect* (Cambridge: Cambridge University Press, 1991), 21–22.
45 Ibid., 23.

I will return to the significance of these critical observations following the discussion of self-esteem, but we can note for the moment that while the first suggests a more complex relationship between the three dimensions of recognition than Honneth admits, the second implies that Honneth's conceptual account of self-respect and, relatedly, his historical story concerning the division of 'honor' into respect and esteem is rather too simple.

Honneth specifies *self-esteem* as a practical relation-to-self in which one's distinct traits and abilities are valued. This practical relation-to-self is formed, Honneth argues, through relations of solidarity in which individuals or groups share a common project or horizon of value. As with respect from which it is gradually disentangled, Honneth argues that the social esteem, is characterized by developmental potentials. He bases this claim on the historical transformation of relations of social esteem, and describes these developmental potentials in terms of processes of individualization and of equalization. Individualization refers to the process whereby social esteem becomes separated out from status-groups and is ascribed to individuals *qua* individuality – that is to say, with respect to their own unique characters or life-projects. Equalization refers to the process whereby social esteem becomes increasingly detached from forms of social hierarchy and interwoven into a pluralistic value framework. Together, Honneth argues, these processes mean that:

the individual no longer has to attribute to an entire collective the respect that he or she receives for accomplishments that fit social standards but can refer them positively back to himself or herself instead. Under these altered conditions, the experience of being socially esteemed is accompanied by a felt confidence that one's achievements or abilities will be recognized as 'valuable' by other members of society. . . . To the extent to which every member of society is in a position to esteem himself or herself, one can speak of a state of societal solidarity.[46]

Today, on Honneth's account, self-esteem is tied to the achievement principle – that is to merit as a productive member of society. I will offer two critical reflections with regard to this account.

We can begin by reflecting on Honneth's identification of esteem with the achievement principle, an identification that helps support

---

[46] Honneth, *Struggle*, 128–9.

the claim that the developmental potentials of esteem can be spelt out in terms of individualisation and equalization. We have, I suggest, reasons to be sceptical of both this identification and the specification of the developmental potentials of esteem. Consider, first, that we esteem individuals for reasons that are not related to their achievements or merit as productive members of society but, rather, to their excellencies of character – for example, their dispositions and capacities for truthfulness and kindness. Here the point is that members of a community characterised by a common horizon of value share an ethical vocabulary that articulates relations of mutual esteem-recognition in terms of the thick ethical concepts that comprise this vocabulary. Within a given modern ethical community of this type, to adapt Honneth's remarks cited earlier, we can say that *the individual no longer has to attribute to an entire collective [or status group] the respect that he or she receives for excellencies of character but can refer them positively back to himself or herself instead. Under these altered conditions, the experience of being socially esteemed is accompanied by a felt confidence that one's excellencies of character will be recognized as 'valuable' by other members of the community.* Now, and here we move to the second point, it is also the case that there may be wide variation between ethical communities (cultural communities being the most obvious example) both with respect to what count as valuable achievements (and how their value is to be ordered) and with respect to what count as excellencies of character (and how they are to be ranked). This matters since, in contemporary societies, there are plural ethical communities – a fact with significant implications for Honneth's account.

The first implication is that the specification of what counts as a valuable achievement can be variable across society according to the cultural evaluation of the achievement in question. This is a point that Honneth appears to acknowledge in recent work,[47] but perhaps does not sufficiently appreciate; indeed, Iris Young has argued that what she calls 'the myth of merit' essentially functions as an ideological mechanism for disguising various forms of oppressive power, including that of cultural imperialism.[48] The second implication is that it is difficult for

[47] Axel Honneth, "Redistribution as Recognition," 155–8.
[48] Iris Marion Young, *Justice and the Politics of Difference* (Princeton: Princeton University Press, 1990), 192–225.

individuals to experience self-esteem insofar as the achievements and excellencies of character valued by their cultural community are not valued by the society in which they are situated. Even if the members of this community enjoy cultural rights justified under the principle of equality, they may still lack the conditions of self-realization insofar as the forms of valuing characteristic of their cultural community are marginalized or denigrated by a dominant cultural community. Under certain conditions, this may lead to the situation that I described in discussing basic self-confidence in which they come to lack confidence in their thick ethical vocabularies and, hence, unable to experience themselves as ethical agents because subject to a form of what we may gloss as 'ethical trauma' (of which nihilism is the most obvious type).

Let me conclude this section by drawing together the criticisms of Honneth's moral psychological account of recognition that have been advanced. The first claim is that basic self-confidence is conceptualised in too limited a way on Honneth's account, and is better expressed in terms of our ability of experience ourselves as agents. On this view, basic self-confidence breaks down when our experience of ourselves as agents is rendered problematic – that is, when we are traumatized in respect of some dimension of our experience of ourselves as agents.

The second claim is that self-respect is not reducible to the form of self-respect that arises from rights-recognition or struggles for rights – and further that struggles for rights involve complex motivational relations to self-confidence and self-esteem. The third claim is that self-esteem is not reducible to articulation in terms of the achievement principle (which is itself riven with problems) and further that the marginalization or denigration of the forms of valuing characteristic of one's cultural community can make it difficult for one to experience self-esteem and can even threaten one's basic self-confidence.

V

The main implications of these criticisms for Honneth's proposal of 'democracy as reflexive co-operation' as a social and political ideal concern, firstly, Honneth's account of the conditions requisite for the pre-political formation of the social consciousness of co-operation that is needed to ground democracy as reflexive co-operation and, secondly, Honneth's account of democracy as reflexive co-operation itself. I will consider each in turn.

With respect to the first issue, there are three points that require attention. The first is that if a just division of labour is to promote consciousness of social co-operation, then it is necessary to transform Honneth's understanding of a just division of labour such that this idea is developed in a way that is sensitive to the cultural (and other identity-related forms of) plurality of contemporary societies. It also seems plausible to suggest that in a culturally diverse society, to promote such a consciousness of social co-operation would require not only a just division of labour but also a mutual willingness on the part of different cultural communities to acknowledge each other's value. On Honneth's own view, this would require introducing a fourth form of recognition to respond to the need of members of non-dominant cultural communities that their cultural forms of valuing are not denigrated or marginalized. As Honneth rightly notes: 'With the demand that a minority communal culture be socially esteemed for its own sake, the normative horizon of both the equality principle and the achievement principle is definitively exceeded.'[49] Moreover, as he goes on to note, 'such a fourth recognition principle would mean that we also have to recognize each other as members of cultural communities whose forms of life deserve the measure of well-meaning attention that is necessary to judge their value.'[50] Honneth is fairly unsympathetic to this claim, but I have suggested reasons to think that he is mistaken in this respect. I also think that he is mistaken in thinking that this development would require a fourth form of recognition as opposed to revision to the first and third of his three forms of recognition. Here it is worth noting that the fact that he now identifies the developmental potential of love-recognition in terms of the identification of new needs on the part of the unique individual who is the object of love or care suggests a way in which this 'fourth' principle can be recast within the terms of (1) a revision of the notion of love-recognition along the lines suggested in the preceding section, and an expansion of this form of recognition to attend also to the needs of a unique community or 'people' combined with (2) moving the

[49] Axel Honneth, "Redistribution as Recognition," 167.
[50] Ibid., 169.

understanding of esteem-recognition away from a simple reduction to the achievement principle in order to incorporate an 'excellencies of character' principle. Given such revisions, Honneth's account could adequately address this dimension of a just division of labour.

The second point refers back to the suggestion that basic self-confidence is linked to trust. If it is the case, as I suggest, that basic self-confidence is at stake in relations of trust, and also that consciousness of social co-operation between citizens and between culturally diverse groups requires mutual trust, then a democratic society needs to be able to generate and sustain relations of trust amongst its citizens and the culturally (or otherwise) diverse groups that compose it. In part, this can be achieved through the social distribution of respect and esteem, but it has recently been observed by Danielle Allen that a crucial category for reflecting on this topic is that of *sacrifice* – that is, of the burdens that politics under non-ideal conditions places on its members or, more pertinently, on specific groups within its membership. Allen's point is that it will be hard to maintain relations of trust unless the demand for sacrifice on the part of citizens is itself equitably distributed over time.[51] Unless this condition is acknowledged and met, it is plausible that the possibility of creating and sustaining a consciousness of social co-operation (and even the basic self-confidence of citizens who are members of an unduly burdened group) would be significantly undermined. Yet, as it stands, Honneth's account of the conditions of social co-operation does not and cannot recognize the significance of this issue, and this refers us back once again to the requirement that Honneth's principle of love-recognition be revised and expanded to address the needs of unique groups.

The third point picks up on the centrality of social trust to a consciousness of social co-operation in relation to the issue of non-moral self-respect and the concomitant sense of self-worth. The key point here is that no one trusts the shameless and the weak-willed, and hence a willingness to engage in social and political co-operation requires the production of citizens who cannot only experience pride and shame, but also generally exhibit a basic level of ethical integrity. Yet Honneth's account of recognition, which is, after all, supposed to articulate the necessary and sufficient conditions of the consciousness of

[51] See D. Allen, *Talking to Strangers* (Chicago: University of Chicago Press, 2004).

social co-operation, does not address the significance of pride and shame except in relation to the principle of achievement in work and this is hardly sufficient. Accommodating this dimension of self-respect would require a development of Honneth's theory of recognition that expanded the notion of respect-recognition from the identification of oneself as a 'morally' responsible agent realised through being a legal person to the identification of oneself as an 'ethically' responsible agent realised through being a person who exhibits ethical integrity – that is, stands in the appropriate relations to both (universal) moral and (personal) non-moral standards.

What of the implications for democracy as reflexive co-operation itself? Two points are especially significant. First, it would seem to be the case that this ideal now needs to acknowledge that the political community is not only composed of individuals but also of culturally diverse groups. However, recognizing this requirement can itself offer further arguments for the ideal of democracy as reflexive co-operation by supplying additional support for the claim that democracy as reflexive co-operation links an understanding of democracy as a political community of co-operation to an understanding of democracy as a way of rationally solving social problems. This is so, though, only if we move away from the residual scientism in Dewey's and Honneth's articulation of an epistemological argument for democracy and towards Aristotle's equivalent perspectival argument for the doctrine of the wisdom of the multitude in which it is the plurality of perspectives brought to bear on a problem that is held to broadly govern the wisdom of the response to it.[52] It is not difficult to see on this Aristotelian model how the diversity of cultural perspectives may help to elucidate different aspect of a social problem and to avoid what may be the significant blind spots of a large but culturally homogeneous public. Second, the articulation of this ideal also requires acknowledging the centrality of the issue of ethical integrity. Specifically, for the salient type of self-respect to a central good for democracy as reflexive co-operation, it must be the case that one's standing within the democratic community is affected by whether or not one exhibits ethical integrity – that is to say, the authority of one's voice within

---

[52] See Jeremy Waldron, *The Dignity of Legislation* (Cambridge: Cambridge University Press, 1999), chapter 5, on Aristotle.

the political discourse of the community is dependent not merely on *what one says* or the reasons one offers for some course of action, but also on *what one is.* Honneth's current formulation of the ideal does not adequately address the salience of this dimension of self-respect, the significance of *who is speaking* in democratic public argument, and this may be because he follows Dewey too closely in considering political problem-solving on the model of a scientific community and thereby treats the individuality of voices as effectively irrelevant. Here again it is not a question of the ideal being undermined but of its being strengthened by modest revisions; precisely because political speech always involves the possibility of the abuse of rhetoric for manipulative ends, acknowledging the importance of who is speaking allows Honneth's ideal to respond to the threat posed by this problem in a way that the residual scientism of the Deweyan model fails to do.

CONCLUSION

In this chapter, I have offered a critical examination of Honneth's proposal of 'democracy as reflexive co-operation' as social and political ideal that demonstrates (1) how this ideal is related to his theory of recognition, and (2) how critical reflection on his theory of recognition affects the plausibility of 'democracy as reflexive co-operation' as an ideal. I have suggested that there are a number of ways in which Honneth's account of recognition is significantly limited, requiring development in relation to each of the three axes of recognition that he identifies and their relationship with one another. On the basis of these critical remarks, I have sought to show that there are significant problems with Honneth's current account of both the conditions requisite for a consciousness of social co-operation and the ideal itself. However, I have also suggested ways in which Honneth's account of recognition could be developed to meet these challenges and how his articulation of the ideal of democracy as reflexive co-operation could be revised in the light of these criticisms in ways that strengthen arguments for it.

My purpose has not been to criticize Honneth's theory of recognition as such but to engage in the more modest endeavour of showing how it might be further developed in relation to certain problems concerning self-confidence, self-respect, and self-esteem as Honneth elaborates these practical relations to self. In the end, I have – somewhat tentatively – suggested that Honneth's ideal can be maintained but only if he makes some significant changes to his understanding of the idea of a just division of labour and relatedly to his accounts of love, respect, and esteem as forms of recognition.

PART IV

AXEL HONNETH ON RECOGNITION AND POWER

affirmation vs. assimilation

self - image vs self - consciousness

13

Recognition as Ideology

Axel Honneth

In the same measure that the concept of recognition has become the normative core of several different emancipation movements over the last several years, so have there also been increasing doubts as to its critical potential. This theoretical skepticism has doubtlessly been fostered by the experience that we live in a culture of affirmation in which publicly displayed recognition often bears the marks of mere rhetoric and has the character of being a mere substitute. The act of praising certain characteristics or abilities seems to have become a political instrument whose unspoken function consists in inserting individuals or social groups into existing structures of dominance by encouraging a positive self-image. Far from making a lasting contribution to the conditions of autonomy of the members of our society, social recognition appears merely to serve the creation of attitudes that conform to the dominant system. The reservations entertained with regard to this new critical approach thus amount to the thesis that practices of recognition don't empower persons, but subject them. We could summarize this objection by saying that through processes of reciprocal recognition, subjects are encouraged to adopt a particular self-conception that motivates them to voluntarily take on tasks or duties that serve society.[1]

[1] Patchen Markell, *Bound by Recognition* (Princeton and Oxford: Princeton University Press, 2003); Kelly Olivier, *Witnessing. Beyond Recognition* (Minneapolis: University of Minnesota Press, 2001); Markus Verweyst, *Das Begehen der Anerkennung. Subjekttheoretische Positionen bei Heidegger, Sartre, Freud und Lacan* (Frankfurt and New York: Campus, 2000).

These fundamental reservations recall the considerations that moved the Marxist theoretician Louis Althusser more than thirty years ago to find the practice of public recognition to be the common mechanism of all forms of ideology.[2] His roughly outlined arguments, which dealt exclusively with state policies, were later taken up by Judith Butler, who, by drawing on Jacques Lacan's work in psychoanalysis, fashioned these arguments into a tenable concept.[3] As is well-known, Althusser made use of the double meaning of the French concept of "subjectivation" in order to elucidate what he understood by ideology: human individuals become "subjects" – that is, persons who are aware of their responsibilities and rights only to the extent to which they are subjected to a system of practical rules and role-ascriptions that lends them a social identity. Once we conceive of the act of subjection indicated by this definition according to the model of public affirmation, that which we could call "recognition" suddenly loses all of its positive connotations and becomes the central mechanism of ideology. To recognize someone would then mean to encourage him by means of repeated and ritual invitations [*Aufforderungen*] to adopt precisely that self-conception that conforms to the established system of behavioral expectations.

However, Althusser never employed this concept of ideology in a critical sense, restricting himself instead to a purely descriptive use of the concept.[4] Without making any normative judgments, he described the institutional act of recognition as a mechanism for creating subjects who behave in conformity with a given social system. For a critical theory of society that seeks to locate its normative foundation in the act of reciprocal recognition, however, Althusser's conceptual determinations pose a difficult challenge, for such a theory is forced to ask whether social recognition might also occasionally take on the function of securing social domination. In this new context, the concept of ideology loses its merely descriptive significance and becomes

---

[2] Louis Althusser, "Ideology and Ideological State Apparatuses," in *Lenin and Philosophy and Other Essays* (New York: Monthly Review Press, 2001).

[3] Judith Butler, "Conscience Doth Make Subjects of Us All – Althusser's Subjection," in *The Psychic Life of Power: Theories in Subjection* (Stanford: Stanford University Press, 1997).

[4] Cf. Raymond Geuss, *The Idea of a Critical Theory: Habermas and the Frankfurt School* (Cambridge: Cambridge University Press, 1981), Ch.1.

a pejorative category, indicating forms of recognition that must be regarded as being false or unjustified because they do not have the function of promoting personal autonomy, but rather of engendering attitudes that conform to practices of domination.[5] Of course, it would be wrong to accuse the theory of recognition of having ignored negative phenomena of subjection and domination from the very beginning. After all, this approach owes its entire critical impulse to its point of departure in social phenomena of lacking or insufficient recognition. It seeks to draw attention to practices of humiliation or degradation that deprive subjects of a justified form of social recognition and thus of a decisive condition for the formation of their autonomy.[6] On the other hand, this way of formulating the issue makes clear that "recognition" was always treated as representing the opposite of practices of domination or subjection. Such forms of exercising power were to be regarded as phenomena of withheld recognition, intentional disrespect, or humiliation, such that recognition itself could never come under suspicion of functioning as a means of domination. This presumption of innocence, however, is no longer self-evident in view of the considerations to which Althusser's concept of ideology gives rise, for the latter draws attention to forms of recognition that can be effective as a means of social domination because they employ methods of ritual affirmation in order to create a self-image that conforms to social expectations; they thus contribute to the reproduction of the existing relations of domination. We could easily cite examples from society's past that demonstrate just how often public displays of recognition in fact merely serve to create and maintain an individual self-conception that is seamlessly integrated into a system based on the prevailing division of labor. For example, the pride that "Uncle Tom" feels as a reaction to the repeated praise of his submissive virtues makes him into a compliant servant in a slave-owning society.[7] The emotional appeals to the "good" mother and housewife made by churches, parliaments, or the mass media over the centuries caused women to remain trapped within a self-image that

---

[5] Ibid., 24ff.

[6] Axel Honneth, "The Social Dynamics of Disrespect," in *The Other of Justice* (London: Polity Press, forthcoming April 2007).

[7] Cf. Gert Raiethel, *Geschichte der nordamerikanischen Kultur*, Vol. I: *Vom Puritanismus bis zum Bürgerkrieg 1600–1800* (Frankfurt am Main: Zweitausendeins, 1995), Ch XXXI.

most effectively accommodated the gender-specific division of labor.[8] The public esteem enjoyed by heroic soldiers continuously engendered a sufficiently large class of men who willingly went to war in pursuit of glory and adventure.[9] As trivial as these examples may be, they do make strikingly clear that social recognition can always also operate as a conformist ideology, for the continuous repetition of identical forms of recognition can create a feeling of self-worth that provides the motivational resources for forms of voluntary subordination without employing methods of repression.

However, these cases all owe their suggestive power entirely to the circumstance that they are equipped with the certainty provided by a retrospective evaluation. The choice of examples itself, indeed the very way they are described, is the result of a moral judgment that can be made only from the perspective of our morally advanced present. Because we live in an era that regards itself as being morally superior to past ages, we are certain that the esteem enjoyed by the virtuous slave, the good housewife, and the heroic soldier was of a purely ideological character. Yet if we put ourselves in the position of past eras, it becomes much more difficult to distinguish between a false, "ideological" form of recognition and one that is correct and morally required, for the criteria of which we were so convinced suddenly become uncertain. Why shouldn't the slave's experience of being esteemed for his submissiveness by his white masters allow him to attain a feeling of self-worth that provides him with a certain degree of inner autonomy? And doesn't the public recognition of women as caring mothers give them a measure of compensation for the disrespect they have endured as a result of their exclusion from roles and offices outside the home? And finally, the set of values comprised by male heroism may have provided men who suffer from social insignificance within their culture as a result of being unemployed or lacking some qualification with an opportunity

---

[8] Cf. Karin Hausen, "Die Polarisierung der 'Geschlechtskaraktere' – Eine Spiegelung der Dissoziation von Erwerbs- und Familienleben," in Werner Conze (ed.), *Sozialgeschichte der Familie in der Neuzeit Europas* (Stuttgart: Klett, 1976), 363–393; Bärbel Kühn, "Vom Schalten und Walten der Hausfrau. Hausarbeit in Rat, Tat und Forschung im 19. und 20. Jahrhundert," in Birgit Bolognese-Leuchtenmüller & Michael Mitteerauer (eds.) *Frauen-Arbeitswelten. Zur historischen Genese gegenwärtiger Probleme* (Wien: Verlag für Gesellschaftskritik, 1993), 43–66.

[9] René Schilling, *Kriegshelden. Deutungsmuster heroischer Männlichkeit in Deutschland 1813– 1945* (Paderborn: Ferdinand Schöningh, 2002).

to become part of a independent, male subculture in which they could gain compensatory prestige and reputation.

In each case, these possibilities of interpretation give us a clear sense of the fact that upon closer inspection of the historical circumstances, a particular *dispositiv* of esteem that we hold in retrospect to be pure ideology can prove in fact to be a condition for a group-specific attainment of increased self-worth. Determining the ideological contents of particular forms of recognition thus seems to become all the more difficult the more we examine them under the socio-cultural conditions prevailing at the time. Only in instances where the concerned parties themselves revolted against dominant practices of recognition do we have any grounds for speaking of mere ideology with reference to that historical period. In general, however, this difficulty diminishes with the increasing period of time separating us from the cases in question, for the greater the historical distance, the more likely we are to possess generally accepted criteria allowing us to distinguish retrospectively between ideological and morally required forms of recognition.

With regard to the present, however, this theoretical problem retains its intricacies. As long as we have no empirical evidence that the concerned parties themselves experience particular practices of recognition as being repressive, constricting or as fostering stereotypes, it is extremely difficult to distinguish between ideological and justified forms of recognition in any reasonable way. This difficulty is a result of the fact that when we speak of acts of recognition, we always refer to the public display of a value or achievement that is to be attributed to a person or social group. Thus to speak in this connection of an "ideology" is to ascribe the negative features of an act of subjection that is free of suppression to a praxis that is intrinsically positive and affirmative, even though this practice appears *prima facie* to lack all such discriminatory features. The question that thereby arises concerns how public displays of a social value, that is, recognition – can nevertheless bear features of domination.

This is the problem I will deal with in this chapter. As an introduction, it would be wise to summarize what we, after a number of recent attempts to clarify this issue, can understand today by a practice of recognition. Here we will see that the concept of recognition possesses a normative character inasmuch as it indicates the rational behavior with which we can respond to the evaluative qualities

[*Werteigenschaften*] of a person or group (Section I). These conceptual considerations, however, only appear to offer a solution to the problem of how to distinguish between ideological and morally justified forms of social recognition, for we will see that it is only in rare cases that ideologies of recognition are simply irrational, but that they instead mobilize evaluative reasons contained within our horizon of values (Section II). A solution to our problem can only be found in the attempt to dissect and spell out the conditions under which forms of recognition are applied, such that the "irrational kernel" of all merely "ideological" forms of recognition will be revealed. I suspect that this irrationality does not lie on the semantic surface of our evaluative vocabulary, but is to be found instead in the discrepancy between evaluative promises and material fulfillment (III).

I

In a certain sense, the problem I wish to focus on here cannot even exist for Althusser. His concept of recognition is one-dimensional in the sense that it doesn't permit any distinctions between "correct" and "incorrect," "right" and "wrong," "justified" and "ideological." For him, every form of recognition necessarily has the character of an ideology, since merely making a demand upon or "calling upon" addressees imposes an imaginary unity on them that they in no way possess as individuals. By contrast, an attempt to distinguish between "ideological" and appropriate forms of recognition must begin by giving a positive definition of "recognition."[10] Although there has been a strong growth in the research literature on the issue of "recognition" in recent years, there remains a great deal of dispute about the conceptual core of this phenomenon. Indirectly drawing on Hegel, the concept is used generally to depict vague attitudes or practices through which individual subjects or social groups receive affirmation for certain specific qualities. Not only does the relation between this notion and the Kantian concept of "respect" remain unclear, but it has also become more apparent than ever that the concept of recognition encompasses semantic

---

[10] Axel Honneth, "Der Grund der Anerkennung. Eine Erwiderung auf kritische Rückfragen," in *Das Andere der Gerechtigkeit. Mit einem neuen Nachwort* (Frankfurt am Main: Suhrkamp, 2004).

components that differ in English, French, and German usage, and that the relation between these various components is not especially transparent. In German, the concept essentially seems to indicate only that normative element that pertains to the act of granting a positive social status, while the English and French usage encompasses the epistemic senses of identifying or recalling something as well. An additional difficulty consists in the fact that in all three languages, the concept can be used to indicate speech acts in which one admits or acknowledges a point, in which case "recognition" has a primarily self-referential sense.[11] Finally, a Wittgensteinian interpretation has come to rival the Hegelian usage of the term; "recognition" here functions as a performative response to the actions [*Lebensäußerungen*] of other people. As a consequence of the writings of Stanley Cavell in particular, which make do without any recourse to Hegel, the category of "acknowledgment" has penetrated into the inner circle of analytic philosophy.[12]

In this thicket of conceptual confusion and unanswered questions, it is only by giving categorial definitions that do not shy away from simplifying the issue or excluding certain elements that we can gain some clarity. Here we must take account of the fact that recognition represents a moral act anchored in the social world as an everyday occurrence. I assume four premises upon which there seems to me to be sufficient consensus. First, it can be claimed that the original mode of recognition consists in the sense that comes to the foreground in the German usage of the term: the affirmation of positive qualities of human subjects or groups. However, this is not to say that we could establish no systematic connections between this and other definitions of the term. Second, there is now general agreement that recognition's character as an action must be emphasized: an act of recognition cannot consist in mere words or symbolic expressions, since it is only through corresponding modes of comportment that the credibility so normatively significant for the recognized subject can be engendered. Insofar as we limit ourselves to intersubjective relationships, we should

---

[11] Avishai Margalit, "Recognition II: Recognizing the Brother and the Other," in *Aristotelian Society*, Supplementary Volume 75 (2001), 127–139.

[12] Stanley Cavell, "Knowing and Acknowledging," in *Must We Mean What We Say?* (Cambridge: Cambridge University Press, 2002).

speak of recognition as a "stance" [*Haltung*] – that is, as an attitude realized in concrete action.[13] Third, we can assume that such acts of recognition represent a distinct phenomenon in the social world, which cannot, therefore, be understood as a mere side-effect of an action aimed at some other goal, but must instead be conceived of as the expression of an independent intention. Whether they be gestures, speech acts, or institutional policies, such expressions or measures are always cases of recognition if their primary purpose is somehow to affirm the existence of another person or group. This basic conceptual choice rules out, for example, defining positive attitudes that are inevitably accompanied by the pursuit of a series of other interests in interaction as being a form of recognition. If I have a strong desire to play chess with another person on a regular basis, I may express a certain amount of esteem for that person's intellectual abilities, but the primary purpose of my action concerns our playing chess together. A fourth premise upon which there is general agreement can be summarized in the thesis that recognition represents a conceptual species comprising a number of various sub-species. "Stances" of love, legal respect, and esteem thus accentuate and display various aspects of the basic attitude we can conceive of generically as recognition.

These four premises only summarize the point of departure for a half-way clear terminological usage. Recognition should be understood as a genus comprising various forms of practical attitudes whose primary intention consists in a particular act of affirmation of another person or group. Unlike what Althusser had in mind, such recognitional stances are of an unambiguously positive character, because they permit the addressee to identify with his or her own qualities and thus to achieve a greater degree of autonomy. Far from being a mere ideology, recognition constitutes an intersubjective prerequisite for the ability to fulfill one's life goals in an autonomous manner.[14] Yet the

---

[13] Heikki Ikäheimo, "On the Genus and Species of Recognition," in *Inquiry* 45/4 (2002), 447–462; Arno Laitinen, "Interpersonal Recognition: A Response to Value or a Precondition of Personhood?" in *Inquiry* 45/4 (2002), 463–478.

[14] A difference becomes apparent here from Althusser's theory whose social-ontological nature lies so deep that we cannot discuss it here in depth. For reasons of principle, Althusser does not concede subjects the possibility of gaining a higher degree of autonomy in their actions and decisions, assuming instead that individuals can

real challenge in clarifying the use of this concept begins once we turn to the epistemic character of such affirmative behavior; the decisive question here is whether we should understand recognition as an attributive or receptive act.

In responding to the question of how we are to characterize appropriately a generic case of recognition, we appear to be confronted with two alternatives concerning our cognitive relation to our partners in interaction. We can either understand the affirmation contained in such an act as an attribution through which a subject is ascribed a new, positive quality, or we can understand this act as a perception, such that the qualities already possessed by a person are somehow strengthened or manifested publicly as a secondary matter. In the first case, what we understand by recognition would be the ascription or addition of a status that the concerned subject could not have previously possessed; in the second case, recognition would be a particular act of perception by which we become aware of an already present status possessed by the subject independent of our perceiving it. Another way of defining the differences between these two ways of viewing the issue could consist in asserting that recognition is productive in the first case and merely reproductive in the second; the status or positive qualities possessed by a person or a social group are either produced in the act of recognition or simply reproduced in a particular meaningful way.

It is not easy to decide between these two conceptual models, because each seems to possess certain distinct advantages. If I see it rightly, the perception or reception model permits us to account better for our intuition that recognition must be an act motivated by practical reasons: we thereby react in a correct or appropriate way to the reasons contained in the evaluative qualities that human beings possess in different respects.[15] By contrast, the attribution model is free of any admixture of this kind of value realism. Here we account for our intuition that recognition is a constitutive act in which we

---

become socially identifiable subjects only by being subjected through public recognition to a web of social rules that does not possess any room for variation with respect to individual autonomy. By contrast, I assume (as does Durkheim) that such social rules of recognition have to be able to be differentiated according to the room for autonomy they open up.

[15] Laitinen, "Interpersonal Recognition."

ascribe particular qualities to a person or group. A disadvantage of this way of seeing the issue lies in the very point that appears to constitute the advantage of the reception model: if the stance of recognition merely attributes determinate qualities to another person, then we will no longer possess any internal criteria for judging the correctness or appropriateness of such acts of ascription. There would be no limits to the permutations that recognition could take, because we would have to regard everything as an ability or status just because it has come about by an attributive act. The only way out of this problem consists in the thesis that the legitimacy of a given act of recognition is measured according to the normative quality of the way it comes about. However, the concept of recognition would then lose all the moral implications that are supposed to distinguish it from a sociological "labeling approach."

Now, at first sight, matters look no better for the other approach, the reception or response model. In order to be able to claim that an act of recognition constitutes a "correct" response to the evaluative qualities of a person or group of persons, we must presuppose the objective existence of values in a way that is no longer reconcilable with our insights into how they are constituted. It may seem right for us to continue to place recognition in the "space of reasons" so that it is not deprived of its character as a moral action, for only if our recognition of other persons is motivated by reasons that we could also attempt to articulate can it be understood as an intentional act of will and thus as belonging in a broad sense to the domain of the moral. The further suggestion that we should identify these kinds of reasons as being "evaluative" is convincing inasmuch as by recognizing others we appear to manifest the value of a person or group. The moral constraints we respect in the act of recognition result from the valuable qualities to which our recognitional behavior gives public expression. The problem starts only when we begin to give a more precise definition of the status of such evaluative reasons. Here we don't seem to have any choice but to fall back upon a kind of value realism that is no longer reconcilable with the remainder of our basic ontological convictions. This unfortunate situation changes, however, once we concede the possibility that these kinds of values represent the certainties of our life-world, whose character can be subject to historical modifications. The qualities we would have to perceive in persons or groups in order to respond to them "correctly" in our recognitional behavior would thus no longer be unchangeable and objective, but historically variable. In order to arrive at a halfway plausible theory, however, we would have to add some further elements to the image of recognition outlined here. We would have to conceive of the life-world as a kind of "second nature" into which subjects are socialized by their learning successively to take notice of the valuable qualities of other persons. This learning process would have to be conceived of as a complex process in which we acquire modes of behavior corresponding to the perception of evaluative qualities, whose particularity would have to consist in the self-evident constraint of our natural egocentrism. As a result, we could then understand human recognitional behavior as a bundle of habits that have been linked to the revisable reasons for the value of other persons in the process of socialization.[16]

However, this line of argumentation has not yet solved the problem that appears to give rise to the real difficulty posed by this type of moderate value realism. We have already said that the valuable qualities we can appropriately recognize in other persons can possess some degree of reality only within the experiential horizon of a particular life-world. Those who have been socialized successfully into the culture of that life-world take these values to be objective givens of their social environment, just as they initially experience other cultural particulars as being self-evidently given facts. This gives rise to the danger of a kind of relativism that is fundamentally irreconcilable with the normative goals of the concept of recognition, because the values against which the appropriateness of our recognitional behavior is measured would then possess validity for only one single culture. As a consequence, the relativism associated with the response or reception model would no longer differ from that of the attribution model. In both cases, the validity of recognitional stances, whether they be described as acts of ascription or as appropriate responses, would be contingent upon the normative givens obtaining in a respective form of life. In my opinion, the difficulty arising for the reception model can

---

[16] John McDowell, "Two Sorts of Naturalism," in *Mind, Value and Reality* (Cambridge, MA: Harvard University Press, 2001); Eva Lovibond, *Ethical Formation* (Cambridge, MA: Harvard University Press, 2002); Axel Honneth, "Zwischen Hermeneutik und Hegelianismus," in *Unsichtbarkeit* (Frankfurt am Main: Suhrkamp, 2003).

be avoided only if we equip this moderate value realism with a robust conception of progress. Basically this would entail supposing there to be a definite direction to the cultural transformations of valuable human qualities, which would allow us to make justified judgments about the trans-historical validity of a particular culture of recognition.[17] Without going into the details of such a conception of progress here, which I am convinced must be defined as a form of reflection of the knowledge by means of which we orient ourselves in the life-world,[18] I would like to limit myself to putting forth the main idea: with the differentiation of the valuable qualities we observe and can take rational account of in other people on the basis of our socialization, the normative level of our relations of recognition rises as well. With every value that we can affirm by an act of recognition, our opportunities for identifying with our abilities and attaining greater autonomy grow. This remark should suffice to justify the idea that our concept of recognition is anchored in a moderate form of value realism.

But before I return to the question of how we can distinguish between ideological and justified forms of recognition, I still need to deal with at least one problem – one that results from speaking of ideologies mostly as transformations of consciousness or evaluative systems of statements whose source lies not in intersubjective behavior but in institutionalized rules and arrangements. We assume with Marx, who held the civil form of the contract to be an institution that produces ideologies,[19] that it is the specific constitution of certain institutions that originally leads to the emergence of illusory or fictionalizing convictions. If patterns of recognition are now also thought to be capable of engendering such ideologies, we will have to clarify the fact that not only persons can grant recognition, but social institutions as well.

---

[17] Axel Honneth, "Redistribution as Recognition: A Response to Nancy Fraser," in Nancy Fraser & Axel Honneth, *Redistribution or Recognition? A Political-Philosophical Exchange* (London: Verso, 2003).

[18] Axel Honneth, "Die Unhintergehbarkeit des Fortschritts. Kants Bestimmung des Verhältnisses von Moral und Geschichte," in Herta Nagl-Docekal & Rudolf Langthaler (eds.), *Tagungsband "Recht – Geschichte – Religion. Die Bedeutung Kants für die Philosophie der Gegenwart* (Berlin: Akademie, 2004).

[19] Karl Marx, *Capital. A Critique of Political Economy*, Vol. I (London: Penguin, 1976), pp. 181–191.

We must therefore shift from the level of intersubjective recognition to the level of institutionally guaranteed recognition.[20]

The point of departure for this transition consists in the observation that institutional rules and practices can contain certain particular conceptions about which human evaluative qualities should receive recognition in which specific way. For instance, the value that a person in his or her quality as an individual with needs should be recognized as possessing is expressed in the institution of the modern nuclear family, while the normative fact that members of modern societies are to be respected as free and equal subjects is expressed in the principle of equality, institutionalized in modern law. In both cases, the respective institution can be understood as an institutional embodiment of the specific form of recognition that subjects accord each other on the basis of specific evaluative qualities. However, we have to distinguish between those institutions in which patterns of recognition find social "expression" and those institutional rules and practices that articulate particular forms of recognition in merely indirect ways or as mere side-effects. In the routines found in all institutions, particular conceptions of human subjects find expressions that don't intentionally accord recognition, but that can be understood nevertheless as crystallizations of patterns of recognition. For example, the rules that regulate the remuneration of labor, protection against illness, and vacation time for workers in certain specific industries reflect forms of recognition that result from social struggles – for example, in the organizational practices and routines concerning the treatment that patients are to receive in hospitals. The schemata of perception and behavior that constitutes the prerequisite for the particular treatment of individuals in these organizations as members or clients can be understood as sediments of practices of recognition in the life-world. Of course, the direction of these sediments can be inverted – for instance, if a certain organization takes on a leading role in the creation or discovery of new evaluative qualities. In cases such as these, modified patterns of recognition are established in the rules and practices of an institution before they find expression in the narrative praxis of a given life-world.

---

[20] Emmanuel Renault, "Reconnaissance, Institutions, Injustice," in *De la Connaissance. Revue de Mauss, Semestrielle No. 23* (2004), 180–195.

This second case of institutional recognition is most likely of special significance for the question of how and in what sense certain specific patterns of recognition possess an ideological character, because of the fact that they give rise to a willingness to subject oneself freely to the prevailing system of rules and expectations.

II

So far, my main concern has been to find an appropriate understanding of the concept of recognition. Confronted with the alternative between an attribution model and a reception model, I have taken the path of a moderate value realism – we should understand recognition as a reaction with which we respond rationally to evaluative qualities we have learned to perceive in human subjects to the degree that we have been integrated into the second nature of our life-world. This suffices to give us a sense of the difference between this conceptual definition and Althusser's suggestion that every form of recognition must represent an instance of ideology. He holds that regardless of how subjects are addressed, the mere ascription of a social status represents an ideological practice because it creates both the illusion of unity and identity as well as the willingness to accept corresponding behavioral expectations. By contrast, the suggestion developed in this chapter assumes the possibility of an appropriate and rational form of recognition that would consist in giving public expression to existing evaluative qualities in a performative way. However, this way of formulating the issue does not yet give us a clear enough sense of why this conception of recognition should indicate a moral act at all. Although we are dealing with an act mediated by evaluative reasons, this by itself in no way indicates that it is necessarily a moral one. Its character as a moral act doesn't become apparent until we take a closer look at the aspect I have already described as a "restriction of egocentrism." In a certain sense this idea builds on Kant, who, when introducing his concept of respect, had said that every idea of a value compels us to impose a restriction on our actions that injures our self-love.[21]

---

[21] Immanuel Kant, *Groundwork of the Metaphysic of Morals*, trans. H. J. Paton (New York: Harper and Row, 1964).

We could continue this line of thought by saying that to recognize someone is to perceive in his or her person a value quality that motivates us intrinsically to no longer behave egocentrically, but rather in accordance with the intentions, desires, and needs of that person. This makes clear that recognitional behavior must represent a moral act, because it lets itself be determined by the value of other persons. When we take up the stance of recognition, the evaluative qualities of the other, and not one's own intentions, are what guide our behavior. If that is the case, then it must be possible for us to distinguish between as many forms of moral action as there are values worthy of recognition. This is why I have come to the conclusion in recent essays that we have to distinguish between three sources of morality corresponding to the various forms of recognition in our life-world, for as I have claimed in agreement with a whole set of other authors, the value horizon of modern societies is marked by the idea that humans, as beings who have needs, who are equally entitled to autonomy and equally capable of achievement, should possess a value to which diverse forms of recognitional behavior correspond (love, legal respect, social esteem).[22]

Before I can pursue this train of thought further, I would first like to turn to the question that actually ought to stand at the center of this chapter. I had said that we cannot exclude the possibility that such forms of social recognition can only possess an ideological function because they encourage an individual self-conception that suits the existing dominant order. Instead of truly giving expression to a particular value, such ideological forms of recognition would ensure the motivational willingness to fulfill certain tasks and duties without resistance. At this point, it probably makes sense to further narrow the set of public value-statements and conceptions of the human subject that could play any role at all in such ideological forms of recognition, for the majority of the evaluative classifications we might currently encounter in our current life-world do not even meet the prerequisites for being credible as ideological forms of recognition.

First, the systems of belief that might be at issue in the case of such ideologies have to give positive expression to the value of a subject or group of subjects. These ideologies are only capable of fulfilling the function ascribed to them if they give individuals the opportunity

[22] Honneth, "Redistribution as Recognition."

to relate to themselves affirmatively, such that they see themselves encouraged to take over willingly certain specific tasks. Thus we must exclude all those classifications that are of an obviously discriminatory character; those systems of belief in which specific groups of persons are denied a certain value – as is the case with racism, misogyny, or xenophobia – cannot take up the role of being ideological forms of recognition, as they normally cause an injury in the self-image of their addressees. Ideologies that are to be effective by virtue of providing social recognition cannot exclude their addressees, but must instead contribute to their integration.

Second, in order to achieve the desired effect, the system of beliefs we are looking for must be "credible" in the eyes of the addressees themselves. If the latter have no good reason to identify with the value-statements addressed to them, then these statements will fail to fulfill their performative function. This limiting condition is not merely trivial, but has a complex side that is not so easy to elucidate. It is obvious that all positive value-statements capable of strengthening the self-image of a person or group of persons have to be realistic in the virtually self-evident sense of being attached to abilities or virtues that the addressees really do possess. It makes just as little sense to praise a police officer for his or her mathematical talents as it does to praise an outstanding mathematician for his or her physical strength, unless both are being honored for achievements unrelated to their respective careers. But even more important than the condition that such recognition must be realistic, the criterion of "credibility" contains a second component related to the expansion of the realm of evaluative reasons: only those value-statements that do not remain on a level of evaluation lower than that which the addressees have achieved in the process of overcoming one-sided or inappropriate interpretations will be acceptable to them. To put it positively, and more simply, we might say that ideological forms of recognition can only employ value-statements that use the evaluative vocabulary of the present. By contrast, statements praising evaluative qualities that have come to be discredited will not be credible in the eyes of the addressees. Alongside the reality component, therefore, the criterion of credibility also contains a component of rationality that unambiguously possesses a historical or temporal index. Today, a woman who is praised for her virtues as a good housewife will have little reason to identify with this value-statement to such a degree that she could regard her own feeling of self-worth as having been thereby reinforced.

Correspondingly, those patterns of recognition we can describe as "normalizing"[23] cannot really be identified as "ideological" forms of recognition, for the term "normalization" in this context means that a person or group has been recognized by virtue of having been defined as having certain qualities or ascribed a certain identity that they themselves experience as a restriction of their sphere of autonomy.[24] Thus a normalizing form of recognition cannot move us to develop an affirmative self-image that would lead us to willingly accept tasks and sacrifices imposed upon us by others. A more difficult situation concerns the case when we only suspect the effect of an act of normalization, without having any empirical evidence that the concerned parties themselves are displeased with or object to such an act. In these situations, the negative judgment operates with the hypothesis that the concerned parties would actually reject the qualities ascribed to them if they indeed knew all the details, for they would have a sense that their autonomy has thereby been restricted. Therefore, this idea essentially amounts to the thesis that a pattern of recognition is "normalizing" if it serves to maintain a restrictive, evaluatively anachronistic ascription of identity in an unjustified manner, while ideological forms of recognition can only maintain their repression-free effect with the aid of contemporary, evaluatively rational value statements.

Perhaps we can name a third condition that has to be fulfilled in order for forms of social recognition to take on an ideological function: such value-statements not only have to be positive and credible, but also contrastive in the sense of giving expression to a particular new value or special achievement. This restriction follows from the fact that individuals have the possibility of identifying with the definitions ascribed to them only if these values give them the sense of being distinguished in a certain way. Thus a value statement that they have to be able to apply to themselves in comparison with the past or with the surrounding social order will have to evince a contrast that provides

---

[23] Carolin Emcke, *Kollektive Identitäten. Sozialphilosophische Grundlagen* (Frankfurt and New York: Campus, 2000); Hans-Uwe Rösner, *Jenseits normalisierender Anerkennung. Reflexionen zum Verhältnis von Macht und Behindertsein* (Frankfurt am Main and New York: Campus, 2002).

[24] Emcke, *Kollektive Identitäten*, 237.

a guarantee that they will feel distinguished in some special way. If an existing form of social recognition is only expanded to include a previously excluded social circle, this aspect of definitive accentuation that elicits the motivational willingness to subject oneself voluntarily will be absent.

With these three restrictions, which are certainly not all of equal importance, I have begun to outline only the conditions under which ideological forms of recognition might potentially be successful. They can evoke an individual self-conception that motivates a subject to accept tasks and obligations freely and willingly only if the value-statements employed are simultaneously positive, credible, and contrastive to a certain degree. But taken together, these conditions for success make clear that such ideological forms of recognition cannot simply represent irrational systems of beliefs; rather, they must mobilize evaluative reasons possessing sufficient power to convince under given circumstances in order to motivate their addressees rationally to apply these reasons to themselves. In contrast to ideologies that have an exclusionary character, and virtually shatter the present's evaluative perceptual horizon by blinding individuals or groups to the evaluative qualities of others, ideological forms of recognition operate within a historical "space of reasons": they only extend, so to speak, the evaluative qualities we have learned to perceive in other humans by adding the accent of a new meaning – one when taken up successfully, however, has the effect of creating a self-conception that conforms to a person's function in society. As with every new accentuation inherent in social recognition, these kinds of rational ideologies are also bound up in the horizon of value that encompasses the normative culture of recognition in modern societies. Thus they also cannot avoid making semantic use of those principles of love, legal equality, or achievement that shape the given conditions of reciprocal recognition all the way down to our evaluative awareness. The question we must therefore pose is how we can draw a distinction between justified and unjustified forms of social recognition. At what point does a new accentuation become an ideology with the function of merely evoking a self-conception conforming to one's social role?

We don't get a clear sense of the full extent of the difficulties we face here until we recall that the historical development of recognition generally occurs as the disclosure of new points of view within the horizon of general principles. By invoking an overarching principle of recognition, one brings a new, previously neglected special value into play whose consideration compels us to enlarge our evaluative horizon of awareness and thereby intensify or enlarge recognition. Thus, in my view, it can be said that during the last two centuries, new needs have constantly been asserted by invoking the normative meaning of "love" – the well-being of the child, the wife's need for autonomy, and so on. These are needs that have gradually led to a deepening of reciprocal care and attention; the same dynamic can be observed in the relations of recognition obtaining in modern law, where legal proceedings pertaining to previously neglected life-situations have brought about an unambiguous increase in legal equality. I would also speak of a dialectic between the general and the particular even with regard to the achievement principle, since here an unbroken symbolic struggle over the meaning of "work" and "pay" has brought us at the very least to the threshold of a broader conception of social contributions and achievements. But the more we become aware of the fact that relations of recognition have been transformed, expanded and improved historically by means of new accentuations of general principles, the more difficult it becomes to identify merely ideological forms of recognition. For who can tell us for sure that an apparently functional, ideological evaluation is not just one of those shifts in accentuation by means of which the struggle for recognition unfolds historically? The issue is simple only in cases where the concerned parties actually resist new forms of evaluative distinction. Here we have at least an initial reason to question the changed form of recognition and to suspect that a mere ideology could be at work. But in the absence of such protest, where individuals seem to attain a stronger sense of self-respect through a new form of recognition, we initially lack all criteria for distinguishing between ideological and justified shifts in accentuation. In the final part of this chapter, I would like to present a recent example in order to at least sketch the first outlines of an answer to the question.

III

As I have already shown, ideological forms of recognition have to represent positive classifications whose evaluative contents are sufficiently credible for their addressees to have good reason to accept them. Any new distinction granted to these addressees has to be able to alter their self-conception in such a way as to promise a psychic premium of heightened self-respect on the condition that they do in fact take over the abilities, needs, and virtues associated with this distinction as being their own. Today, the primary examples of such ideologies appear to be advertisements that set up a schema of recognition in such a way that a specific group of persons sees themselves urged to conform their behavior to a set of given standards. If the corresponding practice can only be carried out with the help of the item they are advertising in a more or less concealed way, these advertisements have attained their goal. However, the example of consumer advertising is only partially sufficient to illustrate the characteristics possessed by ideological forms of recognition, for in general, the content of these advertisements is received with the mental reservation that it only offers mere fictions that cannot really alter our life practices in any substantial way. But if certain specific advertisements cross this threshold and have an actual effect on our behavior, then we could say that they do indeed exercise the same power as ideological forms of recognition: they would then possess the "regulative" ability to engender modes of behavior by promising the advantage of an increase in self-esteem and public affirmation. Thus, in Foucault's terms, the power exercised by ideological forms of recognition is productive and not repressive. By promising social recognition for the subjective demonstration of certain abilities, needs, or desires, they engender a willingness to adopt a web of practices and modes of behavior that suit the reproduction of social domination.[25]

But even by having clarified the type of power represented by ideological forms of recognition, we have not yet answered the question of how they could be identified within the unbroken flow of a many-layered struggle for recognition. Although the comparison with modern methods of advertisement gives us a clear sense of the fact that such ideologies must speak to their addressees in a way that reinforces the former's evaluative credibility, justified demands for new accentuations of social recognition can no longer be made without taking on elements of a symbolic political aim that draws public attention

---

[25] Wolfgang Detel, *Macht, Moral, Wissen. Foucault und die klassische Antike* (Frankfurt am Main: Suhrkamp, 1998), 55ff.

to them. Instead of continuing to address this question on a merely conceptual plane, in what follows I would like to take a look at an empirical example in the hope that it might further clarify matters. From the multiplicity of new patterns of recognition that can currently be found in our social culture – the increased value accorded to female housework in connection with the achievement principle, an appreciation of belonging to social minorities in connection with legal equality, the idea of giving recognition to "public service" [*Bürgerarbeit*] – I would like to select one instance that shows all the signs of being a pure "ideological" form of recognition. By discussing this instance, it should become apparent whether there are any criteria for determining the ideological content of forms of recognition with any certainty.

A far-reaching structural transformation has been taking place recently in the sphere of labor in developed capitalist economies, with the result that employees have come to be addressed in a new way. Current management literature no longer simply speaks of "wage-workers" or the "labor force," but instead of creative "entrepreneurs" of their own labor.[26] The shift in accentuation accompanying this change in nomenclature takes up the discourse of individual self-fulfillment in order to apply it to the organization of labor in the sphere of production and the provision of services. Growing needs for self-fulfillment in the sphere of labor should be accommodated by leveling hierarchies, raising the autonomy of work-teams and providing a higher degree of self-management, thus increasing the chance of conceiving of one's own activity as an autonomous expression of acquired skills. Furthermore, this new nomenclature seems to be accompanied by a whole new way of conceiving of one's own profession, since subjects should no longer regard their labor activity as the fulfillment of a necessity, but as the realization of a "vocation" or "calling." The idea of labeling laborers as employers of their own labor-power urges us to regard every job change or every new change in working conditions as a result of these subjects' own decisions made solely in accordance with the intrinsic value of their respective jobs. Therefore, this modified

[26] Sven Opitz, *Gouvernementabilität im Postfordismus. Macht, Wissen und Techniken des Selbst im Feld unternehmerischer Rationalität* (Hamburg: Argument, 2004), Ch.8; Günter Voß & Hans J. Pongratz, "Der Arbeitskraftunternehmer. Eine neue Grundform der Ware Arbeitskraft?" in *Kölner Zeitschrift für Soziologie und Sozialpsychologie* 50/I (1989), 131–158.

nomenclature also seems to be accompanied by a new accentuation of the old achievement principle, since wage-laborers are required to perform all the autonomous, creative, and flexible activities previously reserved for the classical type of entrepreneur. This new form of recognition asserts that every qualified member of the labor force is capable of planning his or her career path as a risk-filled enterprise requiring the autonomous application of all of his or her skills and abilities.

In this altered manner of addressing employees, it certainly seems reasonable for us to discern the outlines of just that form of recognition I described previously as an "ideology" with regulative power. The suspicion that arises in connection with this example is that the shift in accentuation of recognition primarily has the function of evoking a new self-conception encouraging one to accept willingly a considerably modified work-load. The increased demands for flexibility and the deregulation of labor that have accompanied capitalism's neo-liberal structural transformation require the ability to productively market oneself, an ability engendered productively by referring to workers as entrepreneurs of their own labor-power [*Arbeitskraftunternehmer*].[27] Yet there lies a gap between this initial suspicion and a justified claim, whose overcoming requires a set of criteria that can be developed only with difficulty. If this new way of addressing employees really is to be a case of recognition, we can say that it fulfills the conditions I described earlier as being characteristics of an ideological form of recognition: subjects will have good evaluative reasons to relate the altered distinction to themselves in such a way as to attain a higher degree of self-esteem or self-respect. Therefore, we cannot follow the standard path taken by every critique of ideology, which consists in demonstrating the irrationality of a system of beliefs held to be ideological, for in an evaluative sense at least, the new form of recognition must be sufficiently rational as to be "credible" enough in the eyes of employees for the latter to apply it to themselves. Thus it seems advisable to me to spell out in even greater detail the conditions that must be met if social recognition is to be conferred, so that we might be able to reveal the characteristic deficiencies of ideological forms of recognition. To this end, I must pick up the trail of my argumentation where I last left

---

[27] Sven Opitz, *Gouvernementabilität im Postfordismus*, Ch.8.

it in discussing recognition as a suitably rational, moral response to the valuable qualities of human beings.

At the very beginning of this chapter, I pointed out that recognition may not consist in mere words or symbolic expressions, but must be accompanied by actions that confirm these promises. An act of recognition is incomplete, so to speak, as long as it does not lead to modes of behavior that give real expression to the actual value articulated in the original act. However, recognition can reasonably be said to be "fulfilled" only provided we are dealing with a case of simple interaction in which two people encounter one another. As soon as we switch planes and turn to instances of generalized recognition carried out by social institutions, we may no longer suppose recognition to be consummated in the corresponding modes of conduct or forms of institutional activity. Although institutionally generalized forms of recognition also find expression in transformed habits in the long run, the primary source of their fulfillment lies in the realm of institutional policies and practices. Legal definitions would have to change, other forms of political representation would have to be established, and material redistribution carried out for new modes of generalized recognition to be established.

Hence, alongside the evaluative dimension of the credibility of social recognition, we must also consider the material element, which, according to the degree of complexity of a given social interaction, consists in either appropriate individual conduct or suitable institutional procedures. An altered form of social recognition will only be "credible" if in addition to being rational from an evaluative point of view it also does justice to a new value quality in material terms. Something in the physical world – be it modes of conduct or institutional circumstances – must change if the addressee or addressees are to be convinced that they have been recognized in a new manner.[28]

It is this second, material dimension that provides a key to the difficult task of distinguishing between justified and ideological forms of recognition. As we have seen, the latter are able to develop their

---

[28] This is what John L. Austin (*How to do Things with Words* [Cambridge: Harvard University Press, 1975]) means when he says that specific performative statements count as being successful or completed if something or other happens as a result. With my notion of "material fulfillment," I am applying his analysis of performative statements to the specific case of "recognition."

regulative power only if their evaluative vocabulary is sufficiently rational to reveal credible modes of fashioning a new and affirmative self-conception. Generally speaking, such ideological forms will attain greater success the more fully they account for the evaluative expectations that point the way toward progress in the culture of reciprocal recognition. But the deficiency by which we might recognize such ideologies could consist in the structural inability to ensure the material prerequisites for realizing new evaluative qualities. Thus, between the evaluative promise and its material fulfillment, an abyss opens up that is characteristic in the sense that the provision of the institutional prerequisites would no longer be reconcilable with the dominant social order. If we apply this criterion to the example I illustrated earlier, then my belief will prove to be true. The new manner of addressing employees and qualified workers as entrepreneurs of their own labor-power might contain an evaluative promise of recognizing a higher degree of individuality and initiative, but it in no way ensures the institutional measures that would allow a consistent realization of these new values. Instead, employees are compelled to feign initiative, flexibility, and talents in places where there are no roots for such values. This new form of recognition is not deficient or irrational in an evaluative sense, but it does not meet the material demands of credible, justified recognition, because the institutional practices required for truly realizing the newly accentuated value are not delivered in the act of recognition. But if only those components of material fulfillment that together constitute the rationality of recognition are added, then we can claim that ideological forms of recognition suffer a second-level rationality deficit. Even if they are rational in the sense that they have drawn their terms from the historically changing realm of evaluative reasons, they remain irrational in the sense that they do not go beyond the merely symbolic plane to the level of material fulfillment. A second instance of a novel form of recognition that could prove to be ideological from this point of view is the now fashionable notion of "public service" [*Bürgerarbeit*], whereby a social group is granted a symbolic distinction that could encourage willing subjection without introducing corresponding measures at the institutional level.

Of course, even the criterion formulated here ought not to lead us astray into a hermeneutics of suspicion that is all too certain of itself, for we can never exclude the possibility that the gap between an evaluative promise and its material fulfillment is merely a temporal one causing a delay in the realization of the institutional prerequisites. Just as is the case in simple interaction, on the level of institutional recognition we must often expect lengthy learning processes before the evaluative substance of a new form of recognition can find expression in changed modes of conduct or institutional arrangements. Yet, all in all, the criterion of material fulfillment does provide us with a useful means of testing in advance whether an alteration in a given form of recognition might in fact bring about an increase in regulative power. Those institutional patterns of evaluative distinction lacking any prospect of yielding material change can then in good conscience be called ideological forms of recognition.

14

Rejoinder

Axel Honneth

In recent years, the debate over the philosophical relevance and social-theoretical scope of the concept of recognition has been confronted with two problems, both of which constitute central elements of post-Marxist consciousness. First, there is the question of whether and to what extent the recognitional approach can make more than a merely accidental contribution to our understanding of the conflictual character of societies; second, there is a continuing suspicion that the granting of recognition can always also – or nearly exclusively – turn out to be a means for maintaining social domination. According to some interpretations, these questions are connected, as it is only by noting the character of power inherent in all forms of social recognition that we can account appropriately for the permanent conflictuality of the social.[1]

In their Introduction to this volume, Bert van den Brink and David Owen have reconstructed my own approach with the greatest care and circumspection, up to the point at which these questions arise virtually automatically. They pose the question as to how a theory that conceives of the struggle for recognition essentially as a guarantee of moral progress can respond to the objection that relations of recognition often merely serve to conceal relations of power?[2] With this

---

[1] See Robin Celikates, *Nicht versöhnt. Der Kampf im Kampf um Anerkennung* (unpublished Ms. 2005).
[2] Bert van den Brink & David Owen, "Introduction" (this volume), 31.

provocatively posed question, they open up a collection of essays revolving around the connection between power and recognition, though from very different points of view. Not only are the theoretical perspectives taken up in the individual essays so heterogeneous that a unified focus can hardly be discerned, so are the object domains in which they pursue this central topic. The spectrum ranges from rather conceptual attempts at clarification to social-theoretical proposals that draw upon various authors (Adorno, Hegel, G. H. Mead) or certain forms of recognition (love) as points of reference in order to discuss what they take to be the limitedness or one-sidedness of my approach. Moreover, what is termed here as "power" is defined in the various chapters in thoroughly different ways.

In light of this heterogeneity, I couldn't even think of reciprocating the various authors' efforts by responding in the same depth and length. I will deal with conceptual issues only on the margins, not least because I have already dealt with these questions in greater detail elsewhere.[3] Although many of the objections advanced here essentially have to do with uncertainties as to how we are to understand "recognition" categorially, these problems of conceptual definition should not be detached from the question upon which I take this volume to be centered. In my view, the thematic kernel consists in a problem that is not easy to formulate generally, because the way it is posed varies depending on which object domain and perspective we choose. How, we might ask, is the normative aim of recognition to be preserved if at the same time we must acknowledge that all forms of social recognition, even the institutionalization of entire spheres of recognition, are streaked with inscrutable effects of power? The term "effects of power" is meant to indicate, in accordance with conventional usage going back to Max Weber,[4] all those effects that steer the behavior of certain persons or groups of persons in a direction that serves to maintain the existing social order. This means that relations of recognition possess characteristics of power if they cause a prevalent inequality or

---

[3] Axel Honneth, "Antworten auf die Beiträge der Kolloquiumsteilnehmer," in Christoph Halbig & Michael Quante (eds.), *Axel Honneth: Sozialphilosophie zwischen Kritik und Anerkennung* (Münster: Lit, 2004), 99–121; Axel Honneth, "Nachwort: Der Grund der Anerkennung. Eine Erwiderung auf kritische Rückfragen," in *Kampf um Anerkennung*, Sonderausgabe (Frankfurt am Main: Suhrkamp, 2003), 303–341.

[4] Max Weber, *Wirtschaft und Gesellschaft* (Tübingen, 1972), 542.

disadvantage to be preserved in a particularly successful way – namely, by means of social affirmation. We must ask, therefore, whether we can continue to speak of a "moral grammar" or ascribe an emancipatory meaning to the struggle for recognition once we have realized that recognition as such implies neither freedom from domination nor the absence of power. This is the problem I believe to be the objective core of the essays in this collection.

I will not respond to the many objections and questions advanced in this volume according to any systematic hierarchy or order of relevance. Instead, for the sake of simplicity, I will follow the thematic division used by the editors. First of all, I will briefly go into the more philosophically focused contributions (Section I); then I will respond to the social-theoretical objections (Section II); finally, I will deal with the questions posed within the framework of political philosophy (Section III).

I

With the exception of the chapter by Heikki Ikäheimo and Arto Laitinen, in which the authors propose a conceptual clarification of recognition, the other three chapters in Part I all pursue the same strategy. By giving a new interpretation of one of the philosophers whose ideas I have drawn upon in developing my own approach, they seek to demonstrate that as a result of my selective interpretation of these authors' works, I have either made certain errors or given one-sided interpretations in my development of the notion of recognition. The chapter contributed by my two Finnish colleagues, whose analytical talent for lucid conceptual definition has already caused me to undertake certain revisions in the past,[5] is bursting with astute proposals for further clarification. The point I find to be the most interesting is the idea of identifying forms of disrespect from an "objective point of view," such that distinctions between justified and unjustified claims to recognition can be made in a neutral way. I agree with their proposal that we seek this kind of criterion of validity in the evaluative qualities that people have by virtue of their being members in a lifeworld that

---

[5] See the essays from both authors in "Symposium on Axel Honneth and Recognition," in *Inquiry* 45/4, (2002), 447–462, 463–478.

always already has a certain normative content. What specific claims to recognition can be raised legitimately by the members of a lifeworld is dependent upon the values with which persons in this lifeworld are "objectively" endowed (see Ikäheimo/Laitinen, Chapter 2). Yet how we are to explicate and, above all, defend such a "moderate value realism" is a question that Ikäheimo and Laitinen pose but leave unanswered. Since I will have to return to this problem at a later point, here I will leave it at this short, affirmative commentary.

The other three authors in this part make it more difficult for me than Ikäheimo and Laitinen. If I have understood Robert Pippin correctly, he accuses me of misunderstanding Hegel's argument concerning the social dependence of the individual – her "recognitional dependence" – by interpreting it as an empirical claim about human need. Furthermore, he appears to be convinced that such a false interpretation also has implications for political philosophy, though he doesn't pursue this point in greater detail. As far as his central point is concerned – the appropriate understanding of Hegel's claim about the individual's recognitional dependence – I would formulate the relevant alternatives in the following manner: Does Hegel's theory of recognition intend primarily the conceptual thesis that a subject is capable of autonomous action only if her normative status has already been recognized by the community, in the sense that her intentions and beliefs can be categorized as "social"? Or does his theory aim to develop the significantly more complex, no longer merely conceptual but also empirical (or metaphysical) thesis that subjects need to have every element of their personalities recognized in order to develop their personal autonomy, elements whose activation constitutes a necessary precondition for the articulation of their own chosen ends? These two alternatives not only concern the purpose of the kind of recognition that is seen to be necessary in all respective cases, but also its type and scope.

According to the first interpretation, the one advocated by Pippin, the individual's "normative status" is secured by a single, elementary form of recognition that can best be described with terms such as "respect" or "Achtung." On the second interpretation, which I advocate, the individual's autonomy can be guaranteed only through a multiplicity of forms of recognition, whose particularities vary according to the respective layer of personality to be affirmed. Indeed, the strengths of the first interpretation consist in a certain degree of economic thriftiness, its central thesis's analytical character and proximity to Kant; however, I don't really see how Hegel's multi-level considerations on the problematic of recognition can be reduced to this interpretation. Already in his early writings, Hegel introduced love as an exemplary case of mutual recognition; he then worked on a multi-level model of relations of recognition; and, finally, in the "Philosophy of Right," he explains every ethical institution with reference to a particular form of recognition. This all suggests that he had a comprehensive, perhaps metaphysical theory of recognition in mind. Although moral-psychological considerations don't appear in his theory, speculations on the connection between subjectivity and objective mind certainly do play a fundamental role. It is undoubtedly true that such a differentiated, multi-leveled theory of recognitional dependence has consequences for political philosophy, because we would have to regard the task of the state as consisting not only in the mere protection of individual autonomy, but also in the granting and cultivation of inter-subjective relations of recognition.[6] But didn't Hegel also aim to do more in his Philosophy of Right than to give a refined version of the liberal idea of the constitutional state?

While Pippin's contribution still finds itself in the run-up to the central topic of this collection, the chapters by Bert van den Brink and Patchen Markell lead us right into its center. A satisfactory treatment of their objections would demand more space than is available to me here, since this would require a discussion of their respective interpretations of Adorno and Mead. Thus I will not go into whether I agree with their respective interpretations and instead will deal solely with their critical content. Van den Brink gives Adorno's implicit ethics a slight recognition-theoretical twist in order to derive the necessity of distrusting institutionalized or practiced forms of mutual recognition, as the latter might be dominated by internalized false conceptions about the other. In light of the social tendency towards reification,

---

[6] See Axel Honneth, "Gerechtigkeit und kommunikative Freiheit. Überlegungen im Anschluss an Hegel," in Barbara Merker, Georg Mohr & Michael Quante (eds.), *Subjektivität und Anerkennung* (Paderborn, 2004), 213–227; Joel Anderson & Axel Honneth, "Autonomy, Vulnerability, Recognition and Justice," in John Christman & Joel Anderson (eds.), *Autonomy and the Challenges to Liberalism. New Essays* (New York: Cambridge University Press, 2005), 77–100.

we need to recollect the "rudimentary" form of recognition in which the "difference" of the other's humanity first comes to light. I suspect that the way we approach this difficulty will depend on how we respond to the sociological – or better, social-theoretical – question of whether potentials of mutual recognition really are hindered or suppressed by subjects' self-perception in the light of reified conceptions as mere "things" or "means" for the realization of their own ends. After all, the ethical appeal that we go back behind all existing practices of recognition in order to once again be able to truly perceive the personality of the other only makes sense on the empirical assumption of a comprehensive reification of all social interactions. Because I disagree with this assumption and urge a more careful use of the concept of reification,[7] I don't concur with the moral weight of the demand that we recollect this elementary form of recognition. In my view, the recognition of the personhood of human beings is a social-ontological fact that subjects are capable of violating only in extreme cases of irrational denial or subsequent "forgetting."[8] These forms of "reification" constitute highly unusual states of affairs in which the social bonds that normally hold the human lifeworld together have been broken. Adorno's implicit ethics does not make it entirely clear, however, whether we are to recollect this elementary form of recognition – that is, the primary attitude in which the personality of human beings is given to us, or whether we are to apply a higher-level form of recognition, as he probably intended in talking of "difference." If Adorno had the second alternative in mind, he would not, of course, seek to appeal to something rudimentary, but to the moral product of a sociocultural development, for it was as a response to the principle of equality that the idea of recognizing each and every human person as having a unique individuality first emerged.[9] If indeed Adorno were to appeal to this form of recognition, he would have to demand more moral potentiality of the modern lifeworld than he normally does. He would have to become aware of the fact that he is appealing

---

7 See Axel Honneth, *Verdinglichung. Eine anerkennungstheoretische Studie* (Frankfurt am Main: Suhrkampf Verlag, 2005).

8 Ibid., Ch. IV and VI.

9 See Charles Taylor, *Multiculturalism. Examining the Politics of Recognition* (Princeton: Princeton University Press, 1994).

to normative ideas that have developed over the course of history and continue to prevail over social life.

I don't want to examine how these theoretical implications relate to the remainder of Adorno's philosophy and social theory – for example, to his interpretation of Hegel or his analysis of capitalism. Instead, what I want to make clear is that by making an ethical appeal to the recognition of the "difference" of the other, Adorno would have to ascribe a normative infrastructure to modern society based on diverse forms of the claim to recognition. He could not, therefore, speak of a general "blindness" or a decay of all sociality, but would instead have to concede that certain moral ideas continue to make a claim to validity and thus represent normative instances of critical objection. Under these theoretical circumstances, the question as to how social relations of recognition are constituted in reality also appears in a new light. This question concerns the degree to which prejudices, ideologies, or interests violate claims to mutual recognition in social practices, claims whose normative validity is indisputable. Any claims we make on this empirical level are thus relative to a presupposed conception of factically valid demands for recognition. Only that which violates legitimate claims stemming from currently valid ideals of mutual recognition can be counted as "false," influenced by "power" or obscured by egocentric "interests."

My sole aim in making these methodological considerations is to call to mind that in making an ethical demand for the recognition of difference, Adorno would have to concede more Hegelian premises than he appears willing to do.

Patchen Markell's chapter, which is a fascinating example of how text analysis can be carried out with an interest in systematic questions, deals with what appears to be a wholly different problem. He claims that by turning to a moderate value realism, I drive a wedge between potentiality and actuality in a way that leads to a "condescending" view of the dominated and excluded. By maintaining that the legitimacy of claims to recognition are ultimately measured in accordance with the evaluative qualities potentially contained in a concrete lifeworld, I rob disrespected persons of the chance to gain access themselves to the forms of social recognition they deserve. His objection that I underestimate the danger posed by the effects of dominating interests on the struggle for recognition is raised here from the other side – that is,

Markell doesn't accuse me of ignoring the effects of established forms of recognition that serve to sustain domination, but of placing the excluded in a state of epistemic incapacity by asserting that the domain of potential claims to recognition is accessible only in a theoretical sense. Markell develops this extremely clever and challenging claim in two steps: first, he formulates the objection itself in order to sketch, second, an alternative way of defining the relation between "potentiality" and "actuality" through a new interpretation of the relation between "I" and "Me" in the works of Mead. I will focus only on the first point, since a discussion of his alternative interpretation of Mead would require far too much space.

Indeed, the notion that claims to recognition can be justified only to the degree that they relate convincingly to evaluative qualities previously established and thus "potentially" existent in the lifeworld is bound up with a problem requiring more detailed treatment. As Markell presumes correctly, this "value realist" premise operates on the assumption that we should understand the granting of recognition as an actualization of the evaluative qualities that humans in a particular lifeworld always possess "potentially" in accordance with the horizon of values upon which this world is founded. If this kind of "actualization" is taken to mean a cognitive disclosure, a factical realization, we would be faced with the unfortunate consequence that those affected would not be informed of the normative source of their claims until they have already been recognized. Markell states, "It would seem that to have a justifiable claim to recognition is also to be unable to demonstrate it, at least without the assistance of those who have already actualized their own powers, and so can testify to your equal personhood with unequaled confidence and maturity" (Markell, p. 7).

This objection is only valid, however, if we take "actualization" to mean a type of cognitive realization. This would imply the following: because it isn't until the act of recognition – the "actualization" – that those affected are informed of the evaluative qualities they "potentially" possess in the lifeworld, the justification of their claims are totally epistemically dependent on the subjects or groups of persons that have already been recognized in a corresponding way. This, however, is not the meaning of "actualization" that I had in mind when I took over the concept from Arto Laitinen; rather, I intended this notion to indicate the act by which subjects become capable of identifying wholly with the evaluative qualities of which they are already culturally aware. I believe that if we regard the relation of actualization to potentiality in this way, the problem raised by Markell becomes a moot point, for even though the previously disrespected subjects would then possess (prereflexive) knowledge of the evaluative qualities they possess in accordance with their cultural lifeworld, they would continue to be incapable of identifying with these qualities, because the latter would still lack social recognition. In this case, the distinction between "potentiality" and "actuality" indicates neither an epistemic gap nor a space to be bridged over, but a rift between ethical knowledge and social expression. Through practices of recognition, what all participants are more or less aware of gains social or public expression – namely, the circumstance that even previously excluded persons or groups of persons possess the evaluative qualities previously ascribed only to a smaller circle of persons. In this sense, the struggle for recognition represents a struggle for the social articulation of preexistent knowledge; the positive result of this struggle – "actualization" – consists in the establishment of practices of recognition through which the persons concerned can in fact identify with their evaluative qualities.

Of course, this answer gives rise to new problems having to do with the fact that it isn't yet wholly clear how we are to distinguish between "knowledge" and social practices, for normally we are inclined to link the acquisition of knowledge to the performance of certain practices. The difference that I am concerned with, however, lies on a somewhat different level. For society, this would mean the difference we have in mind when we say that although an individual subject has understood something in an "intellectual" sense, she hasn't yet accepted it "affectively," and thus hasn't yet recognized it. Social practices of recognition express the fact that a transition between these two stages has taken place within society. Thus it is to Markell's astute objections that I owe the need to get clearer about the connections suggested here than I have done previously.

II

While the chapters in Part I have a more fundamental conceptual orientation or are concerned with individual authors in the recognition-theoretical tradition, the objections advanced in Part II all deal explicitly with social-theoretical questions. To put it in my own words, what is open to debate here is how we are to apply the principles of recognition to specific social spheres, without giving rise to false or misleading conceptions about the aims of emancipatory politics. Because such problematic ends can potentially and unintentionally legitimate the injustice of dominant practices or institutions, the discussion in this context once again focuses on the theoretical relation of recognition to power. It is fortunate that the objections contained in these three chapters all focus on the same social domain – the family – because this will allow me to avoid overloading my answer with all too many differentiations. The commonality of their topics, however, mustn't be lead us to ignore the differences in the thrusts of the authors' various objections. While Iris Marion Young and Lior Barshak focus on the question of whether my conception of recognition can appropriately disclose the normative tasks required of a current politics of the family, Beate Rössler's essay takes up the much more fundamental question as to the extent to which recognition can serve as an independent basis for a political ethics or theory of justice at all. Thus it makes sense to start the discussion of Part II with Rössler's objections – not only because of the sequence of the texts, but also for systematic reasons.

Beate Rössler asks whether it is really justifiable to remunerate "family work" – work that is mostly carried out by women – according to achievement, and then uses this question as a prelude to a much more far-reaching problematic. She is concerned about the fact that the normative value of certain types of labor can no longer be judged as a whole if, by concentrating on social recognition, we perceive only the aspect of achievement in them, a perspective that can only take account of the market value of labor, not its alienated or demeaning character. We could summarize Rössler's objection in the following way: by privileging the criterion of achievement, the theory of recognition gives up the opportunity to assess socially established labor conditions according to a comprehensive standard of economic justice, which must also include claims to self-realization and equal liberty. The thrust of Rössler's critique appears to me highly relevant, because it seeks to reactualize and reformulate a topic of classic social critique that is often neglected nowadays. For this reason, I would like to respond in a bit more detail by, first, briefly discussing the principle of achievement (a), and second, by turning to the more comprehensive problem of the normative judgment of social labor (b).

a. I agree in principle with all of Rössler's objections to the complete assimilation of family labor to gainful employment. Not only do we run the risk of cementing the dominant, gender-specific division of labor by financially remunerating a kind of labor that represents a particular type of medium between toil and care, but we also risk promoting the tendency of a pathological deformation of love within the family by subjecting it to a normativity that is foreign to this particular principle of recognition.[10] Rössler appears to assume, however, that I can conceive of the social esteem accorded to the necessary reproductive services of the family only in monetary terms. This assumption is false, for as I have often emphasized, to esteem social contributions by means of financial remuneration is to assert a special case that has many historical equivalents reaching into the present day, from symbolic revaluations (Order of the Federal Republic of Germany [*Bundesverdienstkreuz*] or the Order of the British Empire [OBE]) to social privileges for American war veterans. All these ways of according social esteem represent media through which achievements or contributions to the community are awarded public recognition; financial remuneration constitutes just one type that is common today. In this connection, I can also address the question of whether, as Rössler claims, these forms of financial remuneration really only express the "market value" of a specific kind of labor, and thus hardly convey social esteem. If we take note of the investigations she cites in her chapter, according to which income for certain jobs regularly decreases in the same measure that they come to be filled by women, then this seems to suggest that financial remuneration is calculated according to criteria that are of cultural nature, and thus independent of the market. I would conclude from all this that for the future, family work will require a series of indirect means of social revaluation in order to liberate it from

---

[10] See Axel Honneth, "Between Justice and Affection: The Family as a Field of Moral Dispute," in Beate Rössler (ed.), *Privacies. Philosophical Evaluations* (Stanford: Stanford University Press, 2004), 142–162.

both the curse of a gender-specific division of labor and the stigma of total social disregard. This would require measures for improving public child-care programs, as well as steps towards economic improvement, be it through tax relief or financial assistance based on the number of children. We can only envisage all these measures, of course, if we (in opposition to Pippin and Hegel) assume the existence of a democratic, constitutional state that advocates an active policy of social recognition.

  b. In presenting these defensive considerations, which don't aim to revaluate family work by means of achievement-based remuneration, but by indirect means of economic improvement, I have not, however, touched on the core of Rössler's objections. Her central question concerns whether normative criteria can be formulated within the framework of recognition theory, which would allow us to judge the value of labor itself. She believes that if we don't expand our perspective in this way, we will lose sight of the fact that the ethical relevance of labor is not exhausted by the fact that it constitutes a social contribution, but that the manner in which labor is organized and the degree to which it provides meaning also play a role. In raising this question, she touches on a classic motif of social critique going back to Marx, a tradition that always took it as a given that socially established forms of labor were not only to be judged according to whether their execution is recognized appropriately, but also according to whether their structure and organization provide chances for self-realization. This ethic has been discredited because it appears to presuppose a perfectionism that dictates the pursuits in which people are to find their self-realization. Instead of leaving subjects free to decide how they wish to pursue their happiness under conditions of autonomy, this perfectionism imposes from above the stipulation that it is only if all members carry out meaningful, non-alienated labor that a society is free and just.[11]

Of course, this accusation of perfectionism doesn't justify the fact that meaningful labor is distributed most unequally in our society. Even

---

[11] See the summary of this discussion in Will Kymlicka, *Contemporary Political Philosophy. An Introduction* (Oxford: Oxford University Press, 1990), Ch. 5.

for a liberal theory of justice, the fact that very few people have the chance to sustain a livelihood through work that is satisfying and sufficiently complex remains a moral scandal. Originally, I tended toward a strong perfectionism[12] in responding to this challenge, switching later to a weaker solution amounting to a recognition-theoretical reformulation of the idea of a fair or just division of labor. The central thrust of this theory is not, as Rössler suspects, founded on a normative concept of achievement and merit, but on a conception of legal recognition. If, as I have done in drawing on the ideas of Thomas Marshall,[13] we understand the latter as a dynamic, expansive relation whose normative scope grows along with insights into the necessary preconditions of individual autonomy and involvement, then we will come across the legal norm of equal opportunity by way of a corresponding (justifying) reconstruction. This norm states that a system of mutually accepted rights implies the demand that all have an equal opportunity to acquire necessary qualifying abilities and skills.[14] By framing the principle of legal recognition in this way, we introduce a norm into the social division of labor that exercises constant pressure on the organization of the educational and occupational systems, for this principle demands that schools, other educational centers, and the differentiated occupational system be organized in such a way as to allow every individual not only to develop the abilities he or she deems appropriate, but also to pursue careers that fit with their abilities. I believe that such an extensive interpretation of equality of opportunity is sufficient to take realistic account of the old Marxist intuition today. Although this principle does not directly imply the normative demand that all types of labor be transformed into meaningful, non-alienated activities, it does have an advantage that mustn't be underestimated – namely, that equality of opportunity is to be an institutionalized norm, one that is socially valid and thus effective. In the end, the debate between Rössler and myself comes down to the question of whether a social critique is to have its foundational norms in free-standing ethical considerations, or

---

[12] See Axel Honneth, "Arbeit und instrumentales Handeln," in Axel Honneth & Urs Jaeggi (eds.), *Arbeit, Handlung, Normativität* (Frankfurt am Main: Suhrkamp, 1980), 185–233.

[13] See Axel Honneth, *Struggle for Recognition* (Cambridge: Polity Press, 1995), 107–121.

[14] See Talcott Parsons, "An Analytical Approach to the Theory of Social Stratification," in Parsons, *Sociological Theory* (New York: Free Press, 1954), 69–88.

in reconstructively disclosed principles that have already found institutional anchoring.

A discussion of Lior Barshak's interesting and challenging chapter would demand more space for preliminary theoretical clarifications than is possible in a short response. In the first place, I would have to go into the Kleinian premises in more detail upon which he bases his psychoanalytical assertion of the constitutive role of a "third party" in love relations. His accusation that although I emphasize the horizontal character of recognition, I totally neglect its vertical relation to a superimposed authority, is an accusation that has already been raised against me from the Hegelian corner.[15] Up to a certain harmless point, I can in fact accept this theory, because mutual recognition indeed presupposes a common affirmation of those values or norms in whose light the other is regarded as worthy of recognition – though "vertical" recognition here indicates not so much an affirmation of human qualities or abilities, rather a passive acceptance of facts.[16] It's a big step, however, from the concession that a relationship to a third party constitutes an essential element in all relations of mutual recognition to the assertion that this third party is represented by the "law," a step that Lior Barshak can only take with the aid of Melanie Klein. It would take more than a few pages to clarify whether the latter's highly speculative and extremely controversial theory indeed contains the small kernel of truth that would justify deriving the necessity of a law-giving authority as represented by the father from the need for a generalized third party of ideas and values.

In my discussion of Beate Rössler's objections, I have already gone into some of the questions that Iris Marion Young raises in her chapter, so rich in ideas. Interestingly enough, both authors maintain that to remunerate family work or "love's labor" (Young) according to achievement is to run the risk of depriving these activities of their quality as totally incalculable forms of labor performed out of love and devotion. Because these concerns accommodate my own insistence on a

[15] Walter Mesch, "Sittlichkeit und Anerkennung in Hegels *Rechtsphilosophie*. Kritische Überlegungen zu Theunissen und Honneth," in *Deutsche Zeitschrift für Philosophie* 53 (2005), 349–364.

[16] Andreas Wildt's proposal that we distinguish between "propositional" and "personal" recognition also aims in this direction: "'Anerkennung' in der Psychoanalyse," in *Deutsche Zeitschrift für Philosophie* 53 (2005), 461–478.

necessary differentiation between spheres, I have already mentioned that other, more indirect forms of public esteem appear more sensible than a mere expansion of the achievement principle. At the heart of Young's chapter, however, are doubts as to whether the conception of reciprocal care can serve as a framework for mutual recognition in relationships of love and marriage. If I have understood her correctly, she is suspicious of an all too careless assumption of the possibility of reciprocity in such relationships, behind which she suspects the old ideology of complementarity between the sexes going back to Rousseau and Hegel. Young's mistrust, which is essentially another version of the suspicion of power, is linked closely to the idea that the true structure of care represents an asymmetrical relationship in which one person cares for another being in need of aid (a child or ill person). In her view, however, as soon as we derive from this one-sided relationship the chance of a two-sided, reciprocal relation in which both partners care for each other's welfare, we run the risk of drawing an ideological veil over the relationship by failing to recognize the unequal distribution of burdens and efforts.

Perhaps because of differences in theoretical fields, perhaps because of differences concerning what we are attentive to empirically, my view on the issue differs completely from that of Young's. In my view, the original modus of care represents a reciprocal, symmetrical relation such as is familiar to us in the context of friendship or intimate relationships, while one-sided care and devotion represent a special case of asymmetrical care. I believe that because two-sided, reciprocal care has the idea of symmetry as its internal criterion of validity, this form of care has an inherent possibility of normative improvement, for the more that both partners are able to perceive each other's needs and desires precisely, sensitively, and in an unbiased manner, the more they will be capable of taking care of the other's welfare for the other's own sake. To be sure, love relations in the past have diverged strongly from this ideal because the reciprocal interpretation of needs and desires was oriented toward a fixed, naturalistic schema of the complementarity of male and female roles. Nevertheless, this doesn't change the fact that we can detect such distorted perceptions or self-conceptions as being violations of claims made in love (or in friendship) only if we presuppose the ideal of symmetry I have described as the original modus of care. I don't see, therefore, how Young can justify her own critique of the classical, ideological model of gender complementarity if she suspects the idea of reciprocal care itself of being an ideology.

III

Unlike the chapters in this collection under the heading of "Social Theory," the contributions in the category of "Political Theory" have neither a common theme nor a unified thrust. The intentions of the four authors overlap at very few, rather peripheral points, which compels me to go the not so elegant route of dealing with their positions consecutively. There is only minimal difference between Rainer Forst's position on toleration and my own, though there is all the more that divides us concerning the framework of justification for this issue. While Forst, as he demonstrates impressively in his chapter, grounds the concept of recognition in a Kantian conception of morality, I pursue a strategy of justification that takes its orientation primarily from Hegel, and thus has a stronger reconstructive character. Nevertheless, with regard to the normative placement of the principle of toleration, I am in agreement with Forst. To put it in my own words, the demand for toleration can no longer be justified as a demand for social esteem, nor as a mere act of permission by the state; instead it must be justified as a moral implication of the principle of mutual respect. I don't take this form of moral respect, however, to be a serendipitous element of human nature, as Forst appears to do, but as a relatively late result of a sustained struggle for recognition that has led to a gradual differentiation of the dimensions in which individuals are affirmed.[17]

This touches on the question that Forst poses at the very end of his chapter, to which he responds in such a manner as to open up the way for a critique of my own conception. He asks how and with what conceptual means we can explain the political struggle that led, by way of a critique of demeaning forms of toleration, to the (partial) establishment of "the concept of respect." If I understand Forst correctly, he intends to say that this struggle is not to be understood as having resulted from a striving for recognition, but as an act of defense against (unjustified) power, because the struggling agents had already perceived themselves as subjects of equal moral value. So how could

[17] See Axel Honneth, *Struggle for Recognition*.

this type of struggle have been motivated by a desire for recognition as equals among equals, if those concerned had already been certain of their moral equality before taking up their struggle? Here as well, a satisfactory answer would demand too much space, since this would require a detailed discussion of the historically relevant material, or at least an empirical investigation.[18] Nonetheless, the first part of my response can be culled from my rejoinder to Patchen Markell. The idea of a struggle for recognition doesn't necessarily imply that subjects struggle merely on the basis of a diffuse feeling of being disrespected totally, thus only gaining a clear conception of their actual goal in the course of their social struggle. Rather, what generally motivates these struggles is the still unclear and merely negatively formulated realization that one possesses the same qualities or abilities as those who have already been recognized (institutionally), but without enjoying corresponding public recognition. The starting point of social struggles is characterized by a greater moral diffuseness and perplexity than Rainer Forst would like to believe; otherwise, the often painful experience of these struggles could not represent the source of moral learning processes through which those involved often first acquire the differentiated vocabulary with which they are able to justify their demands publicly. It is along this path, in this recursive relation between experiences of disrespect, political struggle, and moral self-enlightenment, that the idea of equal autonomy for all persons must have originated historically. In any case, I find it highly implausible to conceive of this idea as a serendipitous endowment that all past social actors possessed from the moment of birth. People aren't born into the world as little Kantians, but as competent infants who possess all the capabilities they need to grow into – and perhaps even out of – the moral world constituted by their surroundings. Their parents, for their part, behave like Aristotelians, and assume their children to have all the potentials that they will need, along with the proper care and upbringing, to mature into morally competent adults.

Veit Bader's chapter makes the fact that I don't have enough space to come even close to responding appropriately to all his challenging and highly differentiated considerations even more frustrating than

---

[18] Here I can only refer to Barrington Moore, *Injustice: The Social Basis of Obedience and Revolt* (Armonk, NY: M. E. Sharpe, 1978).

do the other chapters in this collection. He not only links his critique of my monist approach to an already developed pluralistic counter-proposal, but he also develops even more far-reaching thoughts on the social chances and limits for articulating critique. From the many stimulating points in his contribution, I would like to pick out only two that seem to me to be the most in need of clarification. To be sure, a monist strategy that attempts to trace all experiences of social injustice back to a kernel of disrespect runs a risk of which Bader is justified in warning us – namely, that we might neglect the distinctive experience and particular quality of injustice inherent in other forms of disadvantage and discrimination that at first don't appear to fit into the schema of withheld recognition. First of all, I should make clear that there is only one point at which I attempt to link a monist approach with moral pluralism: although all forms of injustice are ultimately analyzed according to the normative pattern of disrespect, at the same time we can distinguish between various dimensions of personality in which persons are justified in feeling disrespected. If we choose to fan out the concept of recognition in this way, we arrive at a threefold division analogous to that on which David Miller bases his own pluralist approach. According to Miller, people can feel disrespected on the basis of the conviction that their needs, rights, or abilities have not found appropriate recognition. I don't see why this threefold schema couldn't also account for the forms of injustice that Veit Bader focuses on in his line of argumentation. In my opinion, it is not until the individual's claim to the product of her labor ("self-ownership") has been institutionalized legally, such that the partial withholding of this product can be condemned justifiably as a violation of her rights, that "exploitation" can be said to represent an injustice, and thus a violation that can be experienced subjectively. As soon as we supplement the monist approach to "disrespect" with a differentiation among needs, rights and capabilities, I no longer see any principal difficulty in analyzing all forms of injustice according to the single schema of a violation of justified claims to recognition.

At this point, however, I must mention a second point on which Bader and I disagree. The degree to which the introduction of forms of disrespect and recognition are to be understood as being dependent upon moral presuppositions that already possess a certain kind of factical validity is greater in my account – this is the Hegelian inheritance of which I have already spoken in my short commentary on Forst's essay. Not only are there certain "meta-ethical" reasons for making the validity of these forms contingent on facticity, but also a moral-psychological consideration that might prove important for the debate between Bader and myself. Subjects experience a given state of affairs as unjust only if it violates claims that they themselves take to be legitimate; these expectations of legitimacy represent moral reasons that rational beings must have in order to be capable of having "moral" experiences at all. This "having," however, should not be conceived of as atemporal knowledge, but as an internalized familiarity, for otherwise this "having" would lack all motivational psychic force. The moral reasons in the light of which subjects experience injustice, therefore, can only be grasped as resulting from their socialization in a social surrounding that already contains the corresponding principles of legitimacy. As a result, theory can only put forth those moral principles that already possess enough factical validity in a social culture as to enable subjects to use them in forming expectations of legitimacy capable of motivating their actions. I'm not certain if this clarification is really relevant for the dispute between Veit Bader and myself, but it seems important that we get clear about the fact that our theoretical classifications of social injustice are not independent of our preexistent presumptions about the factical validity of certain principles of morality or recognition.

Anthony Laden undertakes a rapprochement between the Rawlsian idea of "reasonable deliberation" and my own concept of recognition. His argumentative bridge between these two ideas consists in conceiving of the struggle for recognition as a movement in an overarching political process in which the citizens of a community seek to "co-author" their common identity. Although this proposal immediately "civilizes" my own approach within the context of a constitutional state by subjecting it to the conditions of debate in the democratic public sphere,[19] Laden goes on to develop an idea that appears to me extremely useful and productive. He starts with the claim that I don't distinguish sufficiently within the recognition

---

[19] Jürgen Habermas takes a similar step in "Kampf um Anerkennung im demokratischen Rechtsstaat," in: *Die Einbeziehung des Anderen. Studien zur politischen Theorie* (Frankfurt am Main: Suhrkamp, 1999), 237–276.

framework between "merely basic respect" and "fully equal respect."" While the first form of legal respect merely implies that persons recognize each other mutually as bearers of equal rights, the second form of legal respect implies furthermore that subjects mutually concede each other an equal right to determining the common identity. Now, even in *Struggle for Recognition*, I had included the internal dynamic of the increasing materialization of equality before the law, which proceeds in stages of implementation of liberal, political and social rights. In my debate with Nancy Fraser as well, I went so far as to ascribe a normative surplus to modern law in the principle of legal equality, a surplus that ensures a conflict-laden process of differentiation and materialization of individual rights. Nevertheless, the idea of extending this possibility of an internal progression of law all the way into the "co-authorship" of a common identity seems to me to be genuinely productive and original.

Building on MacKinnon and Foucault, Laden assumes that under conditions of formal legal equality, a (cultural) minority will continue to possess the "constructive, social power" to construct a hierarchy of collective identities by determining the normative relevance of certain categories of features or external characteristics. Laden argues that this asymmetrical distribution of power can be dissolved only if we supplement the principle of legal equality with a dimension of "fully equal respect," such that every member of the community would receive a real chance to cooperate in determining the relevant criteria for the common identity. This kind of cooperative, egalitarian exercise of "constructive power" is possible if institutional conditions of "reasonable deliberation" are established in which members decide what characteristics of the commonly shared identity are desirable in the light of unanimously acceptable "we-reasons." Laden, however, doesn't merely point out the enabling conditions of public deliberations, but adds concrete suggestions as to how institutional arrangements might promote participation in the exercise of constructive power. In this point as well, his chapter seems to me most useful for the purpose of clarifying the internal connection between legal recognition and institutionally enabled participation in public deliberations – far more so than I have done in my own writings.

Finally, David Owen undertakes a penetrating and provocative attempt to convince me of the superiority of a republican model of democracy by thawing and softening up my threefold distinction between self-confidence, self-respect, and self-esteem. Unfortunately I cannot go into all of the very illustrative examples he uses in his attempt to unsettle my quite rigid differentiation between three forms of recognition. Some of the arguments he advances are convincing, and I have meanwhile already made corresponding corrections in my own work.[20] Overall, Owen takes perhaps too little account of the merely analytical character of this threefold division. Yet, his chapter doesn't merely aim at the sum of these smaller objections, but at the consequence he seeks to draw from their synthesis. He claims, firstly, that once we have realized that individual self-confidence (in one's own capabilities as an agent) not only results from the reliability of private love relations but also from the trustworthiness of social relations, and secondly, once we concede that social esteem is not only measured according to the individual's contribution to social reproduction but also according to her "ethical integrity," then the condition of a just, fair division of labor cannot be the only prepolitical prerequisite for democratic cooperation. Instead, this prerequisite must be supplemented with further relations of recognition that don't totally fit into my schema, as they include the extension of love into political trust and the ethicization of social esteem. As a consequence, Owen's line of argumentation amounts to the idea that a democratic culture depends on the self-steering of republican virtues such as willingness to sacrifice and personal integrity, virtues I am forced to ignore because of my attachment to Dewey's ideal of science.

I don't want to deny that David Owen's rhetorical skills almost succeeded in convincing me of the soundness of his republican model. By beginning with slight, immanent corrections to all three forms in my typology of recognition and then combining them into an argument for an Aristotelian notion of politics, he reduces the space within which objections might be formulated. My first doubts arose at the point at which he, by drawing on the ideas of Thomas Hill, Jr., seeks to expand social esteem to cover the ethical excellence of persons. Of course, it is true that in everyday life, we value people higher who act with integrity

---

[20] See the corrections I have made in my threefold division: Axel Honneth, "Antworten auf die Beiträge der Kolloquiumsteilnehmer," in Halbig & Quante, *Axel Honneth: Sozialphilosophie zwischen Kritik und Anerkennung.*

than those who seem to lack sound principles. But do we thereby really assume that the standards we apply here can be generalized beyond our small circle of family and friends? Our ethical esteeming of other persons is based on criteria that are always the expression of group-specific value orientations, whereas I presumed the social validity of my principles of recognition to cover the whole community. To be sure, the achievement principle is always subject to group-specific interpretations, among which those interpretations with the highest degree of "constructive power" (Laden) usually attain primacy. When competing over the appropriate interpretation, however, rival groups always relate to the same institutionalized idea. Owen's conception, on the other hand, ends up in conflict with the social fact of value pluralism, for to esteem certain specific character traits within a society is always to disadvantage those cultural forms of life in which totally different conceptions of personal excellence predominate.

After much reflection, I also have certain doubts about Owen's second proposal. To be sure, a democratic society needs more mutual trust between its members than is found in the narrow, formal bond of mere legal relations. It seems questionable, however, whether we should analyze this increased trust according to the standard of private relationships of friendship or love. In the works of Danielle Allen, upon whose ideas Owen bases his argumentation,[21] it remains unclear as to what type of willingness to sacrifice is expected of the members of society such that it could serve as a foundation for relations of trust. Allen's proposals span from pure legal obligations (such as the acceptance of majority decisions) to the suggestion that we tolerate restrictions on our rights that are so drastic as to require what I would hold to be intolerable sacrifices. In light of these few plausible alternatives, the most promising course seems to be to regard a fair division of labor as the social context of experience in which that measure of mutual trust can develop that constitutes a necessary prerequisite for a cooperative democracy.

As a conclusion to this rejoinder, which has turned out a good deal longer than expected, it remains for me to show my appreciation to the editors both for their willingness and for their efforts in the compiling

---

[21] Danielle S. Allen, *Talking to Strangers. Anxieties of Citizenship since Brown v. Board of Education* (Chicago/London: University of Chicago Press, 2004).

and arranging of this volume. Although the argumentative exchange here has not exactly produced a new theory of the relation between recognition and power, the many objections advanced by the various authors have compelled me to rethink my own position and state it more precisely. This has brought me several steps closer to the goal of developing such a theory. For this I extend my warmest gratitude to Bert van den Brink and David Owen.

Bibliography

Aboulafia, Mitchell. *The Mediating Self: Mead, Sartre, and Self-Determination* (New Haven: Yale University Press, 1986).

———. *The Cosmopolitan Self: George Herbert Mead and Continental Philosophy* (Urbana: University of Illinois Press, 2001).

Adorno, Theodor W. *Minima Moralia: Reflections from Damaged Life*, E. F. N. Jephcott (trans.) (London and New York: Verso, 1974).

———. "Probleme der Moralphilosophie," in *Nachgelassene Schriften*, Vol. 10 (Frankfurt am Main: Suhrkamp, 1996).

Allen, Danielle S. *Talking to Strangers* (Chicago: University of Chicago Press, 2004).

———. "Invisible Citizens: Political Exclusion and Domination," in M. Williams & S. Macedo (eds.), *Nomos* (New York: New York University Press, 2005).

Althusser, Louis. "Ideology and Ideological State Apparatuses," in *Lenin and Philosophy and Other Essays* (New York: Monthly Review Press, 2001).

Anderson, E. *Value in Ethics and Economics* (Cambridge: Harvard University Press, 1993).

Anderson, Joel. "Translator's Introduction," in Axel Honneth, *The Struggle for Recognition* (Cambridge: Polity 1995).

———. & Axel Honneth. "Autonomy, Vulnerability, Recognition and Justice," in John Christman & Joel Anderson (eds.), *Autonomy and the Challenges to Liberalism. New Essays* (New York: 2005) 77–100.

Anzieu, Didier. *The Group and the Unconscious* (London: Routledge, 1985).

Archard, D. "Political Disagreement, Legitimacy, and Civility," in *Philosophical Explorations* IV/3 (2001), 207–223.

Arendt, Hannah. *The Human Condition* (Chicago: Chicago University Press, 1998).

———. "Understanding and Politics," in *Essays in Understanding, 1930–1954*, Jerome Kohn (ed.), (New York: Harcourt, Brace and Co., 1994).

Ariès, Philip. *Centuries of Childhood: A Social History of Family Life*, trans. Robert Baldick (New York: Knopf, 1962).

Austin, John L. *How to Do Things with Words* (Cambridge: Harvard University Press, 1975).

Baars, J. *De mythe van de totale beheersing* (Amsterdam, SUA: 1987).

Bader, Veit, & A. Benschop. *Ungleichheiten* (Opladen: Leske und Budrich, 1989).

————. *Kollektives Handeln* (Opladen: Leske und Budrich, 1991).

————. *Rassismus, Ethnizität und Bürgerschaft* (Münster: Verlag Westfälisches Dampfboot, 1995).

————. "Ethnicity and Class," in Wsevolod W. Isajiw (ed.), *Comparative Perspectives on Interethnic Relations and Social Incorporation* (Toronto: Canadian Scholars' Press, 1997), 103–128.

————. "Culture and Identity. Contesting constructivism," in *Ethnicities* 1/2 (2001), 251–285.

————. "Problems and Prospects of Associative Democracy," in P. Hirst & V. Bader (eds.), *Associative Democracy – The Real Third Way* (London: Frank Cass 2001), 31–70.

————. "Associative Democracy and Minorities Within Minorities," in J. Spinner & A. Eisenberg (eds.), *Minorities Within Minorities* (Cambridge: Cambridge University Press, 2002).

————. "Immigration," in S. Caney & P. Lehning (eds.), *International Distributive Justice* (Cambridge: Cambridge University Press, 2003).

————. "Taking Religious Pluralism Seriously. Introduction," in *Religious Pluralism, Politics, and the State. Special Volume of Ethical Theory and Moral Practice* 6/1 (2003), 3–22.

————. "Pluralism," in A. Harrington et al. (eds.) *Routledge Encyclopedia of Social Theory* (London: Routledge, 2004).

————. "Defending Differentiated Policies of Multiculturalism," Portuguese translation: "Em Defesa de Políticas Multiculturais Diferenciadas," in J. C. Rosas (ed.), *Ideias e Políticas para o Nosso Tempo* (Braga: Universidade Do Minho; Hespérides/Filosofia 4, 2004[2002]), 207–240.

————. & S. Saharso. "Introduction: Contextualized Morality and Ethno-Religious Diversity," *Ethical Theory and Moral Practice* 7/2 (2004), 107–115.

————. "Against Monism: Pluralist Critical Comments on D. Allen and P. Pettit," in M. Williams & S. Macedo (eds.), *Nomos* (New York: New York University Press, 2005).

Barry, Brian. *Justice as Impartiality* (Oxford: Oxford University Press, 1995).

————. *Culture and Equality* (Cambridge: Polity Press, 2001).

Barshack, Lior. *Passions and Convictions in Matters Political* (Lanham: University Press of America, 2000).

————. "The Holy Family and the Law," in *International Journal of Law, Policy and the Family* 18/2 (2004).

————. "Constituent Power as Body: Outline of a Constitutional Theology," in *University of Toronto Law Journal* 57/1 (forthcoming, 2007).

Bayle, Pierre. *Philosophical Commentary*, trans. & ed. Amie Godman Tannenbaum (New York: Peter Lang, 1987).

————. *Historical and Critical Dictionary*, trans. Richard H. Popkin (Indianapolis: Hackett, 1991).

Beck, Ulrich (ed.) *Die Zukunft von Arbeit und Demokratie* (Frankfurt am Main: Suhrkamp, 2000).

Benhabib, Seyla. "Toward a Deliberative Model of Democratic Legitimacy," in S. Benhabib (ed.), *Democracy and Difference* (Princeton: Princeton University Press, 1996), 67–94.

Benjamin, Jessica. *The Bonds of Love* (New York: Pantheon, 1988).

————. "Recognition and Destruction: An Outline of Intersubjectivity," in *Like Subjects, Love Objects: Essays on Recognition and Sexual Difference* (New Haven: Yale University Press, 1995), 27–48.

Berghöfer, A. *An Examination of Beneficiary Participation in Post-Conflict Development Assistance*, master's thesis, ISHSS (Amsterdam: Universiteit van Amsterdam, 2003).

Bernstein, Jay. "Confession and Forgiveness: Hegel's Poetics of Action," in Richard Eldridge (ed.), *Beyond Representation: Philosophy and Poetic Imagination* (Cambridge: Cambridge University Press, 1996), 34–65.

————. *Adorno: Ethics and Disenchantment* (New York: Cambridge University Press, 2001).

Bertram, H. "Arbeit, Familie, und Bindungen," in J. Kocka & C. Offe (eds.), *Geschichte und Zukunft der Arbeit* (Frankfurt/New York: Campus, 1998).

Bion, Wifred Ruprecht. *Experiences in Groups* (London: Tavistock, 1961).

Blasche, S., & D. Döring. *Sozialpolitik und Gerechtigkeit* (Frankfurt am Main: Campus, 1998).

Bohman, James. "Reflexive Toleration in a Deliberative Democracy," in Catriona McKinnon & Dario Castiglione (eds.), *The Culture of Toleration in Diverse Societies*, in *The Culture of Toleration in Diverse Societies* (Manchester: Manchester University Press, 2003), 111–131.

————. "Deliberative Democracy and Effective Social Freedom," in J. Bohman & W. Rehg (eds.), *Deliberative Democracy* (Cambridge, MA: MIT Press, 1997).

Bossuet, Jacques-Benigne. *Politics Drawn from the Very Words of Holy Scripture*, trans. & ed. by Patrick Riley (Cambridge: Cambridge University Press, 1999).

Bourdieu, Pierre. *La Misère du Monde* (Paris: Seuil, 1998).

Boxhill, B. R. "Self-Respect and Protest," in R. Dillion (ed.), *Dignity, Character and Self-Regard* (London: Routledge, 1995), 93–104.

Brandom, Robert. *Making it Explicit* (Cambridge, MA: Harvard University Press, 1994).

Brown, Wendy. "Reflections on Tolerance in the Age of Identity," in A. Botwinick & W. E. Connolly (eds.), *Democracy and Vision* (Princeton: Princeton University Press, 2001), 99–117.

Bubeck, D. E. *Care, Gender, and Justice* (Oxford: Clarendon Press, 1995).

Butler, Judith. "Conscience Doth Make Subjects of Us All – Althusser's Subjection," in *The Psychic Life of Power: Theories in Subjection* (Stanford: Stanford University Press, 1997).

————. "Subjection, Resistance, Resignification," in *The Psychic Life of Power: Theories in Subjection* (Stanford: Stanford University Press, 1997).

Castel, R. *Les Metamorphoses de la Question Sociale* (Paris: Gallimard, 1999).

Cavell, Stanley. "Knowing and Acknowledging," in Cavell, *Must We Mean What We Say: A Book of Essays* (Cambridge: Cambridge University Press, 1976), 238–266.

———. *The Claim of Reason: Wittgenstein, Skepticism, Morality, and Tragedy* (Oxford: Oxford University Press, 1982).

Celikates, Robin. *Nicht versöhnt. Der Kampf im Kampf um Anerkennung* (unpublished ms. 2005)

Chavkin, N., & J. Gonzalez. *Mexican immigrant youth and resiliency* (Charleston, WV: AEL Inc., 2000).

Cohen, G. A. *History, Labour and Freedom. Themes from Marx* (Oxford: Clarendon Press, 1988).

———. *If You're an Egalitarian, How Come You're So Rich?* (Cambridge, MA: Harvard University Press, 2000).

———. & A. Arato. *Civil Society and Political Theory* (Cambridge, MA: The MIT Press, 1994).

Conze, W. "Arbeit," in O. von Brunner, W. Conze, & R. Koselleck (eds.), *Geschichtliche Grundbegriffe* (Stuttgart: Klei Cotta Verlag, 1997[1979ff]).

Cook, Gary A. *George Herbert Mead: The Making of a Social Pragmatist* (Urbana: University of Illinois Press, 1993).

Dahrendorf, R. "Wenn der Arbeitsgesellschaft die Arbeit ausgeht," in J. Matthes (ed.), *Krise der Arbeitsgesellschaft? Verhandlungen des 21. Deutschen Soziologentages in Bamberg 1982*, (Frankfurt am Main: Campus, 1983).

Dante, Alighieri. *Dante's Monarchia*, trans. Richard Kay (Toronto: Pontifical Institute of Mediaeval Studies, 1998).

Darwall, S. L. "Two Kinds of Respect," in R. Dillion (ed.), *Dignity, Character and Self-Regard* (London: Routledge, 1995), 181–197.

Detel, Wolfgang. *Macht, Moral, Wissen. Foucault und die klassische Antike* (Frankfurt am Main: Suhrkamp, 1998).

Deveaux, M. "A Deliberative Approach to Conflicts of Culture," in A. Eisenberg & J. Spinner (eds.), *Minorities within Minorities* (Cambridge: Cambridge University Press, 2002).

Dewey, John. *The Public and its Problems* (Chicago: Gateway Books, 1946).

———. "Self-Realization as the Moral Ideal," in *The Early Works, 1882–1898*, Vol. 4 (Carbondale: Southern Illinois University Press, 1971).

———. "The Reflex Arc Concept in Psychology," in *The Early Works, 1882–1898*, Vol. 5 (Carbondale: Southern Illinois University Press, 1972).

———. "The Public and its Problems," in *The Later Works, 1925–1953*, Vol. 2 (Carbondale: Southern Illinois University Press, 1981).

Dews, Peter. "Communicative Paradigms and Subjectivity: Habermas, Mead, and Lacan" in Peter Dews (ed.), *Habermas: A Critical Reader* (Oxford: Blackwell, 1999).

Doorne-Huyskes, A. V. "The Unpaid Work of Mothers and Housewives in the Different Types of Welfare States," in P. Koslowski & A. Foellesdal (eds.), *Restructuring the Welfare State* (Berlin: Springer, 1997).

Dornes, M. "Frisst die Emanzipation ihre Kinder?" in A. Honneth (ed.) *Befreiung aus der Muendigkeit. Paradoxien des gegenwaertigen Kapitalismus* (Frankfurt am Main: Campus, 2002).

Douglass, Frederick. "The Meaning of July Fourth for the Negro," in Philip
S. Foner (ed.), *The Life and Writings of Frederick Douglass, Vol. 2. Pre-Civil War
Decade, 1850–1860* (New York: International Publishers, 1950).

——. "What Are the Colored People Doing for Themselves," *The North Star*
(July 14, 1848), in *The Life and Writings of Frederick Douglass, vol. 1, Early
Years, 1817–1949*, ed. Philip S. Foner (New York: International Publishers,"
1950).

Du Bois, W. E. B. *The Souls of Black Folk* (New York: Signet, 1995).

Dumont, Louis. *Affinity as a Value* (Chicago: University of Chicago Press,
1983).

Elster, J. "The Market and the Forum," in James Bohman & William Rehg
(eds.), *Deliberative Democracy* (Cambridge: MIT Press, 1997), 3–34.

Emcke, Carolin. *Kollektive Identitäten. Sozialphilosophische Grundlagen* (Frank-
furt/New York: Campus, 2000).

Esping-Andersen, G. *The Three Worlds of Welfare Capitalism* (Cambridge: Polity
Press, 1990).

Fanon, Frantz. *The Wretched of the Earth* (New York: Grove Press, 1963).

Fanuzzi, Robert. *Abolition's Public Sphere* (Minneapolis: University of Minnesota
Press, 2003).

Feffer, Andrew. *The Chicago Pragmatists and American Progressivism* (Ithaca: Cornell University Press, 1993).

Festenstein, M. *Pragmatism and Political Theory* (Cambridge, UK: Polity Press,
1997).

Fetscher, I. "Nachwort," in Karl Marx & Friedrich Engels, *Manifest der Kommunistischen Partei* (Stuttgart: Reclam, 1969).

Folbre, N. *Who Pays for the Kids? Gender and the Structure of Constraint* (London:
Routledge, 1994).

Forst, Rainer. "Foundations of a Theory of Multicultural Justice," in *Constellations* 4 (1997), 63–71.

——. "Die Rechtfertigung der Gerechtigkeit. Rawls' Politischer Liberalismus und Habermas' Diskurstheorie in der Diskussion," in Hauke Brunkhorst & Peter Niesen (eds.), *Das Recht der Republik* (Frankfurt am Main:
Suhrkamp, 1999), 105–168.

——. "The Basic Right to Justification," in *Constellations* 6 (1999), 35–60.

——. "Tolerance as a Virtue of Justice," in *Philosophical Explorations* IV
(2001), 193–206.

——. "Towards a Critical Theory of Transnational Justice," in Thomas Pogge
(ed.), *Global Justice* (Oxford: Blackwell, 2001), 169–187.

——. *Contexts of Justice*, trans. J. Farrell (Berkeley and Los Angeles: University
of California Press, 2002).

——. "A Tolerant Republic?" in Jan-Werner Müller (ed.), *German Ideologies
Since 1945* (New York: Palgrave, 2003), 209–220.

——. *Toleranz im Konflikt. Geschichte, Gehalt und Gegenwart eines umstrittenen
Begriffs* (Frankfurt am Main: Suhrkamp, 2003).

——. "Toleration, Justice and Reason," in Catriona McKinnon & Dario
Castiglione (eds.), *The Culture of Toleration in Diverse Societies* (Manchester:
Manchester University Press, 2003), 71–85.

_____. "The Limits of Toleration," in *Constellations* 11 (2004), 312–325.

_____. "Moral Autonomy and the Autonomy of Morality," in *Graduate Faculty Philosophy Journal* 26 (2005), 65–88.

Fortes, Meyer. *Kinship and the Social Order* (Chicago: Aldine, 1969).

_____. "Pietas in Ancestral Worship," in *Time and Social Structure* (London: Athlone, 1970).

Foucault, Michel. *Discipline and Punish*, trans. Alan Sheridan (New York: Vintage, 1979).

_____. *The History of Sexuality: Volume 1*, trans. R. Hurley (Harmondsworth: Penguin Books, 1979).

_____. "The Subject and Power," in *Michel Foucault: Beyond Structuralism and Hermeneutics*, 2nd ed., Herbert Dreyfus & Paul Rabinow (eds.) (Chicago: University of Chicago Press, 1983).

_____. *Ethics: Subjectivity and Truth. Essential Works of Foucault 1954–1984, volume I*, ed. Paul Rabinow, trans. Robert Hurley et al. (New York: New Press, 1994).

_____. *The Politics of Truth*, ed. S. Lotriner & L. Hochroth (New York: Semiotext(e), 1997).

_____. "What is Critique?" trans. Kevin Paul Geiman, in James Schmidt (ed.), *What is Enlightenment: Eighteenth-Century Answers and Twentieth-Century Questions* (Berkeley: University of California Press, 1996)

Franchot, Jenny. "The Punishment of Esther: Frederick Douglass and the Construction of the Feminine," in Eric J. Sundquist (ed.), *Frederick Douglass: New Literary and Historical Essays* (Cambridge: Cambridge University Press, 1990).

Frank, Jill. "Citizens, Slaves, and Foreigners: Aristotle on Human Nature," in *American Political Science Review* 98/1 (2004), 91–104.

_____. *A Democracy of Distinction: Aristotle and the Work of Politics* (Chicago, University of Chicago Press, forthcoming).

Frankfurt, Harry G. *Necessity, Volition, and Love* (Cambridge: Cambridge University Press, 1999).

Fraser, Nancy. "From Redistribution to Recognition?" *New Left Review* 212 (1995), 68–93.

_____. "After The Family Wage: A Post-Industrial Thought Experiment," in *Justice Interruptus* (New York: Routledge, 1997).

_____. "Socialist Justice in the Age of Identity Politics," in *Tanner Lectures* XIX (Salt Lake City: Univ. of Utah Press, 1998), 1–67.

_____. "Rethinking Recognition," in *New Left Review* 3 (2000), 107–120.

_____. "Social Justice in the Age of Identity Politics: Redistribution. Recognition, and Participation," in Nancy Fraser & Axel Honneth, *Redistribution or Recognition? A Political-Philosophical Exchange* (London: Verso Books, 2003), 7–109.

_____. "Distorted Beyond all Recognition: A Rejoinder to Axel Honneth," in Nancy Fraser & Axel Honneth, *Redistribution or Recognition? A Political-Philosophical Exchange* (London: Verso Books, 2003), 198–236.

_____. & Axel Honneth. *Redistribution or Recognition? A Political-Philosophical Exchange* (London: Verso Books, 2003).

Freud, Sigmund. "Three Essays on the Theory of Sexuality," in *The Standard Edition of the Complete Psychological Works of Sigmund Freud*, Vol. 7 (London: Hogarth, 1953).

_____. "Group Psychology and the Analysis of the Ego," section IX, in *The Standard Edition of the Complete Psychological Works of Sigmund Freud*, Vol. 18 (London: Hogarth, 1955).

_____. "Mourning and Melancholia," in *The Standard Edition of the Complete Psychological Works of Sigmund Freud*, Vol. 14 (London: Hogarth, 1957).

_____. "The Ego and the Id," in *The Standard Edition of the Complete Psychological Works of Sigmund Freud*, Vol. 19 (London: Hogarth, 1961).

Friedan, Betty. *The Feminine Mystique* (New York: W. W. Norton & Co, 1983).

Fromm, Erich. *Escape from Freedom* (New York: Farrar and Rinehart, 1941).

_____. *Man for Himself* (New York: Holt, Rinehart and Winston, 1947).

_____. *The Art of Loving* (New York: Harper, 1962).

Galeotti, Anna Elisabetta. *Toleration as Recognition* (Cambridge: Cambridge University Press, 2002).

Galston, William. "Diversity, Toleration, and Deliberative Democracy: Religious Minorities and Public Schooling," in Stephen Macedo (ed.), *Deliberative Politics* (Oxford: Oxford University Press, 1999), 39–48.

_____. *Liberal Pluralism* (Cambridge: Cambridge University Press, 2002).

Gauthier, David. *Morals by Agreement* (Oxford: Oxford University Press, 1983).

Gerhard, Ute, et al. (eds.), *Erwerbstaetige Muetter. Ein europaeischer Vergleich* (München: Beck, 2003)

Geuss, Raymond. *The Idea of a Critical Theory: Habermas and the Frankfurt School* (Cambridge: Cambridge University Press, 1981).

Goethe, Johann Wolfgang von. "Maximen und Reflexionen", in *Werke* 6 (Frankfurt am Main: Insel, 1981).

Goodrich, Peter. *Law in the Courts of Love* (London: Routledge, 1996).

_____. "Epistolary Justice: The Love Letter as Law," in *Yale Journal of Law and the Humanities* 9 (1997).

Gorz, A. *Reclaiming Work. Beyond the Wage-Based Society* (Cambridge, UK: Polity Press, 1999).

Green, Thomas Hill. *Prolegomena to Ethics*, ed. A. C. Bradley, 3rd ed. (Oxford: Clarendon Press, 1890).

Grell, Ole P., Jonathan I. Israel, & Nicholas Tyacke (eds.), *From Persecution to Toleration* (Oxford: Clarendon, 1991).

Guertler, Sabine. "Drei philosophische Argumente fuer ein Recht auf Arbeit," in *Deutsche Zeitschrift fuer Philosophie* 48/6 (2000), 867–88.

_____. "Die ethische Dimension der Arbeit," in *Deutsche Zeitschrift fuer Philosophie* 49 (2001), 723–41.

Gutmann, Amy, & Dennis Thompson. *Democracy and Disagreement* (Cambridge, MA: Harvard University Press, 1996).

_____. "Democratic Disagreement," in Stephen Macedo (ed.), *Deliberative Politics* (Oxford: Oxford University Press, 1999).

Habermas, Jürgen. *Technik und Wissenschaft als Ideologie* (Frankfurt am Main: Suhrkamp, 1968).

———. *Theorie des kommunikativen Handelns* (Frankfurt am Main: Suhrkamp, 1981).

———. "Die Krise des Wohlfartsstaates und die Erschoepfung utopischer Energien," in *Die neue Unübersichtlichkeit* (Frankfurt am Main: Suhrkamp, 1985).

———. *The Theory of Communicative Action*, Vol. 2, "Lifeworld and System: A Critique of Functionalist Reason," trans. Thomas McCarthy (Boston: Beacon Press, 1989).

———. "Individuation through Socialization: On George Herbert Mead's Theory of Subjectivity," in *Postmetaphysical Thinking: Philosophical Essays*, trans. William Mark Hohengarten (Cambridge, MA: MIT Press, 1992).

———. *Moral Consciousness and Communicative Action*, trans. Christian Lenhardt & Shierry Weber Nicholson (Cambridge: Polity Press, 1993).

———. "Afterword," in M. Deflem (ed.), *Habermas, Modernity and Law* (London: Sage, 1996), 135–50.

———. *Between Facts and Norms: Contributions to a Discourse Theory of Law and Democracy*, trans. William Rehg (Cambridge: Polity Press 1996).

———. "Kampf um Anerkennung im demokratischen Rechtsstaat," in *Die Einbeziehung des Anderen. Studien zur politischen Theorie* (Frankfurt am Main: Suhrkamp, 1999), 237–276

Hacker-Cordon, C. *Our Deliberative Situation* (PhD unpublished dissertation, 2003).

Haeussermann H., & W. Siebel (eds.) *Dienstleistungsgesellschaften* (Frankfurt am Main: Suhrkamp, 1995).

Hausen, "Karin Die Polarisierung der 'Geschlechtsckaraktere' – Eine Spiegelung der Dissoziation von Erwerbs- und Familienleben," in Werner Conze (ed.), *Sozialgeschichte der Familie in der Neuzeit Europas* (Stuttgart: Klett, 1976), 363–393.

———. "Arbeit und Geschlecht," in J. Kocka & C. Offe (eds.), *Geschichte und Zukunft der Arbeit* (Frankfurt/New York: Campus, 1998).

Hegel, G. W. F. *The Phenomenology of Mind*, trans. J. B. Baillie (London: Allen & Unwin, 1966).

———. *Philosophy of Right*, transl. T. M. Knox (Oxford: Oxford University Press, 1967).

———. *Aesthetics: Lectures on Fine Arts*, 2 Volumes, trans. T. M. Knox (Oxford: The Clarendon Press, 1975).

———. *Hegel's Logic*, trans. William Wallace (Oxford: Clarendon Press, 1975).

———. *Phenomenology of Spirit*, trans. A. V. Miller (Oxford: Oxford University Press, 1977).

———. *System of Ethical Life and First Philosophy of Spirit*, trans. and ed. H. S. Harris and T. M. Knox (Albany: State University of New York Press, 1979).

———. "Jena Lectures in the Philosophy of Spirit," in *Hegel and the Human Spirit: A Translation of the Jena Lectures on the Philosophy of Spirit (1805–6) with Commentary*, trans. and ed. Leo Rauch (Detroit: Wayne State University Press, 1983).

———. "Philosophie des Rechts," in *Werke in 20 Bänden und Register*, Vol. 7 (Frankfurt am Main: Suhrkamp, 1990).

———. *Elements of the Philosophy of Right*, ed. Allen Wood, trans. H. B. Nisbet (Cambridge: Cambridge University Press, 1991).

———. "Enzyklopädie der philosophischen Wissenschaften I," in *Werke in 20 Bänden und Register*, Vol. 8 (Frankfurt am Main: Suhrkamp, 1991).

———. "Phänomenologie des Geistes," in *Hauptwerke in sechs Bänden*, Vol. 2 (Hamburg: Felix Meiner, 1999).

Herzog, Don. *Poisoning the Minds of the Lower Orders* (Princeton: Princeton University Press, 1998).

Hill Jr., Thomas E. "Self-respect reconsidered," in Hill, *Autonomy and Self-Respect* (Cambridge, Cambridge University Press, 1991), 19–24.

Hirschmann, Nancy J. *The Subject of Liberty: Toward a Feminist Theory of Freedom* (Princeton: Princeton University Press, 2003).

Hobbes, Thomas. *Leviathan*, ed. Richard Tuck (Cambridge: Cambridge University Press, 1991).

Hochschild, A. *The Second Shift* (London: Piatkus, 1990).

Honneth, Axel. "Arbeit und instrumentelles Handeln," in A. Honneth & U. Jaeggi (eds.), *Arbeit, Handlung, Normativitaet* (Frankfurt am Main: Suhrkamp, 1980).

———. & Hans Joas. *Social Action and Human Nature*, trans. Raymond Meyer (Cambridge: Cambridge University Press, 1988).

———. *Kampf um Anerkennung. Zur moralischen Grammatik sozialer Konflikte* (Frankfurt am Main: Suhrkamp, 1991).

———. *The Critique of Power: Reflective Stages in a Critical Social Theory*, trans. Kenneth Baynes (Cambridge, MA: MIT Press, 1991).

———. "Author's Introduction," in *The Fragmented World of the Social: Essays in Social and Political Philosophy*, ed. Charles W. Wright (Albany: SUNY Press, 1995).

———. "Decentered Autonomy: The Subject After the Fall," in *The Fragmented World of the Social: Essays in Social and Political Philosophy*, ed. Charles W. Wright (Albany: SUNY Press, 1995).

———. "Foucault and Adorno: Two Forms of the Critique of Modernity," in *The Fragmented World of the Social: Essays in Social and Political Philosophy*, ed. Charles W. Wright, trans. Jeremy Gaines (Albany: SUNY Press, 1995).

———. "From Adorno to Habermas: On the Transformation of Critical Social Theory," in *The Fragmented World of the Social: Essays in Social and Political Philosophy*, ed. Charles W. Wright, trans. Jeremy Gaines (Albany: SUNY Press, 1995).

———. "The Limits of Liberalism: On the Political-Ethical Discussion Concerning Communitarianism," in *The Fragmented World of the Social: Essays in Social and Political Philosophy*, ed. Charles W. Wright, trans. Jeremy Gaines (Albany: State University of New York Press, 1995).

———. *The Struggle for Recognition: The Moral Grammar of Social Conflicts*, trans. Joel Anderson (Cambridge, UK: Polity Press, 1995).

_____. "The Perpetuation of the State of Nature: on the Cognitive Content of Elias Canetti's Crowds and Power," in *Thesis Eleven* 45 (1996).

_____. "Recognition and Moral Obligation," in *Social Research* 64/1 (1997), 16–35.

_____. "Democracy as Reflexive Co-operation: John Dewey and Democratic Theory Today," in *Political Theory* 26/6 (1998), pp. 771–2

_____. "Postmodern Identity and Object-Relations Theory: On the Seeming Obsolescence of Psychoanalysis," in *Philosophical Explorations* 3 (1999), 225–242.

_____. *Das Andere der Gerechtigkeit* (Frankfurt am Main: Suhrkamp, 2000).

_____. *Suffering from Indeterminacy: An Attempt at a Reactivation of Hegel's Philosophy of Right*, Introduction by Beate Rössler, trans. Jack Ben-Levi (Assen: Van Gorcum, 2000).

_____. "Zwischen Gerechtigkeit und affektiver Binding. Die Familie im Brennpunkt moralischer Kontroversen," in *Das Andere der Gerechtigkeit. Aufsätze zur praktischen Philosophie* (Frankfurt am Main: Suhrkamp, 2000), 193–215.

_____. "Facetten des vorsozialen Selbst: Eine Erwiderung auf Joel Whitebook," in *Psyche* 55 (2001), 790–802.

_____. & A. Margalit. "Recognition," in *Supplement to the Proceedings of the Aristotelian Society* 75/1 (2001), 111–126.

_____. (ed.), *Befreiung aus der Muendigkeit. Paradoxien des gegenwaertigen Kapitalismus* (Frankfurt am Main: Campus, 2002).

_____. "Between Hermeneutics and Hegelianism: J. McDowell and the Challenge of Moral Realism," in Nicholas H. Smith (ed.), *Reading McDowell. On Mind and World* (London: Routledge, 2002).

_____. "Grounding Recognition: A Rejoinder to Critical Questions," *Inquiry* 45/4 (2002), 499–520.

_____. "Redistribution as Recognition: A Response to Nancy Fraser," in Nancy Fraser & Axel Honneth, *Redistribution or Recognition: A Political-Philosophical Exchange*, trans. Joel Golb, James Ingram, & Christiane Wilke (London/New York: Verso, 2003).

_____. "The Point of Recognition," in Nancy Fraser & Axel Honneth, *Redistribution or Recognition: A Political-Philosophical Exchange*, trans. Joel Golb, James Ingram, & Christiane Wilke (London/New York: Verso, 2003), pp. 237–267.

_____. "Zwischen Hermeneutik und Hegelianismus," in *Unsichtbarkeit* (Frankfurt am Main: Suhrkamp, 2003).

_____. "Antworten auf die Beiträge der Kolloquiumsteilnehmer," in Christoph Halbig & Michael Quante (eds.), *Axel Honneth: Sozialphilosophie zwischen Kritik und Anerkennung* (Münster: Lit, 2004), 99–121

_____. "Between Justice and Affection: The Family as a Field of Moral Disputes," in Beate Rössler (ed.), *Privacies* (Stanford: Stanford University Press, 2004).

_____. "Der Grund der Anerkennung. Eine Erwiderung auf kritische Rückfragen," in *Das Andere der Gerechtigkeit. Mit einem neuen Nachwort* (Frankfurt am Main: Suhrkamp, 2004).

———. "Die Unhintergehbarkeit des Fortschritts. Kants Bestimmung des Verhältnisses von Moral und Geschichte," in Herta Nagl-Docekal & Rudolf Langthaler (eds.), *Tagungsband "Recht – Geschichte – Religion. Die Bedeutung Kants für die Philosophie der Gegenwart* (Berlin: Akademie, 2004).

———. "Gerechtigkeit und kommunikative Freiheit. Überlegungen im Anschluss an Hegel," in Barbara Merker, Georg Mohr & Michael Quante (eds.), *Subjektivität und Anerkennung* (Paderborn: Mentis-Verlag, 2004), 213–227.

———. *Kampf um Anerkennung: Zur moralischen Grammatik sozialer Konflikte*. Mit einem neuen Nachwort (Frankfurt am Main: Suhrkamp Verlag, 2004).

———. *Reification. A Recognition-Theoretical View* [Cambridge: Oxford University Press (forthcoming)].

———. "The Social Dynamics of Disrespect," in *The Other of Justice* [Cambridge, UK: Polity Press (forthcoming)].

Horkheimer, Max. "Traditional and Critical Theory," in *Critical Theory* (New York: Herder and Herder, 1972).

———. & Theodor W. Adorno. *Dialectic of Enlightenment*, trans. John Cummings (New York: Continuum Publishing, 1972).

Ikäheimo, Heikki. "On the Genus and Species of Recognition," in *Inquiry* 45/4 (2002), 447–462.

———. "Taylor on Something Called 'Recognition'," in Arto Laitinen & Nicholas H. Smith (eds.), *Perspectives on the Philosophy of Charles Taylor, Acta Philosophica Fennica 71* (Helsinki: Societas Philosophica Fennica, 2002), 99–111.

———. "On the Role of Intersubjectivity in Hegel's Encyclopaedic Phenomenology and Psychology," in *Bulletin of the Hegel Society of Great Britain*, 49/50 (2004), 73–95.

Irigaray, Luce. *Speculum of the Other Woman*, trans. Gillian C. Gill (Ithaca: Cornell University Press, 1985).

James, William. *The Principles of Psychology*, 2 vols. (New York: Henry Holt, 1890).

Jefferson, T., & J. E. King. "'Never Intended To Be A Theory Of Everything': Domestic Labour in Neoclassical and Marxian Economics," in *Feminist Economics 7/3* (2001).

Joas, Hans. *The Creativity of Action*, trans. Jeremy Gaines & Paul Keast (Chicago: University of Chicago Press, 1996).

———. *G. H. Mead: A Contemporary Re-examination of His Thought*, trans. Raymond Meyer (Cambridge, MA: MIT Press, 1997).

Kambartel, F. *Philosophie und politische Oekonomie* (Goettingen: Wallstein, 1998).

Kant, Immanuel. *Groundwork of the Metaphysic of Morals*, trans. H. J. Paton (New York: Harper and Row, 1964).

———. "An Answer to the Question: 'What is Enlightenment?'" in *Political Writings*, ed. H. Reiss, trans. H. B. Nisbet, 2nd ed. (Cambridge: Cambridge University Press, 1991).

———. *The Metaphysics of Morals*, trans. Mary Gregor (Cambridge: Cambridge University Press, 1991).

Kantorowicz, Ernst. *The King's Two Bodies* (Princeton: Princeton University Press, 1957).

Kaufmann, F. X. *Varianten des Wohlfahrtstaats. Der deutsche Sozialstaat im internationalen Vergleich* (Frankfurt am Main: Suhrkamp, 2003).

Kernberg, Otto F. "Regression in Groups," in *Internal World and External Reality* (Lanham, MD: Jason Aronson/Rowman & Littlefield, 1980).

_____. *Love Relations: Normality and Pathology* (New Haven: Yale University Press, 1995).

Kickbusch I., & B. Riedmueller (eds.) *Die armen Frauen. Frauen und Sozialpolitik* (Frankfurt am Main: Suhrkamp, 1984).

King, Preston. *Toleration* (New York: St. Martin's Press, 1976).

Kittay, Eva. *Love's Labor: Essays on Women, Equality and Dependency* (New York: Routledge, 1999).

Kocka, J. "Arbeit frueher, heute, morgen: Zur Neuartigkeit der Gegenwart," in J. Kocka & C. Offe (eds.), *Geschichte und Zukunft der Arbeit* (Frankfurt/New York: Campus, 1998).

_____. "Erwerbsarbeit ist nur ein historisches Konstrukt," in *Frankfurter Rundschau* (May 9, 2000).

Kompridis, Nikolas "From Reason to Self-Realization? Axel Honneth and the 'Ethical Turn' in Critical Theory," in *Critical Horizons* 5/1 (2004).

Korsgaard, Christine. *The Sources of Normativity* (Cambridge: Cambridge University Press, 1996).

Krebs, A. *Arbeit und Liebe. Die philosophischen Grundlagen sozialer Gerechtigkeit* (Frankfurt am Main: Suhrkamp, 2002).

Kühn, Bärbel. "Vom Schalten und Walten der Hausfrau. Hausarbeit in Rat, Tat und Forschung im 19. und 20. Jahrhundert," in Birgit Bolognese-Leuchtenmüller & Michael Mitteerauer (eds.), *Frauen-Arbeitswelten. Zur historischen Genese gegenwärtiger Probleme* (Vienna: Verlag für Gesellschaftskritik, 1993), pp. 43–66.

Kurz-Scherf, I. "Kritik an Kambartels Arbeit und Praxis," in *Deutsche Zeitschrift für Philosophie* 41/2 (1993).

Kymlicka, Will. *Contemporary Political Philosophy. An Introduction* (Oxford: Oxford University Press, 1990).

_____. *Multicultural Citizenship* (Oxford: Oxford University Press, 1995).

Lacan, Jacques. "The Mirror Stage as Formative of the Function of the I," in *Écrits: A Selection*, trans. Alan Sheridan (London: Tavistock, 1977).

_____. "The Instance of the Letter in the Unconscious," in *Écrits: A Selection*, trans. Bruce Fink (New York: Norton, 2004).

Laden, Anthony Simon. "Outline of a Theory of Reasonable Deliberation," in *Canadian Journal of Philosophy* 30 (2000), 551–580.

_____. *Reasonably Radical: Deliberative Liberalism and the Politics of Identity* (Ithaca: Cornell University Press, 2001).

_____. "Reasonable Liberals, Radical Feminists," in *Journal of Political Philosophy* 11 (2003), 133–152.

Laitinen, Arto. "Interpersonal Recognition – A Response to Value or A Precondition of Personhood?" in *Inquiry* 45/4 (2002), 463–478.

_____. *Strong Evaluation Without Sources. On Charles Taylor's Philosophical Anthropology and Cultural Moral Realism.* (Jyväskylä: Jyväskylä Studies in Education, Psychology and Social Research 224, 2003).

_____. "Hegel on Retrospective and Intersubjective Determination of Intention," in *Bulletin of the Hegel Society of Great Britain* 49/50 (2004), 54–72.

_____. "Social Equality, Recognition and Good Life" (unpublished ms).

_____. "Interpersonal Recognition and Responsiveness to Relevant Differences," in *Critical Review of International Social and Political Philosophy* (March 2006).

Lange, E. M. "Glueck, Sinn und Arbeit," in *Rechtsphilosophische Hefte*, Vol. 5 (1996).

Charles Larmore, "Pluralism and Reasonable Disagreement," in *The Morals of Modernity* (Cambridge: Cambridge University Press, 1996).

Laufer J. et al. (eds.), *Le Travail du Genre. Les Sciences Sociales du Travail a l'épreuve des Différences de Sexe* (Paris: La Découverte: 2003).

Legendre, Pierre. *Law and the Unconscious: A Legendre Reader*, ed. by Peter Goodrich (London: Macmillan, 1997).

Leipert C., & M. Opielka (eds.) *Erziehungsgehalt 2000* (Bonn: Institut für Sozialökologie, 1998).

Levy, J. *The Multiculturalism of Fear* (Oxford: Oxford University Press, 2000).

Lewis, J. David. "A Social Behaviorist Interpretation of the Meadian 'I'," in Mitchell Aboulafia (ed.), *Philosophy, Social Theory, and the Thought of George Herbert Mead* (Albany: SUNY Press, 1991).

Lilburne, John. "Englands Birth-Right Justified" (1645), in *Tracts on Liberty in the Puritan Revolution* III, ed. W. Haller (New York: Octagon, 1965), 257–308.

Locke, John. *A Letter Concerning Toleration*, ed. J. Tully (Indianapolis: Hackett, 1983).

Lovibond, Eva. *Ethical Formation* (Cambridge, MA: Harvard University Press, 2002).

Luhmann, Niklas. *Rechtssoziologie* (Reinbeck: Rowohlt, 1972).

Macedo, Stephen. "Liberal Civic Education and Religious Fundamentalism: The Case of God v. John Rawls?" in *Ethics* 105 (1995), 468–496.

MacGilvray, Eric A. *Reconstructing Public Reason* (Cambridge, MA: Harvard University Press, 2004).

MacKinnon, Catharine. "Difference and Dominance: On Sex Discrimination," in *Feminism Unmodified* (Cambridge: Harvard University Press, 1987).

Mansbridge J., & A. Morris (eds.), *The Subjective Roots of Social Protest* (Chicago: Chicago University Press, 2001).

Marcuse, Herbert. "Repressive Tolerance," in Robert P. Wolff, Barrington Moore, & Herbert Marcuse, *A Critique of Pure Tolerance* (Boston: Beacon Press, 1965), 81–118.

Margalit, Avishai. "Recognition II: Recognizing the Brother and the Other," in *Aristotelian Society Supplementary Volume* 75 (2001), 127–139.

Markell, Patchen. "The Recognition of Politics: A Comment on Emcke and Tully," in *Constellations* 7/4 (2000), 496–506.

_____. *Bound by Recognition* (Princeton: Princeton University Press, 2003).

_____. "Arendt on Democratic Rule" (unpublished ms).

Marx, Karl. "Die deutsche Ideologie," in Karl Marx & Friedrich Engels, *Marx-Engels-Werke*, Vol. 3 (Berlin: Dietz Verlag, 1969)

_____. & Friedrich Engels. *Manifest der Kommunistischen Partei* (Stuttgart: Reclam, 1969).

_____. *Ökonomisch-philosophische Manuskripte* (Leipzig: Reclam, 1970).

_____. *Capital. A Critique of Political Economy*, Vol. I (London: Penguin, 1976).

Matthes J. (ed.). *Krise der Arbeitsgesellschaft? Verhandlungen des 21. Deutschen Soziologentages in Bamberg 1982* (Frankfurt am Main: Campus, 1983).

McDowell, John. "Two Sorts of Naturalism," in *Mind, Value and Reality*. (Cambridge: Harvard University Press, 2001).

McIntosh, Peggy. "White Privilege and Male Privilege," in Margaret Atherton & Patricia Hill Collins (eds.), *Race, Class, and Gender* (New York: Wadsworth, 1995).

Mead, George Herbert. "The Definition of the Psychical," in *The Decennial Publications of the University of Chicago*, 1st series, Vol. 3 (Chicago: University of Chicago Press, 1903).

_____. *Mind, Self, and Society from the Standpoint of a Social Behaviorist*, ed. Charles W. Morris (Chicago: University of Chicago Press, 1934).

_____. "The Mechanism of Social Consciousness," in *Selected Writings*, ed. Andrew J. Reck (Chicago: University of Chicago Press, 1964).

_____. "Social Psychology as a Counterpart to Physiological Psychology," in *Selected Writings*, ed. Andrew J. Reck (Chicago: University of Chicago Press, 1984).

_____. "Suggestions toward a Theory of the Philosophical Disciplines," in *Selected Writings*, ed. Andrew J. Reck (Chicago: University of Chicago Press, 1984).

_____. "The Social Self," in *Selected Writings*, ed. Andrew J. Reck (Chicago: University of Chicago Press, 1984).

_____. *The George Herbert Mead Papers* (University of Chicago: Regenstein Library, Department of Special Collections).

Mendus, Susan. *Toleration and the Limits of Liberalism* (Atlantic Highlands: Humanities Press, 1989).

Menke, C. "Grenzen der Gleichheit," *Deutsche Zeitschrift für Philosophie* 50/6 (2002), 897–906.

Mesch, Walter. "Sittlichkeit und Anerkennung in Hegels *Rechtsphilosophie*. Kritische Überlegungen zu Theunissen und Honneth," in *Deutsche Zeitschrift für Philosophie* 53 (2005), 349–364.

Mill, John Stuart. "Considerations on Representative Government," in *On Liberty and Other Essays*, ed. John Gray (New York: Oxford University Press, 1998).

Miller, David. *On Nationality* (Oxford: Oxford University Press, 1995).

Mills, Charles. *Blackness Visible* (Ithaca: Cornell University Press, 1997).

Moore, Barrington. *Injustice: The Social Basis of Obedience and Revolt* (White Plains: M. E. Sharpe, 1978).

Muirhead, R. *Just Work* (Cambridge: Harvard University Press, 2004).

Müller-Doohm, Stefan. *Die Soziologie Theodor W. Adornos* (Frankfurt am Main: Campus, 2000), 188–198.

Nelson, H., & T. Lasswell. "Status Indices, Social Stratification, and Social Class," in *Sociology and Social Research* 44 (1960).

Nelson, J. A. "Of Markets and Martyrs: Is it O.K. to Pay Well for Care?" in *Feminist Economics* 5/3 (1999).

————. & P. England. "Feminist Philosophies of Love and Work," in *Hypatia* 17 (2002).

Neuhouser, Frederick. *Foundations of Hegel's Social Philosophy: Actualizing Freedom* (Cambridge: Harvard University Press, 2000).

Newey, Glen. *Virtue, Reason and Toleration* (Edinburgh: Edinburgh University Press, 1999).

Nietzsche, Friedrich. *The Gay Science*, trans. Walter Kaufmann (New York: Random House, 1974).

————. *On the Genealogy of Morality*, trans. C. Diethe (Cambridge: Cambridge University Press, 1994).

Nyberg, A. "From Foster Mothers to Child Care Centers: A History of Working Mothers and Child Care in Sweden," in *Feminist Economics* 6/1 (2000).

Offe, C. "Arbeit als soziologische Schluesselkategorie?" in J. Matthes, (ed.), *Krise der Arbeitsgesellschaft? Verhandlungen des 21. Deutschen Soziologentages in Bamberg 1982* (Frankfurt am Main: Campus, 1983).

————. "Anmerkungen zur Gegenwart der Arbeit," in J. Kocka & C. Offe (eds.), *Geschichte und Zukunft der Arbeit* (Frankfurt/New York: Campus 1998).

Oliver, Kelly. *Witnessing: Beyond Recognition* (Minneapolis: University of Minnesota Press, 2001).

O'Neill, Onora. "Practices of Toleration," in Judith Lichtenberg (ed.), *Democracy and the Mass Media* (Cambridge: Cambridge University Press, 1990), 155–185.

Opitz, Sven. *Gouvernementabilität im Postfordismus. Macht, Wissen und Techniken des Selbst im Feld unternehmerischer Rationalität* (Hamburg: Argument, 2004).

Ostner I., & B. Pieper (eds.) *Arbeitsbereich Familie. Umrisse einer Theorie der Privatheit* (Frankfurt am Main: Campus, 1980).

————. & A. Willms. "Strukturelle Veraenderungen der Frauenarbeit in Haushalt und Beruf," in J. Matthes (ed.), *Krise der Arbeitsgesellschaft? Verhandlungen des 21. Deutschen Soziologentages in Bamberg 1982* (Frankfurt am Main: Campus, 1983).

————. & A. Willms. "Arbeits- und Industriegesellschaft," in G. Kneer et al. (eds.), *Klassische Gesellschaftsbegriffe der Soziologie* (Munich: Wilhelm Fink Verlag, 2001).

Owen, David. *Nietzsche, Politics and Modernity* (London and Thousand Oaks, CA: Sage, 1995).

————. & Russell Bentley. "Ethical Loyalties, Civic Virtue and the Circumstances of Politics," in *Philosophical Explorations* 4 (2001).

Parekh, B. *Rethinking Multiculturalism* (Basingstoke: Macmillan Press, 2000).

Parsons, Talcott. "An Analytical Approach to the Theory of Social Stratification," in Parsons, *Sociological Theory* (New York: Free Press, 1954), 69–88.

Perrons, D. "Care, Paid Work, and Leisure: Rounding the Triangle," in *Feminist Economics* 6/1 (2000).

Pettit, Philip. "Complaining about Domination," in M. Williams & S. Macedo (eds.), *Nomos* (New York: New York University Press, 2005).

_____. *Republicanism: A Theory of Freedom and Government*, pb. ed. (Oxford: Oxford University Press, 1999).

Phelps, E. S. *Rewarding Work. How to Restore Participation and Self-Support to Free Enterprise* (Cambridge, MA: Harvard University Press, 1997).

Pippin, Robert. *Hegel's Idealism: The Satisfactions of Self-Consciousness* (Cambridge: Cambridge University Press, 1989).

_____. *Henry James and Modern Moral Life* (Cambridge: Cambridge University Press, 2000).

_____. "What is the Question for Which Hegel's 'Theory of Recognition' is the Answer?" in *The European Journal of Philosophy* 8/2 (August 2000).

_____. *Hegel's Practical Philosophy: Rational Agency as Ethical Life* (forthcoming).

Proast, Jonas. *The Argument of the Letter Concerning Toleration, Briefly Consider'd and Answer'd*, (New York and London: Garland, 1984).

Raiethel, Gert. *Geschichte der nordamerikanischen Kultur, Vol. I: Vom Puritanismus bis zum Bürgerkrieg 1600–1800* (Frankfurt am Main: Zweitausendeins, 1995).

Rawls, John. *A Theory of Justice* (Cambridge, MA: Harvard University Press, 1971).

_____. *Political Liberalism* (New York: Columbia University Press, 1996).

_____. *A Theory of Justice*, rev. ed. (Cambridge: Harvard University Press, 2000).

_____. *Lectures on the History of Moral Philosophy* (Cambridge: Harvard University Press, 2000).

Raz, Joseph. "Autonomy, Toleration, and the Harm Principle," in Susan Mendus (ed.), *Justifying Toleration* (Cambridge: Cambridge University Press, 1988), 155–176.

_____. *The Practice of Value* (Oxford: Oxford University Press, 2003).

Reck, Andrew J. "The Influence of William James on John Dewey in Psychology," in *Transactions of the Charles S. Peirce Society* 20/2 (1984), 87–117.

Renault, Emmanuel. "Reconnaissance, Institutions, Injustice," in *De la Connaissance. Revue de Mauss, Semestrielle* 23 (2004), 180–195.

Rössler, Beate. *The Value of Privacy* (Cambridge, UK: Polity Press, 2004).

Rose, Gillian. *The Melancholy Science: An Introduction to the Thought of Theodor W. Adorno* (New York: Columbia University Press, 1997).

Rösner, Hans-Uwe. *Jenseits normalisierender Anerkennung. Reflexionen zum Verhältnis von Macht und Behindertsein* (Frankfurt/New York: Campus, 2002).

Rousseau, Jean-Jacques. *Emile* (New York: Basic Books, 1979).

_____. *The First and Second Discourses*, trans. & ed. Victor Gourevitch (New York: Harper and Row, 1986).

_____. "Discourse on the Origins of Inequality," in *The Discourses and Other Early Political Writings*, trans. Victor Gourevitch (Cambridge: Cambridge University Press, 1997).

Ryan, Alan. *John Dewey and the High Tide of American Liberalism* (New York: Norton, 1995).

Saage, Richard. *Herrschaft, Toleranz, Widerstand* (Frankfurt am Main: Suhrkamp, 1981).

Säätelä, Simo. "Human Beings and Automatons," in Christian Kanzian, Josef Quitterer, & Edmund Runggaldier (eds.), *Persons – An Interdisciplinary Dialogue*, Papers of the 25th International Wittgenstein Symposium (The Austrian Ludwig Wittgenstein Society, 2002).

Saharso, S. "Female Autonomy and Cultural Imperative," in W. Kymlicka & W. Norman (eds), *Citizenship in Diverse Societies* (Oxford: Oxford University Press, 2000), 224–244.

Saint Augustine, *Letters*, Vol. II, No. 93, trans. W. Parsons (New York: Fathers of the Church, 1953).

Sandel, Michael. "Moral Argument and Liberal Toleration: Abortion and Homosexuality," in *California Law Review* 77 (1989), 521–538.

Sayers, S. "The Need to Work. A Perspective from Philosophy," in R. Pahl (ed.), *On Work. Historical, Comparative, and Theoretical Approaches* (Oxford: Blackwell, 1988).

Scanlon, Thomas. *What We Owe to Each Other* (Cambridge, MA: Harvard University Press, 1998).

Schattschneider, E. *The Semisovereign People* (New York: Holt, Rinehart, and Winston, 1960).

Schilling, René. *Kriegshelden. Deutungsmuster heroischer Männlichkeit in Deutschland 1813–1945* (Paderborn: Ferdinand Schöningh, 2002).

Schlothfeld, S. *Erwerbsarbeitslosigkeit als sozialethisches Problem* (Freiburg: Alber, 1999).

———. "Braucht der Mensch Arbeit? Zur normativen Relevanz von Beduerfnissen," in *Deutsche Zeitschrift fuer Philosophie* 49 (2001).

Schmidt am Busch, H. C. "Marktwirtschaft und Anerkennung. Zu Axel Honneths Theorie sozialer Wertschaetzung," in C. Halbig & M. Quante (eds.), *Axel Honneth: Sozialphilosophie zwischen Kritik und Anerkennung* (Muenster: LIT, 2004).

Schwartz, A. "Meaningful Work," in *Ethics* 92/4 (1982).

Schwarzenbach, Sybil. "Rawls, Hegel, and Communitarianism," in *Political Theory* 19 (1991), 539–571.

Scott, J. *Weapons of the Weak* (New Haven: Yale University Press, 1985).

———. *Domination and the Arts of Resistance. Hidden Transcripts* (New Haven: Yale University Press, 1990).

Seel, M. *Versuch ueber die Form des Gluecks. Studien zur Ethik* (Frankfurt am Main: Suhrkamp, 1995).

Sennett, R. *The Corrosion of Character: The Personal Consequences of Work in the New Capitalism* (New York: W. W. Norton, 1998).

Shapiro, I. *Democratic Justice* (New Haven: Yale University Press, 1999).

Shils, E. "Reflections on Deference," in *Center and Periphery* (Chicago: University of Chicago Press, 1968).

Shklar, J. "The Liberalism of Fear," in N. Rosenblum (ed.), *Liberalism and the Moral Life* (Cambridge, MA: Harvard University Press, 1989), 21–38.

Sigrist, C. *Regulierte Anarchie* (Frankfurt am Main: Suhrkamp, 1967).

Skinner, Quentin. *The Foundations of Modern Political Thought* 2 (Cambridge: Cambridge University Press, 1978).

————. "The Republican Ideal of Political Liberty," in Gisela Bock, Quentin Skinner, & Maurizio Viroli (eds.), *Machiavelli and Republicanism* (Cambridge: Cambridge University Press, 1990), 293–309.

————. *Liberty before Liberalism* (Cambridge: Cambridge University Press, 1998).

Smith, Rogers. "Law's Races," paper presented at the conference on *Identities, Affiliations, Allegiances* (New Haven: Yale, 2003).

Soper, K. *On Human Needs* (Atlantic Highlands, NJ: Humanities Press, 1981).

Stiegler, B. "Mutter, Kind und Vater Staat," in *Digitale Bibliothek der Friedrich-Ebert-Stiftung* (http:/library.fes.de, 2000).

Sunstein, Cass. *The Partial Constitution* (Cambridge: Harvard University Press, 1993).

Taylor, Charles. *Sources of the Self: The Making of the Modern Identity* (Cambridge/New York: Cambridge University Press, 1989).

————. "The Politics of Recognition," in Amy Gutmann (ed.), *Multiculturalism* (Princeton: Princeton University Press, 1994).

Thompson, E. P. *The Making of the English Working Class* (London: Victor Gollancz, 1963).

Tronto, Joan. *Moral Boundaries* (New York: Routledge, 1992).

Trzcinski, E. "Family Policy in Germany: A Feminist Dilemma?" in *Feminist Economics* 6/1 (2000).

Tully, James. *Strange Multiplicity: Constitutionalism in an Age of Diversity* (Cambridge/New York: Cambridge University Press, 1995).

————. "Agonic Freedom of Citizens," in *Economy and Society* 28/2 (1999), 161–182.

————. "Exclusion and Assimilation," in M. Williams & S. Macedo (eds.), *Nomos* (New York: New York University Press, 2005).

————. "Political Philosophy as a Critical Activity," in *Political Theory* 30/4 (2002), 533–555.

Ulshofer Helmut (ed.). *Liebesbriefe an Adolf Hitler – Briefe in den Tod* (Frankfurt am Main: VAS, 1994).

Valadez, J. *Deliberative Democracy, Political Legitimacy, and Self-determination in Multicultural Societies* (Boulder: Westview Press, 2001).

Van den Berg, P. "Be Prestige-Resilient!" in Saharso & Bader (eds.), *Ethical Theory and Moral Practice* 6/2 (2004), 197–214.

Van den Brink, Bert. "Gesellschaftstheorie und Übertreibungskunst: Für eine alternative Lesart der 'Dialektik der Aufklärung,'" in *Neue Rundschau* 108/1 (1997), 37–59.

————. *The Tragedy of Liberalism* (Albany: SUNY, 2000).

————. "Political Liberalism's Conception of Citizenship," German version, in *Deutsche Zeitschrift für Philosophie* 50/6 (2002), 907–924.

Van Parijs, P. *Real Freedom for All. What (if Anything?) Can Justify Capitalism?* (Oxford: Clarendon Press, 1995).

Verweyst, Markus. *Das Begehren der Anerkennung. Subjekttheoretische Positionen bei Heidegger, Sartre, Freud und Lacan* (Frankfurt am Main/New York: Campus, 2000).

Vinken, B. *Die deutsche Mutter. Der lange Schatten eines Mythos* (Munich: Piper, 2001).

Vlastos, Gregory. "The Individual as Object of Love in Plato," in *Platonic Studies* (Princeton: Princeton University Press, 1981).

Voltaire, François-Marie Arouet de. *Dictionnaire Philosophique*, ed. A. Pous (Paris: Gallimard, 1994).

Voß, Günter, & Hans J. Pongratz. "Der Arbeitskraftunternehmer. Eine neue Grundform der Ware Arbeitskraft?" in *Kölner Zeitschrift für Soziologie und Sozialpsychologie* 50/I (1989), 131–158.

Waldron, Jeremy. "Locke, Toleration, and the Rationality of Persecution," in *Liberal Rights. Collected Papers 1981–1991* (Cambridge: Cambridge University Press, 1993).

———. "Cultural Identity and Civic Responsibility," in W. Kymlicka & W. Norman (eds.), *Citizenship in Diverse Societies* (Oxford: Oxford University Press, 2000), 155–174.

———. "Toleration and Reasonableness," in Catriona McKinnon & Dario Castiglione (eds.), *The Culture of Toleration in Diverse Societies* (Manchester: Manchester University Press, 2003), 13–37.

Walwyn, William. "A Helpe to the Right Understanding of a Discourse Concerning Independency" (1644/45), in *The Writings of William Walwyn*, ed. J. R. McMichel & B. Taft (Athens: The University of Georgia Press, 1989).

Walzer, Michael. *Spheres of Justice. A Defense of Pluralism and Equality* (New York: Basic Books, 1983).

———. "Response," in D. Miller & M. Walzer (eds.), *Pluralism, Justice, and Equality* (Oxford: Oxford University Press, 1995).

Weber, Max. *Wirtschaft und Gesellschaft* (Tübingen: Mohr, 1972).

Weinstock, D. "Group Rights: Reframing the Debate," in J. Spinner & A. Eisenberg (eds.), *Minorities Within Minorities* (Cambridge: Cambridge University Press, 2002).

Wetterer, A. (ed.). *Die soziale Konstruktion von Geschlecht in Professionalisierungsprozessen* (Frankfurt am Main: Campus, 1995).

Whitebook, Joel. "Mutual Recognition and the Work of the Negative," in William Rehg & James Bohman (eds.), *Pluralism and the Pragmatic Turn: The Transformation of Critical Theory* (Cambridge, MA: MIT Press, 2001).

Wildt, Andreas. "'Anerkennung' in der Psychoanalyse," in *Deutsche Zeitschrift für Philosophie* 53 (2005), 461–478.

Williams, Bernard. *Ethics and the Limits of Philosophy* (London: Fontana Press, 1985).

———. *Shame and Necessity* (Berkeley: University of California Press, 1993).

Williams, Melissa S. *Voice, Trust, and Memory* (New Haven: Yale University Press, 1998).

Winnicott, Donald. "The Theory of the Parent-Infant Relationship," in Winnicott, *The Maturational Processes and the Facilitating Environment* (London: Karnac, 1990).

Wittgenstein, Ludwig. *Philosophical Investigations* (Oxford: Basil Blackwell, 1958).

Yarborough, Richard. "Race, Violence, and Manhood: The Masculine Ideal in Frederick Douglass's 'The Heroic Slave,'" in Eric J. Sundquist (ed.), *Frederick Douglass: New Literary and Historical Essays* (Cambridge: Cambridge University Press, 1990).

Young, Iris Marion. *Justice and the Politics of Difference* (Princeton: Princeton University Press, 1990).

————. "Communication and the Other," in Seyla Benhabib (ed.), *Democracy and Difference* (Princeton: Princeton University Press, 1996), 120–135.

————. "Difference as a Resource for Democratic Communication," in James Bohman & William Rehg (eds.), *Deliberative Democracy* (Cambridge: MIT Press, 1997).

————. "A Room of One's Own: Privacy and Old Age Residence," in *On Female Body Experience: 'Throwing Like a Girl' and Other Essays* (New York: Oxford University Press, 2004).

Zurn, Christopher F. "The Normative Claims of Three Types of Feminist Struggles for Recognition," in *Philosophy Today* (Supplement 1997), 73–78.

Index

Adorno, Theodor W., 8, 9, 24, 78, 79–99, 259, 352, 353
  and Adelbert von Chamisso, 91
  The Authoritarian Personality, 94
  on cognition and recognition, 95
  on experience and cognition, 93
  on ethical life, 83
  on ethics and morality, 88
  his ethics of resistance, 82, 89
  on false normality, 89, 90
  on the ineffable, 81
  Minima Moralia, 83, 87, 89, 95
  Probleme der Moralphilosophie, 89
  on power through misrecognition, 91
  on rationality, 80
  on recognition as responsiveness, 80, 98
  on reconciliation, 81
  on reification, 81
agency, 57–78, 260
  and incapacitation; *see* power
  three conditions of actualization of, in Hegel, 67
alienation, 9, 81, 151, 155; *see also* work
Allen, Danielle, 317, 369
  on sacrifice and trust, 317, 369

Althusser, Louis, 324, 325, 330, 336
  on recognition as ideology, 324
American pragmatism, 101–132
Anderson, Joel, 310
Anscombe, Elizabeth
  Intention, 72
Arendt, Hannah, 182, 296, 299
Aristotle, 84, 102, 109, 318, 364
  on wisdom of the multitude, 318
atomism, 60
Augustine, 226, 228, 229
authority, 165–188
  of deliberative reasons, 281, 283
autonomy, 7–10, 15, 109, 155, 168, 169, 170, 177, 183, 206, 229, 281; *see also* recognition (in Honneth) and autonomy

Bader, Veit, 28, 364, 365, 366
Barry, Brian, 186
Barshack, 26, 357, 361
Bayle, Pierre, 225, 226, 227, 229, 232, 233
  Commentaire philosophique sur ces paroles de Jésus-Christ 'Contrain-les d'entrer,' 226
  Dictionaire historique et critique, 228
  Moral basis of toleration, 226
  Pensées diverses sur la Comète, 225

391

Bayle, Pierre (*cont.*)
on toleration and religious belief,
225
Beauvoir, Simone de, 205
Benjamin, Jessica, 11
Berger, Peter, 253
Berlin, Isaiah, 255
Bernstein, J. M., 84
Biko, Steve, 311
Bossuet, Jacques Bénigne, 227
Butler, Judith, 2, 324

Canetti, Elias, 176, 178
Crowds and Power, 176
capitalism, 150, 198, 199
and commodification, 151, 209
care, 140; *see also* recognition and
care-work
Cavell, Stanley, 40
on acknowledgement, 40, 329
citizenship, 284–287
skills and attitudes of, 286
shared, 286
communitarianism, 181
corporate body, 174–180
Structure and Communitas,
177–180, 187, 189–212
Critical Social Theory, 1, 7, 8, 220,
236, 239, 240, 244, 248, 252,
259, 265, 323, 324, 344
and "victimizing the victim," 239,
258

deliberation; *see* reasonable
deliberation
dependence, human, 57–78
democracy, 238–269
and community, 297
and good life, 297, 298
and law, 297
and legitimacy, 286
normative theory of, 240
and pluralism, 297, 300
private and public autonomy in,
297
procedural model of, 296–301,
305

as reflective co-operation,
290–320
republican model of, 296–301,
305, 367, 368
and self-government, 290–320
and self-realization, 292
Dewey, John, 29, 100, 101, 114, 117,
118, 119, 120, 124, 127, 128, 368
on communication, 293
on democratic co-operation,
290–320
moral psychology of, 296
"The Reflex Arc Concept in
Psychology," 117
on self-realization, 290, 293
"Self-realization as the Moral
Ideal," 117
on practical deliberation, 293, 294
on problem-solving, 290, 295
on socialization, 290
Douglass, Frederick, 130, 310
"The Meaning of July Fourth for
the Negro," 130
Duplessis-Mornay, Philippe, 223
Dubois, W. E. B., 310
Durkheim, Emile, 175
Dworkin, Ronald, 59

Engels, Friedrich, 150
Ellison, Ralph, 63
Invisible Man, 63
emancipation, 156–163, 215–237
and recognition, 215–237
and toleration, 215–237
equality
legal, 271
material, 239
and (re)distribution, 246
and structural inequality, 239,
240–258

family
in Honneth, 192–212; *see also*
recognition and family; family
work
Fanon, Frantz, 1, 259
feminism, 189–202, 212

Fichte, Johann Gottlieb
  Grundlage, 61
Forst, Rainer, 20, 27, 363, 364
  critical theory of toleration, 220
  right to justification, 229, 234
  see also justification
Foucault, Michel, 2, 7, 8, 9, 21, 89,
  220, 222, 259, 342, 367
Fraser, Nancy, 1, 28, 50, 56, 147, 157,
  184
Freud, Sigmund, 165, 166–188
  The Ego and the Id, 168, 171
  Group Psychology, 168, 173
  Moses and Monotheism, 173
  Totem and Taboo, 173
Fromm, Erich, 167
  freedom, 61, 66, 67, 108
  of conscience, 225, 227
  political 229
  fascism, 182, 183, 185

Galston, William, 255
Gauthier, David, 59
Green, Thomas Hill, 117, 368
  Prolegomena to Ethics, 118
Goethe, Johann Wolfgang
  on toleration, 215, 218, 220
  good life, 147, 149, 155, 229

Habermas, Jürgen, 7, 8, 59, 89, 107,
  112, 151, 155, 266, 296, 299,
  300, 304
  Between Facts and Norms, 299
  on communicative action, 151,
    155, 299
  and democracy, 297, 299
  on lifeworld, 151, 152
Heidegger, Martin, 64
Hegel, G. W. F., 1, 3, 4, 5, 6, 23, 34,
  37, 41, 47–49, 57–78, 102, 107,
  108, 109, 110, 114, 139, 166,
  175, 182, 194, 205, 256, 270,
  272, 286
  on agency and freedom, 57–78,
    108
  on conjugal love, 196, 202,
    203

on consciousness, 70
  Encyclopedia, 68, 76
  and ethical life, 67, 70, 288
  on forgiveness, 76
  Lectures on Aesthetics, 78
  Phenomenology of Spirit, 57–78, 86,
    107
  Philosophy of Right, 68, 76, 352
  on self-consciousness, 69, 70
  Sittlichkeit, 64, 67
  System of Ethical Life, 4
  Master-Slave dialectic, 61, 69
  see recognition; recognitional
    in/dependence
Hill Jr., Thomas, 311, 312
Hobbes, Thomas, 3, 58, 167, 286
Hochschild, 147
Höffe, Otfried, 59
Honneth, Axel, 1–30, 34, 37, 39, 40,
  41, 49–51, 56, 57, 60, 62, 89, 96,
  98, 100–132, 135, 136, 147, 149,
  152, 155, 164, 166–181, 188,
  189–212, 270, 272, 273, 277,
  278, 279, 281, 282, 283, 284,
  286, 288, 289
  "Between Justice and Affection,"
    199
  on democracy, 290–320
  and feminism, 189–202, 212
  critique of, in this volume, 21–22
  The Critique of Power, 2, 300
  his political ideal, 303, 305, 306,
    315–320
  on republicanism, 298
  "Redistribution and Recognition,"
    199
  The Struggle for Recognition, 1, 10,
    17, 96, 107, 164, 195, 272, 290,
    300, 302, 303, 306, 367
  Suffering from Indeterminacy, 60
  theoretical project in context, 6–9
  see also recognition (in Honneth)
Horkheimer, Max, 8, 9
Hradil, Stefan, 253

identity; *see* power and identity
Ikäheimo, Heikki, 23, 33–56, 350

individuation, 182
intersubjectivity, 57–60, 69, 78
  and actualized freedom, 61
  and liberal notions of entitlement,
    69
  and meaning
  and social dependence, 57–60, 61,
    62, 78
  and social independence, 61
  see also recognitional
    in/dependence
Irigaray, Luce, 204, 205
  Speculum of the Other Woman, 204

James, William, 101, 114, 116, 121,
    124, 127
  The Principles of Psychology, 114,
    116, 117, 121, 123
Joas, Hans, 107, 112, 120
justice, 156–163, 194, 235, 237
  and autonomy, 186
  economic, 155
  and injustice, 238–255, 257, 261,
    262, 269
  political, 224
  struggles for, 236, 270–289; *see also*
    recognition, struggle for
justification
  and generality, 230, 231, 235
  and reciprocity, 230, 231, 235
  right to, 229

Kambartel, Friedrich, 136, 149
Kant, Immanuel, 6, 8, 39, 65, 66, 89,
    115, 256, 273, 336, 352, 363,
    367
  "Doctrine of Right," 59
  Rechtslehre, 66
  on toleration, 218, 220, 233
Kantorowicz, Ernst, 174, 181
Kernberg, Otto, 172
Klein, Melanie, 165, 167, 168, 169,
    172, 361
Knight, J. and Johnson, J., 268
Kohlberg, Lawrence, 185
Krebs, Angelika, 142, 149

Lacan, Jacques, 170, 324
Laden, Anthony, 28, 366, 367, 368,
    369
labour, 136; *see also* recognition and
  work
Laitinen, Arto, 23, 33–56, 101, 102,
    103, 106, 350, 355
law, 166–171
  and autonomy, 166, 177, 183, 185
  and social separation, 166–171
Leipert, Christian, 142
Lévi-Strauss, Claude, 170
Lewis, J. David, 126
Lewis, Oscar, 261
liberalism, 3
  and dependence, 63
  political, 296
  and politics of recognition, 57,
    65
  pragmatic justification of, 58
  justification from moral
    entitlements, 59
Lilburne, John, 224
Locke, John, 58, 59, 139, 161, 225,
    226
  Letter Concerning Toleration, 224
love, 10, 17, 26, 27, 41, 164–188,
    189–212, 302
  and care, 189–212
  and egalitarianism, 205
  heterosexual, 204
  political, 184–188
  tripolar structure of, 171–174
  see also recognition (in Honneth)
    and love

MacGilvray, 119
MacKinnon, Catherine, 367
MacIntyre, Alisdair, 62
Maine, Henry, 175
Marcuse, Herbert, 259
Markell, Patchen, 23, 25, 352, 354,
    355, 356, 364
Marshall, T. H., 13, 304, 360
Mead, George Herbert, 1, 25,
    100–132, 349, 352

"The Definition of the Psychical,"
119, 121, 122–123
the "I" and the "me," 101–132, 355
individuality and community, 125,
127, 128, 129, 171
"The Mechanism of Social
Consciousness," 122
Mind, Self, and Society, 121, 122,
124, 125
on self-consciousness, 110
"The Social Self," 122
ultimate goal of human progress,
125
Marx, Karl, 139, 150, 151, 155, 359
post-Marxian theoretical
consciousness, 348
Mill, John Stuart, 58
Miller, David, 187, 365
Milton, John, 224, 225
Mirabeau, Comte de, 218, 220
Montesquieu, Baron de, 225
Moore, Barrington, 254
Muirhead, Russell, 160

Nietzsche, Friedrich, 21, 85

object relations theory, 11
Opielka, Michael, 142
Owen, David, 29, 89, 348, 367,
368–369

Perrons, Diane, 142
Pettit, Philip, 253
Pippin, Robert, 23, 259, 351, 352,
359
pluralism, 257
moral, 255
see also power; recognition
Proast, Jonas, 226, 229
poverty, cultures of, 260, 261
power, 2–30, 238, 241, 348–370
Adorno on, 79–99
asymmetrical/unequal, 207, 240,
243, 244, 265, 267, 276, 277,
282, 287
and the family, 192–212

and gender division on labor,
192–212
and class, 242, 246
constitutive of practical identities,
2
constructive social, 28, 272, 276,
277, 278, 283, 285, 367
and democracy, 238–269
and diversity, 242
and domination, 215, 222, 240,
323, 348–370
and emancipation, 215–237
and family, 167
and freedom, 222, 262
and hidden transcripts of
resistance, 263
and identity, 276, 277, 283,
287–288
and ideology, 323–347
and incapacitation, 239, 240,
258–265, 268, 355
multidimensional analysis of,
239
pluralist account of asymmetries
in, 239, 240–258, 261, 267
and prestige hierarchies, 239, 241,
242, 243, 244, 246, 247
and recognition, 1–22, 30, 79–99,
215–237, 238–265, 269, 274,
323–347
see also recognition
prestige hierarchies and
ascription, 243, 244, 247
see also power
psychoanalytic theory, 165–188, 259
public sphere, 7
and deliberation, 267, 295
and democracy, 297, 299

Rawls, John, 7, 8, 59, 89, 228, 270,
271, 283, 287–289, 297
reasonable deliberation, 270–289,
366, 367
and negotiation, 280
and overlapping consensus, 280
and recognition, 279–282

reasonableness, 28
and disagreement, 228, 250
reasoning, intersubjective, 235
reasons, responsiveness to, 66, 288,
   289
recognition, 1–30, 33–56, 79–99,
   100–132, 135–163, 164
Adorno on, 79–99
and acknowledgement, 34–36, 39,
   52, 132
and actuality, 101, 102, 103, 104,
   105, 106, 109, 111, 113, 118, 119,
   129, 131
and authority, 165–188
and care, 241
and care-work, 140–163, 193–202,
   206, 212
claim for, 65
and constructive social power; *see*
   power
as creative act, 102, 108
and democracy, 238–269
dialogical conception of, 37, 42,
   47–49
and emancipation, 215–237
and family, 167–188
and family work, 136–163, 193,
   357
its grounding as normative
   concept, 101–132
ideal theory of, 248, 250
and identification, 34–36, 39
and identity development, 135,
   222, 272
and incapacitation; *see* power
interpersonal, 37–51
and labor movement, 238
and law, 165–188
and love, 164–188, 193–212,
   241
and misidentification, 51
and misrecognition, 28, 51–56, 91,
   238–255, 258–265, 269, 275,
   277, 284
monological conception of, 37
as moral concept, 135

mutual, 67, 71, 177, 202, 256, 271,
   272, 273, 276, 293
and needs, 241
negative and positive analysis of,
   248–251
one-dimensional vs. multi-
   dimensional conceptions of,
   39–42
and personhood, 102
of persons, 36
political dimensions of, 65,
   184–188, 290–320
politics of, 64, 65, 248–249
and potentiality, 101, 102, 103,
   104, 105, 106, 109, 111, 113, 118,
   119, 127, 129, 131, 355, 356
private and public, 180–184
and psychoanalytic theory,
   165–188, 259
and reasonable deliberation; *see*
   reasonable deliberation
and reconciliation, 57, 71
and redistribution, 185, 248,
   252
and respect; *see* respect, basic;
   respect, fully equal
as response, 102, 108
and responsiveness, 270; *see also*
   Adorno
and "right to be recognized," 65
and rights, 155, 156, 203–204,
   273
and social pathology, 135
struggle for, 28, 55, 110, 135, 147,
   184, 189, 222, 236, 238, 248,
   252, 270–289, 348
and toleration, 215–237
unified frame of, 238
and work, 135–163, 344
recognition (in Honneth), 1–30,
   238–269, 323–347, 348–370
and achievement, 17, 20, 147, 149,
   156, 158, 159, 161, 162, 198,
   201, 206, 313, 314, 316, 340,
   341, 343, 358
and affection, 201

and affirmation, 329, 330, 338,
339, 350
and anthropology, 15
as attitude, 330
attributive and receptive, 331–336
and autonomy, 10, 14, 15, 18, 110,
161, 206, 323, 325, 326, 330,
339, 351, 352, 359
and capitalism, 16, 199, 343
care, 3, 5, 25, 181
and community, 108, 114, 166,
318
and conceptions of the good,
15–20
conceptual core of
"correct" and "incorrect," 332,
333, 340, 345, 346, 347
and Critical Social Theory, 323,
324
cultural, 316
defined, 329
and democracy, 290–320
and disrespect, 325
and division of labor, 17, 343, 345,
358, 359
and dominance, 323, 325
and emancipation, 323, 350
and (formal account of) ethical
life (*Sittlichkeit*), 80, 161, 223,
287–288, 290, 301, 302–306,
314
and ethical theory, 21
and equality, 14, 18, 316
esteem, 3, 5, 10, 22, 41, 181, 193,
196, 198, 199, 200, 202, 206,
271, 273, 304, 317, 326, 337
and evaluative qualities/prop-
erties, 103, 105, 332, 335, 336,
340, 344, 345, 346, 350
and the family, 192–212
and gender division on labor,
192–202, 212
and historical (moral) progress,
104, 105, 107, 109, 114, 206,
273, 332, 333, 334, 341, 348
Honneth's theory of, 2–20

and ideological self-conceptions,
323, 324, 325, 326, 337, 339,
340, 342
ideological and moral forms of,
327, 328
and ideology, 22, 29, 204,
323–345, 347
and individuality, 108, 114, 291
individuality and the common
good, 292, 318
and individualization, 14
and institutions; *see* respect
and integrity, 318, 368
and intention, 330
and life-world, 103, 104, 105, 332,
333–336
and linguistic integrity, 309–315
and love, 10, 17, 26, 27, 41,
164–188, 193, 195, 272, 302,
316, 317, 337, 340, 349
and misrecognition, 15, 22,
238–265, 269, 274, 275, 277,
284
monistic theory of, 22, 239,
240–258, 365
and moral agency, 4, 6, 10, 336
and moral grammar of social
conflict, 2–6
and moral psychology, 301–315
and moral progress, 15–20
parents and children, 18
and perfectionism, 360
performative character of, 329,
345
and physical integrity, 307–315
and pluralism, 300
and political community, 295,
296, 318
political significance of, 290
principles of, 341
and power, 1–22, 30, 238, 274,
323–347, 348–370
and reasoning, 331, 332, 340
regulative in ideology, 342, 344
relations-to-self, 9, 10, 15, 193,
249, 286, 307

recognition (in Honneth) (*cont.*)
respect, 3, 5, 10, 41, 271, 272, 273,
304, 328, 337, 351, 363
and rights, 12, 13, 196, 203–204,
273, 302, 304
self-confidence, 10, 11–12, 302,
303, 306–315, 317, 320, 368
self-esteem, 14–15, 302, 304,
306–315, 320, 368
and self-realization, 290, 292, 293,
302, 303, 343, 345
self-respect, 12–14, 302, 303,
306–315, 318, 320, 342, 368
and socialization, 291, 333
solidarity, 17, 156, 272, 273, 302
and structural changes in modern
societies, 16, 194
struggle for, 6, 11, 15, 109, 159,
164, 236, 270–289, 348, 354
and trust, 317
and value realism, 333, 334, 336,
351, 355
recognitional in/dependence (in
Hegel), 62, 64, 65, 68, 71, 74,
207, 351
and achievement, 67
and human need, 62
and individuality, 62, 67, 68, 71
and intersubjectivity, 62, 67, 302,
303
and misrecognition, 64, 238–265,
269, 271, 275, 277, 284
and normative status, 62, 65, 66
and psychology, 62
and reflective endorsement, 63
and symmetry/asymmetry,
207–212
recognitive attitudes, 33–56
and acceptance, 47–49
and autonomy, 47–49
and action and understanding,
43–47
and feelings and emotions, 46
and internalization, 47–49
and statuses, 49–51, 198, 200
vs. social and institutional spheres,
42–43

respect
basic, 273, 277, 278, 281, 282, 284,
367
fully equal, 273, 277, 278, 279,
282, 284, 287, 367
and institutional recognition, 275,
278, 279, 283–289, 334, 347
Rössler, Beate, 25, 28, 357, 358, 361
Rousseau, Jean-Jacques, 59, 66, 225,
272, 362
amour propre, 189, 192
and relations between men and
women 190–192, 196, 202
on recognition, 189–192, 216
on respect, 190
The Social Contract, 61
Second Discourse, 66
Discourse on Inequality, 189

Sartre, Jean-Paul, 1
Scanlon, Thomas, 231
Scott, James, 243, 254, 261
self, 114, 115, 119, 122, 123, 124
self-determination, 64
self-realization, 64
Shakespeare, William
King Lear, 76
social criticism, 135, 136, 155
social movements, 194, 278, 279,
283, 287, 288, 289
subjectivity, 121
decentered, 111
Sunstein, Cass, 287

Taylor, Charles, 1, 7, 8, 9, 57, 62, 72
teleology, 111
Thompson, E. P. 254
toleration, 27, 215–237, 363
acceptance component of, 216,
233
critical theory of, 220, 239
democratic form of, 221
and disrespect, 219
and domination, 215, 219
as domination, 216
Edict of Nantes, 217, 220
and emancipation, 215–237

and Enlightenment, 215
and ethical beliefs, 232
and ethical judgment, 233
and freedom, 219
and inclusion and exclusion, 218,
 219
of Jews, 220
limits of, 233, 234
and moral judgment, 233
and moral norms, 232
as normatively dependent
 concept, 217
normative justification of, 216,
 219, 227, 229, 231, 233, 234
objection component of, 216, 233,
 234
permission conception of, 219,
 221, 234
and recognition, 215–237
as recognition, 216, 234
rejection component of, 216, 233,
 234
religious, 217
respect conception of, 225
as policy instrument, 219
and power, 215–237
Toleration Act, 218
Union of Utrecht, 223
as virtue, 232
Tully, James, 2, 89
Turner, Victor, 177

Valadez, Jorge, 268
van den Brink, Bert 23, 24, 348, 352
Voltaire, 216, 225

Walwyn, William, 224
Walzer, Michael, 154
Weber, Max, 269, 349
Williams, Bernard, 21, 309
Williams, Roger, 225

Winnicott, Donald, 11
Wittgenstein, Ludwig, 40, 41, 72, 329
 Philosophical Investigations, 40
work, 135–163, 358, 359
and alienation, 150, 156, 162
clean, 154
contract, 138, 139
and care, 140–163
and commodification, 150, 209
and dignity, 154
dirty, 154
family, 136–163
and gainful employment, 137–141
and gender-specific division of
 labour, 144–149, 199, 201–202,
 212
hard, 154
and inclusion, 139
and love, 143
private and public, 138, 146
and property, 139, 160
remunerated, 136–163, 201, 335,
 361
and self-determination, 160
and self-realization, 139, 160
see also recognition and family
 work; recognition and work
Wright, Georg Henrik von,
 Explanation and Understanding,
 72

Young, Iris Marion, 2, 26, 253, 357,
 362
on care work, 206, 362
on conjugal love as ideology,
 203–204
on the family, 192–212
on gender division on labor,
 192–202, 212
on "myth of merit," 314
on Rousseau, 189–192

Made in the USA
Middletown, DE
29 May 2021